THE PRESENT AND THE PAST

Great Britain

Identities, Institutions and the Idea of Britishness

Keith Robbins

LONGMAN
London and New York

Addison Wesley Longman Limited
Edinburgh Gate
Harlow, Essex CM20 2JE
United Kingdom
and Associated Companies throughout the world

*Published in the United States of America
by Addison Wesley Longman Inc., New York*

First published 1998

ISBN 0 582 03138 9 CSD
ISBN 0 582 03119 2 PPR

British Library Cataloguing-in-Publication Data

A catalogue record for this book is available from the British Library

Library of Congress Cataloging-in-Publication Data

Robbins, Keith
    Great Britain: identities, institutions, and the idea of Britishness /
Keith Robbins.
    p. cm. – (The present and the past)
    Includes bibliographical references (p.) and index.
    ISBN 0-582-03138-9 (csd.) – ISBN 0-582-03119-2 (ppr)
    1. National characteristics, British–History. 2. Group identity-Great Britain–
History. 3. Great Britain–Civilization. 4. Ethnology–Great Britain. I. Title. II. Series.
DA110.R66 1997   96-53505
941--dc21   CIP

Set by 7 in 10/12 Sabon
Produced by Longman Singapore Publishers (Pte) Ltd
Printed in Singapore

Contents

Contents

Contents

List of Maps

List of Illustrations

Acknowledgements

The publishers would like to thank the following for granting permission to reproduce illustrative material: the Governor and Company of the Bank of England for fig. 6.2; The British Museum for figs 3.2, 4.2 and 11.1; The British Library for figs 2.2, 2.3 and 4.1 by permission of the British Library; fig. 9.1 from the Royal Commonwealth Society Collection by permission of the Syndics of Cambridge University Library; The Master and Fellows of Corpus Christi College, Cambridge for fig. 1.3; John Giles/PA News for fig. 12.1; Judy Harrison/Format for fig. 13.1; Hulton Getty for figs 7.2, 9.2 and 12.2; Joe Payne/The Berwick Advertiser for fig. 1.2; A.F. Kersting for fig. 2.1; Manchester Jewish Museum for fig. 11.4; Mansell Collection for figs 3.1, 4.3, 5.1 and 7.3; Graham Miller for fig. 10.1; Museum of London for figs 8.5 and 13.2; Museum of Welsh Life for figs 9.3 and 11.2; National Library of Wales for fig. 10.2; National Maritime Museum London for fig. 6.1; National Museum of Labour History for fig. 8.4; Royal Commission on the Ancient and Historical Monuments of Wales for fig. 1.4 (National Monuments Record of Wales Crown Copyright); the Royal Collection © Her Majesty the Queen for fig. 7.1; fig. 5.2 reproduced with permission of the Library Committee of the Religious Society of Friends; Winchester Museums for fig. 1.1.

While every effort has been made to trace the owners of copyright material, we take this opportunity to offer our apologies to any copyright holders whose rights we may have unwittingly infringed.

Preface

Historians who investigate the long past of their own country have both advantage and disadvantage. From childhood onwards they have received a long induction into its conventions and institutions, and have explored its landscape. They may subsequently scrupulously cultivate detachment and seek objectivity, but cannot ultimately escape the influence of their environment. They inevitably absorb, to a greater or lesser degree, its working myths and assumptions by virtue of their own social existence. They know, or think they know, 'their' past as much by intuition and experience as by the fruits of their reading and research. There is the danger, in consequence, that they take that past as normative and miss its oddity. A history written by 'outsiders', on the other hand, can be more sharply aware of national idiosyncrasy, but it also may not 'ring true' because external onlookers may not fully grasp the rules of the national game.

It may be pertinent, therefore, to remark that this historian has spent substantial periods of his personal and professional life in each of the constituent countries of Great Britain. The relative rarity of such a peregrination is perhaps itself a significant indication of how difficult it is, in writing of 'Great Britain' in the present, to do justice to both single and multiple pasts in the same volume. Additionally, however, visiting appointments at the University of British Columbia and the University of Western Australia, and conferences in the United States, have given me an opportunity to think about British history in a context that both was and was not 'British'. Participation in the first major conference on British history held in the People's Republic of China (in Nanjing) helped to make more complicated what might otherwise have seemed deceptively straightforward. It has also been my privilege to take part in conferences in most European countries and to share, personally and professionally, in the ambiguities of British 'Europeanness'.

Such merit as this book has, therefore, derives in part from a fusing of external perception and internal 'ownership'. It could not have been written without a deep indebtedness to a considerable company of friends and historians – happily not mutually exclusive categories – in different parts of Great Britain, and around the world, whose writing and conversation have helped me to grapple with both the British past and the British present.

University of Wales, Lampeter

Prologue

Chapter 1 ....

The Ingredients Assembled

A question of pedigree

The peddling of pedigrees, quite often imaginary ones, has long been perceived to be a vital element in establishing the legitimacy of rulers. Likewise, the people or peoples over whom they have ruled have felt themselves to be 'incorporated' by a belief in a common origin and to have their sense of solidarity buttressed by the retelling of a common history. In this process, over centuries, poets and painters, philologists and philosophers, playwrights and historians have all played their ambiguous parts. A certain nostalgia for the past makes the present seem more tolerable, particularly when it is no longer possible to emulate the deeds of past 'heroes' without global catastrophe. The solace it provides can give new hope, though it can also make the present seem prosaic and the future even more problematic than it necessarily is. There are also likely to be episodes in the past which seem depressing and shameful in the present. Should the guilt of the fathers be inherited by the sons? What does it mean to suggest that the present should 'apologize' or make expiation for the past?

Even though anthropologists and sociologists have largely shunned the concept of 'national character', it has continued to be used in popular and public discourse. Legend and landscape have frequently combined to produce a 'tradition' and an environment which is perceived to be distinctive, if not unique. Composers, too, have drawn inspiration from 'traditional' music and, in turn, their compositions have been seen to carry forward a musical stream which is 'national'. Institutions and associations also take on forms which are seen to reflect the 'genius' of particular peoples. Those very forms, however, may then themselves shape the future. In turn, what once seemed vital and dynamic comes to be seen as marginal and restrictive. Past and present, in short, continually interact. Sometimes change is 'peaceful', sometimes 'violent'. It cannot be avoided.

A pattern of islands

In such a context, the present has sometimes been able to pinpoint, supposedly with precision, a particular moment in the past when the nation was
'born'. It was in 1896, for example, that Magyar patriots thought it appropriate to celebrate 1,000 years of 'Hungary'. No such precision is possible in
the case of 'Great Britain' or 'the British'. The Brythons – whence, at different times, 'Briton', 'British', 'Britain' and 'Brittany' – were a Celtic people
driven westwards from continental Europe, from at least the fifth century
BC. In more modern terms, however, by one definition, 'Great Britain' could
be held to begin in 1603 when James VI of Scotland rode south to succeed
to the English throne. James could claim to be 107th in a line of Kings of
Scots stretching back into a misty past. He himself was of the ninth generation of the House of Stewart to reign over Scotland. By heraldic devices
and, as will be seen, in many other respects, James was determined to stress
that he was the first King of Great Britain and to attempt to advance a notion of Britishness which, if taken seriously, would subordinate, and perhaps
eliminate, the identities which had hitherto been created in the islands over
which he ruled. It was not until 1707, however, that the union of crowns
was followed by the union of countries. In this sense, 'Great Britain' only
came into existence when the unitary state was formed. It is a country,
therefore, which has only been in being for nearly 300 years. In a global perspective that remains a significant period, but, behind 1603 or 1707 there
existed complex pasts and multiple identities which continued to have repercussions on subsequent 'British history'.

A history of 'Great Britain' might therefore logically start with the particular histories of its antecedent component parts and trace their distinctive
evolution from as far back as the historian can go. The focus of this study,
however, begins in the late fifteenth century when, arguably, the 'matter of
Britain' began again to be a major issue. Between 1536 and 1543 the complexities of administration in Wales were 'tidied up' and formal union was
accomplished between Wales and England. In Scotland some minds were
turning in the 1520s to the possibilities which 'Britain' might offer. 'At the
present day', wrote John Major (Mair), the Paris-educated Glasgow professor in
his *Historia Majoris Britanniae* (History of Greater Britain), written in Latin
and published in Paris (1520), 'there are and for a long time have been, to
speak accurately, two kingdoms in the island: the Scottish kingdom, namely,
and the English ... Yet all the inhabitants are Britons ... I say therefore that all
men born in Britain are Britons ...'. It was, after all, possible to 'pass from
England to Wales, and from Scotland, by way of England, to Wales, dryshod'.[1]

---

[1] John Major, *Greater Britain*, ed. and trans. A. Constable (Edinburgh, 1892)
pp. 17–18; R. Mason, 'Kingship, Nobility and Anglo-Scottish Union: John Mair's
History of Greater Britain (1521)', *Innes Review* 4 (1990).

That demonstrated that there were no fundamental barriers of communication which stood in the way of a single kingdom. The implications of these developments will be explored subsequently.

It appears, however, that 'union', whatever the term precisely means, was coming firmly onto the sixteenth-century agenda. The question that has to be addressed at the outset, however, is the extent to which the path to 'Britain' was inherent in what might be called its insular 'geopolitics'. Until the late twentieth century, the prevailing historiographical assumption has been that this process of consolidation was both natural and beneficial. The aggregation of smaller units into a greater whole has been held to lie in the logic of history. It has been a process which has occurred, in varying forms and at different times, throughout mainland Europe and elsewhere in the world. The extent to which such unity has resulted in uniformity has varied. In some cases, pre-existing identities and traditions have dissolved in the states that have been created since the eighteenth century. In others, a strong sense of local identity has survived (or been re-created) and received institutional support, either from the outset or subsequently.

It can be argued that the fact of insularity made 'Britain' an early candidate for consolidation. The sea which surrounded their islands gave the inhabitants of 'Britain' some measure of protection from 'outsiders'. A polity seeking hegemony within the islands could often do so without challenge from an immediate neighbour. A continental polity with comparable hegemonic intentions had no such luxury. Such immunities, however, were relative rather than absolute. Insularity did not intrinsically require unity, though arguably it facilitated it. In any case, it is wrong to think of a single island. There was indeed the major island, but off shore were numerous small islands whose pivotal positions, in an age of sea communication, often gave them a distinctiveness and importance which transcended their size. 'Britain', therefore, could potentially consist of many islands, whose links with each other and with the nearest 'mainland' could be tenuous.

In this context, the position of 'Ireland' becomes enduringly problematic. It is almost a commonplace to remark that in the 'Celtic' world of western 'Britain' and 'Ireland', in terms of contact, the sea united as much as it divided – though it would be quite misleading to posit a pervasive sense of 'pan-Celtic' unity. There is, in fact, in the late twentieth century no state called 'Great Britain' but rather 'The United Kingdom of Great Britain and Northern Ireland'. This title places the present of 'Ireland' alongside the present of 'Great Britain'. It is a reminder – which will be further considered later in the book – of the unfinished business which remains the legacy of a past in which the relationship between the two islands, for good or ill, has been exceptionally close. At certain periods, perhaps most periods, there is an artificiality in supposing that each island has a separate and self-contained history. Developments in 'Ireland' had significant consequences in 'England', 'Scotland' and 'Wales'. This was even more the case in the opposite direction.

Conscious of these complexities, some historians have begun to seek to write the history of 'these islands' in the totality of their relationships – to use the phrase of a modern Irish Prime Minister.[2] There may indeed be one history of the 'British Isles' but to use the term '*British* Isles' loads the interpretative dice in the *British* direction from the outset. 'These islands' is too anonymous a term, while 'Atlantic Archipelago' sounds too artificial and seems to imply that the 'Archipelago' is primarily facing westwards. It is only in recent centuries that such an orientation might be argued. In short, there is no simple solution to these questions of nomenclature, as there is none to the proper framework for handling the 'British'/'Irish' relationship over a long period of time. Not least because there will be a separate volume in this series which will concern itself with 'the present and the past' of Ireland, Ireland will not have an extensive place in this 'British' history.

That said, an outline of the Irish story is necessary at this point. We may begin with the reminder that St Patrick, the fifth-century patron saint of Ireland, was of Romano-British origin. Over subsequent centuries, the island – rarely united under an effective 'high-king' – experienced Viking invasion, subjection and settlement at key points. Even more serious was the Anglo-Norman conquest which, apart from the south-west and the north-west, was complete by 1300. Even so, subjugation was by no means total and over the next two centuries Irish forces regained lost ground. In many cases, too, through intermarriage and assimilation, the conquerors were absorbed into Irish society. The processes at work in this respect were not very different, as will be seen, from those at work in 'England' and 'Scotland'. In consequence, by the early sixteenth century what indubitably constituted 'English' rule was confined to the 'Pale' around Dublin. Whether it would be squeezed even further, or whether the English government would embark on a further attempt at comprehensive conquest, remained to be seen.

Borders and boundaries

A collection of islands might have some measure of unity when viewed externally, but on closer inspection the land mass of 'Britain' was criss-crossed by obstacles – hills and mountains, river estuaries, forests and marshes – which made easy progression across country difficult. In certain areas the landscape was ceasing to be 'natural' as expanding populations shaped it according to their needs. The contrast between 'highland' and 'lowland' zones became more apparent, but it would be misleading to think neatly of the one being 'backward' and the other 'advanced'. 'Britain' simply did not rise in-

---

[2] Charles Haughey is the politician. M. Mansergh, ed., *The Spirit of the Nation: The Speeches and Statements of Charles J. Haughey (1957–1986)* (Cork, 1986) p. 476.

exorably as one moved from the south-east to the north and west. The natural features of the islands had naturally determined the routes of entry, and subsequent passage, of successive invaders over previous centuries. The earthworks, walls, wooden stockades, stone forts and castles of increasing sophistication had in turn defined territory and the limits of authority. By the end of the fifteenth century, this was no *terra incognita* but a country with a rich profusion of place-names. It had been shaped and structured over centuries into units and divisions, using different terms and phrases, which reflected legal, administrative and military convenience. The result was that the boundaries, within 'Britain', of England, Scotland and Wales were established more or less in the alignment which exists at the end of the twentieth century. Both between England and Wales and between England and Scotland, however, were border regions, the 'Marches', whose limits were contested and fluctuating. Wherever the precise frontier was drawn, there was no doubt that a boundary existed. 'Britain' – and by extension Ireland – was not an undifferentiated whole. These boundaries signified zones where distinct societies clashed and mingled – though powerful individuals could transcend them. Behind the boundaries there was indeed great division and complexity, but in front of them stood 'the other'. England, Scotland and, rather more uncertainly, Wales had developed their own identities, institutions and images. It was not clear, however, what ultimate significance the boundaries would have, for they were no more preordained either by geography or 'ethnicity' than many other boundaries in Europe at the same time. Five hundred years earlier they would have been drawn in different places. Seven hundred and fifty years earlier they would have been different again, and so on. The identity of the peoples enclosed within them – insofar as we can speak in such language – would have been different too.

England and the English

The kingdom of England indubitably stood pre-eminent amongst the realms of 'Britain'. Population figures cannot be given accurately, but it is likely that in 1500 there were some thousands in excess of 2 million people living in England and Wales, a heavy preponderance being in England. There may have been half a million in Scotland and some 800,000 in Ireland. It is generally believed that two centuries earlier the figure had been substantially higher but that famine and the Black Death had reduced the population sharply and in 1500 it had only slowly begun to return to a pattern of growth. Some authorities suggest that there were more people living in Roman Britain than in the 'Britain' of 1500. Whatever the exact figures, that the preponderance of the population was in England is not questioned. Population, of course, is only one indication of strength and capacity. However, that such an English population could be sustained points to the relative sophistication of English agriculture and commerce.

In London, too, England had what was clearly a capital city; it was not until 1500 when James IV of Scotland set in train the lavish rebuilding of the Palace of Holyroodhouse that Edinburgh clearly became Scotland's capital. Wales, at this time, had no town to compare. London had an early medieval population of perhaps 25,000. If we take a liberty and include within it Westminster, upstream and separate, it had everything. It was port, trading centre, manufacturing centre and the seat both of the court, the courts of justice and of government (the Exchequer was transferred from Winchester in the twelfth century). The Tower of London, built after the Norman Conquest, dominated the city. Whether or not English people actually visited it, London's buildings and the wealth of its leading citizens were fabled across the country. It was already a magnet which, for better or worse, attracted visitors from all over 'Britain', not just England, and from continental Europe where no other city had quite arrogated to itself such central importance within the state. Bristol, the second city of England, could not seriously rival it, though its merchants too could channel wealth into buildings – as for example the church of St Mary Redcliffe.

'England' had not existed in 500 and the path to its creation could no more have been predicted then than the path to the England of 1500 could have been predicted in 1000. By 1500, it seemed evident that England had firmly arrived. The diverse elements which had impacted on what was to be its territory had been fused or forced together. That there were these diverse strands had not been forgotten. Distinctive elements were discernible and attributable, but the result was England and the English. To assert this is not to suggest a uniformity between, say, Norfolk and Somerset or Northumberland and Hampshire, for that clearly did not exist. Even more was this the case with a 'peripheral' region such as Cornwall where its duke, the eldest son of the King of England, was a quasi-sovereign within his duchy. The duchy had its own charters. When their rights were perceived to be threatened, Cornishmen staged a rebellion in 1497 which brought them to London. The Venetian ambassador to Castile visited Cornwall in 1506 and pronounced it 'a very wild place which no human being ever visits, in the midst of a most barbarous race, so different in language and custom from the Londoners and the rest of England that they are as unintelligible to these last as to the Venetians'. In earlier centuries, however, it would not have been its 'isolation' which seemed the key to Cornwall's identity, but rather its pivotal position between Brittany and Wales and Ireland. Even then, however, the dialects of that world were becoming increasingly divergent.[3] No doubt Cornwall was exceptional in its 'Celtic' inheritance within England, but it was only a marked feature of what was true elsewhere. 'The

---

[3] P. Payton, *The Making of Modern Cornwall* (Redruth, 1992) pp. 46–60.

North' already tended to be perceived from London and the deep South as unstable and uncouth. Northerners in turn took pride in the offence that their directness seemed to cause. These differences had a long ancestry for they were distant refractions of the struggles for supremacy and survival between 'natives' and 'invaders', and then, in turn, between indigenized invaders and later would-be conquerors. They all had a claim to have contributed something to the complexity that was 'England'.

'The English' had, of course, not arrived fully-fledged in the lands they occupied. They emerged from the interaction between Angles, Frisians, Jutes and Saxons – the West Germanic tribes which had conquered and settled in eastern and southern 'England' and then pushed westwards in the period *c.*450–650. Small kingdoms had then emerged, expanding from the entry points of the migrants. Their number fluctuated, but the most well-known became the seven kingdoms of Kent, Essex, Sussex, Wessex, East Anglia, Mercia and Northumbria – the Anglo-Saxon heptarchy. On occasion, the Celtic peoples had proved capable of energetic resistance and, in the south-west and elsewhere, the extension of Saxon power was a piecemeal process rather than a remorseless drive. It was only in the ninth century that Cornish independence effectively came to an end. In the next century, the River Tamar became the boundary between Celt and West Saxon. Cornwall thereafter possessed a king of satellite status, subdued but still distinct. The thirteenth-century Mappa Mundi in Hereford Cathedral divides 'the island of Britain' into four constituent parts: England, Scotland, Wales and Cornwall. Even in 1500 Cornwall was still frequently described as 'West Wales'.

Subsequent historiography, its mind firmly fixed on the entity of 'England', has tended to see its early kingdoms as merely preludes, destined to give way to a unity that was always mysteriously implicit. In the centuries of their existence, their relative status one to another fluctuated. Thinking of the Northumbria of the scholar Bede, for example, we should not make the automatic assumption that the south-eastern kingdoms were more sophisticated than their northern counterparts. In the eighth century it was Mercia which, under successive kings, Ethelbald and Offa, dominated 'England' from its central position. One official document describes Offa as *rex totius Anglorum patriae* (King of all the homeland of the English). It was Offa, too, who had the 150-mile 'Dyke' constructed to the west of his territory. It stretched from the estuary of the Dee in the north to the estuary of the Severn in the south. Whatever its original military purpose, this still substantially extant edifice marked the first boundary between 'England' and 'Wales'.

In the early ninth century, however, Wessex in the south-west exerted a supremacy. Its rulers could normally claim political control south of the Thames. One King of Wessex, Egbert, was hailed by the *Anglo-Saxon Chronicle* as the eighth of the *Bretwaldas* (rulers of Britain). The continued use of this term suggests that some meaning must still have been attached to 'Britain'. Between 871 and 939, under three kings, Alfred, Edward the Elder

1.1 Understanding Alfred: During the South African War, which he ardently supported, Lord Rosebery, Scottish Liberal Imperialist Foreign Secretary and unsuccessful Prime Minister (1894–95), was perhaps an odd choice to put 2,000 English schoolchildren in the picture about 'our Alfred' on the occasion of the unveiling of Alfred's statue in Winchester in 1901. The statue (by Hamo Thorneycroft) celebrated the thousandth anniversary of Alfred's death, though in fact he died in 899.

and Athelstan, Wessex provided the vital leadership of the 'English' in the face of Scandinavian assaults which had begun in the last decades of the eighth century. Vikings made an abortive attempt to settle on the Isle of Thanet in 851, having already established themselves elsewhere around the coasts of 'Britain' and 'Ireland'. The main thrust of the Scandinavian attacks came from the north-east and other dynasties were not able to stand successfully against them. In the late 870s even Alfred was compelled to retreat to the Somerset marshes to survive. Over the next twenty years, however, until his death at the end of the century, the King of Wessex ended the threat posed by the Danes through a combination of diplomacy and clever organization of his resources. Coins struck at the time referred to him as Alfred *rex Angl[lorum]* – King of *the English*. Alfred can properly be called the first English national hero, and was acclaimed as such, from the sixteenth to the nineteenth centuries, and rewarded by statues in Wantage and Winchester.[4]

Any admiration for the achievement of the Wessex kings, however, should not cause the considerable and enduring impact of the Danish invaders to be overlooked. North and east of a line roughly from east of London to Chester, 'England' remained under Scandinavian control. The 'Danelaw' which prevailed for a time in this area therefore applied to approximately half of the country, though it is important to remember that the Danelaw was by no means a contemporary construct. Scholars also point out that there are considerable differences between the impact of the Danes in Yorkshire, Lincolnshire and East Anglia. From the early tenth century, however, West Saxon influence pushed into the 'Danelaw', partly by military means and partly because Danish farmers accepted West Saxon overlordship. By 924, when Athelstan became king, all England south of the Humber was under his control. By the end of the century, however, Scandinavian attacks had been renewed. English military morale crumbled under the ineffective rule of Ethelred. It was almost a relief to receive the Dane, Cnut, as King of all England in 1016. He and his sons ruled until 1042 when Edward the Confessor, of the Wessex dynasty, became king. He was succeeded in 1066 by his brother-in-law, Harold Godwinson, a man with a formidable military reputation. That reputation was to no avail. Nine months later, at Hastings in Sussex, Harold was killed resisting the invading forces of William of Normandy. The first England had come to an end. If the Norwegian king, Harald Hardrada, had been victorious against Harold Godwinson in the battle in Yorkshire shortly before, 'old' England would also possibly have come to an end, under a Norwegian rather than a Norman yoke.

The Normans and the English

Invasion, conquest, settlement – in broad terms this was the pattern which produced Anglo-Saxon England. It should be remembered, however, that the

---

[4] The millenary of Alfred's death was celebrated in 1901 in some style. The battleship *King Alfred* was launched in recognition of the 'founder of the English navy'. Frederic Harrison, the leading figure in the Positivist movement, referred to Alfred as 'the incarnation of all that we must cherish in the national character'. For Lord Rosebery, not himself of Wessex stock, Alfred was 'the ideal Englishman ... the embodiment of our civilization'. The historic continuity of England was symbolized by a commemoration medal with an inscription 'King Alfred the Great 901 AD – Edward VII King and Empr. 1901'. C. Dellheim, *The Face of the Past: The Preservation of the Medieval Inheritance in Victorian England* (Cambridge, 1982) pp. 72–5.

previous Celtic population was not completely dislodged, though it is difficult to say how large it was. Some scholars believe that the Romano-British survivors in 'England' constituted a significant element in the 'unfree' population – a radical distinction being made at the time between 'free' and 'unfree'. Even so, we should be wary of any suggestion that a small number of Anglo-Saxon landlords exercised power over a basically Celtic population. Sometimes, at a late stage in the Saxon consolidation, pockets of Celts were specifically relocated – as happened at Exeter, for example, when the Tamar became the boundary between Devon and Cornwall.

In one sense, therefore, the victory of William of Normandy in 1066 only initiated one more cycle of a predictable kind. After all, England had experienced Danish kings in the person of Cnut and his successors in the immediately preceding decades. Even Edward the Confessor, whose death had precipitated the crisis, had spent his long exile from England in Normandy. It would be quite misleading, too, to think of the Norman Conquest as annexing 'England' to 'France'. The arrival of the Normans was in a sense only one more example of those assaults from Scandinavia on the existing societies and structures of 'Western Europe' and elsewhere which had been going on for some two and a half centuries. It was only in 911 that 'Vikings' had settled in Normandy. They retained their links both with Northern Europe and with the English Danelaw. Their arrival in England 150 years later could be said to be merely another scene of their activity. Yet, wherever they settled, whether in Sicily or in Antioch, it has been noted that they seemed relatively indifferent to their survival as 'Normans' and were prepared to adopt the language and the customs of people they conquered. That happened to a considerable extent in Normandy too in the century and a half after 911.

The year 1066 remains one of the relatively few dates firmly lodged in contemporary British minds as a significant turning point in the history not only of England but of the entire British Isles. Immediately, it took English history in a new direction. The England of 1500 could not have been what it was without the contribution which the Normans made. It was no longer the country developed by the Anglo-Saxons, but equally it survived as an England that was more 'English' than might have been forecast in 1066. The full significance of the conquest has remained controversial amongst scholars. They have debated the extent to which there was 'nascent' feudalism in late Anglo-Saxon society or whether its central features came with the conquest. It is undoubtedly the case that pre-conquest rulers in 'Britain' expected political, administrative and military service from their landed elites. Nevertheless, in the form of knight service – duties performed by well-armed and mounted soldiers for a superior lord in return for land held from him – and in the network of castles where lords resided, other scholars have continued to see the 'feudal system' as a Norman imposition. Much hinges on what the 'essence' of feudalism is taken to be and on this, too, there is no scholarly agreement.

Likewise, the vitality or otherwise of pre-conquest England, taken in the round, has been a matter of dispute. Some writers have been very impressed by the legal and administrative structures which it developed. Sometime during the tenth century, England was divided up into shires and the shires, in turn, into hundreds. Shire courts and hundred courts helped in the administration of royal justice and kept the peace. There has also been admiration for the country's financial sophistication, as evidenced by a reliable coinage. It is argued that England was a wealthy land, full of ardent farmers and arduous farming. It was certainly a land worth conquering and exploiting. There has also been high praise for 'Anglo-Saxon' or 'Early English' vernacular – poems, songs and riddles. In comparative European perspective, the fact that the *Anglo-Saxon Chronicle* (an annual compilation of events) was written in the vernacular was precocious. The Saxon churches that survive in contemporary England attract adjectives like 'solid' or 'sturdy'. On the other hand, the English intellectual climate has been considered stifling, self-contained, even backward-looking. It has also been argued that pre-conquest 'England' was by no means contentedly unified. Was there not lingering resentment, in the former small kingdoms, against the domination of Wessex? There was ruthlessness in Alfred's seizure of London (a Mercian town) and his claim that he was king of all the English who were not under Danish rule. It was, however, that Danish threat rather than any underlying pre-disposition to unite which did bring about 'unification'. An implication of this line of argument is that it was the Normans rather than the English who really created 'England'.

Steadily and ruthlessly, Norman control was exerted and it became apparent that this conquest was no passing cloud. English resistance, which did continue for a time in the north-east, the south-west and along the Welsh border, was dealt with harshly. Settlements were frequently put to the torch. The severity with which resistance was treated no doubt largely explains why it did not last. In 1068, for example, Harold Godwinson's sons, backed by a Viking fleet, were driven off by the citizens of Bristol and the thegns of Somerset, both groups having concluded that Norman supremacy was inevitable. Castles dotted the countryside in strategic positions. Some 500 of these impressive stone-built structures were erected by 1100. The cavalry was of crucial importance. English earls and thegns were deprived of their land and their offices. The famous Domesday Book was compiled in 1086 to enable the king to be certain that all his subjects were paying the appropriate rents and taxes. The consolidation of Norman England was a serious business.

In short, while a certain kind of Englishness did not die, pre-conquest 'England' could not return. The Norman stamp was too vigorous and too omnipresent. The incomers were quickly established in the dominant position in Church and state. It is suggested that land-hunger and a growing population in Normandy may well have been a factor in launching the invasion. Certainly there was no lack of barons and knights prepared to take up position in the new land, though they constituted but a small proportion of the population – perhaps some 15,000 out of around 2 million. Such an imbalance helps to explain why it was so important to establish a clear hierarchy of feudal duties.

The Norman presence was therefore inevitably aristocratic – an alien caste on top of a population which still thought of itself as, in some sense, English. In royal writs, the use of Anglo-Saxon only survived for a few years after 1066. The language was not used thereafter either by government or most of the clergy. There is no evidence, however, that the Normans, either immediately or subsequently, sought to make their kind of French (sometimes a little misleadingly called 'Anglo-Norman') the language of the people of England. Nevertheless, for a further 200 years or so, the French language occupied the dominant position in England. It was the continuing language of the royal court. It was inevitable, too, that scholars, even of English descent, could not resist the attractions of using French. Latin had status for record purposes, though Norman French began to challenge it. It should be noted that some of the many Latin-derived words in the English language came in through the Normans. Romano-British Latin had scarcely any impact on Old English. For some three centuries after 1066, therefore, England was what would now be described as a linguistically plural society, though not in the sense that the entire population was bi- or trilingual. Different languages were used by different people for different purposes with differing degrees of competence. They could not be kept in separate compartments and, over time, there were borrowings and assimiliations.

By the end of the fifteenth century, however, while there was some continuing aristocratic command of French, there was no doubt that England was again an English-speaking country. It was in important respects a 'new' language. Pre-conquest Anglo-Saxon (Old English) had remained a highly inflected language. Its precise form, vocabulary and intonation had varied considerably from one part of 'England' to another. Its loss of the official status which it formerly enjoyed, and its continuing use at a lower social level, probably served to simplify its structure. For several centuries, English had been used in devotional and other texts. The works of Richard Rolle were popular in the late fourteenth century. By the fourteenth century, however, it was a language which had certainly moved out of the hearth and market place. The work of the poet Chaucer (*c.*1340–?1400) showed what it could be made to do – and in the process helped to establish the pre-dominance of the south-eastern vernacular. His *Canterbury Tales* (begun *c.*1387) swiftly established his reputation. It would be a mistake, however, to think that Chaucer was writing for the people he was writing about. He was in royal service and travelled in France and Italy. It was his cosmopolitan frame of reference as much as his use of English which commended him in court circles. The publication of the *Canterbury Tales*, roughly a century later, by the printer William Caxton ensured their popularity in 1500. It was

Caxton who gave Chaucer a laureate status and talked about him reforming the 'rude' language of his ancestors. Chaucer and his contemporary William Langland, author of *Piers Plowman*, gave 'English literature' its pedigree. Their writing, and that of other contemporaries, suggests that English was now the routine language at all social levels.

Scotland and the Scots

The birth of 'Scotland' is even more problematic than the birth of 'England'. Much of its early history is necessarily speculative and cannot be discussed here. A starting point would be the eighth century when the rulers of Fortriu, centred at Scone in Perthshire, had come to be acknowledged as overkings of all the Picts. Who the Picts (*Picti* – painted ones) were has fascinated scholars. They are now increasingly thought to be Celts, but some scholars still endow them with more exotic origins. However, at this point, the western kingdom of Scots (Gaelic speakers who hailed from the north of Ireland) remained distinct under the name of Dalriada. So did the kingdom of Strathclyde, centred on the fort of Dumbarton on the Clyde which was inhabited by 'British' Celts. By the end of this century there were examples of simultaneous 'dual kingships' of the Picts and Scots. In the next century a Dalriadic king, Kenneth mac Alpin, seized the Pictish kingdom and established a dynasty which was to last until 1034.

We can see in these moves some steps which were later to produce, at least to some extent, not only the unification of kingdoms but also the blending of peoples. And authority was acknowledged over peoples rather than specific territory, territory which could fluctuate. For example, the mac Alpin dynasty had its eyes on Durham in 'England', while Anglian Northumbrian aspirations extended into the Lothians of 'Scotland'.

The mac Alpin dynasty shared one problem with the ascendant dynasty of Wessex in southern England: the assault from Scandinavia. Vikings, masters of the sea, found 'Scotland' vulnerable. The Northern Isles – Orkney and Shetland – were lost to the Norsemen early in the ninth century. They also settled on islands in the west of 'Scotland' and in Caithness. The significance of 'Sutherland' is self-evident.

It is easy and, up to a point, convincing to see 'native' rulers up and down the British Isles in these centuries heroically engaged in battles for survival against the Norsemen. The reality appears more complicated. The mac Alpin dynasty, for example, was quite eager to point out to them that the British kingdom of Strathclyde would make a good target. It was also prepared, on occasion, to make marriage alliances with the Vikings. We should not assume, either, that 'the Vikings' were united in their objectives. And, when the Scandinavian threat receded, 'native' rulers did not display conspicuous amity amongst themselves. Eleventh-century 'Scotland' was an uneasy amalgam of peoples. The Norman invasion of England meant that its consolidation as a kingdom was, to an extent, a race against time. Would a Scottish realm be able to display sufficient strength, coherence and sense of common identity to survive before, bit by bit, its territory became an appendage of England?

William of Normandy extended his 'harrying' of the north of 'England' even further in 1072. His expedition was designed to make it clear to the King of Scots that he was not to give support to English nobles who had fled north. It seems that William had no intention of seeking direct control over 'Scotland'. Even so, subsequently, William and successive English chroniclers claimed that the Scottish king, Malcolm Canmore, had done formal homage to the King of England as his vassal. If so, Malcolm's later raids into Northumbria suggested that he had not been inhibited by such submission. The 'border' was contentious then and, as has already been noted, remained so for centuries. By 1500, however, although the 'Marches' still to some extent constituted a law unto themselves, the border between the two countries was broadly constituted by the Solway/Tweed line.

Ambiguity concerning the precise relationship between the kings of Scotland and the kings of England became normal. What it meant depended, in practice, on the relative strengths of the two monarchs at any given time, something which in turn reflected the extent to which their own domains were tranquil. Geographical factors made the control of Scotland particularly difficult. Indeed, some contemporary maps referred mysteriously to the existence of a 'Scottish Sea' which appeared to divide the country into two. Indeed, there was sometimes only a small passage at Stirling which made land communication between south and north in Scotland possible. On the other hand, pressure from Scandinavia, the bane of earlier Scottish rulers, was diminishing. In 1263 the Norwegian king was defeated off the Ayrshire coast in a sea battle. Even so, the Scandinavian element remained significant in the evolution of Scotland, though in the west 'Vikings' were becoming 'Gaelicized'.

The Normans added another factor to the cultural and linguistic complexity of 'Scotland'. By the early twelfth century, there was already a steady pattern of Norman settlement in the Lowlands (though some of these 'Normans' were Flemings). Scottish kings took note. David I (1124–53) and William the Lion (1165–1214) consciously aped Norman ways and methods and sometimes enrolled Normans themselves in their battles against the 'English'. Scottish kings themselves, however, did not become 'Normanized'. Normally they spoke Gaelic and Gaelic language, law and customs were not confined to the Highlands but reached into the Lothians where there was a significant 'Anglian' presence. However, a great Norman family like the Balliols, which also held land in 'France' and many parts of England, did not become 'Gaelicized'. Thirteenth-century Scotland was more variegated than

1.2 Securely ensconced in a Land Rover, the 'Stone of Scone' (or 'Stone of Destiny') comes back across the border at Coldstream in 1996, seven hundred years after Edward I removed it from the abbey of Scone to Westminster Abbey. There it resided under the Coronation Chair on which all subsequent English/British monarchs sat. The removal of this block of reddish-grey sandstone on which, before Edward I of England's acquisition, Scottish kings had formally inaugurated their reigns, perhaps for some four hundred years, symbolized Scottish dynastic subordination. What its return to Scotland symbolized is more problematic.

England was at the same date. Its existence was also more precarious, not least because of the aspirations of its southern neighbour.

Stung by the unwillingness of Scottish nobles to offer him the help that he believed was his due in his campaigns in Gascony, Edward I of England seemed determined to puncture Scottish pretensions permanently. In the background, in Scotland, was a failure to settle the succession to the throne. War began in 1296 and the English forces quickly achieved a victory. The Scots were humiliated: their king languished in the Tower of London and the Stone of Destiny (on which Scottish kings were crowned) was removed to Westminster Abbey, as was Scotland's prized relic, the Black Rood of St Margaret. The Stone was returned to Scotland, with due ceremony, in 1996. Formally, Scotland was not annexed, but an emphatic statement of how the relationship was perceived in London had been made. Even so, in 1297 William Wallace mounted a rebellion which succeeded in defeating English forces which remained in Scotland. In turn, Edward assembled a massive army, invaded again and achieved a major victory at the Battle of Falkirk

17

(1298). Despite the apparently overwhelming nature of the English success, Edward does not seem to have been certain about his next step in Scotland. Should he annex or withdraw, conciliate or coerce? In the event, no clear decision seemed to emerge.

After Edward I's death in 1307, the English position in Scotland fell away quickly under the harassment of Robert Bruce (who reigned 1306–29). Bruce might have been even more effective if he had not had to cope with the divided loyalties and rivalries amongst the Scottish lords, though he himself had committed sacrilegious murder. Paradoxically, it might be said that the fate of Scotland rested with great men, like Bruce, who were of Anglo-Norman descent. The Scottish victory at Bannockburn, near Stirling, in 1314 was decisive. Edward II of England was humiliated, though it did not bring warfare between England and Scotland to an end. In striking language, the Declaration of Arbroath (1320), addressed to the Pope, presented a glowing picture of Scottish kings and people determined to fight for their liberty. Peace of a kind was only agreed in 1328. Even that proved to be a mere interval. When Anglo-Scottish warfare revived in the 1330s it took a more complex form. The English cleverly exploited the rivalry in Scotland between the dominant Bruce and Balliol families. In consequence, they were for a time able to assert their claims to overlordship over Scotland. The Treaty of Berwick (1357) again brought fighting to a temporary conclusion. Before the end of the century, however, a familiar pattern had reappeared: English expeditions reached Edinburgh and Scottish expeditions reached Newcastle.

The fifteenth century, by comparison, was more tranquil. There were fewer direct confrontations across the Anglo-Scottish border. A new dynasty, the Stewarts, had established itself in Scotland and a growing confidence in the viability of the state is discernible. The Orkney islands were ceded to Scotland by the King of Norway in 1472 as part of the dowry of the Danish princess who married James III (1460–88). Scotland had its heroes in the persons of Wallace and Bruce. In the 1370s *The Bruce*, written by John Barbour, achieved the status of a national epic. It would be misleading, however, to suppose that Anglo-Scottish conflict had become a thing of the past. The important town of Berwick was lost to the English in 1482. Yet, under James IV (1488–1513), the Scottish court presided over cultural and building projects of conspicuous brilliance. In 1502 a Treaty of Perpetual Peace with England was signed. It could be believed that a more harmonious future beckoned.

1.3 The Battle of Bannockburn (1314). It was not often that English forces were defeated in Anglo-Scottish military encounters. Bannockburn echoed down the centuries as a conspicuous exception. It was doubly celebrated since the defeat of English forces under Edward II, bent on relieving an English garrison in nearby Stirling, was the only victory over an English king. The Bannockburn triumph (of which this is the earliest known representation) contributed to the survival, precarious though it was, of medieval Scotland.

Wales and the Welsh

In 1485, at the Battle of Bosworth, it is alleged that the blow which finally killed the king, Richard III, was delivered by a Welshman, Sir Rhys ap Thomas, who had thrown his forces behind the claimant, Henry, Earl of Richmond. And Henry was Henry Tudor, son of Owen ap Maredudd ap Tudor, born in Pembroke Castle. The new dynasty on the throne of England was indubitably half-Welsh. It was an outcome which would be described, in contemporary commercial terms, as a reverse take-over.

It was almost a thousand years earlier, in 597, that Saxon forces in the Battle of Dyrham (outside Bristol) had severed the western 'British' Celtic world. What had originally been referred to as 'North Wales' became simply Wales. Something similar happened in the north-west of 'England' when Mercians inserted the wedge which separated Cumbria (and Strathclyde) from 'Wales'. Offa's Dyke, as has been noted, sealed 'Wales' completely. Behind it lay much intractable country divided between tribal units going under various names – Gwynedd, Powys and Deheubarth among them – under a miscellany of rulers. The inhabitants of this territory were referred to by the Saxons as *wealhas* (Welsh) – a word meaning 'foreigner', perhaps originally with the inference that they had been part of the Roman system. Amongst themselves, the inhabitants behind Offa's Dyke used the word *Cymry* – 'fellow countrymen'. The lack of a single territorial description no doubt reflected the fact that for some three centuries the territory they had been inhabiting had been changing substantially. Under Rhodri Mawr (d.878), the northern kingdom of Gwynedd was in the ascendant, and his grandson, Hywel Dda (d.950) of Dyfed, was generally recognized by English rulers as paramount. He instigated the written collection of Welsh customary laws. He is the only pre-Norman Welsh ruler from whose reign a coin survives.

By and large, English rulers had respected, or been compelled to respect, the boundary which Offa's Dyke represented. The Anglo-Normans, however, showed no such restraint and penetrated westwards. They did not mount one comprehensive campaign but rather a series of well-directed raids. In their wake they erected wooden (and subsequently stone) castles at strategically important points. They accrued land and power to themselves and in many places simply took over from Welsh lords. As men of the frontier, however, these Marcher barons were not disposed to yield to the King of England any more than was strictly required by their feudal allegiance to him. For his part, the king needed the security which their activities offered. In this situation, many border barons acted with considerable independence.

Individual Welsh princes, such as the Lord Rhys in the south-west and Owain Gwynedd in the north-west, held great sway in their local area but could not exercise authority throughout 'Welsh' Wales. They both did homage to Henry II in 1163. In practice, the preoccupations, or otherwise, of the

English king determined the scope of the princes' influence in Wales. In the century after 1172, the aspirations of the English Crown, of the Anglo-Norman barons and of the Welsh princes were in reasonable equilibrium. To some extent, in the south-west Anglo-Norman ambitions were redirected to Ireland. Pembroke was the perfect place from which to sail across the Irish Sea. The assault on Ireland began in 1169. Securing the southern sea-route to Ireland became more important than penetrating even further into the inhospitable interior of Wales.

Further action against independent Welsh princes took place approximately a century later. In the interval, Llywelyn 'the Great' (d.1240) had again brought Gwynedd to pre-eminence in Wales. He was careful to acknowledge the overlordship of the English Crown (he married the illegitimate daughter of King John of England) but he nevertheless laid the foundations of what could be a principality of Wales. His grandson, Llywelyn ap Gruffydd, took advantage of turmoil in England to regain ground for the Welsh and obtained recognition as Prince of Wales in the Treaty of Montgomery (1267). A dozen years later, English power reasserted itself. Seeking to turn the tables once again, Llywelyn was killed in 1282. It was clear that Edward I was determined to bring 'Wales' under firm control by military means. Meeting with success, he removed what purported to be King Arthur's crown as a symbol of English supremacy. The Statute of Rhuddlan (1284) set up a new system of shires in Wales on the English model. Together, these new shires formed the principality of Wales. Henceforward, the Prince of Wales would be the eldest son of the King of England. The territory of the Marcher lords in Wales was, however, left unaltered, though in time some of the lordships fell directly into the king's hands.

Administratively, therefore, fourteenth-century Wales consisted of two roughly equal areas – one to the west and one to the east. Wales was not annexed to England but Englishmen began to play an increasingly important part in its administration and in ensuring security. The towns around the major castles – such as at Caernarfon or Conwy, for example – were therefore largely English outposts. A Welsh hinterland surrounded them. It was a situation which required linguistic talent. An official needed knowledge of Welsh, English, Anglo-Norman and Latin. By these measures it appeared that Wales had been successfully subordinated. Its 'foreign' character, however, still seemed very evident to English writers. Welshmen themselves in some cases took comfort from bardic prophecies which foretold that English domination would end. Such prophecies had circulated for centuries and often envisaged a restored 'Britain' under the auspices of the Britons.

In 1400 Owain Glyn Dŵr, a descendant of the princes of Powys, who had previously served the English Crown in London, raised the standard of revolt. What some suggest began as a private grievance certainly turned over the next few years into an uprising which merits the description 'national'. Glyn Dŵr was helped for a time by the Percys, in rebellion in England, by

the French and by the Avignon papacy. By 1405 almost all of Wales was more or less under his control. He obtained recognition for himself as Prince of Wales and in 1404 and 1405 held a parliament in mid-Wales. He had ambitious plans for ecclesiastical and educational reforms. If he had survived and achieved his aims, it seems likely that Wales would have become a modest renaissance state. It has been noted that he neither sought the English Crown nor the revival of 'Britain', but rather placed a novel and striking emphasis simply on 'Wales'. By 1410, however, as English power reasserted itself, Glyn Dŵr disappeared. It is not known where or when he died. In the aftermath, severe laws were passed on Welsh people by way of punishment for the support given to the rebellion. They became, in effect, second-class subjects before the law and were made to obey restrictions which did not apply to Englishmen living in Wales. It is not surprising that the penal laws produced a certain amount of lawlessness in Wales, but there was little likelihood of another major revolt.

It is also not surprising that the appearance of a half-Welsh king on the throne of England in 1485, after all that had happened earlier in the century, seemed a miracle and promised relief. It was a king, moreover, whose ancestors at the beginning of the century had supported Owain Glyn Dŵr. A contemporary Italian writer, for example, saw Henry Tudor's elevation as a revolution: Welshmen might be said 'to have recovered their former independence, for the most wise and fortunate Henry the 7th is a Welshman'. There was a vast amount of symbolism about the fact that Henry gave his eldest son the name Arthur. The likelihood, however, was that the new dynasty would wish to bind Wales even more tightly to England, while perhaps relaxing the discriminatory laws. The new dynasty, by its very antecedents, would symbolize Anglo-Welsh union. The banner of Sir Rhys ap Thomas, new Knight of the Garter, hung in St George's Chapel, Windsor. The king's father was buried in Carmarthen. Wales, it seemed, was moving into the English sun.

The matter of Britain

In outlining the development of England, Scotland and Wales – not to mention Cornwall – the identities that appear to be emerging seem scarcely 'British'.

1.4 Exotic English Outpost: the walled town of Caernarfon, together with the imposing castle begun by Edward I in 1284, stands as a powerful expression of English power in North-West Wales. Caernarfon ('Fort in Arfon') points back to the Roman fort of Segontium built nearby some twelve hundred years earlier. It withstood a siege by Owain Glyn Dŵr and his French allies in 1403–4. Five hundred years later, however, the constituency of which it was a part had fallen to David Lloyd George and, at the end of the twentieth century to Dafydd Wigley, leader of *Plaid Cymru*.

Yet, behind these identities lay the tantalizing and obscure concept of 'Britain'. To explain its appeal and relevance we have to go back even further into the past – to the 'Britain' of the Romans.

As is well-known, fresh from his triumphs in Gaul, Julius Caesar carried out two expeditions in 55–54 BC, landing in Kent. He did not know the interior of the island and had little information about its inhabitants. It was not until AD 43 that 'Roman Britain' can properly be held to begin, when Claudius carried out a successful conquest. The discipline of the legions was too much for the Celtic tribes and their often spirited leaders. It seems clear, however, that from the start a 'divide and rule' policy was operated to good effect by the Romans. It was possible, however, for even Roman power to receive a severe setback, as happened in Boudicca's revolt in 61. Thereafter, stability was maintained, it would seem, by paying more attention to the feelings and aspirations of the Britons. Roman rule pressed on steadily into the interior of 'England' and 'Wales'. In the consolidated areas, the erstwhile tribal territories became self-governing administrative units, centred on either an existing town or a new Roman one. Roads improved communications. Forts ensured security. It seems clear that 'native' aristocracies fitted into the new circumstances without undue difficulty. As time passed, it proved necessary to divide 'Britannia' into two – Superior and Inferior – in 197.

Even so, 'Roman Britain' was not coextensive with the island of 'Britain' as ruled over by James VI and I in 1603. The further north the legions marched, the greater the opposition and the physical difficulties they encountered. In 83 the Roman governor Agricola gained a celebrated victory at Mons Graupius ('somewhere in Aberdeenshire') over the Caledonii, but his recall to Rome entailed the abandonment of plans to subdue the Highlands. The construction of the greatest surviving Roman landmark in contemporary Britain, Hadrian's Wall, was begun on a line roughly from present-day Carlisle to Newcastle. It reflected the view that it was better to build a permanent barrier against the more hostile tribes to the north in 'Caledonia' than to build forts there – though one full legionary fort did exist on the Tay. Twenty years later the Antonine Wall, constructed on the line between the Forth and Clyde estuaries, had a similar purpose. Both of these fortifications, however, were to have very troubled histories, and the latter had only a very short life. Strategies of advance and retreat on this northern frontier followed each other in swift succession over the next 200 years. By around 400, Hadrian's Wall was abandoned. A decade later, 'Roman Britain' was no more: the legions departed. It is now often argued that the departure stemmed from the enormous financial burden of maintaining the imperial army rather than direct military emergency.

The memory of its existence, however, lingered on. One specific example may be given, with all its extraordinary twists. In 383 Magnus Maximus, probably a Spaniard by birth, overthrew the Roman emperor of the west and for five years, until his own death in the Adriatic, ruled Britain, Gaul and Germany from Trier in 'Germany'. By the sixth century, Gildas, author of *The Ruin of Britain* (in Latin), sees him as the man who drained Britain of its Roman troops and let in the Saxons. Three centuries later, he is seen as both the last Roman ruler and the first independent British ruler, from whom various Welsh dynasties subsequently claimed descent. Three further centuries later, the Welsh legend-cycle, the *Mabinogion*, has Maximus spirited away in a dream to a location which, miraculously, can only be at the mouth of the River Seiont opposite the Isle of Anglesey in North Wales. And it is at this spot, near the Roman fortress of Segontium, that Edward I builds his great castle of Caernarfon. It is generally agreed that the inspiration for its design came from the walls of Constantinople, erected in the fifth century. Edward's claim to suzerainty in Wales was thus dramatically reinforced by this attempt to make a link with Magnus Maximus.

'Britannia' had once embraced a very large area of 'England/Wales', but 'Caledonia' had not been absorbed into it. The continuing impressive construction of Hadrian's Wall suggested that a 'frontier' somewhere in this region was 'natural'. The Roman touch in 'Scotland' was much lighter than in 'England/Wales' and, of course, control did not extend to 'Hibernia' (Ireland) at all, though a recent discovery may suggest, contrary to received wisdom, that there was a slight presence. Rome had felt no need to fortify a frontier between 'England' and 'Wales'. What was there to distinguish life in the Cotswolds from life in Gwent? The answer would appear to be 'very little'. It was a life which saw the emergence of a 'Romano-British civilization', blending old and new. Of course, the Roman departure removed the prop of this civilization and the Saxon threat, already evident, intensified and in the end became overwhelming. Just how much 'Romano-British' civilization, particularly urban civilization, survived the departure of the Romans has been much argued over. Whatever view is taken on this issue – and Romanization in Britain was less pronounced than in Gaul – the memory of Rome remained with the retreating 'Britons'. There was irony in the fact that 'Britain' was soon to be a memory most deeply treasured on the periphery rather than in its erstwhile heartland.

And 'Britain' entered into Saxon/English consciousness. In the tenth century, the energetic Athelstan sought to inherit some shadow of it. For practical purposes, by this juncture, Wessex and Mercia under his leadership were one kingdom. This meant that for the first time in 'English' history a southern king could intervene in the north in some strength. Athelstan had his eyes on Northumbria and wished to reduce the power of the Danish kings who still ruled in York. Furthermore, there was 'Scotland' too. In 927, at Penrith in Cumbria, the King of Scots, Constantine II – whose own name is not without significance – together with the King of Strathclyde, swore oaths of loyalty to Athelstan. However, Constantine still harboured hopes of containing Saxon power, if necessary in alliance with the 'Britons' of Strathclyde and the Danes of Dublin. In 937, however, the alliance he formed suffered a devastating defeat at the hands of Athelstan at Brunanburh (somewhere near the Humber). Since he also now controlled York, Athelstan was in a position to contemplate further advance. His victory ended the mac Alpin hopes that the territory of the Scots could extend to the Tyne/Solway line – i.e. roughly to Hadrian's Wall. Moreover, for a time there seemed a real possibility that Athelstan would move into 'Lowland Scotland'. If he had done so success-fully, it might have spelled the end of 'Scotland'. As it was, his navy sailed up the eastern coast and was in action as far north as Caithness. The exten-sion of Athelstan's influence was not confined to the north. The Welsh prin-ces were also persuaded to come to Hereford to swear oaths of loyalty to him. Coins were struck which described him as *rex totius Britanniae* (King of the whole of Britain). This was exaggeration, but it anticipated future events.

In practice, however, it became clear that the maintenance of Athel-stan's 'British' supremacy required constant effort and could not be achieved in perpetuity by a single battle such as that at Brunanburh. In addition, the ambitions of the Wessex/English kings were restrained by the personal and succession problems which afflicted the dynasty after Athelstan's death. Shortly after being crowned in Bath – no mean Roman town – in 973, Edgar was rowed on a royal barge at Chester by Celtic and Scandinavian rulers in symbolic recognition of his overlordship. In reality, that supremacy was slip-ping away. 'Britain' seems not to have been a concept which had particular relevance or attraction for Normans.

Some scholars, however, refused to let 'Britain' die. One such was Geoffrey 'of Monmouth', an Oxford scholar, possibly of Breton rather than Welsh descent. Whatever his ancestry, his Latin prose text *History of the Kings of Britain* (*c*.1138) contributed to a 'British' revival. Claiming that his work was based on a very ancient book 'in the British tongue', Geoffrey gave his readers illuminating accounts of the reigns of no less than 99 British kings, down to the year 689. Most scholars now believe that there was no such original book, though there was some material to draw from. Some of Geoffrey's scholarly contemporaries dismissed the text as fantasy. The suc-cess of his history, however, indicates that many readers wished to include a British past in their England. Geoffrey's most notable suggestion was that Britain had in fact been founded by its first king, Brut (hence the name Bri-tain), who was a descendant, he argued, of Aeneas of Troy. Brut himself had survived and, amongst other things, founded London. Geoffrey was also re-sponsible for giving the career of King Arthur further embellishment. These narratives were still being given currency in the chronicles of the fifteenth century. Edward IV (reigned 1461–83) considered that they buttressed his royal authority. Such a background made the decision of Henry Tudor to name his eldest son Arthur all the more significant. The matter of Britain might be on the brink of revival.

Continuities and contrasts

There is always a danger, in assembling 'ingredients', that the categories employed – the Celts, the Romans, the Saxons, the Danes, the Norwegians, the English, the Normans etc. – become too clear-cut and coherent. Individuals, no doubt on many occasions, behaved in ways which they believed would advance their personal interests, whatever their 'ethnic' identity. For example, Aethelwold, son of Alfred the Great's elder brother, allied with the Danes in Northumbria in 899 and they obligingly made him their king. In the following century, Athelstan himself married one of the sisters of the Norwegian King of York. Long lists of such alliances could be drawn up.

Even before the separation of the Celtic languages of Britain, to take another example, it would be unwise to endow Celtic civilization with a uniformity. The late Roman Empire was very dubiously Roman. The Normans were often Bretons or Flemings. One could go on. Whether, and at what social levels, cultural or ethnic discriminations were of fundamental significance at any given point in time is more problematic. That a conquering people felt itself to be superior to those it conquered goes almost without saying. Yet it has been pointed out, of the Normans in particular, that throughout Europe such ex-Vikings seemed almost indifferent to their own survival as a distinctive ethnic community. We cannot penetrate the minds and feelings of the lower levels of society with any confidence but the 'ethnic' character of their superiors may well have been a matter of relative insignificance. There was great diversity even within the identities that have been outlined, not least linguistically. King David I (1124–53) led a strong 'Scottish' army against English forces in the Battle of the Standard (1138). It was, however, necessary for contemporaries to describe David's force as being composed of 'Normans, Germans, English, Northumbrians and Cumbrians, men of Teviotdale and Lothian, Galwegians and Scots'. When Edward I of England defeated the Scots at the Battle of Falkirk in 1298 his army contained more than 10,000 Welshmen. They made a substantial contribution to the English success, though it is sometimes suggested that they did not fully commit themselves in the battle until it was clear what the outcome was likely to be!

It is the case, however, that Englishmen could on occasion suspect that all non-English peoples of the islands might unite against them and seek to re-establish 'Britain'. As Edward I lay dying in 1307, rumour reached the English court from Scotland that one such attempt was in prospect. In reality the possibility of such a 'pan-Celtic' alliance, including the Irish, was not strong. One of the striking achievements of Owain Glyn Dŵr was his success, albeit temporary, in gathering support throughout a country where geography gave no help to a sense of national unity. As Henry 'of Monmouth', the young Henry V had rather unsuccessfully hunted Owain. As King of England, he was to find Welshmen serving abroad in his army. Shakespeare, indeed, when he came to write his *Henry V*, was at pains to allocate parts in the army of England and St George for a Welshman, a Scot and and Irishman and to endow them with appropriate accents. His Englishmen, however, are made to understand each other's speech more readily in the fifteenth century than was likely to have been the case.

Of course, there existed peoples in these islands before any of the groups that have been identified. 'Albion' seems to have been a pre-Indo-European name for the island. The word 'prehistory' was first used in England in 1851. Periodization by material – stone, bronze and iron 'ages' – then became conventional. Late-twentieth- century archaeology, aided by sophisticated scientific techniques, has refined and altered many assumptions about periodization and population made in the early days of the discipline. The magnificent standing stones of the west of Scotland or the stone circles of Stonehenge and Avebury point to an even greater antiquity in Britain. The fascination of this field of study is enormous, yet we have no written records. 'Who the first inhabitants of Britain were', wrote the Roman historian Tacitus, 'whether natives or immigrants, remains obscure.' Nearly 2,000 years later, the answer still remains obscure.

In any case, a central question remains, both about 'prehistory' and about the 'ethnic' history down to 1500 that has been summarized in this chapter, a question that will recur concerning different periods throughout this book: in what sense, if at all, does it overhang into the present? Naturally, it is not a new question. Over subsequent centuries scholars and writers wrestled with this problem and returned different answers. Individual interpretation is only to be expected, as is the fact that individuals' answers have in turn reflected their understanding of the 'Britain' of their day. A book of this scope cannot hope to provide a comprehensive examination of all such reactions. It is, nevertheless, instructive to give certain examples.

For Victorian Britain, it was Britannia which evoked contrary emotions and attitudes. Intellectuals and politicians were steeped in the history of Greece and Rome. Their concept of civilization was to a considerable extent formed by the classical past. That Britannia had once been 'Roman' was therefore highly pleasing. Just as the Romans built roads in Britain, so British engineers built railways in India. Some commentators also saw significance in the fact that Ireland had not been 'Roman'. Even so, there was a reluctance to suppose that the Romans were 'our ancestors'. On the contrary, the Romans could be seen as the conquerors who had oppressed native Britons. Queen Boudicca, who led the major revolt against the Romans in 59–60, was a heroine. Chariot and all, she received her nineteenth-century memorial on the Embankment in London, close to the Houses of Parliament. She might even be seen as an early version of Queen Victoria, though it was unwise to see the Empress of India as a fomentor of rebellion!

Some writers went so far as to dismiss Roman Britain altogether as a relevant piece of the British past. Thomas Arnold, in his inaugural lecture as

Regius Professor of Modern History at Oxford in 1841, was one of them. He acknowledged a debt to the civilization of Greece and Rome. That was one thing, but Roman Britain was another. The Britons and Romans, he wrote, had indeed lived in 'our country', but they were not 'our fathers'. Caesar's invasions had 'no more to do with us, than the natural history of the animals which then inhabited our forests'.[5] Any past relevant to the present would have to begin later.

A century later, the novelist Rose Macaulay, in her *Life among the English*, approached the issue with more levity. She handled the 'Roman legacy' by picturing 'Latinless, bearded, woaded head tribesmen in remote forest clearings, striding among their swine and hectoring their swineheards in Welsh, deeply and fearfully religious, deeply and happily tipsy on mead'.[6] She did suggest, however, that there might also be found, in these rustic surroundings, an occasional Celtic chieftain who had a smattering of Latin. Rudyard Kipling, decades earlier, had been reading history books and concluded:

> But the Romans came with a heavy hand,
> And bridged and roaded and ruled the land,
> And the Romans left and the Danes blew in –
> And that's where your history-books begin

He omitted to mention that there were Saxons and Anglians who 'blew in' between the Romans and Danes. Such an omission was exceptional since, for many Victorians, 'English history' really began with the Saxons. 'The English nation', wrote William Stubbs, Yorkshireman, bishop and eminent constitutional historian, 'is of distinctly Teutonic or German origin ... This new race was the main stock of our forefathers, sharing the primaeval German pride in purity of extraction ....' Thomas Arnold was even more explicit. 'We', he wrote, 'this great English nation, whose race and language are now overcoming the earth from one end of it to the other – we were born when the white horse of the Saxons had established his dominion from the Tweed to the Tamar.'[7] Thomas Carlyle, however, a Scot latterly living amongst Englishmen, felt it necessary to describe the Anglo-Saxons as a 'gluttonous race ... lumbering about in pot-bellied equanimity'. Alfred Tennyson, conscious, as a Lincolnshire man, of the Danelaw, summed up many Victorian assumptions when he wrote the line 'Normans and Saxons and Danes are we'. Like Sir Thomas Mallory, who had written in English his epic *Morte d'Arthur* in the mid-fifteenth century, and other writers subsequently, Tennyson was also willing to absorb King Arthur and his deeds

---

[5] T. Arnold cited in P. Hinchliff, *God and History* (Oxford, 1992) p. 12.
[6] R. Macaulay, *Life among the English* (London, 1946) p. 8.
[7] W. Stubbs and T. Arnold cited in Hinchliff, *God and History*, p. 16.

into 'English history' and wrote *The Idylls of the King*. Not all writers, how-ever, were willing to accept such a Celtic infusion. 'As to Arthur', stated the poet and critic S.T. Coleridge, 'you could not by any means make a poem on him national to Englishmen. What have we to do with him?'[8] There, per-haps, spoke a true man of Devon – after a thousand years!

G.M. Trevelyan, in his celebrated and best-selling *English Social History* written during the Second World War, would not accept as 'English' anything earlier than the fourteenth century.[9] It was not, it has to be ad-mitted, an appropriate moment to stress the Teutonic origins of England.

So the debate has continued, sometimes even among 'postmodern' historians normally suspicious of the possibility of such linkages. The way in which particular facets of the past have been fastened on for present purposes will continue to be explored in this book. The problem, however, cannot rest with ethnic 'identities', real or imaginary, but must be seen in conjunction with the evolution of ideas and institutions. What happened on the islands of 'Britain' can only be understood, too, in the context of the 'world', great or small, in which the cluster of islands existed. It is these facets of the pic-ture of pre-1500 Britain which will next be explored.

---

[8] Cited and discussed in K. Robbins, *Nineteenth-Century Britain: Integration and Diversity* (Oxford, 1988) pp. 48–57.
[9] G.M. Trevelyan, *English Social History* (London, 1946 edn) p. xii.

Chapter 2

The Framework Established

Entire of itself?

This other Eden, demi-paradise,
This fortress built by nature for herself
Against inflection and the hand of war,
This happy breed of men, this little world,
This precious stone set in the silver sea
Which serves it in the office of a wall
Or as a moat defensive to a house
Against the envy of less happier lands;

Shakespeare gave these famous lines to the dying John of Gaunt in his play *Richard II*. As a statement of retrospective fact, it was scarcely accurate. The 'silver sea' had hardly given the 'sceptred isle' absolute protection against invasion. The ethnic mixture of the islands derived precisely from their subjection to successive invaders. Yet, by the end of the fourteenth century, and even more a century later, there seemed good grounds for supposing that the sea did give 'Britain' a special security and that an island destiny beckoned. It enabled the country to progress in a way that was indeed the envy of other lands which were subjected to continuing invasion and conquest. Individuals – such as Henry Tudor himself who landed in Wales from Brittany – had launched their expeditions from the Continent, but that was different from invasion by a foreign force.

The supposed immunity from invasion, however, should not be taken to indicate that the sea cut off the British Isles from contemporaneous developments on the European mainland. Nor should it even be assumed that a self-contained insular polity was 'inevitable'. John of Gaunt, ironically, was a major figure in European politics in the second half of the fourteenth century. As his name indicates, it was in Ghent in modern Belgium that this

third son of Edward III and father of Henry IV was born. By virtue of his second marriage to Constance of Castile he acquired the title King of Castile and Leon. In addition, from 1390, he became Duke of Aquitaine. Both of these positions entailed deep involvement in war and politics in south-western Europe. Such proliferation of activity was not a novel development. How rulers within 'Britain' saw themselves, and their territories, within the complexity of the Europe of their day had always been a matter of fundamental importance.

Britannia was self-evidently a far-flung part of a complex empire and its fate was bound up with the destiny of the empire as a whole. Britons had no special status but co-existed in what was a multinational conglomeration. The Channel, therefore, had no fundamental importance. Before the Roman conquest, it seems likely that quite strong links between Celtic peoples on both sides of the Channel had been maintained. The last Celtic settlement, that of the Belgae, had occurred only 150 years before the arrival of the Romans. As far as the Saxons and Angles were concerned, they undoubtedly kept contacts across the North Sea with the lands from which they had come, though, in time, a clear distinction existed between 'Anglo-Saxons' and 'German Saxons'. The 'boat grave' discovered at Sutton Hoo in Suffolk, probably that of a seventh-century East Anglian king, revealed Byzantine silver, and coins from 'France' and Scandinavia. Offa of Mercia was able to meet Charlemagne, King of the Franks, more or less on equal terms. There was a British settlement of Roman Amorica – hence Brittany – from the fifth to the seventh centuries, though it is not clear why it took place. A lively contact was maintained with Cornwall. Hywel Dda made a celebrated journey to Rome in 928 or 929. There were other notable continental travellers from the British Isles.

Over the next couple of centuries, it is arguable that the concept of 'insularity' has little value. We have already noted the extent of the Scandinavian incursions in different parts of 'Britain'. It looked as though the islands could be drawn into a Scandinavian orbit – a kind of extended Sutherland. The Danelaw was, for a time, a reality. Later, when Cnut seized the English kingdom by conquest in 1016, it again appeared that England might be an appendage of the Scandinavian world. Cnut became King of Denmark in 1019 and spent much of his time fighting in Scandinavia. However, the empire which he held together disintegrated after his death in 1035. His sons were notably unsuccessful. With their deaths, it can be said that the Scandinavian interest in England was never again so strong. Scotland, however, for

---

2.1 Iona. What survives is not St Columba's original foundation in 563 but one rebuilt in the mid-twelfth century which adopted the Benedictine rule and survived until the Reformation. Vikings sacked the original building in 795. Buried on the island are persons as various as Macbeth, King of Scots and John Smith, brief late-twentieth-century leader of the British Labour Party. In Columba's day it was more populous than in our own and to that extent the image of peaceful isolation is deceptive.

obvious geographical reasons, had greater contacts and it has already been noted that it was not until the end of the fifteenth century that Orkney was formally returned to the Scottish Crown.

On the other hand, the Norman conquest of 1066, as noted in the previous chapter, could itself be regarded as a last Scandinavian throw. The new king, however, excelled his Danish predecessors in vigour, ruthlessness, determination and military effectiveness. William himself, however, maintained a personal preference for his duchy of Normandy and it was in Normandy that he was buried. It was not altogether clear whether William's success in 1066 would inaugurate a new dynasty. He had based his own claim to the English throne on promises which he said had been made to him personally. In the event, a new dynasty was established, but the future relationship between Normandy, France and England was problematic from the outset. England still had a residual continental possession in 1500 – Calais – but at various periods after 1066 England's continental stake, and perhaps its destiny, was much greater.

When Henry II succeeded to the English throne in 1154, he was already Duke of Normandy, Count of Anjou and, as the result of his marriage to Eleanor, Duke of Aquitaine. Ruling until 1189, he and his sons and successors, Richard I and John, left a distinct Angevin mark on English history. Their horizons were not restricted to the English side of the Channel, and indeed they can scarcely be regarded as 'English'. A distinction between 'domestic' and 'foreign' affairs would not have been understood. During his long reign, Henry II spent more time out of England than in it, though it should be stressed that only in England was he king. It is generally agreed that it was prosperous England, where government was efficient and revenue effectively collected, which underpinned all his continental activities. It can only be a matter of speculation whether the lands Henry controlled could have been the basis for a permanent trans-Channel state. Henry himself was a capable ruler, his sons less so.

Richard was crowned in England but was a renowned crusader in the eastern Mediterranean. He did not speak English. His absences not only from England but also from his continental lands certainly contributed to the strengthening of the Capetian dynasty in northern France. The result was that in 1204 his brother, John, was driven from Normandy and his other continental possessions. Some historians take the view that by this juncture the French Capetian monarchy was stronger. For others, however, John mishandled his resources. On this latter view, there was nothing inevitable about the emergence of the separate kingdoms of England and France. The loss of Normandy undermined John's position in England but also emphasized that England itself was the core of the realm. After nearly 150 years, the great Anglo-Norman families came to see, in most cases, that it was in England that their future lay. Even so, there are significant exceptions. William Marshal, a major figure around the English Crown, retained his estates in

Normandy and continued to do homage to the French king. In the former territories, a notion survived for at least half a century that English kings and lords still had a responsibility for 'their people'. The lure of 'France' and a continental role did not therefore disappear overnight. John and Henry III made attempts to recover their ancestral dominions without success. Henry III was left only with the duchy of Gascony, a distinctive region in south-west France, an area far from England. It proved a difficult responsibility and had to be governed through an officer with quasi-regal powers. English kings had to spend more time in England. In 1259 Henry allowed himself to become the liege vassal of the French Crown and for the first time Gascony was explicitly stated to be subject to the suzerainty of the French king. Subsequent English kings failed to find a way of extricating themselves from the consequences of this submission. It was not until 1453, however, after the Battle of Castillon, that English Gascony came to an end.

In the context of 'Britain', it is Edward I as an *English* king that we have encountered in his campaigns in Wales and Scotland. It might be more revealing, however, to think of him as essentially a French-speaking man of Europe. He too was Duke of Aquitaine and for this reason was very willing to spend English treasure to defend his position in Gascony. He was in fact the last reigning English king to visit the duchy. English monarchs continued to claim the throne of France. It was because Edward III pressed his claim in 1337 that what came to be called the Hundred Years War began. However, the triumphs of the English kings in France, when they occurred, became successively more 'English' in tone. That was true, for example, in the case of the famous victory of Edward's archers against the French cavalry in 1346. Thirty years later, however, from an English point of view, the picture in France was bleaker. Gascony was lost and only Calais survived in English hands.

Yet in the fifteenth century Henry V was determined to try again. His celebrated victory at Agincourt in 1415 became the very paradigm of an English victory – something gained against the odds. In a further boost to Englishness, Henry started writing official letters – to the citizens of London, for example – in English. It has been argued that it was not just Normandy but most, or all, of France that Henry aimed to regain for the English Crown, and that contemporaries did not feel this was a fantastic objective. Shakespeare pictures the name of St George being invoked as a battle cry. George, a rather obscure saint, who may have been martyred in Palestine, caught the fancy of English crusaders and became the patron saint of England from the fourteenth century.

In the immediate aftermath of the Agincourt victory there were, in effect, three Frances: French, English and Burgundian. Brittany negotiated between them. English knights and nobles took up substantial amounts of land in Normandy, though they did not keep them for long. There was the prospect of a dynastic union between England and France when, under the

Treaty of Troyes (1420), the French king recognized Henry as his heir and married him to his daughter. Two years later, the youthful Henry was dead – what the longer term consequences would have been if he had survived to become King of France can only be speculated upon. His baby son succeeded in that year to the throne of both countries, though he was not declared of age until 1437. This dynastic union, however, proved short-lived. The French monarchy, with the help of Joan of Arc, recovered and the English were driven out of all of France except Calais by 1453. It did not look likely, at the end of the fifteenth century, that an English king would reopen the issue, except perhaps in an alliance with continental enemies of France. Perhaps John of Gaunt's lavish praise of the sceptred isle at length made sense.

Church and state

Henry V, it was thought, though a man of power, was pious. His son, Henry VI, it was thought, was pious to excess, trembling on the brink of sainthood, but conspicuously deficient in handling power. It was lack of piety which seemed notable in the case of Edward IV, a fact which caused his brother, Richard III, to present himself, not altogether convincingly, as God-fearing. Henry VII seemed confident in handling power. It remained to be seen whether he would be excessively concerned with piety. These fifteenth-century English monarchs, and their Scottish counterparts, were all most Christian kings, ruling over countries which conceived themselves to be Christian in faith and order, life and work.

Jews, active in money-lending and commerce, had been the victims of prejudice and hostility. In 1190 some 150 Jewish men, women and children were massacred in York. Exactly 100 years later, Edward I became the first European monarch completely to expel the Jewish community from his realm. There were probably no Jews in late-fifteenth-century England.

John of Gaunt's son, Henry Bolingbroke, before he usurped the throne, had even assisted in person in the conversion of Lithuania, the last European country to be Christianized. This was one further example of the extent to which 'Britain' fitted into a wider 'Christendom'. Britain was not a special case. Nor should its geographical position lead to the conclusion that its place in Christendom was therefore necessarily peripheral and marginal. The history of Christianity in these islands was inextricably bound up with their political history. The pattern of its development reflected the political, cultural and 'ethnic' turmoil through which they had passed. Of course, this experience was not peculiar to the British Isles. Indeed, it is merely one further example of the inherent tension between the ecumenical, universal aspirations of Christianity, as a faith which knows neither Jew nor Greek, and the world of particular jurisdictions, restricted loyalties, and ethnic and linguistic diversity in which Christians lived. In addition, the organization of Christian society, of the Church, was itself problematic.

The division between East and West was already well-established but even within Western Christianity there was the spectacle, for nearly forty years after 1378, of two rival popes, one in Rome and one in Avignon, both with political backers. The English Crown and the Church in England supported the Roman Pope. The Scottish Crown and the Church in Scotland supported the Avignon Pope. One consequence was that the diocese of Sodor, which extended from the Isle of Man to the Western Isles of Scotland, was split in two! The papal division – the Great Schism – was healed in 1417, with difficulty and not without subsequent lesser schism, by a General Council of bishops which had been meeting for some years in the Swiss city of Constance. A significant feature of the Council was its organization by 'nations'. The 'nations' of the British Isles, while separately identified, were nonetheless grouped together. The 'national' allegiances of the participants were evident in the exchanges. English delegates complained of the French attacks on 'the famous and undoubted English nation, also known as the British nation' – language which is itself revealing. Although a subsequent Council at Basle from 1431 to 1443 was not organized on 'national' lines, the national spirit was still evident as the delegates debated, to put it simply, whether the Church should be governed by the Pope or by the Council itself. A reconciliation with Eastern Christianity also seemed desirable in the light of Turkish (and therefore Islamic) advance in south-eastern Europe. In general, it appeared from the fifteenth-century Councils that the organizational structure of Christianity was in crisis. Whether or not we equate the *nationes* of this period with modern 'nations', it seemed clear throughout Europe – 'Britain' included – that rulers were tending to exert greater control over the Church and, in a sense, to 'nationalize' it. If this process was now in a more acute form, this tension had been present throughout more than a thousand years of Christianity in 'Britain'.

There were Christians in Roman Britain in the third and fourth centuries. Bishops from London, York and Lincoln attended the Congress of Arles in 'France' in 315. In post-Roman Britain, Christianity survived among the Britons and went westwards with them, spreading in a complicated pattern across 'Wales', 'Ireland' and 'Scotland'. Expelled from 'Ireland' in 563, Columba, of Irish noble birth, established his abbey on the island of Iona, which was the inspiration for the conversion of the Picts. Ionan monks later founded the monastery of Lindisfarne in Northumbria and a process of conversion began.

It was in 597 that Augustine came to south-east England on papal instructions to begin the conversion of the English. The hoary story, given us by the Venerable Bede, is that Pope Gregory the Great asked who certain young slaves were in a Roman market. They were *Angli* (Angles). '*Non*

Angli, sed Angeli' (not Angles, but angels) he is said to have replied. Augustine's mission made progress in Kent where he landed. In time, once their king had given the signal, the other Anglo-Saxon kingdoms were also converted, though doubtless for some time Christian and pagan beliefs were conjoined. Augustine brought with him monastic rule which St Benedict had formulated at his monastery at Monte Cassino in central Italy. Canterbury became the first Benedictine foundation in Britain.

It became evident that Celtic Christianity was not quite the same as the fresh Roman implant. The date of Easter was a particular source of contention. It was at the Synod of Whitby in Northumbria in 664 that King Oswy decided in favour of Roman usages. While a different ethos might remain in Celtic regions, Christianity within the British Isles became incorporated within a European ecclesiastical structure centred on Rome. The implications of Christian teaching began to permeate both law-codes and ordinary human behaviour. 'Christianization', however, did not happen overnight and we chiefly learn about its acceptance from the writings of early Christian scholars, most notably from Bede, a man reputed to be the most learned man in the Europe of his age – a claim not easy to test. Such monks were not likely to emphasize pagan survival, though there were undoubtedly many examples of it. Converts could still hedge their bets. Even so, Christianity struck deep and enduring roots.

The extent to which that quickly became the case can be seen in the monastic community at Monkwearmouth in Northumbria where Bede made excellent use of the library assembled by its founder, Benedict Biscop. Bede completed, in Latin, *The Ecclesiastical History of the English Church and People* in 731. It was history with a purpose. As its very title indicates, his vision was that henceforth the English Church and the English people should be bound together. His notion, too, that there was indeed one English people had wide-ranging implications, as rulers of Mercia and Wessex were to spot. Bede's piety, indeed, found an echo in translations from Latin which Alfred the Great undertook. Alfred persuaded the leader of the Danes, Guthrum, to become a Christian. In turn, in the seventh and eighth centuries, Anglo-Saxon missionaries like St Willibrord and St Boniface played a notable role in converting parts of northern Europe to Christianity – Celtic missionaries had been similarly active earlier. In short, the lands of 'Britain' came to see themselves at this time as Christian.

Whether England was also part of 'Christian Europe' is more problematic, since writers within the contemporary Carolingian Empire tended to equate 'all Europe' with Charlemagne's domains. In the person of Alcuin of York (737–804), another considerable scholar, however, he had a leading adviser. Since his empire was itself ephemeral, it perhaps makes little sense to argue the point at length. Over the next two centuries, Christian beliefs and concepts penetrated deeper into English society. The strain of English regal Christian piety – which in some cases had been combined with distinctly unchristian deeds – reached its apogee in the person of Edward the Confessor, king and saint.

William of Normandy conquered with the support of the Pope of the day. In 1070 Lanfranc, an Italian scholar who had made the Norman monastery of Bec famous, came to Canterbury to be consecrated archbishop. He was very much William's man and had notions about the authority of his office which were congenial to the king. He knew no English. In Canterbury itself, and across the country, a programme of church and cathedral building began on a scale comparable to that of the castles. Sensitivity to English feelings was not paramount. At St Albans, Lanfranc's nephew demolished the tombs of his Saxon predecessors to make way for his new building. Durham cathedral was but one massive example of what could be achieved at the end of the eleventh century. Such buildings carried the stamp of a more 'European' Christianity, even if we attach the label 'English Romanesque' to their style.

To return briefly to Canterbury: strenuous efforts were made to secure its paramountcy in the English Church and hence, inevitably, to make the archbishop's relationship with the Crown of fundamental importance. Lanfranc was followed by another Italian, Anselm, also from Bec, a brilliant theologian and teacher. His relationship with William II Rufus, however, was very different from that of Lanfranc with William I. The Church in England experienced the impact of an increasingly centralist papacy which opposed lay investiture and forbade churchmen to do homage to laymen. The Cluniac monastic order (Bec was a Cluniac abbey), still in its prime, was equally centralist in tendency. Anselm insisted on what he conceived to be the rights of his Church and rejected royal discipline. He appealed to the Pope and would not be judged in a secular court. A sequence of exiles and returns followed, before a compromise was reached with Henry I in 1107. However, the very complexity of the transnational Church and the growing emphasis on legal form continued to produce disputed jurisdictions and conflicts.

The most celebrated English crisis involved Thomas Becket, made Archbishop of Canterbury by Henry II in 1162. Becket, who had been Henry's Chancellor, opposed the king's attempts to bring the Church within the jurisdiction of the courts. He insisted that only ecclesiastical courts should try cases involving the clergy. This struggle led to Becket's murder in his cathedral in 1170. His tomb swiftly attracted pilgrims from all over Europe and still did so in 1500 (conversely pilgrims from England were travelling elsewhere in Europe at this time, to Compostela in Galicia in north-west Spain, for example). In penance, Henry was forced to make some concessions, but the issues did not go away.

The centuries immediately after 1066 also saw fresh emphases in the world of monasticism. New abbeys and priories were built which became a feature of the landscape over the next couple of centuries. In the eleventh century, in Benedictine houses, most abbots came from France, but thereafter they tended to be recruited in England. The great monastic orders –

Carthusians, Cistercians and others – all established houses. The new abbey at Rievaulx in Yorkshire was but one example of Cistercian enterprise. The first Dominican friars arrived in England in 1221 and the Franciscans in 1224. These developments, stimulated by 'mother houses' on the European mainland, served to strengthen links both across the British Isles and to emphasize the European character of Christianity. English abbots travelled abroad annually to the general chapter of their order. It is noteworthy, however, that these new movements originated outside the British Isles. Only the small twelfth-century Gilbertine order actually emerged in England itself.

An Englishman, Nicholas Breakspear, who had made his career in widely different parts of the Continent, became Pope as Adrian IV (1154–59). Other leading English clerics studied and taught abroad. In Oxford, which received a charter from the papal legate in 1214, and then in Cambridge, England had two universities which took their place in a European network. New colleges continued to be added to these foundations.

Was this, then, an 'age of faith'? Such a concept, of course, begs many questions. Society appeared to have been 'Christianized' to outward appearance but in some cases the uniformity of public profession may have masked indifference or frank disbelief. William II Rufus may have been an unbeliever. It has been noted that Henry II took his Christianity in a rather detached and carefree way, warning the Pope that he would rather become a Moslem than have Thomas Becket as Archbishop of Canterbury. Arguably, before the twelfth century the great mass of the laity was too ignorant of Christianity to reject it. It was also dangerous to do so. The complex layers of actual Christian belief, its changing expression, and indeed content, must be kept in mind when 'Christendom' is talked of in these centuries.

It does appear to be the case, however, that in the late Middle Ages England was perceived by Rome to be somewhat prone to heresy. A thousand years earlier it was a British monk, Pelagius, probably from Wales, who had caused problems in Rome by heretically asserting that salvation could be attained by the exercise of the will. There was, however, no continuous history of dissent or heresy in medieval England. John Wycliffe (*c*.1330–84), a Yorkshireman and an Oxford theologian and philosopher, changed the picture radically. He argued strongly against the clergy's right to property and the Church's interference in matters he deemed temporal – views which commended him to John of Gaunt, but not to the Pope, who condemned his subversive opinions in 1377, but to no great effect. Two years later, writing on the Eucharist, Wycliffe denied the doctrine of transubstantiation. He was expelled from Oxford. The Lollards, reformers both clerical and lay who took Wycliffe's ideas further, in particular his emphasis on the Word of God as revealed in the Bible as the only certain source of authority, aroused both political and ecclesiastical ire, not least for their attacks on worldliness and luxury. Wycliffe translated the Bible into English and the Lollards tried to spread the manuscripts through an elaborate network. Although not a Lollard, Henry VI possessed a copy! Wycliffe was scathing about the cult of images, pilgrimages, and devotion to the saints. The statute *de heretico comburendo* (1402) made holding heretical views a political crime, punishable by death.

The intimate relationship between Church and state could not have been made plainer: it was to take many centuries for the notion to be abandoned that the enforcement of religious uniformity was a responsibility of the secular power. Even so, Lollardy survived into the fifteenth century, though its strength and distribution are not easy to determine. How far Lollardy should be seen as a specific precursor of the Reformation has remained contentious, but it had revealed a laity suspicious of ecclesiastical power. Whatever its significance, however, it would be unwise to take Lollardy's appearance as a signal that 'orthodox' Christianity was in terminal decline. The link between 'Britain' and papally centred Western Christianity had not been broken.

The earlier participation from the British Isles in the Crusades reminds us of an insular eagerness to see 'Britain' in a pan-European/pan-Christian context. Crusaders, whether to the Baltic, the Near East or the Iberian peninsula, came from England, Scotland, Wales and Ireland (and roughly in that order of participation). Richard I 'Coeur de Lion' gave inspired leadership to the third crusade. No Scottish king went on crusade. Needless to say, motives of British crusaders were mixed, but there was certainly a commitment to a concept of 'Christendom'.

King and country

Henry VII not only called his own son Arthur but went to further lengths to express his homage to that elusive early 'King Arthur', one-time King of England, whose career, by the end of the fifteenth century, had been given so many different twists. Henry had caused to be hung in the Great Hall at Winchester a revamped version of the Round Table. At its heart, however, lay not the Holy Grail but the Tudor Rose. Geoffrey of Monmouth, in his *History*, had succeeded in wrenching Arthur out of his previous identity as a Celtic hero into a man any English king would be glad to acknowledge as the very pattern of kingship. Geoffrey's Arthur had gone conquering and campaigning in Europe. This new model, with his court and knights, entered into European romance, but Arthur still had a special place in kingship as conceived in England. Richard I was fortunate enough to go off to the Crusades wielding Arthur's famous sword Excalibur. Some subsequent monarchs were compared, to their detriment or otherwise, to the illustrious Arthur. Only the victor of Bosworth, however, could capitalize on both prototype and developed version.

2.2   King Arthur, Once and Future King: Geoffrey of Monmouth in the 1130s transformed the Arthur of Celtic legend into a figure of European stature as conqueror of a host of kingdoms (enumerated in this picture beneath Arthur's feet). The illustration is from Langtoft's Chronicle (1307–30) [British Library, Royal MS. 20 A II f.3r]. The device on the shield represents the Virgin and Child. Rarely has any 'historical' figure led such a transmuted existence as Arthur. For example, the nineteenth-century poet Tennyson a little optimistically imagined that Prince Albert, Victoria's German consort, would find in King Arthur 'some little image of himself'.

The real Arthur, if he ever existed, may have been a Romano-British sub-king. Kingship was ubiquitous throughout the early British Isles. In the Celtic societies, kings existed in some profusion. Their territorial authority was circumscribed and rarely stable. To some extent, kings were graded in status in relation to each other, particularly in Ireland, but in the last analysis, a king only had the status which his capacity as a war-leader brought him. Law-giving and 'government' remained secondary. The picture does not seem very different amongst the Anglo-Saxons, where fighting ability was likewise paramount. Succession, in almost all cases, posed problems since primogeniture was not the customary practice. Fights and murders between claimants were common. Eligibility could be liberally interpreted. A son of Offa of Mercia is believed to have been the first king to be anointed, in 786. By the late tenth century, a coronation ceremony had been elaborated. After 1066 English monarchs were almost invariably crowned in Westminster Abbey using the crown of Edward the Confessor (the coronation place of Scottish kings was less settled). They were equipped with orb and sceptre, though there was considerable speculation on the significance of coronation and the degree of divinity which might hedge about a king. Such symbols of power, however, did not ensure that they could in fact exercise it. Some medieval kings knew very well that even the adoption of primogeniture in the eleventh century did not ensure smooth successions.

In short, royal authority rested upon personal qualities in an environment given to suspicion and treachery. If the king's behaviour, or a perception of weakness, alienated unduly those magnates who owed him allegiance, that allegiance was likely to be frail. If the king, on the other hand, sought to be overbearing or to demand excessive revenue, that too could cause trouble. The trick, apparently, was to maintain a shrewd balance between these two approaches. In this light, it is not possible to characterize English medieval kingship, as such, as inherently 'weak' or 'strong'. The late Sir Geoffrey Elton was tempted to see something providential in the sequence of English kings. A disastrous occupant, it seemed, appeared just when monarchy appeared likely to become despotic and a rather competent person appeared when monarchy seemed on the brink of disintegration. Naturally when all things did still depend upon the king, it mattered intensely whether he lived too long or whether he ascended the throne as a minor.

Kings were deposed and murdered in both England and Scotland, though some did die peacefully. They were knights in a company of knights, following a code of chivalry, but they were also in an exceptional position. Edward I, warrior extraordinary, was anxious to use his curative powers as a monarch. Probably a couple of thousand people were 'touched for the king's evil' per annum, presumably with beneficial consequences. His grandson, Edward III, was also smitten with Arthurian enthusiasms. When he established the Order of the Garter in 1348, he was only the second European ruler to establish a secular order of this kind. It has to be said, however, that his chivalric military enthusiasms were expensive and undermined the financial autonomy of the Crown. The preservation of the rights of the Crown was normally seen as a primary duty by all monarchs. At his coronation, Edward I reputedly took off his crown and swore that he would not wear it again until the rights and lands his father had granted away had been recovered. That was a dramatic gesture, but it was proper for a king to want to live 'off his own'.

2.3   A step too far: A humble Essex tiler (?), Wat Tyler dominated English politics in June 1391 in extraordinary fashion when he marched into London at the head of Kentish rebels, lynching prominent figures and occupying the Tower of London. This illustration, from a later fifteenth-century copy of Jean Froissart's Chronicles [British Library, Royal MS. 18 E. if. 175], combines two scenes: the killing of Tyler at Smithfield by the Mayor of London, William Walworth (*left*), and, afterwards the fourteen-year-old king's spirited appeal to the assembled peasants to disperse (*right*). The rebels are shown bearing the arms of St George, indicating their professed loyalty to the king himself during the rebellion. After Tyler's death the peasants' revolt swiftly collapsed. It was all over by August.

England, Scotland and Wales were rarely 'at peace' for long. Revolts and rebellions of one kind or another punctuated what tranquillity there was. 'Northern revolts', of varying degrees of gravity, disturbed many reigns. Yet the frequency of battle should not lead to the conclusion that vast armies were involved or that endemic warfare prevented the continuance of 'ordinary life'. The Battle of Bosworth itself, from one perspective, was a modest little affair. Henry's army probably amounted to a mere 5,000 men, while Richard's was scarcely double. Only eight peers deigned to fight for their monarch and a mere three for his rival. Clearly a lot of sensible men stabled their horses. For roughly thirty years before 1485 raged the 'Wars of the Roses', as Sir Walter Scott first termed them in the nineteenth century. It is not altogether to deny the disruptive and debilitating consequences of these civil wars between the houses of Lancaster and York for the English Crown to point out that fighting only took place for a total of fifteen months in that period and, again, that the armies involved were small. It cannot, even so, be said that England in this period was altogether 'the envy of less happier lands'. In comparative perspective, however, the condition of the British Isles was neither significantly more nor significantly less conflict-free than other European lands at this time. Shakespeare, however, in Henry Tudor's speech at the close of *Richard III*, was determined that a line should be drawn:

> England hath long been mad, and scarred herself;
> The brother blindly shed the brother's blood;
> The father rashly slaughtered his own son

The future would be different:

> Now civil wounds are a stopped; peace lives again.
> That she may long live here, God say 'Amen'.

Parliament and people

Kingship, clearly, required constant reinterpretation if it was to serve as the central means, in the societies of 'Britain', both of linking past and present in symbolic fashion and of being the effective *locus* of power. Such accommodation required a degree of consultation, which in turn came to require some kind of representative institution, though one possibly only to be summoned on occasion. As commerce became more important, such consultation could not be restricted to clergy or nobility, though the effective power which the latter might wield could still be decisive. The emergence of such consultation was a European-wide phenomenon, though the institutions and processes naturally varied in form and function.

Even so, to an extent, English developments can be thought at least precocious if not exceptional. It may well be, as some historians, both British and foreign, have argued, that it was the fact that England (though not Britain) was a truly unified state much earlier than any continental kingdom which explains its 'advanced' character. For some writers, too, this approach broadens out into a thesis which emphasizes English 'individualism' and sees the English social, economic and legal system as distinct. In its extreme form, however, such a viewpoint has not carried the day. It is the case, however, that the pedigree of even contemporary English institutions can be examined over an almost uniquely lengthy period.

The later Anglo-Saxon kings had certainly gathered about them the principal ealdormen, thegns and bishops to witness charters and other acts of royal administration. This *witenagemot* (gathering of wise men) was, however, occasional rather than regular. The extent to which it constituted an effective check on royal power is debatable. Some writers go so far as to argue that the Anglo-Norman kings could not ignore the fact that such gatherings had come to be expected. There are, however, few signs of parliamentary enthusiasm on their part.

The Magna Carta signed in 1215 has been described as the oldest European document on the liberties of the estates of the realm and the municipalities and, as such, the remote ancestor of the parliamentary system. While there is some truth in the claim, the 'remote ancestor' looks suspiciously like the 'Adam' reached by enthusiastic medieval genealogists. The charter concerned was called *Magna* (Great) not so much because of its constitutional significance as because of its length (and complexity). As a charter, too, it was not unique. Having lost Normandy, and having failed to reconquer it, King John was discredited. He was confronted by rebellious barons who might ordinarily have turned to another member of the royal family. John, however, was the only adult Plantagenet. In these circumstances, the answer seemed to be to present specific demands. John, hoping for better days, conceded them. The Charter's extensive clauses guaranteed, amongst other things, every free man security from illegal interference in his person or property and justice for everyone. It limited the power of the king in matters of feudal taxation. A council of twenty-five barons was to monitor the implementation of the Charter. If the king overrode the law, the barons were to 'distrain and distress him in every possible way'. The peace thereby achieved lasted only a few months before fighting broke out again. The following year, John died.

His son, the boy Henry III, was persuaded to issue what turned out to be the first of a number of modified charters. It was that of 1225 which really gained the status of fundamental law. Subsequently, critics of the Crown placed themselves, as they saw it, in the tradition of Magna Carta. That was true of the 1258 Provisions of Oxford which pressed for further limitations on royal power. In the struggle which then ensued, in which Simon de Montfort was prominent, the Crown largely maintained its position. Edward I, however, subsequently conceded some baronial demands. By the early fourteenth century, a situation was emerging in which royal power remained formidable but was to a modest extent restrained by baronial influence. The balance of power, however, depended at any given time on the personalities involved.

The Provisions of Oxford had attempted to subject the Crown to magnate supervision. A Parliament was to meet on three occasions in the year, to give a specific context for consultation. The attempt failed. Parliaments were summoned by subsequent monarchs but at times and with individuals of their choosing. In 1295 Edward I needed resources for his wars and for this reason summoned a Parliament. Amongst those attending on this occasion were not only earls and barons, but also leading clergy and two knights from each shire and two representatives from each borough. In the next half-century, the king's Parliament did begin to take on a more formal structure, though whether 'the Commons' was part of Parliament or separate from it is somewhat problematic. By the reign of Edward III, however, it was clear that Parliament had come to have two chambers. From 1376, the Commons elected their own Speaker (though he was a servant of the Crown) and met separately from the King's Council, a body which evolved into the House of Lords.

The power and influence of these bodies must be intimately related to the resources of the Crown and the demands of warfare. Unlike some continental states, the English Crown did not need to maintain a standing army for defence. Therefore, when wars were embarked upon, particularly in France, the Crown needed extra resources to finance them. It was in these circumstances that the advice and consent of the Lords and Commons proved useful, even necessary. The risk for the Crown, in return, was that it would be subjected to unwelcome criticism. Historians generally suggest that Parliament is still best seen at this time as an adjunct of royal government rather than an alternative to it. Even so, by the mid-fifteenth century, it was emerging that legislation and taxation derived its authority not simply from the Crown but from the Crown in Parliament. It was this aspect of the evolving polity that Sir John Fortescue, the constitutional writer, had in mind in the 1470s when he distinguished between an 'absolute' and a 'limited' monarchy.

By the time Henry VII came to the throne, therefore, it is not fanciful to see a kind of participatory, but nevertheless still hierarchical, structure of government evolving. Use of the word 'evolving', however, should not imply an inevitability. The new king might take a new course. As things stood, however, barons and knights, perhaps themselves evolving into lords and gentry, together with merchants and yeomen, shires and boroughs, were all now in a sense 'represented' in Parliament. And it was the Parliament of an England which, unlike contemporary France or other countries, did not contain within its borders semi-independent entities of considerable power.

Concentration on the late-medieval evolution of Parliament is important, in view of the institution's subsequent centrality in British public life, but its evolution has also to be seen in a wider social context. 'Pure' feudalism, if indeed it ever existed, was crumbling and being replaced by a 'bastard' version whereby lords paid annual retaining fees and daily wages in return for services rendered rather than granting land to tenants to hold for life. In some cases, too, retaining fees were paid to royal judges in order to buttress private interests and the dominant position of the aristocracy. Hence, allegedly, the 'overmighty subject' and the turmoil of the fifteenth century. How widespread this latter practice was, however, and whether it did have the effect supposed, has remained controversial. In any event, the social order was in difficulties. Social revolt was in the air.

The most well-known rising was the 1381 'Peasants' Revolt' associated with the plain English names of Wat Tyler and John Ball. It has been variously explained. Some historians have argued that it was a rebellion of 'rising expectations'. Men sought to throw off the archaic restrictions of a social world that was coming to an end. Others have pictured a peasantry which, ruthlessly exploited, could no longer tolerate the burden imposed on it and revolted in despair. Whatever may be the underlying structural discontent, however, it is unlikely that the revolt would have occurred but for the poll-tax imposed during the minority of Richard II and the associated governmental incompetence. Rebel forces from Kent and Essex seized London and appeared to have servants of the Crown (some of whom were executed) at their mercy. The boy king agreed to the abolition of serfdom, a concession he later revoked. The tables were turned. John Ball, the priest rebel who asked the revolutionary question

> When Adam delved and Eve span,
> Who was then the gentleman?

was hung, drawn and quartered. The social and political order survived. Serfdom – the legal condition of personal servitude – did not end in the fourteenth century. The serf was not a slave, however, and was protected by customary rights even though such rights could only be upheld before the manorial court. Labour shortages in the next century led some serfs to flee their lords' estates or to make deals which gave them their freedom. It is generally agreed that we can at this time discern a pattern of rural population which was to endure for some three centuries – freeholders, tenant-farmers, and landless or virtually landless labourers.

The importance of the revolt lay in the fact that it was not another fight within an elite, but an attempt to overthrow the ruling order by popular action. As things stood, the possibility of a *jacquerie* (peasant rising) could not be altogether excluded and it induced a certain caution about taxation. In 1450, however, there was another rebellion, again involving men from Kent. This time gentry, too, enrolled under the leadership of a certain Jack Cade. A considerable force assembled on Blackheath once more in protest both about high taxation and failure in France. Henry VI fled London. In the event, this rebellion also failed but again constituted a warning.

It would be unwise, however, to paint too strong a picture of social instability or lawlessness – though it seems almost to have been regarded as a matter for national pride that in the fifteenth century English highway robbers were both more numerous and bolder than anywhere in Europe. And the use of force was not confined to land. The English also had a certain reputation for piracy. As European trade expanded, so the prizes became more attractive. The Earl of Arundel seized a great Flemish, French and Spanish wine-fleet in 1387. In 1449 a Hanseatic fleet of some hundred ships was seized by an English squadron in the Channel. English seamen, for their part, denied that they were exceptional in their predatory zeal.

On the other hand, it was certainly the case that, domestically, the machinery of justice could be thought 'advanced'. Since the early thirteenth century, if not earlier, professional lawyers functioned within a frame-work of common law – common in the sense of being the same throughout the land and applicable to all. The Inns of Court in the next century, with the training they provided, contributed to the increasing consolidation of the precedents and procedures of a 'common law' system. There were those, however, who wondered whether it really did constitute an intellectually rigorous 'system'. Roman law, as taught and expounded on the European mainland, was significantly different in its manner of reasoning: a battle or at least a skirmish lay ahead.

Both England and Scotland were firmly linked into the complex pattern of exchange which constituted late-medieval European and Near Eastern Trade, but the hub, or hubs, lay elsewhere. And it may, indeed, be almost meaningless to speak so generally of England and Scotland in this way. It was particular regions of both countries and the commodities which they produced or extracted – wool (and finished cloth) and fish notably – which profited most clearly. Small towns with river access expanded and developed from this export trade – Hull in England, for example, or Perth and Berwick in Scotland (still). The splendour of the parish churches of the Cotswolds or East Anglia testifies to a prosperity that was regional. It could be said that in a commercial sense East Anglia, London and south-east England 'belonged' in the dynamic economic world shared with the Low Countries and northern France. In England, Scotland and Wales the economies of their respective highland regions differed considerably from their lowland regions. More contentiously, it might be said that Flanders was in the driving seat. Foreign merchants were granted specific trading rights and privileges but these later became very unpopular and were whittled away. In the early medieval period, to take another example, foreign-owned ships and foreign crews carried Scotland's exports abroad. Financial sophistication and innovation were associated chiefly with Italian merchants – though Edward III's failure to repay capital or interest on the loans from two major Florentine houses resulted in their bankruptcy in the mid-fourteenth century.

Individual English merchants could become men of very great wealth. In the early fourteenth century, for example, William de la Pole made a fortune in Hull out of the wool trade and was advancing money to the Crown. His daughters married into noble families and his son became the first Earl of Suffolk. It looked as though any opprobrium attached to 'trade' could be easily erased if the fortune was sufficient – but of course it would be unwise to erect one particular family's experience into a general principle.

On the edge of a new world?

Taken in the round, in 1500, in a comparative sense, the countries of 'Britain' somewhat baffled European contemporaries, that is insofar as their rulers, scholars or merchants ever troubled to reflect on this distant island grouping. There was, of course, no single European vantage point from which anything like a comprehensive judgement could be made, and it is this fact which makes a general comment on the backwardness or precocity of 'Britain' hazardous. Concerning the fifteenth century, commentators have sometimes fastened simultaneously on the extent to which it can be seen to epitomize both the 'good' (growth of Parliament) and the 'bad' (civil war) and have not been sure which feature was most pregnant of future significance.

If 'success' at this point in time is measured in the extent to which 'nation-states' were being consolidated, England can be put in a 'leading group' in a still territorially complex Europe, alongside France, Spain and Sweden. In Central Europe, by contrast, small units achieved sovereignty. It was not clear, however, whether 'France' or 'Spain' – it was in 1492 that the Moors were expelled from Granada and the Kingdom of Aragon straddled across to include southern 'Italy' – were yet complete. The same was true of England/Britain. Was a 'Britain' to be created – also in some manner embracing Ireland – which would stand in pan-insular unity in contradistinction to the structures of the European mainland, and if so, under what conditions and with what consequences? It is the chequered path to unity and its institutional and ideological accompaniments which will be explored in the next two chapters.

The creation of Britain was not, as things turned out, the only question, and perhaps not even the most important one. The nature of the 'world' was changing dramatically in the last decade of the century. Astronomers, mathematicians and shipbuilders combined to make possible feats of navigation and discovery. The Cape of Good Hope was reached. Christopher Columbus, a Genoese hoping to reach Asia, 'discovered' 'America' in 1492 for the Crown of Spain. Two years later the term 'New World' was applied to his discoveries. In 1499 Vasco da Gama completed the first round trip to India.

The lead in this activity clearly came from the Iberian peninsula. However, in 1497 John Cabot – not an Englishman but a Genoese – sailed from Bristol down the tortuous River Avon on a voyage which might reveal that it was possible to sail to Japan by a North Atlantic route. Quite apart from the benefit to Bristol, it was anticipated that the resulting traffic would make London a more important mart for spices than Alexandria. The commercial world could be turned upside down. Sadly, it became clear that the new island of Newfoundland was not even on the outskirts of China or Japan. What the 'new world' actually was, or could be made to be, however, had a profound bearing on what 'Britain' in turn was or could be made to be.

Part One

Great Britain: Creation, Crisis,
Consolidation *c.*1500–*c.*1750

Chapter 3 ....

Designs and Accidents: Making Great Britain *c.*1500–*c.*1700

An observer in 1500, one recent historian has concluded, might reasonably have forecast that the ties between southern England and the rest of the British Isles would remain 'largely commercial in character'.[1] There is, if this view is accepted, no reason to presuppose that union between Scotland and England (and Wales) followed inexorably from the fact that the two kingdoms shared one island. The island of Ireland, contentiously, is currently divided. There are other insular examples in the contemporary world, as there have been in the past, where two or more states co-exist. Our initial chapters, however, have made it clear that the possibility of a single 'Britain', whatever that might mean, was part of the island's tangled history. There were factors in turn-of-the-century politics which Professor Kearney's 'observer in 1500' might not altogether have taken into account.

Comparative analysis, simply put, suggests that there are two routes to political union. One state, in one scenario, is conspicuously stronger – politically, militarily, economically – than its neighbour. Its rulers, should they so desire, are therefore in a position to coerce that neighbour into a union. If necessary, they can deploy force and anticipate overcoming resistance, if it is offered. Whether a state thus conquered acquiesces in its new status depends upon a host of factors. In a second scenario, a union comes about because the rulers of neighbouring states conclude over time, perhaps for complex reasons, that it is to their mutual benefit (and the assumed benefit of their people) that a union should take place. There may, or may not, be a long antecedent history of hostility. The basis of the union and the arrangements which follow from it may, however, vary very considerably and it may or may not endure. The making of 'Great Britain', however, does not conform precisely to either pattern, though it contains elements of each. There is both

---

[1] H. Kearney, *The British Isles: A History of Four Nations* (Cambridge, 1990) p. 108.

53

design and accident, coercion and consent, in the processes which combined to bring it about over some 200 years. It is the purpose of this chapter to explain and explore them.

England, Wales and Scotland in the Sixteenth Century

In 1502 Henry VII of England concluded a full peace treaty with James IV of Scotland, the first since 1328, and 'perpetual peace' between the two kingdoms was in prospect. Under the treaty, James was to marry Henry's daughter Margaret, which he did the following year. It was an arrangement which came as near as any contemporary agreement could to inaugurating a new era in relationships between the two countries. James had in the recent past given encouragement to the English 'Richard IV', the pretender Perkin Warbeck. Henry could hope that support for English rebels would not be offered again. In his own lifetime that proved largely to be the case, but four years after his death in 1509, English and Scottish forces were again on the battlefield. At Flodden the Scottish army suffered a severe defeat. A plaintive lament for the Scots who fell has resounded down the centuries.

Quite why James should have risked such a fight remains a mystery, but the outcome was a disaster, though still one which did not place the Scottish kingdom in total jeopardy. It did mean, however, that in some Scottish quarters questions were being asked about the country's long-term future. If Scotland cultivated French support, as had been done in the past, such support might give protection against England. On the other hand, it might not be sufficient and would be considered in London to be provocative. The alternative was to return to the notion of 'perpetual peace' with England, though recognizing that an amicable relationship might equally, over a longer term, place a question mark against Scottish independence.

After Flodden, Henry VIII was more immediately interested in trying to make England a force to be reckoned with on the European mainland than in 'settling' Scotland. He did not make a direct attempt to annex Scotland. Temporarily, too, the French king had no interest in trying to use Scotland as a means of putting pressure on England. It was understandable that James V of Scotland gave no leadership when he succeeded his father, who had been killed at Flodden. He was only seventeen months old. Leading nobles were concerned and James's mother Margaret worried what her brother might do. A French garrison appeared in Scotland to deter any English attack from the south. James V, who successfully escaped from his protectors in 1528, was determined to prove that he had a will of his own, but was ever mindful of his English uncle.

Henry, however, had other things on his mind after 1529 than the condition of Scotland. It was in that year, after the failure of his attempt to obtain from Pope Clement VII the annulment of his marriage to Catherine of Aragon, that Henry summoned Parliament. There followed a series of measures over the next seven years which, culminating in the dissolution of the monasteries in 1536, had the effect of destroying papal authority in England.

Also in 1536 (with a further measure in 1543) the English Parliament passed measures to accomplish the union of England and Wales. They had no direct bearing on contemporary Anglo-Scottish relations but the fact of union nevertheless constituted a kind of precedent. Henry VII had in part exempted Welsh people from the 'penal legislation' imposed a century earlier but appears in general not to have been driven by sentiment. He gave life to a Council of Wales and the Marches based at Ludlow and installed the Prince of Wales, young Arthur, there in 1501. It was also there that Arthur died in the following year and with him the revived Arthurian myth. The problems of jurisdiction and justice on the Borders, with their lordships, were formidable and unresolved. Given that the principality remained separate, Wales as a whole was, from an administrative point of view, distinctly untidy.

It was claimed by a Welsh historian later in the century that Henry VII gave to Prince Henry a 'special care' of his own countrymen, the Welsh. If so, Henry VIII took the view that this was best achieved by the incorporation of Wales. The legislation enacted can be viewed from two perspectives. On the one hand, Welshmen achieved full equality with Englishmen before the law. On the other hand, the law was English law not Welsh. English was to be the language of the reorganized court system in Wales. Primogeniture was to become the system of inheritance. New counties replaced the lordships and all of Wales was now shired on the English model, with the right to return Members of Parliament in London. The Council at Ludlow flourished over the next half century. Wales was made outwardly uniform as never before but, paradoxically, in the act of being absorbed into England. It was unclear whether, over time, Welsh language and culture could flourish or even survive. However little Henry VII's son and grandchildren made of the Welsh element in their ancestry, it can be argued that the Tudors could take the loyalty of the Welsh for granted. It was that same Protestant Welsh historian who wrote in 1590 that 'No country in England so flourished in one hundred years as Wales hath done ...'. It had changed from evil to good and from bad to better.[2]

In Scotland there was the possibility that James V might follow Henry's example and dissolve the monasteries. Henry would have liked this to happen, since it would assist his own security in his quarrel with the papacy and have the incidental benefit of worsening Franco-Scottish relations. He

---

[2] For more on Owen see B.G. Charles, *George Owen of Henllys* (Aberystwyth, 1974).

attempted to create a pro-English faction in Scottish politics. However, James was not to be drawn into dissolving his monasteries. Perhaps he was too busy arranging for five of the wealthiest abbeys and priories to be granted to his under-age bastard sons – there were nine such sons to choose between. Instead, his thoughts turned to France.

In 1537 he married Madeleine, daughter of Francis I of France, in Paris, and following her death within the year he married another French bride, Mary of Guise-Lorraine. Two sons died in infancy. Lack of a legitimate heir, however, was by this time not his only difficulty. Henry VIII, who had been having his own protracted problems in producing a male heir, had grown increasingly irritated by Franco-Scottish intimacy. In what were his last years, he turned again to war with France (and captured Boulogne) and to war with Scotland. In 1541 James had declined Henry's invitation to an avuncular discussion in York and war clearly threatened. The Scottish king had great difficulty in mustering a sufficient force from his magnates to cope with such an attack. When the two armies did meet on the Border at Solway Moss in November 1542, the battle proved to be another Scottish disaster. James V himself escaped, but died in the following month, leaving as his successor his one-week-old daughter, Mary.

Henry followed up military success by diplomacy, making use of Scottish nobles who had either been in exile in England or had been captured at Solway Moss. His plan was for his five-year-old son Edward to marry baby Mary. She would move to England at the age of ten with this objective in mind. The Treaty of Greenwich (July 1543) embodied this plan, but before the year was out the Scottish Parliament repudiated the treaty, suspecting that it would be a step, perhaps an irreversible step, which would lead to political union. The political opinion that mattered in Scotland was bitterly divided on this issue, compounded as it was by clerical rivalries and the new complication of possible Protestant infection. A baby queen could not help. Henry reacted fiercely to the repudiation of the treaty, sending forces north by land and sea which harried the eastern Lowlands of Scotland viciously over the next few years. It is not for nothing that Henry's 'courtship' of Scotland at this time is known as the 'Rough Wooing'. In addition, he tried to exploit Gaelic disaffection in the Western Isles and to promote a pro-English 'fifth column' elsewhere in Scotland by bribery.

This policy was followed, after Henry's death in 1547, by a more ambitious attempt to create a fortified English 'Pale' (analogous to the Pale that existed in Ireland around Dublin). Haddington, but a short distance from Edinburgh, became the English military headquarters in the Lowlands. The Battle of Pinkie (1547) was another substantial Scottish defeat in this same area. Yet the English forces did not succeed in reaching Mary, the queen, in Stirling. In July 1548 she departed for France where it had been agreed that she should marry the Dauphin, Francis, son of the King of France. The corollary of this marital arrangement, set out in the Treaty of Haddington, was that French troops and mercenaries of other nationalities should be sent to Scotland in what would become a concerted effort to drive out the English. Over the next few years – in the context of a wider politico-military struggle between the two countries – both England and Scotland spent a very great deal in financing their armies and fortifications in Scotland. By 1550, the outcome was a clear Franco-Scottish victory. The English government withdrew its garrisons from Scotland, promised not to attack in the future, and acquiesced in the marriage of Mary to the Dauphin of France.

It seemed, therefore, that the independent survival of Scotland was guaranteed. It could also be said, however, that Scotland had merely exchanged the threat of English control for the reality of French control. The new French king, Henry II, could well use Mary's claim to the English throne for his own purposes. In addition, when Mary and the Dauphin were married in 1558, the accompanying treaty promised that her husband would take the Scottish Crown in the event of her death. In this way, Scotland might be absorbed into the French monarchy as Brittany had been absorbed fifty years earlier. In Scotland itself, Mary of Guise became Regent for her daughter from 1554. Franco-Scottish intimacy, at least at a certain level, had never been greater. Scotsmen in France were to be treated virtually as naturalized Frenchmen, and Frenchmen living in Scotland were to be treated likewise. A notable case in point was that of George Buchanan, historian, political theorist and Latin poet, pupil of John Major, who had studied and taught in Paris for a decade as a young man and returned there in the 1550s.

Even so, beneath official concord and amity lay the crisis of the Reformation which was dividing both France and Scotland internally and to which we shall subsequently return. John Knox, Scottish Protestant preacher, had been captured by French forces when they had attacked St. Andrews castle – a centre of disaffection – in 1547. On his release in 1549 he settled for safety in England and became a chaplain to the king, Edward VI. He went on his travels on the Continent when Mary Tudor, a Roman Catholic, became Queen of England in 1553 after the death of the youthful Edward. He kept his eye on events in his native land. There, in the later 1550s, the 'Lords of the Congregation', magnates who had taken up the Protestant cause, pressed for changes in a Protestant direction, but to no avail. On his return to Scotland, Knox, together with the Protestant lords, mustered sufficient support to depose Mary of Guise as Regent in 1559 – though, having done so, it was questionable whether they would themselves be able to stay in control. A few months earlier, the Regent's daughter, Mary, had become Queen of France on the death of her father-in-law. In her own mind, she was now queen of four kingdoms: Scotland, France, England and Ireland.

Elizabeth I, Queen of England and Ireland since November 1558 when she succeeded her sister Mary, naturally objected. Despite the fact that the Treaty of Câteau-Cambrésis had ended the war with France which Elizabeth

3.1 John Knox and Mary, Queen of Scots. A word in your ear, ma'am: Lawyer, tutor, church reformer, temporary galley slave, John Knox famously delivered a *First Blast of the Trumpet against the Monstrous Regiment of Women* (1558). He held that women should not rule. In the event Mary, Queen of Scots contrived by her behaviour to give some plausibility to the contention. Knox returned to Scotland in 1557 and Mary was deposed in 1567. Engraving after the early Victorian Edinburgh artist Sir William Allan, the first Scottish painter to research and accurately portray the dress of the period in his 'historical' canvasses.

had inherited from Mary, a French army still remained in Scotland. There was a widespread fear in London, whether justified or not, that if the Protestant rebels in Scotland were overcome, the French would then invade England and put Mary, Queen of Scots, on the throne of England. A counter-stroke was required. After having made contact with the Protestant lords in Scotland and having made sufficient military preparation, an English land and sea campaign began in the spring of 1560, focusing on Leith, the port of Edinburgh, where a French garrison was quartered. The expedition had many shortcomings and was met with fierce resistance, but eventually it achieved its objective. The Treaty of Edinburgh, signed in July, brought the 'Auld Alliance' of France and Scotland to an end. The natural death of Mary of Guise in Edinburgh Castle came, as it were, on cue. Both French and English troops were to withdraw from Scotland. Mary, Queen of Scots, was required to remove the arms of England from her insignia and thus, in effect, to recognize that Elizabeth was indeed Queen of England.

It is, of course, only in retrospect that the Treaty of Edinburgh appears so significant. Mary might not be Queen of England, but she was still Queen of France and Queen of Scots. Surely, the French investment in Scotland over the previous decade and more could not simply be abandoned? The position of the Protestant lords was still precarious, despite the fact that the Scottish Parliament had formally abrogated the Roman supremacy. Religious allegiances were fluid and Protestant supremacy was by no means assured.

However, it was the outbreak of the 'Wars of Religion' in France itself which largely made it impossible for the French monarchy to contemplate the restoration of its strength in Scotland. There was also one further unforeseen turn of events. Francis II of France sustained an ear infection and died in December 1560. Mary came back to Scotland to reign there for seven stormy years, both in her private life and in the affairs of the realm. Internal turmoil climaxed in what amounted to a domestic revolution and Mary was compelled to abdicate in favour of her son, James, in 1567. She escaped from her captivity in Scotland in the following year and fled abroad for safety – to England. She left behind her a civil war of significant ferocity, into which English forces would again be drawn. In England she inevitably became the focus of intrigue and disaffection amongst those circles who regarded her as the legitimate Queen of England. She never returned to Scotland. A life which has attracted more than the usual quota of literary and operatic attention ended with her execution in 1587.

By this date, her son, James VI, now twenty-one, had begun to rule effectively after a childhood and youth in which he had been overshadowed by the ambitions of powerful men. He had been tutored by George Buchanan who came back to Scotland in 1561. James was a Protestant. It had not escaped his notice that, since his cousin Elizabeth had resolutely refused to marry, only his mother had stood between himself and the throne of England. He dutifully protested to Elizabeth about his mother's execution, but resisted routine notions in Scotland that he might, in consequence, invade England. He had recently agreed a 'good neighbour' treaty with England whereby each country promised to come to the aid of the other in the event of a third-party invasion.

England and Scotland in the seventeenth century

James's authority and acceptability grew steadily in Scotland in the 1590s, but as time passed it was the prospect that he would succeed to the English Crown which began to concentrate men's minds, both north and south of the Border. Sir John Harington, Queen Elizabeth's godson, prudently sent James VI the present of a lantern at New Year in 1603. It was adorned with a crucifixion scene and the words of the good thief to Jesus on the cross were meaningfully inscribed: 'Lord, remember me when thou comest into thy Kingdom'. Elizabeth died on 25 March 1603 and, having confirmed the news from London, James allowed it to be released in Edinburgh that he had ascended the English throne. Harington's lantern would no doubt help James find his way among the English.

Of all the possible outcomes to the tangled relationship between England and Scotland as it had evolved over the centuries, this was the most unexpected. The 'in and out' involvement of the English in Scotland, fluctuating in intensity as we have observed, might have been expected, at some stage or other, to culminate in the final conquest of Scotland by an English king and by his installation either as King of Scotland or as King of 'Great Britain'. The circumstance of a Scottish king coming to London, to be accepted as King of England, was therefore without precedent and, to some English observers, a bizarre turn of events.

At one level, this outcome was merely an example of what might happen in a dynastic age as a result of unpredictable births, deaths and marriages. At another level, however, it was a development which had profound, enduring and largely uncalculated consequences for the two kingdoms which now, somewhat uncomfortably, found themselves sharing one monarch.[3]

The paradoxes of the arrangement did not escape contemporaries. After 1560, from an English perspective, it was arguable that Scottish options had narrowed. The experience of French power in Scotland, at least for Protestants, diminished enthusiasm for the revival of the 'Auld Alliance'. Without that alliance, however, Scotland had no substantial diplomatic negotiating hand in its dealings with England. Some historians have also evoked geopolitical factors in explaining the weakening of the Franco-Scot-

---

[3] J. Wormald, 'The Creation of Britain: Multiple Kingdoms or Core and Colonies?', *Transactions of the Royal Historical Society* Sixth Series 2 (1992) pp. 175–94.

tish connection. The long sea voyage between the two countries was a formidable problem, not to mention difficulties of language and culture. Without constant and substantial French support, Scotland might yet survive in a struggle with England because the past again suggested that, even if it was in part conquered, Scotland was too expensive in men and resources for a conqueror to subdue permanently. The prospect of never-ending warfare across the Border was not altogether enticing; men did occasionally tire of fighting, even there.

It was not clear, however, what kind of union this 'union of crowns' would entail, particularly since, contrary to the expectations and perceptions in the two kingdoms, it was Scotland, if only in the person of the monarch, which was 'on top'. Even from an English perspective, however, there might be advantages. If the 'union of crowns' congealed into a more fundamental union of the kingdoms, it would no longer be necessary to worry about the security of the Border or the direct conquest or subjection of Scotland. The prospect of intervention by France, or any other continental power, in insular affairs, would also be removed. Viewed from such perspectives, there was a good deal to be said for the way in which things appeared to be working out.

In practice, whether viewed from Edinburgh or London, matters were not as straightforward as these general assessments might suggest. In a dynastic era, the union of crowns was not unprecedented – but there was no uniformity about the arrangements that followed or guarantee that they would endure. Did both kingdoms continue as before, merely sharing a monarch who divided his time appropriately between them? But what was 'appropriate'? Alternatively, should a deliberate attempt be made, at the moment of the union of the crowns, to forge a new kingdom out of its component parts – a new kingdom which would have new institutions and practices, though naturally drawing upon previous precedents? Perhaps the new kingdom would have a new name. The year 1603 could be a turning point; past and present could part company.

James himself cannot be accused of neglecting these matters. At one point, he seems to have thought that it might a a good idea to change his name to Arthur (though the fate of Henry VII's son Arthur was not encouraging). Such a step would have enrolled the British past comprehensively. On his Great Seal there would be a place for Cadwallader (reputedly the last Celtic 'King of Britain'), together with Edward the Confessor, positioned alongside the arms of England and Scotland. Heralds worked away, ultimately unavailingly, at a flag which satisfactorily combined the crosses of St George and St Andrew on an equal footing.

Heraldry apart, the king was conscientious in a practical way in ensuring that there were appointments for Scots in his court at Whitehall. It soon became apparent, however, that what James thought was fair, and what English courtiers thought was fair, did not necessarily coincide. These steps, symbolic and practical, were necessary to give meaning to the fact that on

20 October 1604 King James VI and I proclaimed himself 'King of Great Britain, France and Ireland'. It was claimed that this title rested on records of great antiquity. On this level, at least, it looked as though the 'perfect union' of the two kingdoms, to which James aspired, was in the process of being realized. In seeking to put the new relationship on an elevated basis, however, James was moving ahead of both his English and Scottish subjects, none of whom seemed ready to contemplate the kind of integration which he proposed.

The long reign of Elizabeth had witnessed a consolidation and deepening of English identity which will be further explored subsequently. Anything which smacked of a Scottish take-over would be resisted. Since the wars of Edward I, at least, common soldiers, both English and Scots, had developed an image of their opponents which was less than flattering. The prospect of a Scottish king in London could be tolerated – on condition that he was not accompanied by too many Scotsmen. While such feelings existed, it is not surprising that it was with some reluctance that the English courts decided that those born in Scotland after 1603 should have the rights of an English subject. An act of the Scottish Parliament gave Englishmen the rights of Scotsmen. James would like to have established free trade between his two kingdoms, but could not get his way – there were too many English fears that cheap Scottish goods would flood the market.

The Scottish Parliament was not happy with the pace of change either, alleging that Scotland was being treated as though it were a conquered province. If the king had returned regularly to Scotland, as it had originally been supposed would be the case, Scottish complaints would have been less strident, but although James was to reign until 1625 he made only one return visit to his native country, in 1617. Such lengthy absence did not assist the smooth running of the Scottish body politic. It was questionable, indeed, whether in the longer term 'Scotland' could survive if its monarch was an absentee. Quite apart from politics, the departure of a royal court from Scotland had a grave impact on literary and musical life. Loss of patronage was a serious blow, though the Scottish universities, more numerous than the English, continued to testify to the high regard in which learning was held.

James personally was regarded by some Englishmen as a curiosity. It was somewhat alarming that he had written books. The dubious impression left by his expressed early views on the nature of kingship was compounded by the trenchant *Counterblaste to Tobacco*, a volume which upset English smokers. James suffered both from the disadvantages of being a Scot and from his intellectual aspirations. His physical appearance and supposed indifference to soap and water occasioned barbed comment. James had his private compensations and in public pressed on with his 'British' design, studiously refraining, so far as possible, from talking about either 'England' or 'Scotland'. After all, did not a common Protestantism now undergird the two countries?

In Scotland itself, James's court had been noticeably unsympathetic to lingering elements of Gaeldom. Attitudes in Edinburgh towards the alleged 'incivility' to be found in the Highlands and Islands resembled many contemporary English attitudes towards remote regions of the British Isles. It was not unreasonable, therefore, to think that the English and the Lowland Scots could coexist. In practice, however, although he spent most of his time in England, James himself remained too much of a Scot 'with an insatiable thirst for theology' and 'a dreary penchant for pedantry' to satisfy the English. At this juncture, at least, it was apparently impossible to be a genuinely British monarch, able to reconcile the ambitions and perceptions of his two kingdoms to their mutual satisfaction. Historians have generally concluded that James was a successful king in Scotland (at least before 1603) but a failure in England.[4]

James's son and heir, Charles, was born in Scotland, in Dunfermline, but he came to England with his father when he was only three years old. It was therefore in the English court that he was raised, though we may speculate that the difficulty of deciding whether to speak with an English or a Scottish accent may account for the stammer from which he suffered. Succeeding his father as king in 1625, he reached Scotland to be crowned in 1633 and to oversee the first Scottish Parliament of his reign. However, he made an adverse impact in Scotland within weeks of his accession by announcing his intention, by an Act of Revocation, to require all former church lands which were now in the hands of lay proprietors to be surrendered to the Crown.

James, famous for the dictum 'No Bishop, No King', had revived a kind of episcopacy in Scotland, thereby upsetting Scots of Presbyterian disposition. His arrangements were designed to buttress royal power. His son, however, inconveniently believed in episcopal government as essential to the

---

[4] M. Lynch, *Scotland: A New History* (London, 1991) pp. 238–9; J. Wormald 'James VI and I: Two Kings or One', *History* Vol. 68 no. 223 (June, 1983) splendidly illustrates contrasting perceptions of the monarch: James wanted to establish a 'representative court' and in 1607 pointed with satisfaction to the 'Irish, Scottish, Welsh and English, divers in Nation, yet all walking as subjects and servants within my Court'. N. Cuddy, 'Anglo-Scottish Union and the Court of James I', *Transactions of the Royal Historical Society* Fifth Series 39 (1989) p. 122.

3.2 Over: Solemn and Binding?: The National Covenant (1638) was a manifesto and bond of alliance signed by those opposed to Charles I's religious policies in Scotland. The 'Covenanters' ruled Scotland until 1651. The Solemn League and Covenant (1643) was an agreement between the Covenanters and the English Long Parliament designed to uphold the peace and safety of the three kingdoms: England, Scotland and Ireland. It delivered a Scottish army into England but did not succeed, as the Scots had hoped, in imposing Presbyterianism in England and Ireland. After 1662, when Episcopal government was restored in Scotland, the Covenanters sought to uphold the original National Covenant.

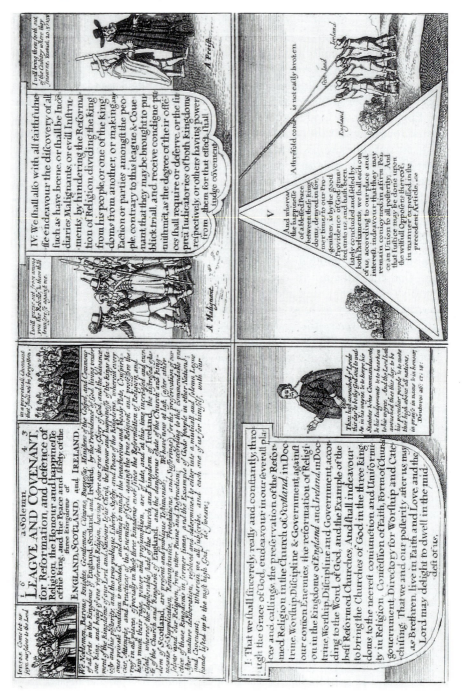

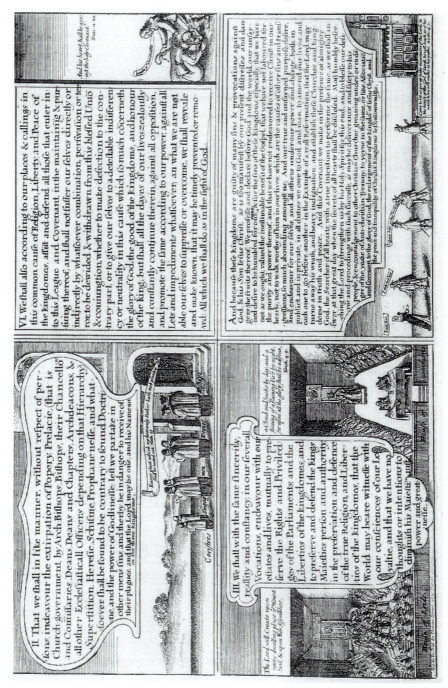

65

Church. The stage was therefore set for a confrontation in Scotland. The issues were frequently seen in black and white – the black Genevan gown opposed to the white Anglican surplice. There were other particular sources of irritation. Charles wanted a new Prayer Book (which would be based on an English model) and seemed to think that Edinburgh taxpayers would welcome the opportunity to fund both the conversion of the Kirk of St Giles into a cathedral and the erection of a new parliament building.

The religious issues in Scotland must be taken seriously in themselves as sources of disaffection, but they also form part of a wider discontent with the way the country was now being governed. A strong body of opinion wished to resist a 'Church of Britain' which would, in effect, mean the extension of the Church of England into Scotland. A 'National Covenant' was therefore drawn up in Scotland early in 1638. At the end of the year, Glasgow Cathedral was the scene of a month-long free Assembly which defiantly culminated in the rejection both of the 1637 Prayer Book and of episcopacy. What was taking place in Scotland constituted, in Lynch's words, 'a self-consciously national revolt'. Charles was determined not to give way to the Scots, but his overall financial and military position was weak. After the second of the so-called 'Bishops' Wars', the king was forced to agree to the Treaty of Ripon in October 1640. In the subsequent negotiations, which extended into 1641, the Covenanters were largely able to get their way. They also had to be paid handsomely to persuade them to leave the part of northeast England which they had come to occupy.

At one level, this struggle can be seen as one between 'England' and 'Scotland' but it had already taken on fresh dimensions. Charles had been forced to call the Long Parliament in London from November 1640 and over the months that followed he was compelled by his opponents to acquiesce in the execution of Strafford, his chief minister over the previous eleven years. There were also clear threats to the powers he believed himself legitimately to possess. A Catholic Irish rebellion against the settled English or Scottish families in the 'plantation' in Ulster added a further element to an already tense situation in England and Scotland. Events in London moved ever closer to a crisis as both the king and his parliamentary opponents sought to enlist Scottish support in order to strengthen their own positions. In August 1642 civil war began in England.

However, recently, it has become common to emphasize that this was not merely the 'English Civil War' but rather a struggle in which English, Scottish and Irish elements all intertwined. Forty years on, King James's 'Great Britain' did not appear to be a very firmly based or durable creation. Certainly, discussions between the Scottish Covenanters and the English parliamentary commissioners referred to their mutual desire for 'a perfect amity and a more neere union than before'. However, it might be doubted whether, as they suggested elsewhere, 'unity in religion and uniformity in church government' would provide a special means of preserving peace. It was clear that neither in Scotland nor in England was there agreement on what that unity and uniformity should be.

As the war continued, it looked at one stage as though forces from outside England might settle the outcome in England itself. In September 1643 Charles signed a truce with the Irish rebels, thereby releasing troops for service in England. In the same month, Parliament signed a 'Solemn League and Covenant' with the Scots. In return for a somewhat ambiguous promise to set up the Presbyterian system in England, the Covenanters marched south of the Border in January 1644. Their army played a significant part in determining the outcome of the war in the north of England, particularly at the Battle of Marston Moor, when they fought alongside Cromwell's Ironsides. Other wars raged within Scotland itself and it was to the Scots that Charles gave himself up in May 1646. He remained their hostage for nearly nine months. During this period, it became clear that Cromwell's army would not accept the imposition of Presbyterianism in England to which the parliamentary commissioners had agreed in 1643. The voice of the Independents – who stressed the autonomy of each local Christian congregation – had become too influential.

The Scots, having been paid for their services, handed Charles over to English Presbyterians (though he was to fall into the hands of the New Model Army) and returned home to Scotland. It was not long before elements among them wondered whether they had done the right thing in doing so. Before the end of the year, the Scottish Parliament signed an 'Engagement' to come to the rescue of 'their' king (who had escaped to the Isle of Wight) on the understanding that if they did rescue him he would give Presbyterianism a trial in England for three years.

The second Civil War began with various regional risings in Wales and the north of England. The army of the Scottish 'Engagers' crossed the Border but was destroyed by Cromwell at Preston in August 1648. Scottish opponents of the 'Engagers' welcomed Cromwell when he reached Edinburgh, and for a short time a new Covenanting regime in Scotland seemed willing to comply with his wishes. However, the execution of Charles in January 1649 shocked the Covenanters. In consequence, the Scottish Parliament proclaimed his son king as Charles II and invited him to Scotland, where he obligingly signed the Covenants.

In England, however, the monarchy was abolished. Cromwell advanced into Scotland and defeated a superior Scottish army at Dunbar in September 1650. It was then to be a further year before the fighting came to an end, partly owing to Irish problems and Cromwell's illness. A Scottish army tried a last despairing invasion of England in 1651 – the fourth since 1649 – but was defeated at the Battle of Worcester. Charles II, who had been crowned at Scone, was lucky to escape and flee to France. Other Cromwellian armies had been relentlessly mopping up in Scotland and by the end of 1651 English garrisons were installed in all the big Scottish towns and royalist resistance was at an end, except perhaps in the mysterious fastnesses of the West Highlands. It was an extraordinary conclusion to an extraordinary series of events.

This summary by no means does justice to the full complexity of the issues and the bewildering shifts of alliances and alignments both within England and Scotland and between England and Scotland. During the course of these events, the politics and religion of both countries had become thoroughly mixed up to an unprecedented degree. Now that Cromwell was comprehensively in charge, north and south of the Border, would a new model 'Britain' emerge from the conflict, integrated as a single state to an extent not previously attempted?

In October 1651 the English Commonwealth appointed commissioners for Scotland. The Scottish Parliament ceased to meet. The objective was to ensure that Scotland 'be incorporated into and made one Commonwealth with England'. Ordinances issued by Cromwell and his Council in April 1654 referred to Scotland and England being united in a happy union. It was the intention that 'the people of Scotland be made equal sharers with those of England in the present Settlement of Peace, Liberty and Property'. It should be noted, in this phraseology, that the term 'Britain', so clearly associated with the Stuart monarchy, was avoided. The Scots were granted the free trade they had been denied half a century earlier. They were allocated thirty seats in the Commons at Westminster. A Council for Scotland was set up in 1657. However, the English army of occupation remained in place. Forts and garrisons across Scotland, extending even into the Highlands, provided central government in Scotland with a degree of control over the country which had become unusual over the previous decades. It was an expensive operation which was not covered by Scottish revenues and it did not altogether prevent rebellion. It seemed that Scotland did not wish to be the kind of godly society desired by Cromwell. The 'happy union' still seemed some way off when the Cromwellian order in turn came to an end.

The Restoration of Charles II in 1660 was the restoration of a monarch to two kingdoms. Pleas to the Westminster Parliament that the Cromwellian union should be maintained, but on better terms for Scotland, were ignored. However, it was not clear what the restoration of a Scottish Parliament and judiciary would actually entail. Even more was this the case with the religious settlement, which provided for the return of bishops. Episcopacy was clearly the ecclesiastical polity which suited monarchy. It was, however, a solution which was too English for a substantial body of Scottish church ministers who would not be reconciled to it. The Covenanters, whether in open rebellion, as in 1666 and 1679, or in sullen defiance, constituted a formidable reminder, despite their own internal divisions, that the new order in Scotland was still not acceptable. The Sanquhar Declaration of 1680 disowned Charles Stuart, describing him as a tyrant 'on the throne of Britain'. The 'killing time' which followed showed the determination of government to maintain control. From a southern perspective, Scotland was still unstable.

The accession of James VII and II in 1685 brought new problems and shifts in alignment. James's Roman Catholicism occasioned a revival of 'no popery' agitation, though a Protestant revolt under Argyll was a failure. The countrywide rebellion which the events of the previous half century in Scotland might have suggested did not materialize. When James's short reign came to an end in 1688, the sequence of events which led to his fleeing the country has been convincingly described as 'an English crisis, with its roots there, and it is hard to find any trace of the same in Scotland'. William, Stadholder of the Netherlands, husband of James II's daughter Mary, landed in Torbay and, together with his wife, accepted the Crown.

In England, the transfer of power was relatively smoothly accomplished. It was in Scotland that there was some resistance. Supporters of James, chiefly with Highland troops, led by John Graham of Claverhouse, Viscount Dundee, were victorious at the Battle of Killiecrankie in July 1689. Dundee's death from injuries in the battle was a disaster for the Jacobite cause and the Highlanders failed in another encounter with William's troops at Dunkeld in the following month.

Even so, the Jacobite threat in Scotland remained real and formed the background to William's political and ecclesiastical settlement there. He would have liked bishops but the bishops did not like him. The result was a Church of Scotland which was Presbyterian in government. Seemingly, the vexed Scottish church question had been finally settled. The General Assembly of the Church – its highest authority – was restored. William agreed to the abolition of the Committee of the Articles, a means by which royal influence over business had been maintained, but he did retain the right to appoint what ministers he pleased. Consolidation of control in the Highlands was another priority. Chiefs were required to take oaths of allegiance to William and Mary by 1 January 1692. MacDonald of Glencoe came late for this purpose. The massacre that ensued, carried out by forces from the Campbell clan, whatever its precise causes, was taken as a sign that the new order meant business.

Fifteen years later, in 1707, the Act of Union joining Scotland and England/Wales was passed. Scholarly opinion generally takes the view that, whatever might be said about its long-term likelihood, there was little in the events from 1688 to make it inevitable. Needless to say, however, there is no unanimity amongst commentators concerning the relative importance of the factors which did in fact bring about the union.

Some have emphasized the controversy surrounding the failure of the attempt to establish a Scottish colony at Darien on the Isthmus of Panama (1698–1700). The fact that a Scottish relief expedition to help the colonists was refused supplies in the English colonies in the West Indies rankled deeply in Scotland. But, while it embittered Scottish relations with England, the failure of the colony and the circumstances surrounding it pointed up the inherent problems in commerce and colonization which derived from there being two countries and one Crown. Could these complications go on indefinitely?

More generally, there was concern over the succession to the throne. William III had died in 1702 and was succeeded by his wife's sister, Anne. Although a Stuart, the new queen seems to have felt herself thoroughly English and indeed had only ever spent a few months in Scotland, and not very enjoyable ones. Her last child had died before she ascended the throne. The likelihood was that the Crown would pass to Sophia, Electress of Hanover, or her Protestant descendants. Could the Scottish Parliament have a say in the fact that the succession would go to the House of Hanover? Steps were taken in each kingdom which were regarded in the other as provocative. A Scottish Act indicated that Scotland would not take part in any foreign war into which Anne's successor might enter. An English Aliens Act (1705) was designed to treat all Scots as foreigners and to ban the export of their cattle, coal and linen to England. Emotions were running high on both sides of the Border. In the background was a Stuart Pretender to the throne who might be aided by French land and sea power. It was in this context, liberally lubricated by bribery and enlivened by rapid changes of front on the part of the politicians concerned, that the negotiations for union began.

The treaty was an act of state negotiated and concluded, naturally, by political elites on both sides. It might, or might not, be a settlement to which 'hearts and minds' gave their assent. There is no way of judging what popular opinion, north and south of the Border, felt in detail about the issues. It was not called upon to express a view. There were certainly dissenting voices in Scotland who suspected that too much had been conceded and who feared for the future of the nation. On the other hand, the agreement could be presented as the climax to a process which we have seen at work over centuries, or at least since 1603. It is indeed arguable whether 'two kingdoms, one Crown' was an arrangement which could have survived indefinitely. Yet the century between 1603 and 1707 had been so turbulent and prodigal in its constitutional possibilities that it would be rash to assume there was some unstoppable momentum behind unification. It has rightly been stressed that in its immediate context the Union was the result of an aristocratic pact, north and south of the Border, arising out of the nature of post-1688 monarchy and government. In short, neither a stress upon long-term factors nor a stress only upon short-term factors is fully persuasive. There was both design and accident in the process.[5]

And indeed the 'Great Britain' that emerged, a state with two churches

---

[5] B.P. Levack, *The Formation of the British State: England, Scotland and the Union, 1603–1707* (Oxford, 1987).

and two legal systems but with one Parliament, was not necessarily stable. The possibility of a Jacobite restoration was a lively one. How such a state would actually be governed remained something of a mystery and it was not clear whether, and with what significance, its inhabitants would regard themselves as 'Britons'. Was Scotland as inescapably subordinate within the new state as Wales appeared to be, subject to conscious or unconscious pressures of 'Anglicization', or was this a partnership of give and take, albeit between unequal partners, from which would emerge a country which was, in a real sense, new?

It is important to remember, too, that this was not just some kind of insular national laboratory experiment. The 'new world' which had only beckoned in 1500 had become a reality. 'Great Britain' was no longer simply an island set in a silver sea. The sea had opened up undreamed of possibilities of overseas expansion, and not simply in the Americas. Even so, during the 200 years which have been considered in this chapter, the island could not be detached from the influences and threats perceived to come from mainland Europe. The communities of Britain had all changed internally during these centuries of interaction. To different degrees, their institutions, ideas and assumptions had undergone dramatic changes since 1500. It is this inheritance of the new United Kingdom of 1707 which will be considered in the next chapters.

Chapter 4 ....

Precedents and Rights: The British Body Politic, *c.1500–c.1750*

Crowns and constitutions

The 'precedents' presented by the past became ever more important as weapons in the present in the eyes of both supporters and critics of Tudor and Stuart monarchs. Debate and argument began to broaden, and the emphasis in historiography began to change. 'During the sixteenth century', writes Sir John Hale, 'the emphasis on what history taught shifted from morals to wisdom, and in particular, political wisdom. From being a repertory of sins punished, it became a storehouse of historical parallels.'[1] Lawyers began to make a deeper study of law and government. Magna Carta was first published in 1499 and translated into English in the mid-sixteenth century, though it was the reissue under Henry III rather than the Charter of John's reign which was used.

The sense grew that documents provided a reliable picture of the past. Antiquaries like John Leland (?1506–52), William Camden (1551– 1623) and Robert Cotton (1571–1631) guarded such treasures as they could get their hands on. Camden bullied high officials into letting him look at state papers. A Society of Antiquaries was formed in 1572. It was claimed that it would not be 'hurtful to any of the Universities ... for this Society tendeth to the preservation of history and antiquitie of which the universities, long busied in the arts take little care or regard'.[2]

Of course, the interest of heralds, genealogists and lawyers in the antiquity of the office of Lord Chancellor, or of Christianity in England, could have more than 'antiquarian' implications. Their interest in the past was itself stimulated by the events in England in the first half of the sixteenth century. Their con-

---

[1] J. Hale, *The Evolution of British Historiography from Bacon to Namier* (London, 1967), p. 10.
[2] Cited in H. Butterfield, *The Englishman and his History* (Cambridge, 1944) p. 32.

clusions could be politically explosive. The same processes were also at work in Scotland. Published in 1582, George Buchanan's *History of Scotland* has been described as 'the most influential work ever written in Scottish history'.[3] It met a need to place the events of 1567 – when Mary, Queen of Scots, was forced to abdicate in favour of her son, James VI – in a satisfactory framework, from a Protestant perspective.

Tudor monarchy

In both England and Scotland in the early modern period, monarchy remained personal. The monarch exercised authority over the affairs of state. Its governance therefore continued to reflect the monarch's individual qualities and capacities. Hence the question of succession remained of central significance. Historians in Tudor England needed little encouragement (though they received it) to contrast the reign of Henry VIII or of Elizabeth with the faction, civil strife and disputed successions of the fifteenth century. In the case of Henry, it was the first time since 1422 that a new monarch had not been more or less immediately faced by a rival for the throne. Between them, in their long reigns, Henry VIII (1509–47) and Elizabeth (1558–1603) provided stability, whatever else they provided, for almost an entire century. In both cases, however, their marriages, or failure to marry, left the succession in difficulty and had profound political consequences. Even so, in the cases of James I (James VI of Scotland) (1603–25) and of Charles I (until 1640) monarchy remained secure, without the kind of coup d'état that had occurred in 1399 or 1485.

In Scotland, the long reigns of James V (1513–42) and James VI (1567–1603) likewise presented the outward image of continuity. In neither country, however, would this picture be altogether convincing. In Scotland, Mary's intervening reign had been punctuated by strife, culminating in her deposition. In England, the short reigns of Edward VI (1547–53) and Mary (1553–58) had been, in different ways, acutely contentious. Their experiences made it clear how much the security of their position was intimately related to the religious issues which now divided the nation. Elizabeth began her reign, in some eyes, as a bastard and a heretic. Mary, Queen of Scots, stood ready and there was the possibility, until her death, that she would attract sufficient support both from within England and from abroad to make a determined effort to seize the Crown. The fact remains that she did not do so.

It would be wrong, however, to suggest that there was no violent opposition or dissent between 1509 and 1640, though some historians take rebellion more seriously than others. The 'Pilgrimage of Grace' and the

---

[3] M. Lynch, *Scotland: A New History* (London, 1991) p. xviii.

Lincolnshire Rising of 1536 affected seven counties north of the Trent. Likewise the rebellion of 1569 was in the north and involved the earls of Northumberland and Westmorland. These rebellions were in part in protest against religious change, but other writers have interpreted them as a 'last fling' by a conservative aristocratic order in the north. They were defeated without undue difficulty by the Crown, a success which reinforced the authority of kingship in general and also emphasized that the north was not a 'no go' area beyond the Crown's control.

The fact remains, however, that no major internal strife did occur. The advantages of order seemed too conspicuous to too many. It was a message delivered with much vigour, skill and insight by William Shakespeare in the last decade of the sixteenth century. His history plays, depicting as they did discord and division, seemed to point to the advantages of order and concord. And in *Troilus and Cressida* he has Ulysses picture a world which observed 'degree, priority and place':

Take but degree away, untune that string,
And hark what discord follows!

As John Morrill has noted, 'The period from 1569 to 1642 was the longest period ever without a major rebellion; the period 1605 to 1641 the longest without the conviction of a peer of the realm for treason ...'.[4] Judged comparatively, the English kingdom could bid to be the most peaceable in Europe.

The maintenance of peace and order is not unduly difficult if it is imposed by a despotic king or queen with adequate power to enforce obedience. Henry VIII has remained a major figure in subsequent popular consciousness because of his brutal disposal of inconvenient wives rather than because of his skill as a musician. Whether or not he deteriorated into a bloody autocrat or was from the beginning an unscrupulous manipulator of men and women can be argued over. It is indisputable that he was a man of great energy, determination and ingenuity. He was fascinated by guns and women. He was ruthless and cruel. He drove the English state down a particular path with consequences that remain in the present. Even Thomas Cromwell, his devoted servant in implementing many changes, was himself eventually beheaded.

Yet the terminology to be used to describe this past remains contentious. We can speak, with a positive emphasis, about a Tudor 'revolution' in government and the establishment of the sovereignty of the king in Parliament or, with a negative emphasis, about 'Tudor despotism' and bloodsoaked tyranny and plunder. Either way, royal authority was successfuly asserted. One interpretation, particularly associated with Sir Geoffrey Elton, has suggested that it was in the 1530s that the 'modern' state was created.

---

[4] J. Morrill, *The Nature of the English Revolution* (London, 1993) p. 5.

The preamble to the Act of Appeals (1533) declared that the realm of England was 'an Empire, and so hath been accepted in the world, governed by one Supreme Head and King having the dignity and royal estate of the Imperial Crown of the same ...'.[5]

In 1547 it was upon a nine-year-old boy, Edward VI, that this awesome responsibility descended. For two years, the realm was effectively in the hands of his uncle, Edward Seymour, created Duke of Somerset, a man sometimes seen as the embodiment of tolerance. To contrast him with Henry in this respect would not be difficult, but even so Somerset's use of his prerogative powers was high-handed. Moreover, his use of them was also incompetent. Protestantism, though apparently firmly in place, was in fact not deeply entrenched. Somerset was succeeded as Protector in 1549 by the Duke of Northumberland who was able, through the Council, to establish more effective government during a period of economic and social difficulty – there had been riots in southern England in 1548 and 1549. However, the succession question could not be avoided. By 1553, Edward's precarious health was failing. He was childless. If Mary Tudor, a Catholic, was to be prevented from succeeding, drastic measures would be needed. However, the plan, which involved Edward himself, to place Lady Jane Grey on the throne failed. Mary, basing her claim on statutory succession, raised forces in East Anglia. Northumberland, Lady Jane's father-in-law, had to capitulate in Cambridge and was subsequently executed.

The restoration of a Catholic realm had to reckon with one reality. It would be politically impossible to restore ex-Church lands to the Church. Papal dispensation in this regard was obtained. Otherwise, in the first couple of years of the reign Parliament was persuaded, without undue reluctance, to repeal all the religious legislation of Edward's reign. It had clearly been designed to stamp England as firmly Protestant. In effect Catholicism under a royal supremacy was restored. Mary was adamant that it should be firmly Catholic. Her decision to marry Philip of Spain, son of the Emperor Charles V, provoked a major rebellion in 1554 in which 3,000 Kentishmen under Sir Thomas Wyatt marched on London. However, although the rebels were defeated on this occasion, Mary could not feel safe. Taking the country to war against France in the Habsburg cause in 1557 proved a disaster. The following year Mary died without an heir. If she had lived longer or produced an heir, she might have realized her hopes and successfully restored Catholicism. She well knew that her half-sister Elizabeth would not do so.

A daughter whose mother has been executed on the orders of her father is likely to have some sense of the precariousness of life. Elizabeth was never safe. She was a woman and men were not lacking who found that fact unpalatable. Plots, intrigues and the prospect of rebellion had all to be taken in her stride. Her response was to project her maternal care for the nation;

---

[5] Cited in G. Elton, *England under the Tudors* (London, 1955) pp. 160–1.

she was the Virgin Queen, Mother of her people, in her own estimation, and did not hesitate to inform them of that fact. A monarch, at least a female monarch, needed to reach out and be loved. Whether genuine sentiment lay behind this projection or whether it was merely an act, it worked – for a long time. 'Gloriana' was the very model of an English queen. Yet, for all her brilliance and skill in her prime, in the last fifteen or so years of her reign she found it increasingly difficult to maintain her earlier authority. Faction at her court mounted, as did financial and military problems, and bad harvests. By the time of her death, one historian goes so far as to argue that she was 'unloved, and almost unlamented'.[6] Political and constitutional problems were put off rather than solved. All was certainly not well, but there had been moments of magic in the life of 'Good Queen Bess' which merited rehearsal in subsequent centuries.

Stuart monarchy

The new king was a stranger to the Elizabethan pageant. In Scotland, he had had to take note of serious men who thought hard about kingship and what right of resistance to it there might properly be. George Buchanan, his early tutor, argued that if a ruler were tyrannical, then the right of resistance belonged to the people as a whole and was not restricted to elected representatives. Moreover, the people had not handed over sovereignty unconditionally. A sovereign ruled only on the basis of his good behaviour. The arguments on these matters carried further positions that had been advanced by Huguenot writers in France. James rejected these views in Scotland, but knew that he had to take them seriously. He rejected them in England too, telling Parliament in March 1610 that 'Kings are justly called gods for that they exercise a manner or resemblance of divine power upon earth. For if you will consider the attributes to God, you shall see how they agree in the person of a king ... And to the King is due both the affection of the soul and the service of the body of his subjects.'[7] The affection that James showered on George Villiers, the favourite who was made Duke of Buckingham, did not make it easy for others to offer the king the affection of their souls which he believed his due. Given the mounting financial problems, the king's capacity for conspicuous consumption caused further criticism. Perhaps it was the excitement of living in a richer country. It has sometimes been argued that the problems of the monarch stemmed from his ignorance of England. Of course, he was not English, but no one could claim

---

[6] C. Haigh, *Elizabeth I* (London, 1988) p. 164.
[7] Cited in R. Lockyer, *The Early Stuarts: A Political History of England 1603–1642* (London, 1989) p. 10.

that he did not make an energetic attempt to understand England by reading, writing and disputing at length. Perhaps he would have done better not to have tried so hard to understand. Even so, it was a testimony to his kingship that he kept England at peace with itself.

There seemed no immediate reason to believe that Charles would upset the stability preserved by the new Stuart monarchy when he ascended the throne in 1625. He had attended the Upper House in both 1621 and 1624 and therefore knew something of the working of Parliament from the inside. However, the continued influence of the Duke of Buckingham caused offence in Parliament. The behaviour of the Parliaments in 1625, 1626 and 1629, when they refused to grant the king the money he asked, caused him mounting displeasure. He dissolved the second session of his third Parliament and a period of 'Personal Rule' began until 1640, during which time no further Parliament was called. Charles, sensitive to what he believed to be the prerogatives of monarchy, did not believe that he was acting illegally. Parliament had refused the money that the Crown needed and he therefore had no alternative but to seek other means of raising it. Parliament was affronted. Charles had succeeded in alienating men who mattered. In the crisis that lay immediately ahead he was to find himself without the friends and support he needed if he was to survive as king. How this impasse had been reached can only be understood if we consider the self-understanding of Parliament as it had evolved over 150 years.

Parliament and the Tudors

Henry VII called but six Parliaments during his reign and none after 1497. It is quite clear that there had been no change in the basic assumptions of kings. Parliaments met only when they were needed – to approve taxation or declare law. Historians sense, however, though it is difficult to prove, that the status of Parliament was increasing, at least in the minds of those who spasmodically attended it. The 'Reformation Parliament' (1529–36), which had eight sessions over seven years, clearly stood out for its exceptional significance. What that significance precisely was, however, has been a subject of enduring debate. At various points in subsequent history, it has been convenient to see the Reformation Parliament as a major step in the rise of Parliament. A wise king took Parliament into partnership to display the unity of king and people. It is a view that Sir Geoffrey Elton has been at pains to dismiss. Royal supremacy did not depend for its existence on Parliament but on divine appointment. Parliament's role was to make possible the prosecution at law of those who opposed royal policy. However, because Henry and Cromwell had to employ Parliament and statute for this purpose, wittingly or unwittingly, they embarked on a course whose longer-term consequence

QUEEN ELIZABETH IN PARLIAMENT

A. L.ᵗ Chanceller. B. Marquises, Earles &ᶜ. C. Barons. D. Bishops. E. Iudges. F. Masters of Chancery. G. Clerks. H. Speaker of ẙ Comons.
I. Black Rod. K. Sergeant at Armes. L. Members of the Commons house. M. S.ᵗ Francis Walsingham Secretary of State.

was to establish that there was nothing which an act of Parliament could not do. It was futile for Sir Thomas More, or anyone else, to claim that it contradicted natural law or some other transcendent principle.

The extent to which the longer-term consequences were perceived can be disputed, but the role of Parliament was enhanced in the process. The king was fully engaged with its debates and discussions, secure in the general knowledge that the feeling of members was not hostile to his wishes on central matters. Henry's later statement to Parliament in 1543 has been frequently quoted. He declared that 'we at no time stand so highly in our estate royal as in the time of parliament'. This sentiment, however, confirms that the king did not stand outside of Parliament. He was king in Parliament and by no means indifferent to ways in which he could influence its decisions. At the same time, however, membership of the Commons increased and became more prized. In procedural matters, too, members sought to regularize their own affairs. Sir Thomas More, Speaker in 1523, formalized the right to free speech on questions which were legitimately before the House. In the reign of Edward VI, through the Statute of Uniformity (1549), Parliament asserted its authority in doctrinal matters – in this case the Prayer Book of the same year. It has already been noted, however, that Parliament was largely willing to do Mary's bidding, except in the matter of church lands. It would be wrong, in other words, to believe that Parliament was evolving on a clearly ordained path with its members anxious, at every turn, to 'win the initiative'. It was the case, however, that its place in the political life of the state was becoming steadily confirmed.

Elizabeth was not enthusiastic about calling Parliament. She did so only thirteen times in her long reign and, with one exception, largely for purposes of supply. She did not require busy lords and gentry to spend time at Westminster in idle debate or in contemplating new legislation. She needed to tax for particular purposes. Nevertheless, there were occasions when her wish to see business speedily transacted was not sufficient. Members did have local and private interests and, on occasion, wished to discuss them at some length. It may be the case that some of them would have liked lengthier and more frequent Parliaments, but it has been noted, for both houses, that attendance declined quite sharply as a session wore on. Through her councillors, Elizabeth had no hesitation in seeking to influence the composition of particular Parliaments. Pressure and patronage combined were a

---

4.1 Queen Elizabeth in Parliament. Every man in his place: Elizabeth looked down with some disdain on a man's world. She had no enthusiasm for summoning Parliaments and only did so sparingly. Parliament was left in no doubt that she was God's anointed queen and, on occasion, unwelcome discussion was stifled. Elizabeth also recognized, however, the need to prepare speeches carefully. In this contemporary engraving, members of the Commons gather in the foreground around the Speaker (H). Elizabeth herself is flanked by her Lord Chancellor on her right and Sir Francis Walsingham, Secretary of State, on her left.

powerful weapon, but it could produce situations in which it was not easy for the queen to control her councillors. She did, however, develop her speeches to Parliament into a fine art and thus influence matters directly. Yet, particularly on religious matters, she did encounter difficulties from a persistent parliamentary minority. The current view, however, is that it is misleading to envisage the queen locked in a permanent battle with Puritans. Instead, attention has switched to emphasize the growing difficulties for the Crown if the members of the Council sought to enlist Parliament in their desire to follow a particular policy. Emphasis also continues to be placed on the legislative, as opposed to the political, role of Parliament during the reign of Elizabeth.

Parliament and the Stuarts

The fact that, within forty years of Elizabeth's death, civil war raged in which 'King' fought 'Parliament', has naturally led to a protracted examination of the status and function of Parliament during these decades. It was an argument, not unexpectedly, which began in the works of seventeenth-century writers themselves and has continued into the present. It has been noted that early parliamentary histories stressed that their cause was based on historical foundations.[8] To have admitted otherwise would have been to concede that they were rebels. James I and Charles I had abandoned the 'parliamentary way' followed so prudently, it was claimed, by Elizabeth. Royalist writers, on the other hand, claimed that it was the Crown which had continued to uphold a traditional understanding of the place of Parliament and it was the parliamentarians who were advancing seditious and anti-monarchical principles which were new and unpalatable. In his reply to the Nineteen Propositions advanced by parliamentary leaders in the summer of 1642, Charles reiterated that laws were 'jointly made by a King, by a House of Peers, and by a House of Commons chosen by the people'. The Propositions, whose effect would have been in practice to create a system of government carried on by privy councillors, appointed by and responsible to Parliament, and only nominally to the king, were subversive of the fundamental laws and excellent constitution of the kingdom. Anarchy threatened and the Stuart monarchy might crumble before a latter-day Jack Cade or Wat Tyler.

Raising the stakes so high could not easily have been predicted in 1603. James had been in the habit of summoning his Scottish Parliament roughly every three years. The English Parliament summoned in 1604 remained in existence, with breaks, until 1610. The brief Addled Parliament

---

[8] R. Richardson, *The Debate on the English Revolution* (London, 1977) p. 11.

was held in 1614. The third Parliament met in 1621 and the last in 1624. Averaged over James's English reign, Parliament met just over seven weeks per year, nearly three times Elizabeth's yearly total. Charles I held three Parliaments before the beginning of his 'personal rule' in 1629. A Short Parliament was held in the spring of 1640 to be followed by the Long Parliament in the November. It is evident that in the preceding decade a formidable body of opposition had built up amongst those who now sat in the Lords and the Commons. Charles's foreign policy, with its seeming subservience to Spain, had been a major source of discontent with his rule. Indeed, from London merchants to country gentry, there seemed scarcely an interest group which he had not succeeded in offending. However, the constitutional issues which surfaced when the Long Parliament met had also been present under James. He had been pleased to say that he found it convenient to rule with Parliament but he had no doubt that its role was to advise. He was not bound by it. Any historian knew that monarchy came before Parliament. He resented the notion that he had to trade concessions for money. Even so, the language of 'contract' between ruler and ruled was in the air, though it could not altogether be made to stick.

Early in his reign, too, Charles was confronted by a Petition of Right from the Commons. His financial needs were acute, though objectively capable of solution – but the mood of MPs was such that they were unwilling to grant him supply without an assurance concerning what they termed the preservation of their liberties. The king with difficulty succeeded in linking his commitment to the just rights and liberties of his subjects with his own just prerogative. The debate which had taken place revolved around issues of sovereignty; it did not resolve them.[9] In discussing these matters, historians differ in the stress they place on these far from subterranean rumblings. There is little controversy, however, about the degree to which Charles had alienated support by 1640. The king left himself with no large or powerful class or interest group willing to back him when resistance began.[10]

In this scenario, fear of tyranny and fear of anarchy were present in almost equal measure. From the royal perspective, Charles was standing up for royal prerogatives, like other contemporary European monarchs, against the turbulent spirit of his Parliament – which would lead to anarchy. From a parliamentary perspective, the thrust of Parliament's endeavours was defensive rather than aggressive, designed to restore rather than innovate, and to prevent monarchical tyranny. From this perspective, it is difficult to decide who, if anybody, is being 'revolutionary'. In any case, it is not easy to discern conspicuous 'popularity' attaching to either 'side' at the outbreak of hostilities.

---

[9] J.P. Sommerville, for example, writes: 'Royal financial problems were objectively soluble. It was ideology which made them so intractable.' *Politics and Ideology in England 1603–1640* (London, 1986) p. 237.
[10] Morrill, *English Revolution*, p. 10.

Nonetheless, generations of historians have been willing and felt able to align themselves and their interpretations in such a way that 'Parliament' has been considered to open up the path to the present. Even if this is the case, in a general sense, it will be seen in subsequent discussion that the path has not been straight. It is important, however, to try to preserve the distinctive flavour of a conflict in its own time. Whatever the importance of the 'afterlife' of events, however much particular occurrences gain significance over a long period, it remains important for historians to stress the uniqueness of the past. Hence there has been an emphasis on what are believed to be the distinctive features of a mid-seventeenth century crisis that was not, of course, confined to Britain. Although it has been difficult for historians to resist the temptation, the 'English Revolution' should not be seen in its origins as an 'early' version of the French Revolution of 1789 or the Russian Revolution of 1917. However, the words 'in its origins' are used advisedly. What happened subsequently in the 1640s and 1650s was a different matter.

The execution of King Charles and the abolition of the monarchy and of the House of Lords in 1649 can only be described as a radical break with the past. In one sense, given that the 'revolution' lasted but a decade, it may seem to be 'freakish', meriting attention only as illustrating a route into the present which has not been taken. In late-twentieth-century Britain, the formal elements in the constitution remain – monarch, Lords and Commons – whatever changes have taken place in their respective power and authority. It appears, therefore, that it is this institutional continuity which characterizes contemporary Britain and makes it unique among the major states of Europe.

However, from the perspective of 1707, that is from the date of the formation of the British state, the upheavals were but half a century in the past. It was by no means certain that the 'old order' had been securely restored. Indeed, as will be noted, the 'Restoration' of 1660 was itself followed, in 1688, by a further 'Revolution' which some deemed 'Glorious', which replaced one monarch by another and required a further 'settlement'. The events of the 1640s and 1650s, in other words, made an indelible impression on subsequent British history. They pointed to both the danger of obduracy and the unpredictability of change, once embarked upon. It is arguable that both of these facts have had a profound impact upon the political elites who controlled the subsequent direction of British politics.

Parliament and the Protectorate

The sight of a king on a scaffold was certainly a shock. Although it was doubtless of little consolation to Charles, such an outcome appeared to vindicate his own comment in 1645 that Parliament was bent on 'extirpating the royal blood and monarchy of England'. In fact, however, the great majority of parliamentarians had no such intention at this time, though the clash between the Crown and Parliament led to the emergence of radical ideas. John Lilburne and Richard Overton emerged from obscurity to question the need for monarchy and the social, political, economic and ecclesiastical hierarchies associated with it. Their objectives merit the description 'democratic'. 'Levellers' gained support in London but, with few exceptions, the emergence of such ideas caused apprehension in Parliament and the army. The hierarchical basis of society, as traditionally understood and upheld, now seemed in jeopardy. Fears on this score lay behind the attempts, which in the end proved unsuccessful, to find the basis for a settlement with the king after the Second Civil War of 1648. In December 1648 the Commons was 'purged' by Colonel Pride – MPs still favourable to negotiation were removed – and two months later it voted to abolish the House of Lords. The office of king was held to be unnecessary and dangerous to the liberty, safety and public interest of the people. England was proclaimed a Commonwealth governed by the representatives of the people in Parliament. It was, of course, only a 'Rump' which could claim this authority, less than half its former membership.

The figure of Oliver Cromwell moved inexorably to the centre of the political stage. In recent scholarship, historians have emphasized the complexity of Cromwell's background, character and beliefs.[11] Both devious and impetuous, he saw himself, under God, as a man with a troubling and puzzling mission – to bring about a godly reformation. That mission did not commit him to any specific constitutional scheme. His action against the Levellers was confirmation to the propertied classes that Cromwell's was a reformation of character and conduct which did not entail sweeping social transformation. It is not easy, however, to attribute consistency to Cromwell's conduct in the years immediately after 1649. His military campaigning has already been noted and his successes in this respect inevitably increased his own stature. It seemed that he was increasingly being placed in a position in which he had to choose between the army and the Rump Parliament. In April 1653 he forcibly dissolved the Parliament – though it is a matter of debate whether he did so because the Parliament's plans for electoral reform went too far or because they did not go far enough. A 'Parliament of Saints' – Barebone's Parliament – replaced it, but in turn Cromwell became disillusioned with its conduct. He shied away from the millenarianism of the Fifth Monarchy Men which had once had some attraction for him. He was alarmed both by the sectarian disposition to attack fellow-Protestants and threaten thereby the liberty of religious conscience to which he was attached, and also by an anti-military mood. Yet he also denied that he wished to establish what would now be described as a permanent military dictatorship.

---

[11] B. Coward, *Oliver Cromwell* (London, 1991); J. Morrill, ed., *Oliver Cromwell and the English Revolution* (London, 1990).

4.2 Bare-faced cheek: satirical Dutch medallion (1655) showing the French and Spanish ambassadors competing to kiss Cromwell's backside as he lies with his head on Britannia's lap. According to the (French) inscription, the French ambassador is claiming the privilege for Louis le Grand. 1655 was a difficult year for Cromwell. Forces which he had sent to the Caribbean as part of the Western design failed humiliatingly against the Spanish at San Domingo: God had sorely chastened the English for their sins. It was in this mood that a defensive treaty was made with France in October 1655. Nevertheless, although the pose is hardly flattering to the Lord Protector, this satire testifies to his political standing amongst the European powers at the time.

Indeed, initially at least, such a description has an anachronistic ring.

In December 1653, accepting an Instrument of Government which attempted to set out his power and that of Parliament, Cromwell became Lord Protector. The Instrument of Government had brought about a major change in the parliamentary constituencies and the MPs who were returned by them, but Cromwell appears to have shown little interest in wooing MPs. Indeed, he felt himself increasingly driven to courses of action which would now be described as 'authoritarian'. In a declaration published in October 1655 he stated that 'the Supreme Magistrate' should not be 'tied up to the ordinary rules'. Such statements reflected his belief that the 'godly cause' was under attack in England and abroad. He had just appointed eleven major-generals to supervise the government of the English provinces. The sole end of these appointments, apparently, was the suppression of vice and the encouragement of virtue. Parliament did not like that very much and refused to pay for their upkeep. The experiment ended early in 1657.

Proposals for a new constitution – the Humble Petition and Advice – were put to Cromwell in March 1657. They included provision for a limited hereditary monarchy and for parliamentary approval of taxation and appointment to the great offices of state. Having agonized, however, Cromwell rejected the Crown but accepted an amended version of the petition. In all probability, Cromwell refused to become King Oliver not only because he feared opposition from the army but because such a title would constrain him in his still continuing quest for a godly reformation. Nevertheless, there were elements of quasi-regality in his final years as Lord Protector. There were also growing calls for a return to 'the ancient constitution'. Cromwell himself died in September 1658. His son Richard succeeded him in the protectorship but resigned in May 1659. He had proved himself unable to control the rivalry between the restored Rump and the army. Fear of anarchy and a possible uprising led the propertied classes to look to the king over the water.

The Cromwellian experiment was remarkable. As has been noted, in the end it became clear that Cromwell was 'concerned not to establish constitutional government, a balanced polity in which those who exercised authority were accountable to those they governed. The destruction of divine right kings was to make room for a divine right revolutionary.'[12] The regime that resulted, in all its twists and turns, could be variously represented as tyrannical and bigoted or enlightened and open-minded. A provincial farmer and businessman from the open lands of eastern England had shown himself to be a remarkable soldier with a distinctive though opaque vision of England's destiny, under God. Iconoclast and 'betrayer of the people', his mark on English history could not be erased, ambivalent though it was.

In successive centuries, Cromwell continued to evoke both fear and admiration in political discussion.[13] In the nineteenth century, for Thomas Carlyle, Cromwell was the archetypical hero which his own century needed to reproduce. In 1940, at a time when Britain did need a hero, Leo Amery quoted in the Commons from Cromwell's speech to the Rump Parliament: 'You have sat too long for any good you have been doing. Depart, I say, and let us have done with you. In the name of God, go!' Neville Chamberlain did go.

---

[12] Morrill, ed., *Cromwell*, p. 18.
[13] T. Mason, 'Nineteenth-Century Cromwell', *Past and Present* 40 (1968).

In other quarters, however, the reaction in subsequent centuries to Cromwell's name and record remained hostile. The Victorian movement to erect a statue was controversial – as was its eventual location outside the Houses of Parliament. It seemed, to some, an odd place to commemorate a man whose rule, in the event, was as 'personal' as that of Charles I. In the twentieth century, George V demurred at the suggestion, even when it came from Winston Churchill, that it would be appropriate to name a battleship in the Royal Navy *Oliver Cromwell*. In short, 1640–60 could not easily or swiftly become a 'common' past. Just as, in the late-nineteenth-century words of W.S. Gilbert, every boy alive was born a Liberal or a Conservative, so 'Roundhead' and 'Cavalier' symbolized a divide that was still to resonate across the centuries. It was a divide which was as much 'religious' as 'political'. How that religious division had in turn arisen will be considered subsequently.

Restoration and a national equilibrium?

The general view is that the 'Great Rebellion' largely collapsed from within. Once again, the possession of military power was a significant factor. After Cromwell's death, General Monck, latterly his commander-in-chief in Scotland, marched south and entered London in February 1660. In turn, his decisive position was made possible by divisions within the army in England. The MPs excluded from Parliament by Pride's Purge in 1648 were brought back. The restored Long Parliament dissolved itself and in an election held on the pre-1640 franchise, a 'Convention' Parliament assembled. In May 1660 it recalled Charles II to the throne.

The previous month Charles had issued the Declaration of Breda in Holland which facilitated his return. Amongst other things, he indicated that he would pardon all those who returned to their duty to the king within forty days, saving only those excepted by Parliament. Parliament would likewise play its full part in determining religious and land settlements. More immediately, the arrears of army pay would be met. In the light of all that had happened it would be foolish to assume that the king's return was universally popular. Nevertheless, amongst the political forces that mattered, only a restored monarchy offered the prospect of stability.

Legitimacy was also important, for Cromwell had failed to find a firm foothold in his constitutional experiments. Instead, the Convention Parliament and the 'Cavalier' Parliament that followed it took a very different course. There was a strong disposition to believe that an enduring settlement which would take the country forward could only be achieved by eradicating the recent past. The general spirit of what was settled did indeed embody that aspiration, but it could not do so completely. The House of Lords was restored, complete with bishops, and soon proved that it was of a mind to act vigorously. The changes made to the electoral system in the 1650s were abandoned. However, Star Chamber and other prerogative courts, the abolition of which Charles I had consented to in 1641, were not resurrected. Similarly, the Crown could not resort to extra-parliamentary taxation. Yet, although Parliament had to be called every three years, the powers of the Crown remained very significant – in the control of foreign policy and the maintenance of the security of the state, and in the appointment and dismissal of ministers.

Unsurprisingly, what had emerged was not an ideal balance, as dreamt of by political writers, but a working solution to an immediate set of problems. Perhaps even more important than the specific constitutional provisions was the degree to which the new regime was firmly underpinned by families who had also been 'restored' to something like their old status and position. Undoubtedly, some did regain their former possessions, but there were also many who never fully regained either their estates or their wealth. Charles genuinely tried to help royalist families who had suffered but there were limits to what he could do personally. He himself had been granted for life an excise on liquors. Nevertheless, it did not take long to become clear that the resources of the Crown were stretched and would continue to be so even if the king had shown less inclination to extravagance.

In other words, the problems which had contributed to the Civil War had not gone away. In this respect, too, the settlement was backward-looking. It was more important, from a parliamentary perspective, to keep the Crown on a tight rein than to give it the financial freedom which would enable it to conduct an ambitious foreign policy and thereby enhance the country's standing in Europe and indeed in the world. The equilibrium established in 1660–62 remained precarious. It was, moreover, still a system which inevitably depended on the attitude and aptitude of the king himself.

Civil wars, in any society, inevitably leave behind them bitterness and recrimination, and also the possibility that they will trigger an apparently endless sequence of coups and counter-coups as defeated parties seek revenge. By this yardstick, the British, or at any rate the English, experience of restoration was remarkably successful. There was not to be another civil war. In retrospect, it can be seen that rival armies were never again to tramp about the English countryside for extended periods, though the possession of military force, as events were to show, remained significant in subverting or upholding the political status quo. It was desirable, however, to restrict the size of the army and its role in politics. There was to be no need to repair and reconstruct the great castles of an earlier era which had sometimes been badly damaged during the fighting. England/Wales, if not Scotland, was on the verge of becoming a 'peacable kingdom', precocious again amongst European states in this respect. How far, if at all, a deep-seated aversion to fanaticism and addiction to compromise, supposedly identified as fundamental to 'national character', can be traced to this era in British history can be asserted but not conclusively proved.

Revolution?

That these trends suggested possibilities for the future rather than certainties was demonstrated by the crises of the last decades of the seventeenth century. Indeed, in the face of a series of sectarian/republican plots, some writers have seen Charles II as almost in a state of panic. The problems of 'managing' Parliament became more acute. Religious issues, which will be returned to, became extremely contentious again in the 1670s. Attacks on the king's ministers, hitherto somewhat sporadic, became more organized. Financial problems were almost always present, though it would be wrong to see the picture as one of steady and inexorable deterioration. In a variety of areas, the imprecision of the settlement became steadily more apparent in matters directly involving the royal prerogative. The king himself, though clever, indolent and 'merry', displayed an increasingly careless admiration for things French. He had no legitimate heir. He declined to legitimize the Duke of Monmouth, who was indubitably Protestant. In 1678 Titus Oates 'revealed' the existence of a Jesuit plot to assassinate the king – a revelation which proved congenial to a country always ready to believe in such a possibility. And it could not be denied that the heir to the throne, James, Charles II's brother, was a Catholic and had recently married a Catholic second wife. Catholic sons might prevent the two Protestant princesses, Mary and Anne, born to James's late first wife, from succeeding to the throne.

The 'Exclusion Crisis', in its various phases, lasted from 1679 to 1681. It was a trial of strength between the Crown and a parliamentary opposition which seemed, at several points, on the verge of achieving an Exclusion Bill to prevent James from succeeding to the throne. In the end, it was outmanoeuvred. Part of the difficulty of the opposition was that it could agree on the exclusion of James but not on who should be the alternative monarch. Royal supporters, too, gained ground when they put the question 'Whether a civil War is more dangerous than a Popish successor'.[14] When he dissolved the third Exclusion Parliament held at Oxford in March 1681, Charles had clearly 'won'.

The implications of that victory, however, were disputed at the time and have remained so in the interpretations of subsequent generations of historians. It is not in doubt that there was a period of 'reaction', particularly at the municipal level, but opinions differ as to how far Charles initiated or

---

[14] Cited in W. Speck, *Reluctant Revolutionaries: Englishmen and the Revolution of 1688* (Oxford, 1988) p. 37.

merely presided over this 'reaction'. Yet, in the final years before Charles's death in 1685, alarm at increasingly 'arbitrary' government and the detection of 'absolutist' tendencies was less important politically than concern amongst the elite that there should not be another civil war. Despite the Triennial Act, in 1684 Charles was allowed to get away with not calling a new Parliament. Indeed, whatever might have been the case four years earlier, James succeeded to a very powerful position. The rebellions against him – by the Earl of Argyll in the West of Scotland and the Duke of Monmouth in the West of England – came to nothing.

Hard-working and less 'merry' than his brother, James had little need for a Parliament. His overall financial position has been described as being better than that of any monarch since Henry VIII. Indeed, between March 1681 and January 1689 Parliament sat for less than two months. The 're-modelling' of the charters of parliamentary boroughs and the interference with the judiciary were taken to be but two examples of an absolutist disposition. In addition, the capacity of the army to intimidate – an army which James could finance without recourse to Parliament for extraordinary supplies – caused increasing concern. That, together with the 'professionalization' of officialdom and restrictions on press liberty, seemed to suggest that England was steadily becoming like most continental states where parliamentary institutions were atrophying. Historians dispute whether these developments point in an 'authoritarian' or an 'absolutist' direction, but they do not generally dispute that there was what one might call a 'royalist consolidation'.

It might have succeeded, too, if James's perceived centralizing disposition had not threatened the political and social supremacy of local elites, and if he had been content, although a Catholic, to leave the supremacy of the Church of England alone. His actions in both of these aspects, however, alienated critical sections of the political nation. Even so, commentators have been at pains to point out that conspiratorial opposition was not widespread. In December 1687 James's internal position still seemed so strong that his parlous circumstances a year later could not have been foretold. There was no countrywide rebellion in prospect.

This points to the importance of the 'external factor' in the person of William of Orange, Stadholder of Holland, Zeeland and other Dutch provinces, who was both the king's nephew and son-in-law. His wife, Princess Mary, was first in the Protestant line, but King James had a male heir in June 1688. William had for some years displayed great caution in the matter of England, but at length, in response to an 'Invitation', he issued a 'Declaration' in late September which, amongst other things, pressed for 'a free and lawful Parliament'. The strength of his own hopes for the Crown has been variously estimated. No doubt his chief concern was to consolidate England behind the Protestant cause in a war with France which could be anticipated. William's forces landed at Torbay in November 1688 and superior royal forces moved to Wiltshire to defeat them. In the event, however, James chose not to fight, and over the next couple of months he in effect chose not to save his Crown.

The sequence of events, which cannot be described in detail, was so unexpected that it again took time to digest the full implications. When historians used the 300th anniversary of these events in 1988 to discuss their significance, it was evident that these implications remained problematic.[15] There is irony in the fact that this 'Glorious Revolution', amongst whose indirect consequences was to be, as we have seen, the creation of the British state, was at one level a coup d'état achieved by a foreign adventurer whose army consisted of Dutchmen, Brandenburgers, Swiss and the occasional Englishman.

The direct consequence was the enhancement of the authority of Parliament and the confirmation of its freedom and regular assembly. Although there were various ways in which the succession to James could have been resolved, on the assumption that the throne was indeed vacant, it required Parliament to offer the Crown jointly to William and Mary for their position to be legitimate. The Crown, in theory, had not been 'seized'. A 'Declaration of Rights' – subsequently formalized into a 'Bill of Rights' – was presented to William and Mary at the same time as the Crown was offered to them. Historians have debated ever since whether this 'package' amounted to a contract and thus made monarchy subject, as it were, to formal terms and conditions of service.

In 1938, in *The English Revolution 1688–89*, a book written to commemorate its 250th anniversary, G.M. Trevelyan identified 'an agreed contract ... between Crown and people' which William had been required to accept. That was the essence of the matter, which made it a determining event in the history of England. 'Divine-right' monarchy was henceforth dead. Subsequently, such a view has been dismissed as 'Whig mythology', only in turn to be to some degree resurrected. Certainly, William did not trumpet his acceptance on these terms and in some respects wished, and attempted to act, as though they did not exist. Equally, however, it is difficult to argue against the proposition that after 1689 Parliament ceased to be an event and became an institution. It was in the legislature, in which king, Lords and Commons all had a part, that sovereignty resided. The monarchy was limited and, apart from the right of veto, now lacked discretionary power in relation to legislation. That there remained some ambiguity was a reflection of the circumstances. There was again sufficient compromise within Parliament and between the Crown and Parliament to produce a settlement which would allow the regime to solidify.

---

[15] Speck, *Reluctant Revolutionaries*; J. Clark, *English Society 1688–1832* (Cambridge, 1985); L. Schwoerer, *The Revolutions of 1688–89: Changing Perspectives* (Cambridge, 1992).

It is not difficult to indicate some areas of continuing monarchical power but not such as to render inapplicable the concept of 'limited' monarchy. It was that notion, stripped no doubt of exaggerated hyperbole, which nonetheless was to be the underlying basis of the British state when it came into existence two decades hence. As such, therefore, in comparative European terms, it meant that Britain would not be likely to follow the 'absolutist' pattern which predominated elsewhere. The 'exceptionalism' of Britain was therefore firmly established, insofar as any set of political relationships can ever be firmly established, after half a century of rebellion, restoration and revolution – all terms capable of varying emphasis and interpretation.

Never again, however, would a foreign adventurer, in this case William of Orange, albeit equipped with an English wife, land an army in England and be in a position to force a settlement in his favour. Although such things could not have been known at the very end of the seventeenth century, the context for the future evolution of the British state had been set.

Yet, around the events of 1688–89, there remains much ambiguity. One recent historian has repeated the claim that 'No one who studies British history before and after the years 1688–89 should fail to be aware that in passing from one period to another we are crossing one of the great divides on the entire landscape of "early modern" and modern times'.[16] For others, however, the notion of a 'great divide' is spurious – for a variety of reasons. Searching for a 'real' revolution, and supposing the word 'revolution' to mean the overthrow of an established social and political order, some historians believe that that term should only apply in the 1640s and 1650s – even though, eventually, 'revolution' failed. By comparison, 1688–89 was a minor matter.[17]

Alternatively, it has been thought appropriate to push the 'great divide' into the nineteenth century when, some argue, the 'confessional state' broke up. It has also been pointed out that if 'Liberty and Property' were the watchwords of 1688, the emphasis soon came to be placed on the latter, with harsh penalties for offences against it. Property was upheld by what was arguably the severest penal code in Western Europe. Enthusiasm for Parliament should not be mistaken for enthusiasm for 'popular sovereignty'. One in four adult English males had the right to vote. It was a sufficiently large number to give the business of Parliament a resonance in the country at large, though it was, of course, a propertied electorate.

The 'Bill of Rights' was not the embryonic assertion of the need for a constitution – it was a substitute for it. Indeed, for Macaulay, what was 'glorious' about the revolution was as much that sense of the word which implied a return to a starting point as a sense of innovation. The main prin-

---

[16] G. Holmes, *The Making of a Great Power: Late Stuart and Early Georgian Britain 1660–1722* (London, 1993) p. 212.
[17] For a discussion see R. Beddard, *The Revolutions of 1688* (Oxford, 1991) pp. 96–7.

ciples of English government had been 'engraven on the hearts of English-men during four hundred years' – no arbitrary legislation, no taxation, no regular soldiery, no arbitrary imprisonment. These were the 'fundamental laws' and 'a realm of which these were the fundamental laws stood in no need of a constitution'.[18]

William and Mary, Anne and two Georges

William III, though he had an English mother, had been Stadholder of the Netherlands for seventeen years before becoming King of England, Scotland and Ireland. Not even conforming to the Church of England could erase his Dutch past and the memory of the wars against the Dutch was still strong. In addition, until her death in 1695, William was an unusual king in that he reigned jointly with his wife, Mary. Inevitably, too, he was very well aware of the great risk that his own adventure to England had been. It was now not in his own interests to encourage the view that his action had created a precedent for others to emulate. The security of the monarchy was therefore his prime concern, and he succeeded in establishing it, even if the 'revolution' framework which embraced him was not entirely to his liking.

Anne, his sister-in-law, succeeded in 1702. None of her many children had survived into maturity. The previous year the Act of Settlement had been passed which stipulated that the succession should pass to the Electress Sophia of Hanover, granddaughter of James I through her mother, Elizabeth, or Sophia's Protestant descendants. Further, the sovereign was to undertake not to leave the country, or go to war to defend foreign possessions, without the consent of Parliament. Membership of the Church of England was another requirement.

The new queen reigned for a dozen years, applying herself diligently and obstinately to affairs of state. Only at the very end of her reign did circumstances require her to modify her determination, which had also been William's, not to be beholden entirely to one party in forming her ministries. It was clear that she had favourites. Sarah, Duchess of Marlborough, held pride of place until 1710 when Abigail Masham took her place. The political repercussions of this switch were considerable; a monarch's preferences mattered. The Union of 1707 was something of a surprise for the queen, but during her remaining seven years she did not feel called upon to visit her Scottish subjects in person.

George, Elector of Hanover, who became king in 1714 was not best equipped to develop 'Britishness' except insofar as he was a complete out-

---

[18] Cited in J. Black, *Convergence or Divergence? Britain and the Continent* (London, 1994) p. 134.

sider with no partiality. He neither spoke, nor read, nor understood English beyond a few words. As required, he did become an Anglican, an allegiance compatible with being a Lutheran in Hanover. His wife could not repair his British deficiencies, having been divorced for adultery and locked up in a German castle. Hanover remained close to his heart and it was there that he died and was buried. George II came to the throne in 1727. He had achieved some fluency in English. He reigned for thirty-three years – in itself an important stabilizing factor. Father and son both survived the Jacobite rebellions which threatened their position.

The Jacobite question

The continued existence of Jacobitism after 1707 meant that a challenge might still be mounted to the new British order and its constitutional apparatus. James Edward Stuart, the 'Old Pretender', son of James II, was recognized as king by Louis XIV of France. In 1708 a French squadron was off the east coast of Scotland. The supposition was that it would link up with a Scottish army poised for action. Bad weather – it was March – caused the enterprise to be abandoned. Scottish nobles suspected of involvement in the plot were rounded up and taken to London. It was hardly a serious military challenge, but from a London perspective the evidence of Scottish disaffection was disturbing.

The difficulty for Jacobites lay in moulding that disaffection into effective opposition, an opposition which could unite the diverse strands of Scottish opinion. It was amongst the Episcopalians that their support was greatest, but such a base was inadequate. Even some Presbyterians, hostile to the Union, might support, or at least not actively oppose, a Catholic Pretender, but that could not be relied upon. Although James had Protestants at his exiled court, his own Catholicism remained ardent. In addition, was it feasible to think that there could be a Jacobite restoration in Scotland alone? Some Scots thought so and could once again envisage separate monarchs and separate kingdoms. For most, however, England held the key to Scotland's release. Only by concerted action in England and Scotland could the enterprise succeed. In effect, therefore, it would be for English Jacobites to determine whether or not the enterprise succeeded.

Historians, however, have not agreed about the strength of Jacobitism outside Scotland. Obviously men were reluctant to declare their support for James publicly, but equally obviously a Jacobite nod or wink might be worthless. It was one thing to toast the Pretender on bended knee, as gentry gathered in Aberystwyth, mid-Wales, were said to have done in private in 1710, another to be ready to fight for him. Clandestine clinking throughout Britain was a dubious indicator of military potential, but clandestine correspondence with the exiled court suggested that some were indeed willing to flirt with treason.

Much clearly depended upon the smoothness of the Hanoverian succession in Britain as a whole. In theory, everything had been well arranged in advance of Queen Anne's decease, but the transition could go wrong. Even the childless queen was in touch with her step-brother, James Edward. Yet, although the garrison of Edinburgh Castle wisely started to dig a ditch round its eastern walls on hearing of her death in August 1714, its anxiety was unnecessary. The arrangements previously made for a regency council did indeed work smoothly. George I was installed in Britain before any rebellion occurred. This comfortable transition further complicated the task of would-be rebels, as had James Edward's reiteration that he would not contemplate becoming even a nominal Anglican for the sake of the throne.

Nevertheless, challenge there was. The initial plan envisaged a major rising in England and a secondary one in Scotland. In the event, the leading English plotters were detained before their preparations were complete. It was left to the Earl of Mar, formerly one of the Secretaries for Scotland and erstwhile leading architect of the Union, but now dismissed and disaffected, to flee back to Scotland. Raising his standard in the north-east in September 1715, he attracted strong support there, though not, as he had hoped, from the western clans. Even so, he gathered an army of some 15,000 men. It could have been an effective force if Mar had been a soldier as well as a politician. Argyll, with fewer troops, held him in check at Sherrifmuir in November. Even the arrival of the Old Pretender himself at Peterhead in the following month could not reverse the rebellion's prospects. He departed dolefully back to France in February 1716. In the meantime, a sideshow in Lancashire had come to nothing when a mixed Scottish and English force – possibly a third of the men were English Catholics – was defeated at Preston. At the very least, it showed how difficult it was to fuse together an effective English/Scottish combination. The forces at the disposal of the British state had survived a challenge which could have been much more serious than it turned out to be.

On this occasion, France was not involved – though there was another plot at the exiled court which might have been more effective if it had come to fruition. The death of Louis XIV was a setback for the cause. It looked increasingly likely, however, that another attempt could only succeed if an invasion was backed from abroad. And, for a time, after 1715 it was Spanish rather than French interest that was aroused. A well-equipped fleet set sail for Scotland from Cadiz in March 1719, only to be scattered in a violent storm. A small diversionary force did reach Stornoway, on the Isle of Lewis, but the unexpected presence of 307 Spanish infantrymen and miscellaneous Jacobites did not cause the clans to rise. The dispirited Spaniards surrendered after a perfunctory fight.

The somewhat farcical conclusion to this particular affair should not lead to the conclusion that the Jacobite threat was over. For several decades plots and conspiracies were still in the air. A problem for Jacobites was that, for their own reasons, neither France nor Spain now wished to contemplate war with England. They could not be enticed to finance expeditions. Replacing their support with assistance from Peter the Great of Russia was distinctly difficult. Within Britain itself, Jacobitism could still attract disgruntled spirits, but its positive attraction, as time passed, weakened. It looked ever more likely that the Hanoverian regime could only be overthrown if a significant foreign army could assist an internal rebellion. In 1743–44 it looked briefly as though this might happen, only for the plot to be discovered and the initial preparations to be nullified by storms at sea. It was evident from this episode, however, that France was once again willing to assist.

It turned out that the 1745 rising, which began in the Outer Isles of Scotland in July and ended thirteen months later, both prospered and ultimately foundered from the French connection. On landing, Charles Edward, the Young Pretender, gained widespread but not complete support in the Highlands but he did not carry all Scotland with him. The young David Hume, philosopher and historian, was one of those prepared to march out of Edinburgh to confront the prince's army. A Jacobite victory, of a kind, was achieved at Prestonpans in September. The decision to move south into England was then only taken with the narrowest of majorities in the Jacobite war council. Such division revealed ambivalence about the aims of the enterprise. The invasion of England might well encourage French participation but it might also bring defeat. Was it not better to consolidate in Scotland?

In the event, within a month of crossing the Border, the Jacobite army had reached Derby in the English Midlands by early December. In its progress south it had side-stepped rather than defeated Hanoverian armies. London lay before it – but then the decision was taken to turn back. Commanders refused to believe Charles Edward's assertions that the French were about to invade. It appears in retrospect that the French did have serious intentions, though they were again frustrated by the weather. English support was wavering.

The long road back ended in the final military disaster at Culloden, outside Inverness, in April 1746. What would have happened if the Young Pretender had gone on from Derby remains one of the speculative mysteries of British history. The Young Pretender never did come back again. Although traces of Jacobitism still lingered, the Jacobite threat to the Hanoverian British state was effectively at an end. Culloden was to be the last military action on Scottish soil; the Battle of Sedgemoor in 1685, when the Duke of Monmouth's rebellion was crushed, was the last military action on English soil. The Stuart dynasty faded into the past and into mythology.[19]

---

[19] D. Szechi, *Jacobitism and Tory Politics 1710–1714* (Edinburgh, 1984); E. Cruickshanks, ed., *Ideology and Conspiracy: Aspects of Jacobitism 1689–1759* (Edinburgh, 1982); F. McLynn, *The Jacobites* (London, 1985).

The BATTLE of CULLODEN, near Invernefs in *SCOTLAND*, 16ᵗʰ April 1746.

The King's Army Commanded by the Duke of Cumberland was drawn up in three Lines, into the left of which the Rebels attempting to break with
Swords and Targets were repulsed; when Kingston's Horse attack'd the left Wing, and the Dragoons the Rear; which compleated the Rout of the
Rebels, who had 2500 Men kill'd in the Battle, 1500 in the Pursuit and 1800 taken Prisoners.

Printed for & Sold by CARINGTON BOWLES, at his Map & Print Warehouse, Nᵒ 69 in Sᵗ Pauls Church Yard, LONDON.

Stability?

The mid-eighteenth century, therefore, marks the point at which the ebb and flow of battle, which had determined the outcome of so many political struggles in the long centuries of the British past, was at an end. England would not be again invaded from Scotland or Scotland from England. A pattern had been broken. In September 1745, in a London theatre, the 'national anthem', 'God save the King', was probably first sung publicly and perhaps somewhat apprehensively. The following year, it could be sung with gusto. The British state had survived its severest internal test.

It would be difficult, however, to describe the constitution at this juncture with precision. The early Hanoverians had arguably established themselves not because they were men of conspicuous merit but because the status quo was acceptable to propertied society. To opponents of Whigs, however, the Hanoverian kings were still essentially Whig creations. No doubt, if the Jacobites had succeeded, the opponents of Tories would have felt that the Crown was in Tory hands. Certainly, Whigs lost no time in branding Tories as Jacobites, or potential Jacobites, and thus consolidating their own power. There was still some way to go before the Crown constituted a symbol above and beyond politics. It was still intimately enmeshed in the complex world of 'party'.

Despite all that has been written on the subject, it is still not a straightforward matter to talk about 'party' at this time. There is no firm line that divides 'faction' from 'party' and there is nothing inherently 'bad' about the one and 'good' about the other. Some historians have felt that it is impossible to speak of 'party' before 1679 but that in the politics of the Exclusion Crisis of this period the first 'genuine' political parties can be found both in the country and in Parliament. Others have not been convinced. Likewise there has been disagreement about the extent to which the 'principles' which 'parties' defend have real substance. 'Every party', wrote the cynical Lord Halifax in *The Character of a Trimmer* (1688), 'when they find a maxim for their turn they presently call it *Fundamental* ... no feather hath been more blown about in the world than this word *Fundamental* ... For all men would have that principle to be immovable that serves their use at the time.'[20]

Even so, the roots of Parliament now spread far and relatively wide. It is probable that between 1689 and 1715 the voting population of England and Wales was growing faster than the population as a whole. Professor

---

[20] Cited in Butterfield, *Englishman and his History*, p. 90.

4.3 Bitter End: In April 1746 the Jacobite army under Charles Edward Stuart, some 5,000 strong, was defeated (in some forty minutes) by the superior forces ranged against it under William Augustus Duke of Cumberland on a moor by Inverness. Jacobite casualties were very heavy but the losses of their opponents very few. Culloden was the last significant land battle fought in Britain.

Holmes has suggested that in the three general elections of 1710, 1715 and 1722, a higher percentage of English adult males voted than at any subsequent election before 1868.[21] Thereafter, however, under Walpole and his successors as 'prime ministers', election results diminishingly expressed the 'national will'. The passage of the Septennial Act (1716), decreeing that Parliaments were to last seven rather than three years, is important in this connection. Patronage was crucial to the functioning of the system. The Duke of Newcastle controlled government patronage for some forty years after he became Secretary of State in 1724. His passion for arranging elections never waned and, in alliance with the major borough patrons, he could be virtually certain to deliver the election result which the government wanted.

Elections, however, were expensive affairs for those who indulged in them. Rivals were sometimes driven to the verge of bankruptcy. However, not all elections were contested – in the mid-eighteenth century only some 30 per cent were. Elections were not secret affairs, quite the contrary, and there were ways and means for non-electors to make their views known. Whether the lack of an election angered voters is not easily determined. The size of the constituency followed no particular logic. Nor did the regional distribution of seats. 'Party' was important, but so was the notion that a particular 'interest' or locality should be represented.

Scholarly interest in the House of Commons, with an eye to its future parliamentary dominance, has almost invariably led to a neglect of the House of Lords. Most major contemporary political figures – with some outstanding exceptions – sat in the upper house. The relationship between the two houses was indeed under considerable strain at the beginning of the century, not least because, on balance, there was more talent in the upper than in the lower house. After the mid-1720s, however, as the party balance shifted in favour of the Whigs, the Lords declined. Between 1721 and 1754, except for a few months, the First Lord of the Treasury ('Prime Minister') sat in the Commons. Of course, no absolute contrast should be drawn between the two houses. There were many sons of peers in the Commons and many parliamentary seats over which peers exercised a commanding interest. The term 'aristocratic century' is certainly not without force.

The management of this political system required skill and ruthlessness. Men such as Sunderland, Godolphin and Harley 'managed' business by mediating effectively between the requirements of the Crown and the mood of Parliament. Afterwards, in somewhat different circumstances, Robert Walpole carried 'management' to an even higher level as First Lord of the Treasury from 1721 to 1742. Scholars balk at the notion that he was the first Prime Minister but their caveats are to no avail in face of a hallowed public perception. It may be more plausible, however, to regard Walpole as the last in a long line of royal servants who established their own fortune

---

[21] Holmes, *Making of a Great Power*, p. 330.

and dynasty. His subtle, and not so subtle, manipulation of men by place and pension excited both admiration and hatred of 'Robinocracy'. After 1733, in particular, he was never secure in office, surviving ministerial crisis after ministerial crisis only with the Crown's support, until the end came in 1742.

Thirty years ago, Sir John Plumb traced what he called the 'growth of political stability' in Britain in the half century before 1725.[22] How had this come about? Plumb suggested that it was because there was a common sense of identity amongst those who wielded power, together with an acceptance by society at large of its political institutions and those who made them work. For other writers, the achievement of 'stability' extended over a longer period and Walpole himself was part of that process. It has been urged that there was even a kind of 'yearning' for stability which politicians sought to achieve above and beyond their ordinary manoeuvres.[23] Stability, however, like liberty, is an elusive concept and is never achieved on a 'once and for all' basis.

And, if the new Britain in the decades after 1707 had reached such a plateau, at least for a time, perhaps it only did so because it suited the interests of a small political elite. The 'Age of Oligarchy' which some have seen dawning is, in this perspective, too bland a term for an arrogant and rapacious 'Old Corruption' concerned to serve its own interests.[24] Offices in the early eighteenth century were still regarded as pieces of property and their holders still relied for payment on fees and gratuities of one kind and another.[25] Eighteenth-century administration has been aptly characterized as an extraordinary blending of the old and the new, the useless and the efficient, and what was corrupt and what was honest.[26]

Britain as a 'modern bureaucratic state' was still some way in the future but the 'Britain' of 1500 with its separate kings, Parliaments and peoples already seemed a long way in the past. Paradoxically, however, political unity, and

---

[22] J. Plumb, *The Growth of Political Stability in England, 1675–1725* (Oxford, 1967).

[23] Holmes, *Making of a Great Power*, p. 387.

[24] 'Not to put too fine a point on it', write two authors, 'the State [was] a racket, run by particular groups within the ruling classes largely for their own benefit.' P. Corrigan and D. Sayer, *The Great Arch: English State Formation as Cultural Revolution* (Oxford, 1985) p. 89.

[25] G. Aylmer, 'From Office-Holding to Civil Service: The Genesis of Modern Bureaucracy', *Transactions of the Royal Historical Society* Fifth Series 30 (1980), p. 106. Aylmer notes that the term 'civil service' has not been found before 1816. See also G. Aylmer, 'The Peculiarities of the English State', *Journal of Historical Sociology* 3, 2 (June 1990).

[26] Moreover, it is sometimes argued that the century as a whole witnessed not the resolution but the deepening of social and intellectual contradictions. P. Monod, *Jacobitism and the English People 1688–1788* (Cambridge, 1989) pp. 348–9.

its accompanying governmental structures, coincided with the fragmentation of that Christianity which had formerly at least aspired to transcend the structures of the state. After 1500, however, out of one now came many. The diversity that emerged during the Reformation and after in some respects buttressed British identity but in others rendered it fragile and incomplete. It is the purpose of the next chapter to explore the nature of this paradox.

Chapter 5

Truth, Uniformity and Toleration: Making a British Compromise? *c.*1500–*c.*1750

Henry VII, on coming to the throne, had no difficulty in maintaining vigilance against the lingering 'Lollardy' which still occasionally surfaced. In 1498 the king himself gained great credit for converting a priest from his heretical opinions so that the man 'died as a Christian'. Grateful for papal support, especially in the years immediately after 1485, Henry gave no encouragement to religious innovation. It would have been inconceivable to him that, 200 years later in 1689, there would be a Toleration Act which would modify the penal laws against religious Dissenters, though it still did not abolish them. The notion that the state had an obligation to 'establish' a particular expression of the Christian religion was not dead even then. Religion was not merely a private and personal matter, it was frequently the expression of national values and aspirations. Debate about the form of the Church and the content of theology, seen in this context, was fundamental not incidental. 'Reformation' was not so much an instant replacement of one creed by another as a protracted process, ebbing and flowing, in which the claims of truth, uniformity and toleration coexisted and conflicted in an uneasy trinity. The interaction between these concerns shaped the Britain of 1750.

Ecclesia Anglicana

Papal unwillingness to nullify the marriage of Henry VIII to Catherine of Aragon, which had not produced a male heir, had dramatic repercussions. The king, who had in 1521 composed a treatise against Luther, the leading German reformer, and established to his satisfaction that papal authority was divine, took a series of steps from 1529 onwards to make himself by 1534 'Supreme Head' of the English Church. Henry divorced Catherine and their daughter, Mary, was declared illegitimate. The dissolution of the monasteries followed (1536–40). On the pretext that they had become lax, some eight hundred monastic houses were swept away, resulting in a substantial augmentation of royal revenue. Within a century, however, most of the appropriated land was to be sold off, creating a laity which had a vested interest in the new status quo.

The significance of these measures remains puzzling. It is arguable that what Henry attempted was not so much 'Reformation' as conceived elsewhere in Europe (though that, too, was not a uniform phenomenon) but a 'Reform'. He did not want the Church to be simply a company of the 'elect' but he did want it to be purified. Scripture was superior to both papal law and canon law. The first legal translation of the Bible into English was authorized and a copy was ordered to be placed in every parish church. A proper emphasis upon the Bible, however, did not mean that the historic continuity of the Church was to be discounted. The Pope of Rome was not yet Antichrist, but his upstart pretensions had to be reduced.

It was not clear how the resulting Church should be defined: *Ecclesia Anglicana*, as a term, had a history which long anteceded the Reformation Parliament but its English translation could carry various shades of meaning. In the sixteenth century, however, 'Anglican Church' would not be among them. The crucial issue was to what extent it was the '*Church* of England' or the 'Church of *England*'. Legislation on doctrine, worship and governance swung first one way and then another over subsequent decades. Under Edward VI, the broad tendency was 'Protestant', though it is important to remember that the protest in 'Protestantism' was conceived to be positive rather than negative.

In 1549 Cranmer's First Book of Common Prayer maintained some continuity in that the liturgical structure followed closely that of the Mass and could even be taken to imply traditional Eucharistic doctrine. That of 1552, however, removed any reference to the divine presence in the Eucharist. The altar was brought down into the nave. The change in the language to English made the liturgy much more accessible to the laity. The laity would have been conscious of a narrowing of the gulf between itself and the priesthood. Clergy could marry and the laity could receive both the bread and the wine in the Communion. A very great emphasis was now placed upon the sermon, the preaching of the Word. Indeed, one might speak of a shift from a visual to a verbal culture. It would have been the sweeping changes which took place inside a church building which made most immediate impact as chapels, altars, statues and ornaments were removed. In cathedrals, where the pattern of services was most elaborate, change could be comprehensive as ten services each day were reduced to three. At Canterbury in February 1550, the government ordered the handing over of all service-books of the Latin liturgy for their destruction; the defacement of windows and images had already been under way.

Under Mary, naturally, a Catholic restoration was swiftly attempted. Traditional worship and papal authority were both restored. For worshippers, it was a case of 'as you were'. At Canterbury, for example, we read that the rood was swiftly re-erected, and in short order processional crosses, ornaments and vestments were back in use – perhaps suggesting that they had been prudently hidden rather than destroyed. It was more difficult to equip the choir with plainsong service books. By 1557 the cathedral was almost its 'Catholic' self, minus its shrines and relics. Heresy was stamped out. In the city of Canterbury between July 1555 and November 1558, there were no less than seven separate spectacular burnings in which a total of forty-one people perished. Thomas Cranmer, Archbishop of Canterbury, Prayer Book compiler, was burnt in 1556, together with other leading Protestants.

It was against such a background that Elizabeth, after Mary's death in 1558, sought a settlement which could endure. It remained the assumption that the solution should be 'national'. In the event, the 1559 Acts of Supremacy and Uniformity made Elizabeth 'Supreme Governor' of the Church and promoted an ecclesiastical establishment which had elements which could appeal to the various shades of opinion that had emerged over the preceding thirty years. Mary's laws against heresy were repealed. Liturgically, the queen steered a path between the Prayer Books of 1549 and 1552. A form of words to be used in the Eucharist was found which would be acceptable, on the whole, to those with different understandings of the sacrament. It was a *via media* (middle way) of a kind. In its Elizabethan version, the Prayer Book established itself in the minds and hearts of English worshippers. There is evidence that its replacement in 1645 caused great resentment and that it continued to be used clandestinely. A new Prayer Book came out in 1662 and continued to be used for a further 300 years. Its uniform use throughout the kingdom was itself thought to be a representation of divine harmony.

In other aspects, however, over the decades of the queen's reign there was much continuing controversy as first one faction and then another tried to steer the Church in the desired direction. Controversy centred on clerical vestments, on the term 'communion table' as opposed to altar, and, in some quarters much influenced by continental Calvinism, on issues of Church government, including the legitimacy of episcopacy itself.

The Thirty-Nine Articles, the doctrinal standard of the Church of England, received parliamentary sanction in 1571, though all controversy was by no means stilled. A quarter of a century later, in his *On the Laws of Ecclesiastical Polity*, Richard Hooker vigorously and 'judiciously' justified the structure that had emerged both against Rome and against Presbyterianism. An 'Anglican' mode of discussion and temper of mind was crystallizing. The Book of Common Prayer gave form and focus to the Church's worship. The use of the Creeds placed Anglican worship in the context of the long Christian past. It was a Church, apparently, in some sense both Catholic and

Protestant – a very English creation – governed, not without symbolic significance, by a 'Virgin Queen'.

It was even found possible to work out a new synthesis in the work
and worship of cathedrals. It was the queen's personal wish that, so long as
the sense of the words which might be adopted for any appropriate part of
the Prayer Book service was not obscured, 'modest and distinct song' was
appropriate. Music was a 'laudable science' and should not be banished.
And, more generally, at the beginning and end of Morning and Evening
Prayer, a hymn or such like song might be sung in the best sort of melody
and music that could be devised. By such means, past and present were to be
reconciled.

The significance of what had happened can be considered at a variety
of levels. Historians, on the whole, have looked in vain for a pervasive popular enthusiasm for the changes that took place. There was no general desire
either to press on to a more thorough-going Protestantism or to return to
'papacy'. The 'Englishness' of the ecclesiastical enterprise was also ambivalent. Unlike the variegated pattern that was prevailing in mainland Europe,
the Church of England was a thoroughly 'national' affair. No specific theological label could be attached to it, although both Lutheran and Calvinist
ideas were present. On the other hand, particularly for those who had spent
time abroad, the English Church as a Protestant Church was not an isolated
insular phenomenon. In Edward's reign, after all, an Alsatian (Bucer), an Italian (Peter Martyr) and a Pole (Lasko) had all given the Archbishop of Canterbury the benefit of their advice. 'Our' religion belonged in the European
Protestant world.

Some Protestant writers, however, felt that Providence had a particular
care for the English nation. Hugh Latimer, later to be burnt at the stake, rejoiced in 1537 on the news of the birth of Prince Edward in these terms:
'verily [God] hath shewed himself God of England or rather an English God,
if we consider and ponder well all his proceedings with us from time to time
...'. The English were an Elect Nation and even, in the eyes of some, *the*
Elect Nation. The fires of Mary's reign smouldered in English hearts long
after her decease. Mary's marriage to Philip of Spain contributed to the fusing of Protestantism and patriotism. 'O lord', prayed one pamphleteer in

---

5.1 Testament Newydd/New Testament: Translations of the Bible into English are
associated with William Tyndale and Miles Coverdale in the 1520s and 1530s. A
Welsh New Testament was translated by William Salesbury and Richard Davies in
1563–78 and the Bible by William Morgan in 1588. The English 'authorized version'
of James I was the work of 1604–11. Various Welsh revisions followed the early
work. The ornate title page of this 1620 Welsh New Testament indicates that it was
produced in London by printers to the king. A Scottish Gaelic New Testament appeared in 1767 and a complete Irish Gaelic Bible in 1810. The timing of these translations is significant not only in British religious history but also in linguistic and
cultural history.

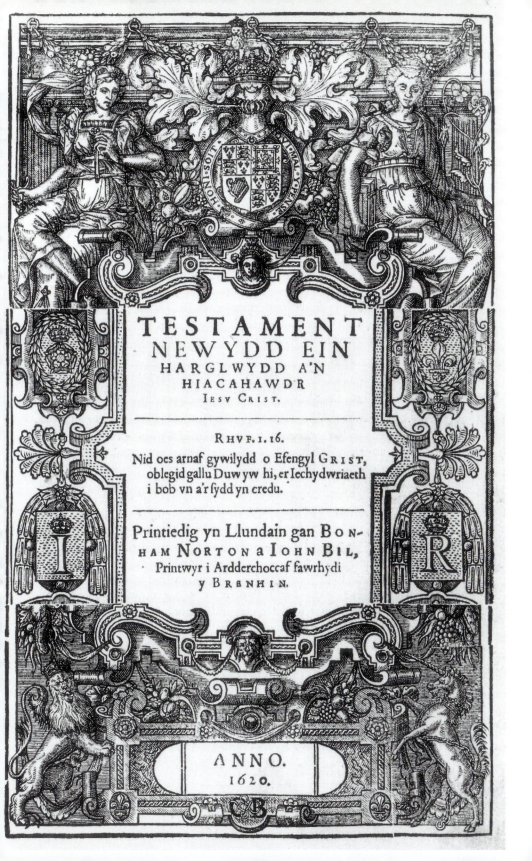

TESTAMENT NEWYDD EIN HARGLWYDD A'N HIACAHAWD'R Iesv Crist.

RHVF. 1. 16.

Nid oes arnaf gywilydd o Efengyl GRIST, oblegid gallu Duw yw hi, er Iechydwriaeth i bob vn a'r fydd yn credu.

Printiedig yn Llundain gan Bonham Norton a Iohn Bil, Printwyr i Ardderchoccaf fawrhydi y Brenhin.

ANNO. 1620.

1554, 'defend thy elect people of Inglond from the handes and force of thy enemyes the Papistes.'[1] It was one of Elizabeth's apparent virtues that she was 'mere English'.

A Welsh *Ecclesia Anglicana?*

During his rebellion, Owain Glyn Dŵr had resurrected the claim to autonomy on the part of the Welsh Church: a Welsh Archbishop of St Davids should be independent of Canterbury. However, the failure of his revolt meant that this long-cherished ambition made no further progress. It was inevitable, therefore, that Henry VIII should follow through in Wales the policy he had embarked on in England. It would seem, in general, that his reform policy did not meet great opposition in Wales. The Edwardian changes, however, affecting as they did so many visible aspects of church life, were very unpopular in Wales. Even zealous Protestants were alarmed that the speed of change might provoke revolt. The brief revival of Catholicism under Mary seemed more acceptable than extreme Protestantism.

The arrival of the Prayer Book and the emphasis placed by reformers on the Bible caused particular difficulties in Wales. The Prayer Book was in English, a language still not readily accessible to the bulk of the population. Since English was the only language permitted in churches, it meant that the language was now heard throughout Wales as it had never been before. The new order was dismissed by one Welsh poet as *Ffydd Saeson* (the English faith). In 1563, however, Parliament passed an act which allowed the Scriptures and the Book of Common Prayer to be translated into Welsh. They would be used in Welsh-speaking areas. A New Testament and Prayer Book in Welsh appeared in 1567. It was in 1588 that the complete translation of the Bible by William Morgan appeared. It was a critical juncture because, with the decline of its official status, Welsh was dividing into dialects. It was the Bible which gave a common standard. No translation into any other Celtic language occurred in the sixteenth century. Morgan, however, was primarily a Protestant clergyman, latterly a bishop, not a language conservator. Without the Bible in their own language, the Welsh might return to Catholicism. Protestant bishops indeed argued with some success that the new ecclesiastical order was closer to the Ancient British Church than to the Roman. The Reformation, therefore, though imposed from without, could be held to have an 'authentic' flavour which it lacked in England. And it was a British

---

[1] Cited in D. Loades, 'The origins of English Protestant Nationalism' in S. Mews, ed., *Religion and National Identity: Studies in Church History*, vol. 18 (Oxford, 1982) pp. 302, 304. In the same volume see also A.J. Fletcher, 'The Origins of English Protestantism and the Growth of National Identity'.

dynasty that was responsible. By the end of the century, it did largely appear that Welsh adherence to the Church of England had been secured. Ecclesiastical uniformity therefore reinforced the 'Acts of Union' on English terms but also in a way that gave Welsh people a religious breathing space.

Ecclesia Scoticana

It was not until 1560 that the Scottish Parliament swept away papal authority and jurisdiction and revoked the legislation against 'heretics'. The Mass was banned. It was an extraordinary outcome which would have been inconceivable forty years earlier. Some English Lollards had fled to Scotland, and Lutheran ideas came in through seaports, but it is generally agreed that their impact was modest. The advances made by Protestants subsequently cannot be divorced from the complexities of Scottish politics. Religion was used by pro-French and pro-English factions for their own ends, though it would be too cynical to suppose that only politics was involved in the allegiances and alignments that emerged. The conservative and controlled Henrician reform was not without its attractions for some Scottish nobility but, in the event, Scotland was not to follow the English pattern.

The person of John Knox was one of the reasons why this was not the case. Ironically, however, although often portrayed as *the* Scottish reformer, his lasting impact could equally well have been in England. It was there that he fled in 1549 after his release by the French who had made him a galley-slave, following their capture of St Andrews Castle where Knox was preacher to the Protestant garrison. He was very active in supporting the Edwardian Reformation but fled to Frankfurt and Geneva when Mary came to the throne. Knox, thinking of Mary of England and Mary of Guise in Scotland, published in 1558 his *First Blast of the Trumpet against the Monstrous Regiment of Women*. It was evident that he did not think women should rule – a view that was not likely to commend him to Elizabeth. He returned to Scotland as the clerical leader of the Protestant anti-French camp which triumphed in 1560. His influence over the ensuing decade was powerful.

Ecclesia Scoticana was more clearly Calvinist in theology than *Ecclesia Anglicana* was allowed to become. For decades, however, a struggle ensued over the structure and government of the Church. Where was the boundary to be drawn between Church and state? The General Assembly asserted its spiritual independence. Reformed scholars saw no basis for bishops in the Word of God. In 1596 Andrew Melville, an enthusiast for the Presbyterian system as it evolved in Geneva and France, told James VI that there were 'two kings' and 'two kingdoms' in Scotland. In Christ's kingdom, the Kirk, the king was no more than a member. It was an issue which was still unresolved when James became King of Great Britain in 1603. The monarch knew very well that Reformation in his two kingdoms had indeed occurred but it had taken different forms and embodied different beliefs.

Dissenters: Catholic and Protestant

It should not be assumed that the forms of Protestantism endorsed by the state in England/Wales and in Scotland in the sixteenth century settled religious issues to universal satisfaction. Before the Henrician Reformation, English Christians had not been notably ardent in their enthusiasm for the papacy as an institution or for the popes of the day. Nevertheless, after the break with Rome, outward conformity within the new structures often disguised adherence to the old faith. In the mid-century, however, the Council of Trent forbade such occasional conformity by Catholics. In addition, in 1570 the Pope excommunicated Queen Elizabeth. He further decreed that her subjects should not obey her or her laws. The arrival in England of missionary priests further heightened feelings. The government suspected Catholic plots – particularly with the presence of Mary, Queen of Scots, a Catholic claimant to the throne – and proscribed the Catholic faith in a series of drastic measures. Catholics seemed to have a simple and stark choice in these circumstances, to support the Pope or the queen, and many of them agonized inconclusively. The enthusiasm of some Jesuit priests for the Spanish 'Enterprise of England' was unbounded and made the charge of treason seem well-founded. Some other Catholic priests tried to dispute the Pope's authority in civil as opposed to religious matters as a way out of the dilemma. By 1585, any Catholic priest active in England and Wales was, by definition, guilty of treason. There could be no clearer affirmation that the state was hostile to Catholicism. It was 'Roman', not a creed for the people of England and Wales. However, Catholic 'recusants' who refused to conform still existed in some parts of the country – in Lancashire in England, in Flintshire in Wales, for example – though not in large numbers. Despite the restraints and restrictions to which it was subjected, the old religion was not completely eliminated.

The same was true in Scotland. In Aberdeenshire, Ayrshire and elsewhere, there was considerable opposition to the progress of Protestantism, but by the end of the century the old faith only survived locally when supported by prominent families. In some parts of Scotland – in the Western Highlands and Islands, for example – there was for a time a kind of religious limbo, even for decades, as parishes existed without either Catholic priest or Protestant minister.

It was not only Catholics, however, who were outside the new Established Churches of 'Britain'. In England, Protestant Separatists argued that the Church of England was only a half-way house. It contained too many features of the old religion. In the last decade of the sixteenth century a specific Act against Separatists had been passed to counter the threat they also posed. Their ideas evolved rapidly. They argued that the Church should not be, in effect, a branch of the state. It should be a 'gathered community' of believers, a 'communion of saints' identified by a radical Christian discipleship and a personal commitment. Some Separatists fled to the Netherlands where their views were further elaborated. Their notions of what a church should be challenged the prevailing assumptions of the Church as a national, all-embracing institution embedded in the structure of the state. It was also the case amongst such Baptists that their ecclesiastical ideas had political implications. If no hierarchy was needed in the Church – they saw no need for bishops – why was one needed in the state?[2]

At the beginning of the seventeenth century, therefore, Protestant Separatists, like Catholics, constituted only a small minority of the population, but the continued existence of both communities suggested that religious uniformity was in difficulties. The failure of the attempt by a few Catholic gentry to blow up James I, the Lords and the Commons at the opening of Parliament on 5 November 1605, however, provoked further anti-Catholic outbursts and restrictions. Every year, subsequently, Gunpowder, Treason and Plot was never to be forgot. In structure, doctrine and liturgy, it could scarcely be said that the Church of England and the Church of Scotland were of one mind, but it seemed undoubted that this uneasy Episcopalian/Presbyterian combination underpinned the throne of King James VI in 1603 and gave 'Britain' its diverse but pronounced Protestant ethos.

Half a century later, however, that could not be said with confidence. The breakdown of established authority during the Civil Wars and the advent of the Commonwealth saw the mushrooming of radical groups operating under various names with strong religious/political agendas. Amongst them, for example, were the 'Friends of Truth' who followed George Fox in rejecting sacraments and the idea of 'professional' clergy. 'Quakers', as they came to be called, dressed distinctively, refused to swear oaths and rejected distinctions of rank. Oliver Cromwell was himself a 'Dissenter', although a precise denominational label cannot be attached to him and little is known about his religious practice. What he did seek, however, was a 'reformation of manners' and the growth of a 'godly nation'. The label 'Puritan', however, whether applied to Cromwell or to sectarians *en bloc*, can be misleading. The Protector ordered forty-eight violins and fifty trumpets for the wedding celebrations of his daughter, Frances. At the occasion, there was 'much mirth with frolics'.[3]

---

[2] C. Hill, *The World Turned Upside Down* (London, 1972).
[3] J.C. Davis, 'Cromwell's Religion' in J. Morrill, ed., *Oliver Cromwell and the English Revolution* (London, 1990) pp. 181–208; B. Coward, *Oliver Cromwell* (London, 1991) pp. 105–6.

The proliferation of such groups confronted Cromwell with a problem. He claimed for himself liberty of conscience but grappled with the extent to which it constituted some kind of absolute principle. Confronted by competing claims to truth in matters ecclesiastical and theological, he did not resort to bland indifference but neither did he espouse a comprehensive toleration. There could be, in his eyes, a unity in diversity amongst the conscientious godly, but who were the conscientious godly? It was certain that Catholics were neither conscientious nor godly. Under Cromwell, however, some Jews began to congregate in London and a kind of semi-official permission to settle was extended. It should not be thought, even so, that their advent represented a triumph for toleration. Some Puritan divines thought that their presence would hasten the Second Coming of Christ. It is possible that Cromwell tried to resolve the dilemmas confronting him by promoting not 'church unity' but the unity of the 'godly nation'. The notion of a 'particular plan' for England already had an ancestry, as has been noted, and Puritans gave the idea renewed emphasis.

Restorations

After 1660, however, there was an inevitable 'Restoration' of religion to accompany the restoration of Charles II.[4] The Church of England had undoubtedly suffered during the period of Puritan supremacy, paying the price for the 'Laudian' era in the 1630s when Archbishop Laud stood close to Charles I. Laud himself had been executed. 'Anglicanism' had implanted itself in many minds and hearts over the course of a century; there was, for example, considerable opposition in the 1640s to the proscription of the Book of Common Prayer. The period also saw the abolition of episcopacy and church courts. Hundreds of Church of England clergy were ejected from their livings. A turning of the tables could scarcely be avoided.

Between 1660 and 1662, in externals at least, the Church of England regained its pre-Civil War position in the state and society. Once again, the king's subjects were compelled to accept a state-imposed uniformity. However, attempts were made, unavailingly as it proved, to reach a wide degree of doctrinal and ecclesiastical comprehension in the re-established Church of England. The king, whose personal religious zeal was not pronounced, would probably have welcomed a 'broad church'. However, the discussions

---

[4] I. Green, 'Anglicanism in Stuart and Hanoverian England' and M. Mullett, 'Radical Sects and Dissenting Churches' in S. Gilley and W. Sheils, eds, *A History of Religion in Britain* (Oxford, 1994); J. Miller, *Popery and Politics in England 1660–1688* (London, 1973); G.V. Bennett, *The Tory Crisis in Church and State 1688–1730* (Oxford, 1975); J. Walsh, C. Haydon and S. Taylor, eds, *The Church of England c.1689–1830* (Cambridge, 1993).

failed and the 'Great Ejection' occurred in August 1662. One-third of London clergy, for example, refused to give unqualified subscription to the newly drawn up Prayer Book. The Uniformity Act, passed earlier in the year, required assent to the Thirty-Nine Articles, but they declined to give it.

There were undoubtedly men on both sides who profoundly regretted this separation, but they could not prevail. The ejected clergy found their way into various dissenting bodies and a new clear divide was established in English life. Dissenters who insisted on maintaining their convictions were subjected to penalties of varying severity. Amongst their number was John Bunyan, the unordained tinker, who wrote *Pilgrim's Progress* during his twelve years in prison (1660–72) for holding Baptist religious services. It seems clear, however, that in many localities these penalties were not exacted with enthusiasm and in some cases scarcely at all. Even Charles II, for reasons that are obscure, made some effort to ensure that Dissenters could at least worship in peace. Shut out of the two English universities, the Dissenters turned their energies to schools and academies. There were periodic suggestions that a reconciliation with the Church of England could be achieved but they came to nothing. Dissent would stick it out. Many Anglican bishops and clergy, however, still thought that Dissent could be reduced to an ineffective rump.

The advent of James II to the throne put these issues into a new context. The political ramifications of his Catholicism have been noted in the previous chapter. The ecclesiastical ramifications were no less significant. The Church of England was alarmed by his manifest wish to produce a policy of 'toleration', a policy which would undoubtedly assist his fellow-Catholics. It was also supposed, however, that he would not stop there. Bishops and laymen in the country at large, who had come to feel comfortable with the Restoration ecclesiastical settlement, now became alarmed. Protestant Dissenters, however, were a little tempted by the fact that a 'toleration' designed to assist Catholics would also release them from comparable penal laws. Their mutual exclusion gave Catholic and Protestant Dissenters a shared discomfort, though they were in other respects far apart. In the event, James's manoeuvres failed. Historians who believe that he would have created an England which refrained from penalizing on grounds of religion express regret. They suggest that the episode brings out how limited was the 'freedom' allegedly brought by the subsequent 'Glorious Revolution'. Other historians, however, believe that the 'toleration' James desired was only envisaged as a first step which would lead to the reimposition of Catholicism.

Under William and Mary, the 1689 Toleration Act allowed Dissenters to worship without penalty in licensed meeting-houses, provided the doors were left unlocked during services. Dissenting ministers were relieved of penalties previously imposed, provided they subscribed to the specifically doctrinal articles of the Thirty-Nine Articles. They were also required to take the oath of allegiance. Baptists were exempted from the article relating to infant baptism.

Quakers were no longer to be penalized for refusing to swear on oath. Relief, however, did not apply to Catholics and non-Trinitarian Dissenters. The 1662 Uniformity Act, however, still remained on the statute book. Parliament was not committed to any view that toleration was desirable and religious pluralism inescapable. It was becoming apparent, however, that the Church of England was not likely to be again the Church of the whole English nation, though that is still what its hierarchy would have liked.

It was unlikely, too, that the Church of England would be the Church of the whole Welsh nation. Puritanism in Wales before the Civil War can only be described as marginal, but twenty years later, in radicalized form, it had become a key element in Welsh religious life. The 'Welsh Saints' endeavoured to liberate their countrymen from what they considered a 'swarme of blind superstitious ceremonies'.[5] The extent to which Wales had a special place in Christian history was again stressed. Energetic evangelization took place, in both languages, in barren places.

Naturally, in 1660 an attempt was also made to restore the proper order. Several hundred Welsh Quakers, for example, were locked up in Welsh castles. However, the immediate past could not be obliterated completely. The 1662 Great Ejection also gave fresh life to Welsh Dissent. Dissenting meeting- houses proliferated: this was more than a movement of the 'lower orders'. Clergy of the Established Church tried energetically, in some cases, to restrict the spread of Dissent, but could not invariably rely upon the support of the gentry for their efforts. It should be noted, however, that it was in Merionethshire in 1677 that it was last seriously proposed that heretics, in this case Quakers, should be burnt at the stake. Those who administered the restored religious and political order could not forget the time when modest itinerant preachers presumed to speak with authority on religious matters and had turned the world upside down. It was becoming clear, however, that in Wales Dissent could be restricted, but not stamped out.

In Scotland, as noted in the previous chapter, Crown and Church had been in virtually constant conflict in the period leading up to the Civil Wars. There had then come a point when the Scots sought to impose a Presbyterian order in England. The restoration of Charles II turned the tables once again. The king would not accept a purely Presbyterian system in Scotland and insisted upon episcopal restoration, though he indicated that a kind of mixed system might be acceptable. However, any notion that 'bishops with presbyteries' might satisfy all shades of opinion was shattered by the armed resistance offered in south-west Scotland by the 'Covenanters'. The fighting was savage, meriting the description applied to the period, 'The Killing Time'. It seemed that there could be no compromise in the ecclesiastical politics of the country.

---

[5] Cited in P. Jenkins, *A History of Modern Wales: 1536–1990* (London, 1990) p. 111.

King James VII and II made some attempt to woo Presbyterians in Scotland with notions of toleration, as he wooed Dissenters in England, but again to no ultimate effect. Scotland, however, played little part in the events in southern England which led to the king's downfall. Naturally, though, his departure was the signal for another attempt by Presbyterians to gain the ascendancy.

William – declared king and his wife queen by the Scottish Convention of Estates in March 1689 – was a Dutch Calvinist and hence Presbyterian expectations were high. In the event, 'prelacy' was abolished in Scotland and the Presbyterian system of Church government reinstated. The first General Assembly of the Kirk to meet in Scotland since 1653 reaffirmed its Calvinist Confession of Faith. Lay patronage, another contentious issue from the past, was also abolished.

These steps signified the final failure of successive Stuart kings to impose a uniform and episcopal ecclesiastical structure in their two kingdoms. In Scotland, an Episcopalian rump remained, subjected to severe restrictions, particularly in the north-east, as there remained a Presbyterian residue in England, but the outward image was of a Presbyterian Scotland and an Anglican England (and English Dissent had no precise counterpart in Scotland). Thus, oddly, on the eve of what turned out to be the union of the two countries, it was their difference rather than their convergence which was emphasized in their ecclesiastical settlements. This was not a marginal matter since both the Church of England and the Church of Scotland were perceived to embody attitudes and values characteristic of their respective nations.

Equilibrium?

In both England/Wales and Scotland, therefore, the principle of uniformity still held sway, but in a somewhat precarious fashion. The Church of England was bitterly divided. For some of its leading figures, the Toleration Act was only an unfortunate and temporary concession to Dissent. Its provisions should be strictly enforced and compliance monitored. Parliament surely did not intend the nation to be rent by permanent religious schism. Others believed that 'toleration' was inevitable and might indeed extend to complete equality for Dissenters, both Catholic and Protestant, at some stage in the future. 'High Church' and 'Low Church' factions divided on this and other issues, and these factions broadly corresponded to the political divisions between 'Tory' and 'Whig'. There were 'Non-Juror' clergy who broke away or were deprived of their posts because they believed in divinely instituted authority and could not approve of the consequences of the 'Glorious Revolution'.

More generally, in the early eighteenth century, the effects of more than half a century of religious turmoil were to be seen in decaying churches and depressed and penurious clergy. The Church of England was not as a whole sinking into a mire of absenteeism, clerical pluralism and ignorance, but there were sufficient examples of this condition to suggest that there was a kind of crisis. Convocation, the Church of England's own 'parliament', in two houses, had been suspended in 1689. After it was restored in 1701 the two houses clashed vehemently. Bishops, whose political colour had been the prime determinant in their appointment, were expected to assist in the passage of government business in the House of Lords – an activity which some of their number found more interesting than their diocesan responsibilities.

During Anne's reign, the High Church Party was resurgent and the queen herself created a 'Bounty' to augment poor clerical livings. In 1709–10 Dr Sacheverell, a Tory High Churchman, referred to Dissenters as 'a nest of vipers' and presented a picture of the Church in danger.[6] In 1711 the Occasional Conformity Act tried to prevent Dissenters from 'occasionally' conforming to the Church, and thereby evading the provisions of the Test Act, though it was repealed eight years later. Such occasional conformity had enabled Dissenters to obtain offices from which they would otherwise have been excluded. The disagreeable Convocation was scrapped again in 1717: there was no place in which 'the Church' could express a mind of its own, even if it had a mind to express.

George I was naturally not well-versed in the ethos of the Church of England. He was happy to accept Walpole's advice that the Church would be best buttressed by the appointment of Whig bishops. Edmund Gibson, Bishop of London, was the chief ecclesiastical instrument of Whig policy, but he was also an earnest churchman, with ambitious reforming schemes. Perhaps, in any case, the Church was not in as parlous a condition as was once thought. Historians are now ready to interpret the complaints made by contemporaries as evidence of rising expectations on the part of the laity rather than declining standards on the part of the clergy.

In a general sense, the majority of the population still conformed to the Church of England and expected it to provide rites of passage on demand. Perhaps 10 per cent received the sacrament on the rare occasions when it was administered – likely to be only four times a year. 'Parish Anglicanism' was a reality. The parson, when he was in residence, was not enclosed within an ecclesiastical compound but continued to be involved in a wide range of public activities. Local community life, in many instances, still revolved around squire and parson. It could therefore still seem that Church and state in England/Wales were but different sides of the same coin.

The Anglican hysteria of the early century may reflect uncertainty

---

[6] G. Holmes, *The Trial of Doctor Sacheverell* (London, 1973).

THE QUAKERS MEETING

5.2 Plain Truth: 'The Quaker's Meeting', mezzotint engraved by Isaac Bowles after the painting by Egbert von Heemskirk (late seventeenth century). George Fox founded a religious group in the 1650s which sought the Inner Light and shunned liturgical and sacramental worship. Members of the 'Religious Society of Friends', nicknamed Quakers, refused to swear oaths or pay tithes to the Established Church or honour contemporary notions of rank and status. Their dress was plain but distinctive. They rejected a professional ministry and members waited quietly in worship until one of their number felt moved to speak. It was not unusual (though frequently considered unbalanced by those outside the society) for women to feel so moved. Quakers, though always small in numbers, were noted in subsequent centuries for their philanthropy, business acumen and pacifism.

---

about the actual size of the Protestant Dissenting community. Daniel Defoe, Dissenter after a fashion himself, came up with a figure of 2 million – around a third of the English population. It is a figure which has been drastically scaled down by modern historians to around a third of a million. It must be remembered, however, that Dissent, almost by definition, was not a united body. In this light, the 'threat' posed by Dissent appears less substantial, though in certain localities – for example, the city of Bristol – Dissenters were clearly more numerous than their national percentage suggests.

Presbyterians, Congregationalists, Baptists and others did not, in fact, advance in the early decades of the century. The same was true of Quakers, whose distinctive beliefs, practices and dress always marked them off from other Dissenters. The title of a 1730 volume, *An Enquiry into the Causes of the Decay of the Dissenting Interest*, is significant. In part, decline was caused by the departure of some of their socially elevated members. More fundamentally, however, their difficulties stemmed from the very nature of their independent polities. Although 'the Dissenting interest' could be mobilized, both locally and nationally, to protest against the restrictions still placed upon them, theological differences could be acutely divisive. Presbyterians, still probably the largest group, found their congregations being deeply divided on the doctrine of the Trinity.

Catholic Dissent remained under greater disability than Protestant Dissent. Catholic proprietors had to pay a supplementary land tax. There was no legal form of Catholic marriage. Attendance at Protestant worship was required of any Catholics who served in the armed forces. Catholics could only hold office under the Crown in the rare event that they were willing to deny the spiritual and temporal authority of the Pope and the doctrine of transubstantiation. The Catholic community survived, however, numbering some 70,000 in England at the beginning of the eighteenth century, and a smaller number in Scotland – in both countries with continuing regional concentration. When George I came to the throne some prominent English Catholic laymen, led by the Duke of Norfolk, asserted that the Pope did not influence them in political matters. Even so, while the Jacobite threat or bogey remained, there was no disposition in Parliament to remove Catholic disabilities, north or south of the Border.

Compromise?

Voltaire, the famous French *philosophe*, spent some time in England in the late 1720s. He came to the conclusion that there was a close link between the religious structure of the country and its political institutions and values. If only one religion had been allowed it was likely that the government might well have become arbitrary – he did not think it was. If only two religions had been allowed, their adherents would have cut each other's throats. However, since he calculated that there were thirty, they all lived in happiness and in peace. There may have been a tinge of exaggeration in this latter assessment – in Scotland, for example, the Kirk was still battling hard to get Episcopalians out of Highland parishes. It resented the Act for the Toleration of Episcopacy (1712), claiming that it was a measure inflicted upon Scotland by *English* High Tories in the *British* Parliament. Nevertheless, Voltaire's view that the British state had reached an unusual accommodation of opinion and belief – as compared at least with France and many other European countries – had substance. It was clear that at least some element of mutual forbearance had entered into the mainstream of British culture and thinking.[7]

It is not too difficult to understand how this condition, which so excited Voltaire's admiration, had been reached. Controversy and unchristian conflict over theological and ecclesiastical matters had certainly not been stilled, but there was some sense of exhaustion and some sense of their futility. Voltaire himself certainly took the view that sectarian fury had finished in England with the Civil Wars. There were ecclesiastics, of varying opinions, who shared the political cynicism of Lord Halifax, the 'Trimmer', writing in the 1680s: 'In a corrupted age, the putting of the world in order would breed confusion'. He believed that a rooted disease, whether in the body politic or in the Body of Christ, was better stroked away than kicked away.[8]

In addition, some leading minds looked to a Christianity which would, above all, be 'reasonable'. There was a disposition to discount 'revelation' and to stress, rather, the 'naturalness' of religion. Christianity could perhaps be shown to be 'as old as the creation'. It was not 'mysterious' but was, in essence, straightforward. John Locke expounded *The Reasonableness of Christianity* (1695). The way was open for variations on orthodoxy: Deists, Arians, Socinians, Unitarians and others all advanced new (or perhaps they were 'rediscovered') interpretations of the person and place of Jesus Christ. Mr Chubb, for example, a modest Salisbury glover, firmly expressed the view in 1734 that 'the epistles of the Apostles *were not* written by divine inspiration' but were 'the *produce* of the *judgment* of each writer.'[9] Even Apostles could get things wrong. Only a few decades earlier, by contrast, ministers of the Kirk in Edinburgh had seen no reason why a student, Thomas Aikenhead, should not be hanged for blasphemy. By the mid-century, however, the 'Moderates' had established control over the General Assembly of the Kirk and rather different attitudes, for a time, prevailed.

In short, it was beginning to appear that the authority of the past, whether to be found in the Bible or in an ecclesiastical hierarchy, was suspect. Indeed, in the second half of the seventeenth century England experienced what is sometimes called a 'scientific revolution'. The Royal Society was incorporated in 1661. There is no need, however, to suppose that 'science' was opposed to 'religion'. A number of front-rank Anglican divines were early Fellows of the Royal Society. Nevertheless, after decades of dogmatic assertion and counter-assertion in religious matters, a 'scientific method' of detached anaysis, backed up, where possible, by experimental proof, was attractive as an alternative way of arguing.

---

[7] Voltaire, *Letters from England* (Harmondsworth, 1980) p. 41.

[8] Lord Halifax cited in H. Butterfield, *The Englishman and his History*, (Cambridge, 1944) p. 90.

[9] Cited in D. Pailin, 'Rational Religion in England from Herbert of Cherbury to William Paley', in Gilley and Sheils, eds, *History of Religion*, pp. 211–12.

Finally, historians have followed Voltaire in emphasizing the importance of 'commerce', in all its facets, as a vital clue to the understanding of
Hanoverian society. Commerce, he said, had made men free, and freedom,
in turn, had enhanced the nation's commerce. In a sense, to a degree unknown elsewhere in Europe, there was an emerging 'market' in religion.
Churches, denominations and sects had to put their wares before a public increasingly used to making choices between suppliers of the goods they
desired.[10]

Liberty

If truth was a little enigmatic, uniformity perhaps unobtainable and tolerance still a little suspect, perhaps some other watchword was needed as the
defining characteristic of Britain. The word which served was 'Liberty'.
Many writers were willing to supply the necessary rhetoric. One of the most
enthusiastic was James Thomson, poet son of a Lowland Scots Presbyterian
minister. He pictured liberty walking 'unconfin'd' in the 'Island of Bliss'. In
a substantial poem, *Liberty* (1735–36), he set out the *British* ancestry of this
noble condition.[11]

His vision, however, was not merely a flight of domestic fancy. Visitors
from mainland Europe – Montesquieu and Voltaire among them – all readily confirmed that England was apparently 'passionately fond of liberty'.
Englishmen would go to any lengths to defend what they conceived to be
their liberty. In 1728 Voltaire wrote of the harmony that prevailed between
the Commons, the Lords and the Crown. A 'happy blend' had been
achieved. The English were the only people on earth who had succeeded in
controlling the power of their monarchs by directly resisting them. Effort
after effort had been then required to achieve a wise system of government,
but now the deed was done. The king was all-powerful for doing good,
Voltaire believed, but his hands were tied to prevent him doing evil. English
aristocrats were without arrogance.[12] The people shared in the government
without confusion. Twenty years later, Montesquieu stated that the English
were the one nation in the world for whom political liberty was the direct
object of their constitution.

Some historians since have not been slow to puncture these opinions
by arguing that the much-vaunted 'English Liberty' was a privilege of the

---

[10] Voltaire, *Letters from England*, p. 37: N. McKendrick, J. Brewer and J.H. Plumb,
*The Birth of a Consumer Society: The Commercialization of Eighteenth-Century
England* (London, 1983).

[11] J. Sambrook, *James Thomson, 1700–1748* (Oxford, 1990); H.T. Dickinson, *Liberty and Property: Political Ideology in Eighteenth-Century Britain* (London, 1977).

[12] Voltaire, *Letters from England*, pp. 45–7.

propertied. For some, the 'despotism' of James II appears amateurish beside the measures of George I and his Whig ministers. Amongst other repressive measures, they mention the Riot Act (1715) and the 'Black' Act (1723). The former was introduced following pro-Jacobite riots in London. If a riotous assembly of a dozen or more persons failed to disperse after the Riot Act was read, those concerned would be guilty of a felony, an offence punishable by death.[13] The latter had its origins in the activities of particular gangs taking deer rather than in any attempt to suppress 'legitimate protest'. It joined many other measures making offences against property punishable by death. However, while the legislation does indeed suggest that a propertied class felt a deep need for security, the draconian punishments available were not invariably imposed. So, when the necessary caveats have been made, the 'liberty' thought characteristic by foreign observers was not mere rhetoric. A kind of compromise between liberty and order had been reached.

> *Britain was doom'd to be a slave*
> *Her frame dissolv'd, her fears were great*
> *When God a new supporter gave*
> *To bear the pillars of the State.*[14]

So wrote the Dissenting hymn-writer Isaac Watts (1674–1748), reflecting on the history of the early eighteenth century. It had only been by a narrow margin, in his opinion, that Britain had escaped 'slavery' but now the future could be looked forward to with confidence:

> *Our God, our help in ages past,*
> *Our hope for years to come,*

The 'our' in the hymn was symbolic of a national unity which transcended the gulf between Church and Dissent. Isaac Watts's father had been imprisoned as a Dissenter in the later years of Charles II. His own Dissenting convictions did not waver yet he was granted a memorial in Westminster Abbey. Was that the best way to bury the past?

---

[13] E.P. Thompson, *Whigs and Hunters: The Origin of the Black Act* (London: 1975); E. Cruickshank and H. Erskine-Hill, 'The Waltham Black Act and Jacobitism', *Journal of British Studies* 24 (1985): J. Sharpe, *Crime in Early Modern England* (London, 1984).
[14] Cited in E.A. Payne, *The Free Church Tradition in the Life of England* (London, 1944) pp. 80–1.

Chapter 6

New World Power: A British Vision? *c.*1500–*c.*1750

Angles of approach

A country's conception of itself is never static. The 'space' it believes itself to occupy shifts constantly. Institutions and ideas deemed to be characteristic only become so by comparison and contrast with what is believed to prevail elsewhere. In turn, that external world reinforces or destroys indigenous assumptions and aspirations. What is 'core' and what is 'periphery' is likewise fragile. Perceptions of order and location, deemed immutable, quake and disintegrate in the light of new knowledge and fresh contexts. Yet the past still asserts itself in the mental maps of any age and people resist the 'relocation' which the present seems to demand. The experience of the British Isles between 1500 and 1750 bears out these dicta admirably.

Mental maps among the political and intellectual elite were increasingly being determined by physical maps. The work of cartographers became more sophisticated as they struggled to assimilate the new knowledge made available by explorers. Yet every map has a message, implicit or explicit. A mapmaker has to start somewhere. There is still a need to tell a story. So, from this perspective, for continental mapmakers, the British Isles remained peripheral in their conception of 'Europe', and ways of making this apparent were not lacking. But the boundaries of 'Europe' were as problematic to them as they were to their political masters.

The concepts of 'Christendom' and 'Europe' coexisted in the sixteenth century in uneasy juxtaposition, sometimes being held to be synonymous, sometimes pointing to different realities. The fall of Constantinople to the Ottoman Turks in 1453, and their previous and subsequent conquests in the Balkans and Hungary, raised one question about 'Europe'. The rupture of the Reformation raised another about 'Christendom'. At Lepanto in 1571 the combined strength of Venice, Spain and the Pope defeated the fleet of Selim II, but the Ottoman challenge was not yet over. The 'Christian' states had not been conspicuous in displaying unity when confronted by it.

It was in this context that, over two centuries, European political theorists and lawyers, such as the Dutchman Hugo Grotius and the Frenchman Jean Bodin, struggled to elaborate and clarify the law of peace and war and definitions of sovereignty and order, in a continent apparently prone to protracted periods of conflict. To put matters very simply, there was a struggle between continuing notions of empire, that of Charles V of Spain (1519–56) being the most conspicuous example, and notions of state sovereignty. The result was seemingly endemic warfare, particularly in the early decades of the seventeenth century, extending from the Baltic to the Balearics – the Thirty Years War.

The Peace of Westphalia (1648) which brought this phase to an end does indeed have certain features which represented an advance in 'peacemaking' but the liberty of states remained paramount. If an imperial order was either not desirable or not achievable it seemed that order of a kind could only be established through the notion of a 'balance of power', a theory attributed to various authors. It was a mechanical concept which could require rulers to ignore religious or other convictions in pursuit of an equilibrium. Alliances and alignments shifted first one way and then another. Stability was transient, but this was perhaps the best that could be hoped for in a world in which war was a rational/barbaric enterprise, whether for territory, dynasty, trade or booty. The century after Westphalia was to witness many more wars both in Europe and, increasingly, between European powers overseas.

Interests: dynastic and national

'Britain' could not escape this European/Christian upheaval but geography could determine the nature and extent of its involvement in a manner not open to mainland states. It needs to be constantly remembered, however, that there was no single 'European' pattern and that the sea was both barrier and highway. It is also important to stress that geography only offered certain options; it did not compel conclusions. This was particularly the case in an era when dynastic considerations could frequently be paramount. Monarchs could not conceive that the interests of the realm could be different from their own personal interests. For Henry VII, after Bosworth, the task was clear – to establish himself and his descendants securely on the throne. It was a project which had both a domestic and a foreign agenda. By the time of his death in 1509 it could indeed be claimed that England had gained a position in Europe which had scarcely ever before been attained. What was probably more important to Henry was that he had succeeded in establishing his house amongst the royal houses of Europe. There is, of course, a certain artificiality in even making such a distinction, since a 'national mission' which was not royal was scarcely conceivable. The monarch, as a matter of prudence, had to seek to carry his people with him in his adventures, but the fundamental decisions were in his hands.

England lost Calais in 1558, and although the English forces in Dieppe and Le Havre in 1562–63 may have been aspiring to regain it in collusion with French Protestants, in general it was not part of subsequent foreign policy to seek to regain a continental toehold. And this particular adventure turned out to be a disaster.

In this sense, the sea made it possible, then and later, for English policy-makers to distinguish, in broad terms, between an offensive and a defensive strategy. Few European states had the same freedom. The English and Scottish governments did not dispense entirely with their armies but their chief purpose was still to prepare to fight each other or to intervene, with internal allies, in each other's domestic affairs. Scottish soldiers roamed far and wide in Europe seeking employment, and so did some bellicose Englishmen, but English and Scottish armies did not.

It was not until 1585 that Queen Elizabeth could be persuaded to send another army across the Channel – again, ostensibly in the Protestant cause, to aid Dutch Protestant rebels in the Northern Netherlands against Philip II of Spain. Even then, the Earl of Leicester, captain-general of the army for the Netherlands, was explicitly instructed 'to make a defensive rather than an offensive war'.[1] Behind the expedition lay Elizabeth's fears that Spain would dominate both France and the Low Countries and then be in a position to invade England. However, it cannot be said that she supported her army with much enthusiasm or that it accomplished a great deal in the Netherlands. Troops remained there until 1603. Although expensive to maintain, soldiers were not the kind of chaps anybody was particularly anxious to see return home. English forces, however, did operate in Normandy and Brittany in 1589 and 1591, supposedly to assist the new Protestant King of France, Henri IV, but to no great effect. Elizabeth seems to have become resined to the fact that there were always men who wanted to fight and she could not invariably restrain them.

Sea power

The navy was a different matter. Under Sir John Hawkins, Treasurer of the Navy from 1578 to 1595, a considerable programme of building and modernizing took place. The English fleet, supported by armed merchant ships, could hold its own both in the Channel and in the Atlantic. The piratical exploits of the 'sea-dogs' – Drake, Grenville and others – passed into national

[1] C. Haigh, *Elizabeth I* (London, 1988) p. 130.

consciousness. Readers of *Stirring Sea Fights for British Boys* (1908) joined the ranks of those in previous centuries who had thrilled to the description of the glorious battle in 1591 between Sir Richard Grenville and the Spaniards. Who but an Englishman would fight when the odds were fifty-three to one against?

The supreme example of naval success was the defeat of the Spanish Armada in 1588. Some subsequent historians have suggested that the purpose of the Spanish expedition was to force the English out of the Netherlands rather than to conquer the obstinate island. Such an interpretation, however, runs contrary to received national wisdom. In a wider perspective, the defeat of the Armada probably ensured that the Counter-Reformation would not completely succeed – the Duke of Parma could not defeat the rebel Dutch provinces. In the short term, however, despite the display of English bravado, it was the island's vulnerability which was most worrying. Indeed, in the 1590s, Philip was again able to mount expeditions against England and Ireland. Brittany was the base from which Spanish invasion was most to be feared. Shakespeare's 'sceptr'd isle' might more accurately be described as a beleaguered isle. Nevertheless, in a struggle with Spain which lasted for a quarter of a century, England survived by a judicious handling of resources and determination of priorities.

Europe: the seventeenth century

In the seventeenth century, however, serious threats of foreign invasion largely disappeared. In part, this was because the Stuart kings decided that discretion was the better part of valour. James I reached what he believed was an honourable arrangement with Spain in 1604 and tried to be an active peacemaker in Europe, keeping on good terms with both Protestant and Catholic powers. He married his daughter to the Protestant Elector of the Palatinate and sought a Spanish Catholic match for his sons. Such a pursuit of balance stemmed from an awareness of the fact that the country was in no mood and in no condition to become engaged in the European quarrels that climaxed in 1618 in what became the Thirty Years War. The difficulties that arose when England was at war with Spain between 1625 and 1630, and with France between 1627 and 1629, confirmed the merits of detachment.

The advent of Cromwell and the Commonwealth caused under-standable consternation in European royal circles, but the possibility of a European monarchical combination against the regicide regime was not strong. By the late 1640s, as the Thirty Years War came to an end, internal revolts in France and Spain precluded any such possibility. For his part, although Cromwell inherited a well-established Puritan concern for the Palatinate and

talked of the 'Protestant cause' in Europe, he was circumspect in policy. Some historians have attributed to him 'a novel and sophisticated recognition of the strategic use of force'.[2] He too could not escape the perennial need to balance France and Spain, though there are those who argue that his decision against Spain accelerated the growth in the power of France – the country that was to prove England's real rival.

The restored Stuarts confronted this problem by mending fences with France. Charles II had to face the embarrassment of a Dutch 'raid in force' up the Medway in 1667 – it was scarcely an invasion. The three Anglo-Dutch wars (1652–54, 1665–67 and 1672–74) showed the extent to which commercial rivalry was replacing an earlier sense of religious kinship between England and the Netherlands. Despite the lack of sophistication, both politically and operationally, with which these wars were fought, they have been seen as 'modern' conflicts. That is to say they extended beyond the North Sea into America, the West Indies, Africa and East Asia. They also involved the only two major European states which still possessed representative institutions. This meant that 'public opinion' could not be altogether ignored. However, it can be argued that none of these Dutch wars was really 'national'.[3] A war policy fitted into the schemes of ambitious ministers. Charles II himself, partly out of financial need, allowed himself to be drawn ever closer to the French king. A clause in the Secret Treaty of Dover (1670) can be taken to mean that he was prepared to make use of a foreign army to re-establish Catholicism in England. It is, therefore, scarcely possible to see England as the chief protector of the 'Protestant interest' in Europe – France was England's ally in the Third Anglo-Dutch War which broke out in 1672. Naturally, this was even more the case in the reign of James II. Then, foreign and domestic policies interacted to produce that heightened Protestant alarm which led to the 'Glorious Revolution'. A Dutch ruler was hardly likely to be indifferent to the fate of his homeland. His new kingdom had a good deal to offer him from this perspective and it might be that England

---

[2] D. Hirst in J. Morrill, ed., *Oliver Cromwell and the English Revolution* (London, 1990) p. 147; M. Breslaw, *English Puritan Views of Foreign Nations 1618–1640* (Cambridge, Mass., 1970).
[3] J.R. Jones, *Britain and Europe in the Seventeenth Century* (London, 1966) and *Britain and the World, 1649–1815* (Glasgow, 1980).

6.1 Too Close for Comfort: In 1666 English government was weakened by the great plague, by the fire of London and by the near-bankruptcy of Charles II. In 1667 the fleet was laid up at Chatham. Dutch ships exploited their opportunity in June, sacked Sheerness, sailed up the Medway and destroyed docked English warships. They then proceeded to blockade the Thames. The English government concluded a peace at Breda in the following month which ended the second Anglo-Dutch War, a conflict which largely stemmed from trading rivalries. Painting of the Medway raid by Willem Schellinks.

would be drawn deeper into European affairs to an unwonted and unwanted degree.

In the 1670s William, as much as anyone, could claim credit for successfully galvanizing resistance in Europe to French ambitions. When the Spanish king died, it looked as though the United Provinces, Spain, the Austrian Habsburgs and some German states would find themselves at war with France. From William's perspective, even though the English population was only roughly a quarter the size of the French, England's naval, commercial and financial resources might be crucial.

William was in a position to declare war on France in May 1689. Scotland joined in too, demonstrating that since 1660 the notion that Edinburgh could conduct a foreign policy significantly separate from England had faded. The declaration of war was a risk. England/Scotland was dubiously a 'Great Power', at least in comparison with the France of Louis XIV. English troops had to be tutored by the Dutch on how wars were conducted on the Continent. The English had been away too long – the biggest English force to fight there between 1604 and 1690 was a detachment of the New Model Army at the Battle of the Dunes in 1658 consisting of some 6,000 men.

With the Dutch wars as precedent, a two-year war might have been envisaged. In fact, it lasted for nine years. From a 'British Isles' perspective its importance lay in the fact that Ireland was recovered. Both before and after the Battle of the Boyne (1 July 1690) the struggle between James II's Franco-Irish army and the even more mixed force which William deployed was hard. The Battle of the Boyne continues to echo down the centuries in the contested histories of Britain/Ireland. In Europe, the Treaty of Ryswick, which concluded this Nine Years War, left unresolved the future of the Spanish Empire and, with it, the European balance of power.

It was clear in 1707 and for a long time thereafter that the new 'Britain' was forged in a context in which France was 'the Other'.[4] It was a continuity of antagonism which produced stereotypes and images which, as will be seen, powerfully reinforced respective identities. The extent to which 'Jacobitism' was both an internal and an external problem has already been noted.

In 1689, however, there was little suggestion that this was the beginning of a struggle for mastery between the two countries which would be carried on worldwide for more than a century. In part, no doubt, this was because 'foreign affairs' was still something which only engaged the attention of a small minority – though by the end of the century the rapid growth of newspapers contributed to an interest in foreign affairs. Professor J.R. Jones suggests that the total number of people, at this time, who can be said to be directly involved in making foreign policy was only around a hundred.

---

[4] J. Black, *Natural and Necessary Enemies: Anglo-French Relations in the Eighteenth Century* (London, 1986).

Even so, in the country at large, general sentiments and prejudices about matters foreign certainly existed. For example, news that the Turks were at the gates of Vienna in 1683 was seen in some quarters primarily as a gratifying indication that the end of popery was at hand.[5] William himself was irritated by English arrogance. The English seemed to carry on, he wrote to the Netherlands in 1698, as if 'no other country existed but this island and that it need not concern itself with what happened elsewhere in the world'.[6]

In fact, increased concern with what happened elsewhere in the world was inescapable. Starting with the authorization of an expeditionary force to the Continent of 11,000 men in 1689 (and another 9,000 for Ireland), Parliament was voting for an army for service abroad of 48,000 men by the end of the Nine Years War. It also authorized the employment of 20,000 foreigners. These numbers increased during the War of the Spanish Succession (1702–13) to an average strength of around 120,000 men – roughly a tenth of the adult male population. The navy expanded in similar fashion and, in numbers and in quality, it has been reckoned the largest and strongest in Europe at this time. Even so, the army of France was a formidable force.

In the War of the Spanish Succession, however, in the person of John Churchill, later Duke of Marlborough, England threw up a soldier of genius whose strategic vision was combined with the organizing and diplomatic ability necessary to conduct coalition warfare. His victory at Blenheim (1704) saved Vienna from the French. It was followed by celebrated successes at Ramillies (1706), Oudenarde (1708) and, less clear-cut, Malplaquet (1709).

The navy, too, played its part, though criticized initially for failing to prevent the losses of English merchant ships. The French navy proved reluctant to engage in full-scale combat. The complexities of the campaigns and the diplomatic negotiations which produced the treaties of Utrecht (1713) cannot be followed through here. However, France did recognize the Act of Succession which would bring a Hanoverian king to Britain. It also ceded territory in North America. Spain ceded Gibraltar and Minorca to Britain, together with the contract to supply slaves to Spain's New World territories for thirty years. There was to be no union of the French and Spanish crowns.

Within a period of some twenty years, therefore, there had been a dramatic transformation in Britain's standing as a European state. England and Scotland became a United Kingdom just at the point when it could be

---

[5] J.R. Jones, 'English Attitudes to Europe in the Seventeenth Century' in J.S. Bromley and E.H. Kossman, eds, *Britain and the Netherlands in Europe and Asia* (London, 1968) p. 40; K.H.D. Haley, *The British and the Dutch: Political and Cultural Relations through the Ages* (London, 1988).

[6] A. Carter, 'Britain as a European Power, From Her Glorious Revolution to the French Revolutionary War' in Bromley and Kossman, *Britain and the Netherlands*, p. 112; J. Bromley, 'Britain and Europe in the Eighteenth Century', *History* 66, (Oct. 1981).

claimed that the new state was a European Great Power. The terms of the Utrecht settlement and the 'Barrier' treaty of 1716 made it clear, whatever may have been the case in 1689, that it was British interests not Dutch interests which determined British policy. Even so, Louis XIV of France still dominated Western Europe, though not perhaps to the same degree as in former decades. The Utrecht settlement appeared to confirm that Britain's main interests were commercial and colonial. In one year Walpole was able proudly to assert that there were 50,000 men slain in Europe but not one of them had been an Englishman.

'Foreign affairs', in the wake of these developments, became of sustained and engrossing interest rather than spasmodic significance. The British diplomatic service became more sophisticated. The role of the Secretary of State in the formulation of policy was to some extent clarified. Yet it was not ultimately the case that there was a straight alternative in foreign policy between 'trade' and 'war', so mixed up were they. By 1739 it was felt that it was time to teach Spain a lesson. Amongst other things, there was resentment in Britain at what was held to be improper Spanish interference with British merchantmen. It was anticipated, however, that the war could be fought at sea and in the colonies. It would not entail a return to the battles which British forces fought in Europe.

Things were not so simple. By the time of Walpole's resignation in 1742, the colonial conflict with Spain had merged into the War of the Austrian Succession which had begun in 1740 and was to continue until 1748. Francophobia was never far below the surface in these years. In 1738 the London theatre-going public made things so unpleasant for the *Comédie Française*, then playing in the capital, that the company was forced to flee back to Paris.

France declared war on Britain in March 1744. The conflict centred on North America and India. It was during this war, of course, that the Young Pretender tried his luck in Scotland. Peace was reached at Aachen in 1748, but it was a patched-up affair. Britain had, however, upset the Dutch and the Austrians. Louisburg, the great French fort on Cape Breton island, which, if retained, would have enabled Britain to dominate the approach to French Canada, was given up in exchange for Madras in southern India in the overall settlement. The war, from a British perspective, had not gone smoothly and only in its final stages was British naval superiority effectively deployed. It is perhaps excessive to regard another round between Britain and France, in what was a global struggle, as inevitable. Nevertheless, in 1750 it was impossible to believe that a *modus vivendi* had been reached. And so it proved.

It would be misleading, however, to conclude from this global shift that the British Isles in the seventeenth century existed in a political, economic or cultural vacuum cut off from European intellectual, cultural or religious developments. The upheavals of the mid-seventeenth century meant that political debate could not be confined to one country. It was in exile in France, for example, that the English political philosopher Thomas Hobbes, author of *Leviathan* (1651), made the acquaintance of Galileo, Gassendi and Descartes. Even so, marked divergences were also observable. The Common Law tradition in England differed significantly from continental legal theories and practices, though the law of Scotland continued to draw heavily upon them. Scottish lawyers were frequently educated in France and the Netherlands. Stair's *Institutions* (1681), the first systematic treatise on Scots law, shows strong Dutch influence. The arrival of French Protestant refugees after the revocation in 1685 of the Edict of Nantes, which had guaranteed their position in their homeland, provoked strong interest in what was going on in Europe.[7] Although the biggest concentration of Huguenots was in London, they were also to be found in Bristol, Edinburgh, Dublin and elsewhere. And, at another level, England and Scotland were 'European' in sharing with the Dutch Republic and Spain and Portugal a sense of the world beyond Europe.

'The world'

It could not be said that in the unravelling of the 'New World' – a world 'discovered' on the supposition that it was the 'known' world of China – the English had taken the lead. Cabot's 1497 Atlantic voyages apart, the names that resonate are Bartholomeu Dias, Christopher Columbus, Vasco da Gama, Vasci Nunez de Balboa, Ferdinand Magellan, Hernan Cortes, and Francisco Pizarro. Confronted by the reality of Iberian predominance, Englishmen at first lamented that they had not adequately availed themselves of opportunities that were literally golden. In any case, it took time in the sixteenth century to realize that North America might itself be not without interest. It was still the wealth of Asia that attracted. In 1527, for example, John Rut found substantial quantities of ice in Labrador rather than the Great Khan. The possibility of finding the elusive north-west passage still gripped the imagination of English merchant adventurers from the 1570s onwards – Frobisher, Davis, Gilbert and Chancellor. Richard Hakluyt clung tenaciously to the opinion that the passage might 'easily, quickly and perfectly be searched out'. Dr John Dee, London Welsh wizard, proliferated volumes on the perfect art of navigation. He envisaged the creation (or recreation since apparently the Welsh Prince Madoc had set the ball rolling in

---

[7] R.D. Gwynn, *Huguenot Heritage: The History and Contribution of the Huguenots in Britain* (London, 1988); B. Cottret, *The Huguenots in England: Immigration and Settlement c.1550–1700* (Cambridge, 1992); J. Black, *The English Press in the Eighteenth Century* (London, 1987).

North America in 1170) of an 'Incomparable Islandish Empire'. In the first instance, therefore, colonies were envisaged as little more than bases for further exploration. Virginia in 1585 and 1587 turned out to be a disaster for Sir Walter Raleigh and did not encourage the belief that colonies had their own intrinsic importance. When Queen Elizabeth died in 1603 she had only a handful of subjects in Northern America.

Re-founded in 1606, however, Virginia proved much more successful. There were, though, questions which the English could no more avoid than could the Spaniards. In *A Good Speed to Virginia* (1609), Robert Gray asked by what right the English entered the land of savages, took away their rightful inheritance and planted themselves in their stead. The answer lay in the advantages brought by Christianity and civility. In a sermon before the Virginia Company in 1609 Robert Johnson indicated that *Nova Britannia* would endeavour to bring the inhabitants from their base condition to one that was far better. He suggested that without Julius Caesar and his Roman legions 'wee had continued brutish, poore and naked Britanes to this day'.[8] It is far from clear that native Indians drew much comfort from this analogy.

Virginia was followed, in the 1620s and 1630s, by New Plymouth, Massachusetts, New Hampshire, Maryland, Rhode Island and Maine. In the 1660s came Carolina, New York and New Jersey – the latter two captured from the Dutch. In the 1680s came Pennsylvania (where William Penn was exceptional in trying to integrate Indians into the life of his new colony) and Delaware. Around 200,000 English settlers emigrated to North America during the century and reproduced themselves rapidly. In aggregate, these territories could be said to constitute the 'Empire' in North America, but even from the outset each had its own characteristics. Massachusetts, for example, had a Puritan ethos which reflected its origins as a shelter for English religious Dissent – the 'Pilgrim Fathers'. They could not be said to be governed uniformly as part of an English 'imperial system'. In this new world the British Crown did not exercise the power wielded by the Spanish. *Nova Britannia* was indeed the reproduction and extension of 'Great Britain', but not in a simple fashion.[9] Diversity was inescapable. Emerging government in the colonies emphasized participation. Claims to legislative authority were viewed with suspicion in London. Development tended to be haphazard, reflecting what some historians see as the absence, before the mid-eighteenth century, of anything that can be described as a coherent British colonial policy. Colonies fell within the orbit of the Board of Trade

---

[8] Cited in J.H. Elliott, *Britain and Spain in America: Colonists and Colonized* (Reading, 1994) pp. 4–5, 7–8; J.P. Greene and J.R. Pole, *Colonial British America* (Oxford, 1984).

[9] J.P. Greene, *Peripheries and Center: Constitutional Development in the Extended Polities of the British Empire and the United States, 1607–1788* (Durham, N.C., 1986).

whose President was not normally in the inner circle of government. Their location within a commercial department testifies to the perspective from which they were approached. The colonies were subjected to restrictions on their freedom to trade and manufacture – the Molasses Act (1733) was the most controversial – but legislation could be one thing and implementation another. Smuggling was rife.

Late in the day, in 1698–99, there was an attempt, which proved abortive, not least through English actions, to establish a Scots settlement on the Isthmus of Darien (Panama). Failure resulted in anti-English riots in Edinburgh but perhaps also in the realization that Scottish commerce could only prosper if it gained access to the English trading system.

Outside North America, islands in the West Indies were steadily acquired, Barbados amongst them (1627). Oliver Cromwell had seized Jamaica from Spain in 1655. Charles II's Portuguese bride brought him the present of Bombay. English forts and stations appeared elsewhere on the coasts in Asia and Africa. The East India Company had been in existence since 1600. It was followed by the post-Restoration Royal African and Hudson's Bay Companies.

All of this signified, in the last half of the seventeenth century particularly, a major expansion of trade, both by weight and by value: textiles, tobacco and sugar. It has been calculated that imports from Asia and America into London, as a proportion of total imports, rose from nil in 1600 to around a third by the end of the century. Successive legislation (the 1660 Navigation Act, the 1663 Staple Act, the 1673 Plantation Duty Act and the 1696 Navigation Act) sought to maximize the benefits of these developments. Englishmen (or Irishmen), for example, had to own the ships that carried on the import or export trade. Three-quarters of a ship's crew had to be English. Goods from mainland Europe destined for the North American plantations had to come to England first and be transferred to English vessels with English crews. The 1696 Navigation Act insisted that all colonial as well as English shipping should be registered in London.

Comfortable identity?

Such regulations were indications of the extent to which the capital of England was beginning to see itself in a new role. England was in the process of extending itself westwards – and, of course, by plantation, in Ireland as well. Such an orientation, on this scale, was without precedent. It is no accident that Sir Walter Raleigh, courtier, explorer and colonizer, not only wrote *The Discovery of the Empire of Guyana* (1596) but also embarked, in prison, on a *History of the World*, though sadly he did not live long enough to chronicle the contribution of the English themselves. Rampant commercialism was inexorably leading to reflection on the place of England *in the world* as more and more came to be known about the nature of that world. In particular, was Great Britain/*Nova Britannia* destined to be an enduring reality?

At the beginning of the eighteenth century there was renewed interest in the problem of international order. It was increasingly but not universally believed that Britain could only achieve security, as a Protestant state in which liberty flourished, by some degree of engagement with, rather than detachment from, the affairs of the neighbouring mainland. Daniel Defoe was one of a number of writers to address the problem. 'Every King in the World', he wrote in 1703, 'would be the Universal Monarch if he might, and nothing restrains but the Power of Neighbours; and if one Neighbour is not strong enough for another, he gets another Neighbour to join with them, and all the little ones will join to keep the great one from suppressing them. Hence comes Leagues and Confederacies.'[10] The problem was that such leagues and confederacies were never static. The Treaty of Utrecht was in fact the first international treaty to make explicit reference to the 'balance of power', but the pursuit of equilibrium was a perpetual merry-go-round. The 'balance' principle was one which Jonathan Swift believed functioned effectively both within and between states. Some writers thought that the new Britain would have to 'balance' its European and American interests.[11]

There was little sign, however, that the King of Britain was bent on becoming the Universal Monarch. 'Empire', however, was a concept very much discussed, though no easier to handle then than now. Political theorists across Europe were inclined to see the notion of a 'world monarchy' as a threat to individual liberty. Montesquieu, for example, claimed that 'a Great Empire necessarily supposes a despotic authority in he who governs it'. Over the preceding century, too, Spanish imperial achievement, once so lauded, had come to be perceived as a mixed blessing. In 1613 Samuel Daniel, an English writer, suggested that it was Spain's exploitation of the New World which had 'opened a way to infinite corruption'. A century later, many Spaniards might have accepted that verdict. The Spanish Empire had been a great curse. By the 1730s it had brought financial ruin to a country which squandered its resources on retaining colonies that were in practice already independent.[12]

A British 'empire' might therefore be a dangerous and destructive enterprise. Yet, while some voices still urged caution, it looked as though the

---

[10] P. Langford, *A Polite and Commercial People: England 1727–1783* (Oxford, 1989) pp. 171–2 finds the idea of a colonial policy 'misleading' but K. Wilson, 'Empire of Virtue' in L. Stone, ed., *An Imperial State at War: Britain from 1689 to 1815* (London, 1994) pp. 128–36, disagrees.

[11] Cited and discussed in M. Sheehan, 'The Development of British Theory and Practice of the Balance of Power before 1714', *History* 73 no. 237 (Feb. 1988) p. 36.

[12] A. Pagden, *Spanish Imperialism and the Political Imagination* (London, 1990) pp. 7–8.

die had been cast. Some kind of new world order was evolving and Britain was part of it. That was all very well, but wars were expensive and had to be paid for. Governments used excise duties and a land tax to bring in yields never before achieved which were sufficient to enable forces to be supplied and paid regularly. They were also successful in raising loans. Some historians have talked about a 'financial revolution' to describe the innovations of this period. They have highlighted the creation of both the Bank of England (1694) and the Bank of Scotland (1695). The English bank became in effect a state bank with a crucial role in the funding of government needs. In addition, the National Debt – use of the word 'national' is significant – was introduced when the House of Commons was persuaded to guarantee the interest needed to pay annuities to investors who loaned to the government. The National Debt moved inexorably upwards. It has been suggested that interest payments to service the debt were about half the value of total exports. Even so, it meant that war could be funded, though that is not to say that it could be rashly entertained.[13]

It remained the normal assumption among thinking Britons that war was both legitimate and an unavoidable aspect of the human condition. William Penn, an admiral's son and Quaker, meditated on peace in Europe in his experimental Pennsylvania in 1695, though could offer no conclusion which his countrymen would accept. 'Properly and truly speaking', Penn wrote sadly, 'men seek their wills by war rather than by peace, and ... as they will violate it to obtain them, so they will hardly be brought to think of peace unless their appetites be in some way gratified.'[14]

There were indeed frenzied investors in 'the City' whose appetites might be satisfied by other than bellicose means. A bemusing variety of instruments tempted the speculator. In came new specialized merchant banks, a market in mortgages, bills of exchange, insurance and a stock exchange. There was a good deal of boom and bust – the collapse of the South Sea Company in 1719–20 being a spectacular case in point – but some authorities suggest that in this period Britain was about a century ahead of France in evolving modern financial institutions and instruments. Such 'new finance' nevertheless engendered much suspicion. Jonathan Swift, for example, was one of those unable to believe that so many millions in stocks and annuities counted as real wealth in the nation.[15] In some quarters, too,

---

[13] D.W. Jones, *War and Economy in the Age of William III and Marlborough* (Oxford, 1988); P.M.G. Dickson, *The Financial Revolution in England: A Study in the Development of Public Credit, 1688–1756* (Oxford, 1967); W.R. Ward, *The Land Tax in the Eighteenth Century* (Oxford, 1953); J. Brewer, *Sinews of Power: War, Money and the English State, 1688–1783* (London, 1989).
[14] Cited and discussed in F.H. Hinsley, *Power and the Pursuit of Peace* (Cambridge, 1963) p. 41.
[15] P.J. Cain and A.G. Hopkins, *British Imperialism: Innovation and Expansion 1688–1914* (London, 1993) p. 65.

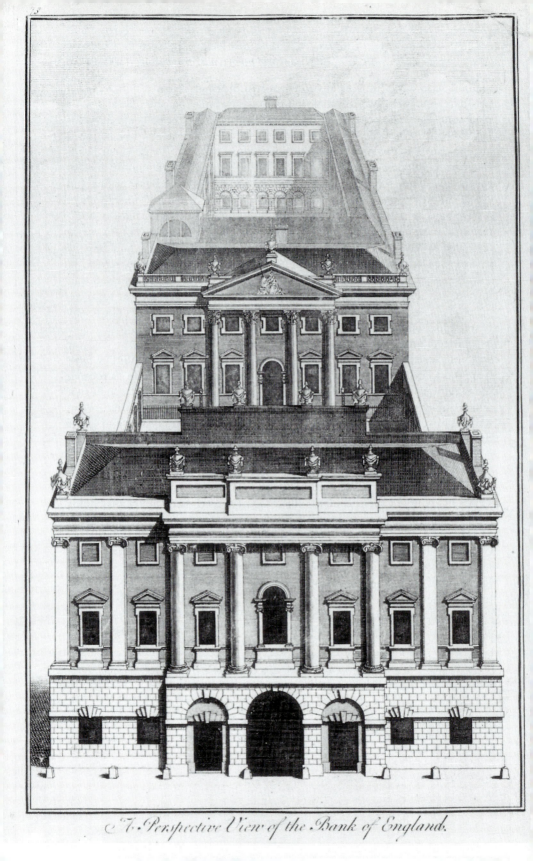

A Perspective View of the Bank of England.

suspicion of these innovations extended to any aspect of British overseas projection. Joseph Addison makes a country squire declare in 1716 that he had always been against all treaties and alliances with foreigners. Trade was an altogether inconvenient business and Britain would be the happiest country in the world if Britons could live 'within ourselves'.[16]

Looking back on the two centuries since Columbus, William Paterson, the extraordinary Scotsman who founded the Bank of England, remarked that the fruits of the discoveries of the Spaniards had 'made far greater alteration in Christendom than the sword'. It was in this spirit that in 1757 David Hume regretted that he had not begun his *History of England* with the reign of Henry VII because it was properly then that modern history commenced.

Home fires

Between 1500 and 1750 'England' had indeed undergone significant change. If there was an emerging British vision of a new world order, it was not the product of a country which had obliterated its own internal diversity in its pursuit of an external mission.[17] Yet the physical and intellectual landscape was changing. There was a relationship between that mapping of England and the mapping of the world which continued with increasing sophistication from the sixteenth century. No one was more acutely aware of the potential of cartography than William Cecil, Lord Burghley. Christopher Saxton was set to work to produce not only county maps but also one of *Anglia* (1579) to be followed by *Britannia Insularum in Oceano Maxima* (1583). This wall-map was designed to be mounted for hanging. Anglia/Britannia 'came

---

[16] Cited in G. Holmes, *Making of a Great Power: Late Stuart and Early Georgian Britain 1660–1722* (London, 1993) p. 254.
[17] A. Everitt, *Landscape and Community in England* (London, 1985). His essay 'Country, County and Town: Patterns of Regional Evolution in England' reminds us that perhaps the only regional name in contemporary use which has a continuous history is East Anglia.

6.2 Safe as Houses: The Bank of England was founded in 1694 and the first transaction in the newly-completed building was made forty years later, in June 1734. Designed by George Sampson, the foundation stone was laid in 1732. An act of 1708 had confirmed the Bank of England's privileged position. It not only carried on ordinary banking business but became the banker to the exchequer and the main government departments. It subsequently administered the national debt. These facades emphasized its pre-eminence and the impression of security – in a financial world which was not without its volatility. The bank was subsequently rebuilt to designs by Sir John Soane (1788 onwards), some of whose work still survives in the much-altered building of today.

alive' for contemporaries as it had never done before. The market towns, parish churches, country houses, parks and other features all stood in clear relation to each other enclosed within the structure that was the county.[18]

It was still not impossible to believe that 'This England' was what it had always been. Henry VII's world was one in which the past may not have seemed too remote because it could be conceived as occurring in a landscape which had itself not fundamentally changed. Of course, there had been fresh settlement, but there remained large tracts of the country covered by forest. Millions of sheep had inexorably nibbled away over centuries, causing as much change to the environment as that brought about by human beings. The fragility and vulnerability of human life was still very evident.

It is impossible to be precise, but the Black Death, the bubonic plague that reached England and Wales in 1348 and Scotland a year later, probably reduced the population by around one-third over subsequent decades. The impact of this terrible experience was still evident a century or so later. Population only began to recover in the late fifteenth century. The population of England and Wales doubled in the sixteenth century, reaching around 4 million in 1600 – the population of Wales was less than a tenth of that total. By 1750 the England/Wales population was around 5¾ millions, still below what some writers believe was the figure in 1300. Even when the million or so Scots are added after 1707, the British population was still substantially below the figure for France. It is impossible to be dogmatic about these figures and they hide troughs and peaks, but they do not suggest a country so disorientated by population growth as to lose contact with the landscape of its past.

Even so, there was dramatic change. London, reduced to a population of around 50,000 in 1500, grew tenfold in the next century and a half. The density of its housing – now breaking out beyond the walls – made its population vulnerable to disease. The last great plague occurred in 1665. A year later, reconstruction and redevelopment after the Great Fire of 1666 began to change the city's face. London was rightly perceived by contemporaries to be an extraordinary phenomenon. Men came into the capital in search of work from distances even of 200 miles. It seemed that every facet of English – and increasingly British – life was centred upon the capital: politics, trade, 'society', finance. The need to supply this city had a significant consequence – in effect, a national market. Its centrality was such that, for most purposes, the capital's elites congregated there and 'spoke for' the nation from a posi-

---

[18] Dr Morgan notes that it was only in the 1570s and initially to meet the needs of the central government that the internal morphology of England, both topographical and political, was finally determined. V. Morgan, 'The Cartographic Image of "The Country" in Early Modern England', *Transactions of the Royal Historical Society* Sixth Series 2 (1979) pp. 153–5. He expresses scepticism about the extent to which the work of Saxton and others should be seen as the efflorescence of national sentiment.

tion of unchallengeable superiority. In due season, however, some of that elite was to be found in the new 'spa' towns, of which Bath stood pre-eminent.

In England, only Bristol, Norwich and Yarmouth had populations exceeding 10,000 in 1700, and they did not approach London's stature. Historians have stressed the extent to which function determined the character of towns – for example, the dockyard towns of Deptford and Chatham. In Wales, only Carmarthen, with a population of less than 5,000, could be said to be a town – a fact which reveals the extent to which life was lived within small and scattered communities.

Emphasis upon London is inevitable as the focus of 'national' life but it should not lead to the conclusion that Bristol and Norwich, to take the two most significant examples, saw themselves as merely 'provincial'. In 1700 Bristol was twice the size (around 20,000) it had been in 1550. The first authentic map of the city was made in 1568, drawing attention to its medieval walls and powerful castle. Prominent also, however, are its rivers which took its ships and merchant venturers now into far more distant seas than their predecessors had contemplated a century earlier. After London, Bristol was the major Atlantic port in England. Before the mid-fifteenth century Gascony had been Bristol's principal market – Bordeaux had not been a 'foreign' port. The 'discovery' of the Atlantic helped both to revive and re-orientate Bristol's commerce. It is a reminder of the extent to which geography, for good or ill, could determine the fortunes of particular communities – the exploitation of the Atlantic had no commensurate benefit for Norwich whose fortunes depended on other factors.[19]

Civic pride and county feeling – and Bristol was distinctive in being since 1373 both a city and a county – did not stand hostile to a sense of being part of a greater whole. Saxton's maps brilliantly articulated a sense that England was a country whose constituent parts fitted together harmoniously. Some historians, noting amongst other things the fashion for county histories and a marked tendency amongst the gentry to marry within the county, have argued, in Professor Everitt's words, that mid-seventeenth century England was a kind of union of partially independent county-states. On the other hand, the 'independence' seems in practice to be very limited. It is perhaps more convincing to see pride in locality coexisting with a strong sense of legal and constitutional uniformity. Pride in the English language is a conspicuous feature of the sixteenth century. No doubt the accents of the west of England were not easily comprehended in Yorkshire, but it was the same language. It was used with brilliance and eloquence by Spenser, Marlowe, Webster, Shakespeare and Donne, to name only a few.

The self-confidence, even the arrogance, of English sentiment did not

---

[19] D.H. Sacks, *The Widening Gate: Bristol and the Atlantic Economy, 1450–1700* (Oxford, 1991).

sit easily alongside 'Britain'. It did, however, give zest to colonizing. In one sense, as has been pointed out, colonizing in North America built upon and shared many of the assumptions which had informed English policy in Ireland.

The Britain of 1750, therefore, remained a country which would have been puzzling in many of its features, but nevertheless possible to comprehend, from the perspective of 1500. Although England was a country whose commerce and settlement extended across the Atlantic, it remained one of small settlements, by later standards. Despite the burgeoning stage-coach services of the mid-seventeenth century, it was not easy to travel from one end of the country to the other. Scotland was not easily or speedily reached over land from England. Whether this new 'Britain', in these circumstances, constituted a front-rank power, in European terms, could still be debated. That it was almost uniquely placed by geography, commerce and the consolidation of stable government to *become* a major power was a reasonable speculation. Moreover, the English, at least, had such a strong sense of identity to sustain such a role that foreigners supposed them to be distinctly xenophobic.

Part Two

Great Britain: World Power
c.1745–*c*.1945

Chapter 7

Preservation and Progress: Representing the People *c.1745–c.1845*

Oligarchy to democracy

In 1948, under the Representation of the People Act, all plural voting and the university seats were abolished. Henceforth, with only insignificant exceptions, each man and woman in the United Kingdom over the age of twenty-one was entitled to cast one vote in elections to determine the composition of the House of Commons. In the space of 200 years, the British polity moved from 'oligarchy' to 'democracy'. The fact that it was a Labour government which introduced the above measure seemed to confirm that at length 'the people' had triumphed. The long struggle for the franchise had come to an end.

On the other hand, the House of Lords, with a membership restricted to hereditary peers and certain Anglican bishops, was still in existence. It still possessed the power to delay – reduced in 1949 to one year – measures passed by the House of Commons. Much could be said for the manner in which the Lords conducted its business, but the constitutional position was not altogether consonant with democratic theory. Anglican bishops had their place as befitted a Church which was still established. King George VI sat securely on the throne, the very model of a constitutional monarch.

There was a good deal of contemporary satisfaction with this state of affairs. Writing in 1942, Sir Ernest Barker had explained to readers across the world anxious to hear more about the extraordinary qualities of the British people that they had 'perhaps served civilization best in the art of politics'. Writing on 'the genius of British parliamentarism', he suggested that the British had created 'a system of government, responsible government based upon representative institutions, which has been one of the sources and supports of modern democracy everywhere'.[1]

---

[1] Sir Ernest Barker, *Britain and the British People* (London, 1942) p. 28.

It was not easy, in these circumstances, to disentangle continuity and change, past and present. While one new landmark had been reached, the surrounding political and constitutional landscape still contained many old and familiar features. In fact, as this chapter and its successor suggest, there was no inexorable predetermined path from 'oligarchy' to 'democracy'. At almost every turn, choices had to be made between preservation, reform and progress. Old outward forms disguised revision and adaptation. Foreigners found this British mode of change difficult to understand, and they were not alone in their incomprehension. The British appeared simultaneously to have a nostalgia for the past and, with it, a large capacity for make-believe, but at the same time to espouse rampant commercialism. They also possessed an intense belief in the virtues of common sense.

In addition, Great Britain in these centuries was not an obscure insular laboratory in which political experiments could take place for the benefit of mankind. It was a major power, increasingly responsible for the government of a large part of the world. Any changes in the British polity had a bearing on that task. However, the central paradox did not escape some contemporaries. There was an inescapable tension between a domestic system founded upon the 'representation of the people' and an imperial system which operated on a different basis.

The sense that monarchy encapsulates and embodies the national past and brings it into the present lies at the heart of its appeal. Yet the nature, form and function of monarchy changes even as its existence gives emphasis to continuity. For 200 years after 1745, the Crown stood at the apex of the symbolic and functioning structure of the British state, almost without challenge. Indeed, for legal purposes it could be argued that the Crown was the state. Nevertheless, at any given time, what monarchy actually signifies has depended upon a multiplicity of factors – the personality of the monarch being not least among them. Monarchs have had to accommodate themselves, reluctantly or otherwise, to changing perceptions of their role and function. While not necessarily representative of their peoples, they have nevertheless had to represent them. Throughout these centuries, in a world where monarchy preponderated, the British state had a personal face at its symbolic heart.

Kings

It was, of course, not altogether convenient that George II, as King of Great Britain and Ireland, retained a conspicuous interest in Hanover where he was Elector. Indeed he returned there regularly in the summer. Together with his then minister, Carteret, he had taken Britain into the War of the Austrian Succession with enthusiasm. At the Battle of Dettlingen in 1743 he commanded British, Hanoverian and the Austrian troops against the French and Bavarians. It was alleged that he had no particular concern for the welfare of his British troops. No British monarch would henceforth be required to hold field command. George II could not escape the suspicion that, like his father, he approached European issues from a Hanoverian rather than a British perspective. That was a handicap.

Some historians speak of George's virtual withdrawal from active domestic politics in the 1750s. They see this as another 'landmark' in the evolution of constitutional monarchy. Others, however, are less convinced. George's expressed remark that 'in this country Ministers are Kings' has been seen as self-pitying and not even accurate. George, they point out, continued to assert vigorous control over military and household appointments. It was not so much a fundamental constitutional shift that was taking place as the fact that at this stage in his life a particular king experienced difficulties with particular politicians. Things could change under a successor keen to play an active political role.

'Born and educated in this country', declared the 22-year-old George III in his speech from the throne in 1760, 'I glory in the name of Briton.' This ringing affirmation was significant in more than one respect. The king was letting it be known that his perspective was gratifyingly insular. He was young and did not have the profound German attachments of his grandfather and father. Indeed, he never went to Hanover. Moreover, the choice of the word 'Briton' was very deliberate. He reigned as King of Great Britain, not merely King of England. The inhabitants of his kingdom were 'Britons', though the English, in particular, were disinclined to use the word to describe themselves, whatever the king might say. George III may also have been wishing to emphasize the extent to which the Crown represented a patriotism which transcended 'party politics'. Something may have been lifted here from the Jacobite Bolingbroke's *The Idea of a Patriot King* (1738). Others suspected the influence of George's tutor, Lord Bute. Not only was Lord Bute the king's favourite, he was a Scotsman and therefore a legitimate target for English politicians.

It became one established interpretation among historians that in his clumsy and largely unsuccessful political interventions in the decade after 1760, George III consciously set out to 'put the clock back' and regain power for the Crown. It is an interpretation, however, that only makes sense if '1688 and all that' had indeed tightly circumscribed royal prerogative. If it had not in fact done so, George III was not trying to 'overturn' anything, but rather to assert legitimate rights which his grandfather had been unwilling or unable to do.[2]

Yet, whatever George's aspirations, and whatever his state of mind, the

---

[2] I. Christie, *'George III and the Historians* – Thirty Years On', *History* 71 no. 232 (1986).

politics of the next twenty years demonstrated that the ability to carry on successful government depended not so much on whether the king or a particular minister held the upper hand, in terms of abstract principle or right, as on a rather more intangible sense of mutual confidence. In the absence of this confidence, as was amply shown in practice, there was political instability and occasional crisis. However, a minister who lost the support of the Commons could not survive even if he was supported by the Crown. If the king wished to alter a ministry which did not please him but which had sufficient support in the Commons, he had to appeal to the electorate in the hope that a more congenial Commons would be forthcoming. That was demonstrated in 1783–84 in George's battle with the Fox–North coalition.[3] By this date, incidentally, the king had given up his power to remove judges and had lost control of his own civil list.

In short, although the king still had horses and men, the old Crown could not be put together again. A century after 1688, it appeared that understanding had moved on beyond the rhetorical reiteration of 'the Revolution Settlement'. Where 'ultimate authority' rested was unclear. What the constitution actually was almost appeared to be what the leading political actors pragmatically agreed it to be. Defenders of this foggy state of affairs were content to argue that it seemed to work reasonably well – and no doubt it was congenial to the propertied classes.[4]

The Hanoverian monarchy gave more than a cloak of respectability to that society but it was difficult to argue that the monarchy was 'above party'. Tories still tended to regard the Hanoverian dynasty as a Whig creation. No doubt, if the Jacobites had succeeded, Whigs would have regarded the restored dynasty as a Tory creation. To what extent monarchy could or should be a symbolic guarantee of national unity remained contentious. While George III did not find it possible to reassert royal authority in policy-making – though he could block, for example, further measures of Catholic emancipation – he nevertheless became a 'conspicuous king'. He created what Linda Colley calls 'an assertively nationalistic royal image'.[5] It was an image which did not help in handling the aspirations of the American colonists, as will be discussed subsequently. As with Elizabeth I, the sheer length of his reign – sixty years – made it impossible for contemporaries to think of Britain without him. There was, however, a certain irony in the fact that it was in the later decades of his reign, as he descended into madness, that his popularity appears to have grown. In the wars both against Revolutionary France and against Napoleon, George III could be presented as an exem-

---

[3] J. Cannon, *The Fox-North Coalition: Crisis of the Constitution 1782–84* (Cambridge, 1969).
[4] P. Langford, *A Polite and Commercial People: England 1727–1783* (Oxford, 1989) pp. 681–2.
[5] L. Colley, *Britons: Forging the Nation 1707–1837* (London, 1992) p. 207.

7.1 Homecoming: George IV liked palaces and contrived to spend a great deal both from the Civil List and his own funds on extending Windsor Castle and Buckingham Palace. The refurbishment of the Palace of Holyroodhouse in Edinburgh was equally congenial. In 1822 he became the first British monarch to visit Scotland in 171 years. Moreover, he was dressed in flesh-coloured tights and kilt. It was only in 1782 that the kilt, banned after the 1745, had been permitted. It was only prudent for George to choose the Stewart tartan. In Sir David Wilkie's picture, however, the king wears the uniform of a Field-Marshal but with the judicious addition of the ribbon of the thistle and the stars of the Garter and Thistle. He is about to receive the keys of the palace from the tenth Duke of Hamilton, its hereditary keeper.

plary constitutional monarch. It was this institution which guarded Britain against both revolutionary insanity and the tyranny of genius.

Even such a presentation, however, was not altogether 'above party', as will subsequently be seen. Nevertheless, since it was becoming clear that government in Britain presupposed the continued existence of distinct and competing 'parties' and since it was also becoming clear that there could be no return to religious uniformity, the notion that monarchy could nevertheless embody a transcendant symbolic unity was clearly open to George III's nineteenth-century successors.

It was not evident that George IV comfortably embodied such a unity. He had demonstrated the customary Hanoverian disposition to quarrel with his father. He had become Prince Regent in 1811, because of George III's incapacity. If it was the function of monarchy to exemplify the highest standards of family life, George IV conspicuously failed. His attempt to divorce his wife Caroline of Brunswick and to exclude her from his coronation occasioned much scurrilous comment. Although at Brighton he had a stately pleasure dome decreed, it was scarcely sufficient to rescue him – and the monarchy as a whole – from ridicule.

He was succeeded in 1830 by his brother William IV, the 'sailor king', so called because of his extensive naval service. Prior to his marriage in 1818, his lengthy liaison with an actress had produced a large family. He came to the throne at a time of political crisis over 'Reform'. The wider ramifications of that crisis will be discussed in more detail subsequently. It necessarily involved the monarchy since the new king made no secret of his opposition to the proposed extension of the franchise. The House of Lords resisted the Reform Bill with the encouragement of the Crown. The Whigs, returned to power after a dissolution, persuaded the king that he should create sufficient peers to enable the Reform Bill to pass if the Lords again rejected it. However, he changed his mind and tried to form another Tory ministry but failed. In due course, the Reform Bill passed and the limitation on royal power was exposed. Even so, in 1834, William IV required Lord Melbourne to resign as Whig Prime Minister, though he still had the confidence of the House of Commons. It was the last time the royal prerogative of dismissal was exercised. Peel's Tory government, which replaced that of Melbourne, lasted for a hundred days. After the general election in 1835, Peel could not command a Commons majority and William was forced to ask Melbourne to form a new government. The royal preference for Peel was to no avail.

Monarchy, therefore, seemed a showpiece example of the British capacity both to preserve and to change – as much fortuitously as by conscious decision – a central institution.

Reform or revolution?

It was also tempting to look back over the century and to see the franchise reform of 1832 as the logical climax of an inexorable process of political change and constitutional development which was also quintessentially British, not least in the extent to which it diverged in its 'peacefulness' when compared to the upheavals which characterized the development of other major European countries.

Comparatively, such purring satisfaction may have appeared particularly justified in 1845, but it disguised the extent to which there were periods during which the transition from one political order to another occasioned acute tension. There was a keen awareness that 'peaceful change' could hardly be said to characterize British history before 1745. There was no reason to assume that the violence of the previous century had been ruled out for all time. Indeed, in the late eighteenth and early nineteenth centuries, some writers were haunted by their knowledge of the past and wondered whether, in their generation, they were wiser.

One such was the historian Macaulay. 'Time', he wrote in an review in 1828 of Hallam's *Constitutional History*, 'is bringing round another crisis analogous to that which occurred in the seventeenth century. We stand in a situation similar to that in which our ancestors stood under James I. It will soon again be necessary to reform that we may preserve. It remains to be seen whether two hundred years have made us wiser.' He distinguished between the 'fundamentals' of the constitution and its 'subordinate parts'. Every useful institution 'endeared by antiquity and noble associations' could be preserved by introducing improvements which harmonized with what he liked to consider the 'original plan'. It was his opinion as a historian that compromise early and graciously made invariably prevented a great revolution. But when was that compromise best reached and was it really possible to distinguish between what was 'fundamental' and what was merely 'subordinate'? Certainly, defenders of the existing status quo suspected that tinkering with reform precipitated calamity.[6]

'To reform that we may preserve' stood therefore uneasily alongside 'To reform that we may change'. It is a tension that can even be seen in the building of the new mid-nineteenth-century Houses of Parliament. Augustus Pugin, assistant to their architect Sir Charles Barry, could not be restrained in his enthusiasm for what he conceived to be the medieval past. A convert to Roman Catholicism, he looked back to a golden past and found its values, expressed in art and architecture, infinitely preferable to those of industrial, commercial, urban Britain. He did not want the Houses of Parliament to be democratic temples. They should look backwards rather than forwards in their design and form.[7]

Bagehot, political analyst and editor of *The Economist*, wrestled with these paradoxical aspects of mid-nineteenth-century Britain in *The English Constitution* (1867). He recognized that in British public life the 'dignified' parts and the efficient parts were jumbled together. There was indeed a boundary between them, but it was not easy to determine and in any case was constantly shifting. That his own treatment of the constitution was essentially descriptive rather than analytical is itself significant. He believed that he had 'caught' a working mechanism at a particular point in time, but nothing was permanent. A system had been inherited and adapted from the past. It was not the embodiment of a specific theory concerning the nature of representative government. There was, therefore, an untidiness about it all, even an absurdity, but its incongruities had to be accepted with good hu-

---

[6] *The Works of Lord Macaulay: Essays and Lays of Ancient Rome* (London n.d.) pp. 104–5.
[7] R. Quinault, 'Westminster and the Victorian Constitution', *Transactions of the Royal Historical Society* Sixth Series 2 (1992).

mour precisely because 'the past' was like that. It was better to have such a constitution, he implied, than dogma and the relentless application of 'principles' which were supposedly eternal but which were in fact transient. Bagehot's genial but perhaps self-indulgent wisdom reflected a mid-Victorian confidence that it was possible to change and yet avoid the specious attraction of revolution. 'Gradualness', however, was not the inevitable characteristic of the preceding century of British history and there still remained some storms ahead.

Reform of the constitution *c.*1760–1832

'Reform of the constitution' had surfaced as a political cry in the 1760s. From then until the early 1780s, clubs, societies and associations had pressed for 'reform', though there was no unanimity about what precisely that entailed. Some reformers continued to argue that there had indeed been a glorious English parliamentary past which had functioned in the way that the contemporary Westminster Associations of Radicals wanted it to function in the present – that is to say on the basis of universal manhood suffrage, annual parliaments and equal parliamentary constituencies. They also desired the abolition of the property qualification and the introduction of payment for MPs. Other contemporary reformers, however, began to weary of this supposed 'past' as a weapon in their current political struggle. They suggested that there were 'natural rights' which all men – and, some believed, all or at least some women – possessed. That being the case, the political task was simply to convert these abstract rights into effective civil rights. In the event, however, even a modest measure of parliamentary reform, which had seemed at least a possibility at the beginning of the 1780s, no longer appeared feasible by the end of the decade.

The years 1788–89, as things turned out, showed how complicated change could be. At first sight, the time was ripe in 1788 to celebrate and 'claim' the 1688 'Glorious Revolution'. The Radicals who formed the Revolution Society argued that the principles of 1688 had been betrayed by the practice of subsequent decades. It was now the moment to insist on the 'sovereignty of the people', a doctrine which they claimed to be at the heart of the 1688 constitutional settlement. Richard Price, for example, a leading Radical Dissenter, spelt out what this would mean in an address, subsequently published, in November 1789. Other pamphleteers and agitators pressed for the repeal of the Test and Corporation Acts which entrenched Anglican privilege. There seemed a great deal to be gained politically by jumping on the '1688' bandwagon.

Also in 1789, however, there were extraordinary events in France, events which became more extraordinary by the month. The King of France was humbled and the 'natural' and inalienable 'rights of man' were proclaimed. The Catholic Church was to be 'disciplined' and the aristocracy stripped of its privileges and status. British Radicals were delighted to see what they interpreted as the 'ardour for liberty' catching and spreading, as Price put it. However, the general British reaction to events in France was predictably much more mixed. Some suggested that what the French were apparently seeking to achieve had in fact already been achieved in Britain. If this was all that was happening, there was no cause for apprehension. Yet were the French really just 'catching up' on Britain? It was difficult to believe that the new Constituent Assembly in France was exactly like the House of Commons, and strangely did not even seem to want to be like it. That was disturbing if the British constitution was indeed the perfection which its supporters believed it to be. Some Radicals, on the other hand, drew the conclusion that events in France proved the need for drastic change in Britain too. So what was really happening in France?

Edmund Burke, Irishman in England, published his celebrated *Reflections on the Revolution in France* in 1790. He was joined by other writers who elaborated on the dire consequences which would follow in Britain if the established order were tampered with because of an abstract doctrine. Pamphleteers of this persuasion had no doubt that the British constitution represented an acceptable balance. Its merits derived from real experience in the past. Such experience was infinitely more reliable than the elevation of universal principle. Such universal principle showed every sign of descending into anarchy, tyranny and terror. Burke argued his case with eloquence and insight, but cruder propagandists had little time for subtle argument. Men like the poet Wordsworth, who rejoiced to be alive at this new French dawn, were, in their eyes, suffering from a dangerous innocence.

On the other hand, 'Jacobins' throughout Britain were strong in their conviction that a state of bliss had indeed arrived in France, or was at least imminent there. Thomas Paine's *The Rights of Man*, published in two volumes in 1791 and 1792, powerfully argued in favour of 'natural rights' and a constitution in Britain which would uphold the civil rights which flowed from them. He expounded the benefits which the poor could expect to gain in Britain once the need to support an extravagant monarchy and aristocracy had been removed. Paine himself was a republican, though this was still a step too far for other British Radicals who supported the general thrust of his views. The 'war' between Burke and Paine was repeated by lesser titans in newspapers, pamphlets, tracts and sermons. 'Loyalist' and 'Jacobin' political clubs contended for support. Historians have variously estimated the strength of their respective adherents. It does seem clear, however, that 'popular' opinion was by no means hostile to the defence of the British constitution against 'French' notions.

The fact that it was in France that the great drama of 'revolution' was taking place inevitably complicated British reactions. That there was a long

149

history of past conflict between France and Britain (or at least England) needs no further rehearsal at this point. The merits, or otherwise, of 'revolution' could not therefore be argued over as though that history did not exist. It was a debate into which other Franco-British considerations inevitably obtruded.

In one sense, initially, the turmoil in France was a source of comfort to British politicians. The strength of France, and the 'threat' she had traditionally posed, would be reduced by 'her own intestine Commotions', as the British Foreign Secretary, the Duke of Leeds, sagely noted. Therefore, so long as British Radical 'sedition' could be kept in check, then the international hand of British government was considerably strengthened. There was an initial supposition that any action against France could safely be left to alarmed governments elsewhere in Europe. In 1792, for example, it was assumed that the Duke of Brunswick, with support, would be able to destroy the 'democracy' of France. Disturbingly, however, that turned out not to be the case. On the contrary, French armies were in the Austrian Netherlands. General war began in February 1793.

The conflict that followed, and which lasted, with brief intermission, until 1815, could not be a straightforward matter since 'ideological' and 'national' elements intermingled from the start. The defeat of the French revolutionary armies, from one perspective, was a matter of safeguarding traditional British interests in the Low Countries and beyond. From another perspective, however, their defeat was important because the armies carrying 'revolution' were, in a manner of speaking, only incidentally French. Peace might either be achieved by the establishment of a 'balance of power' or it might require the overthrow of the revolution and the restoration of the Bourbon monarchy.

If the war against France was 'ideological' it necessarily followed, or was supposed to follow, that British sympathizers with French 'revolution' had to be suppressed. What was taking place was a kind of European civil war. Indeed, armed with fresh legislation, the government's determination and capacity to stamp out what it regarded as sedition was quickly apparent in England, Scotland and Wales. Even so, some British Radicals continued to flirt with the idea of insurrection or other revolutionary activity. Once again, the significance of this activity has been differently assessed. In West Wales,

---

7.2 *'French Liberty and British Slavery'* (1792): James Gillray (1757–1815) turned to caricatures after he began his career as an illustrator of books. He latterly concentrated upon topics in the politics of his time. However, his broad stance was equivocal. As in this case, neither revolutionary fervour nor conservative complacency, embodied in national images, gained his allegiance. His satire punctured both. His unwillingness to be unequivocally enlisted was perhaps closer to much contemporary opinion than partisans of either side in the debate caused by the French Revolution allowed. It may be, however, that such savage detachment drove him to the insanity that clouded his final years.

for example, though there was a good deal of political and religious radicalism in the 1790s, the rather odd French force which landed at Fishguard in 1797 did not precipitate an insurrectionary surge. It was the last foreign invasion of Britain.

These circumstances produced a classical squeeze of 'middle opinion'. Those contemporaries who deplored specific revolutionary excesses in France, but who continued to argue in favour of 'reform' in Britain, had little impact. In the end, it was the patriotic appeal which was most persuasive. In Scotland, even Robert Burns, in asking himself in a poem *Does Haughty Gaul Invasion Threat?*, reluctantly concluded that 'Gaul' did. Charles James Fox stirred himself in the House of Commons, on occasion, to argue in favour of what he described as a 'balanced constitution' but made little progress towards achieving it. In 1797 his follower, Charles Grey, unsuccessfully moved a resolution for reform. He would have to wait a quarter of a century, through continued war and its troubled aftermath, before, as Earl Grey and British Prime Minister, he successfully achieved the passage of the 'Great Reform Act' of 1832.

Crisis of the *ancien régime* (1): the significance of 1832

The years between 1827 and 1832 have been seen by some historians as marking the crisis of the *ancien régime* in Britain. Here was the break with the past which ushered in 'modern Britain', a break which might paradoxically have occurred half a century earlier had the existing structure not been given a longer lease of life by the French Revolution and the ensuing wars against France. The notion of an *ancien régime* of course extends beyond constitutional structures, defined narrowly. Indeed, arguably, as will subsequently be considered, it was 'religion' in the shape of the passage of the Catholic Emancipation Act in 1829 which really broke the dam and which inaugurated the 'constitutional revolution'. Nevertheless, the issue of parliamentary reform came to be the test of whether the old order could hang on and adapt or would find itself swept away.

The Cabinet formed by Earl Grey in November 1830 did not suggest an inclination to undermine the pillars of society. Of its thirteen members, nine were peers who sat in the Lords. Additionally, Lord Palmerston, merely an Irish peer, sat in the Commons. There was no doubt, however, that Grey would embark on some measure to reform 'representation'. The issue had revived just before and after the ending of the Napoleonic Wars. The only British Prime Minister to have been assassinated, Spencer Perceval, met that fate in 1812. There was a good deal of economic distress. The 'Luddites', who engaged in machine-breaking, have been seen by some historians as reviving the insurrectionary tradition of the 1790s. In 1819 a major political meeting in Manchester got out of hand when an attempt to detain the speaker, 'Orator' Hunt, led to military intervention and what became known as the 'Peterloo Massacre', when eleven people were killed. The determination on the part of government to maintain law and order, and to suppress radicalism, can be seen in the subsequent 'Six Acts' which limited the right to hold public meetings and extended newspaper stamp duties. The restrictions were considerable but it has been pointed out that, looked at in comparison with the power exercised by the state in mainland Europe at this time, the Six Acts appear 'distinctly mild rather than draconian'.[8] It would be wrong, too, to envisage constant and widespread popular agitation for 'reform' throughout the 1820s. Tory governments managed to survive without addressing the issue directly.

The advent of the Grey government in 1830 coincided with widespread rural discontent across southern England. Demands for better wages and better Poor Law payments were accompanied by machine-breaking and the torching of ricks. Such agitation was in a sense political but it was not a concerted political campaign. The Whigs gave as high a priority to the maintenance of law and order as their Tory predecessors had done. Grey's intention to press on with 'reform' was not the product of panic. It represented the culmination of a long conviction that some change in the basis of representation was necessary.

It was not easy to see any clear principles undergirding the existing confused jungle of constituencies and franchises. Over previous decades there had been spasmodic though abortive efforts to tinker here and there. Something more fundamental was now required and the Cabinet set up a committee of four to draft a measure. Its brief was to produce something which would be acceptable to 'public opinion' while at the same time ensuring that property remained the basis of the right to vote. 'Public opinion' in this instance did not of course mean the male population of the country, let alone the female. It meant the existing small electorate and a wider, though ill-defined, section of the 'respectable' population. The committee in due course came forward with a scheme whose most striking aspect was the intention to disfranchise no less than 168 small boroughs and redistribute the seats concerned to London and unrepresented larger towns, and to the counties, in roughly equal measure. The committee also suggested use of the secret ballot – later not pursued – together with a standardization of the householder franchise.

The notion that the measure could be pushed through quickly had soon to be abandoned. When put to the House of Commons in March 1831 it passed by only one vote – the MP responsible committed suicide a few months later. Nevertheless, difficulty at the committee stage of the bill led Grey to ask for a dissolution, which the king reluctantly conceded. Campaig-

---

[8] N. McCord, *British History 1815–1906* (Oxford, 1991) p. 20.

ning focused on a single issue – the Reform Bill – to an unusual extent. The measure of the government's victory can be gauged from the fact that the Reform Bill passed its second reading with a majority of 146 votes. Both in town and country there was a tide running for reform and in urban areas non-voters could possess a powerful influence in determining particular electoral outcomes. The Duke of Wellington was not alone in again looking to history at this juncture. He too had the sense that the mood in the country seemed very like what it had been before the commencement of the seventeenth-century Civil War.

Having completed its stages in the Commons, the bill came before the Lords in October and was there defeated by forty-one votes. On this occasion, Wellington went even further back into English history. Told on all sides that the country was on the brink of revolution, he reposted that such a revolution could only be produced by force and violence. He would defy those who would use such violence. 'History shows', he confidently asserted, 'that a great change has never, since the wars of the Houses of York and Lancaster, been produced in England by any authority but Parliament ...'.[9] There were riots in Nottingham, Derby and Bristol. Law and order might be on the brink of breaking down. The 'Political Unions' which had sprung up in major cities would not let the matter rest. The government could not and would not abandon its policy. Since it was also unable to make sufficient peers change their minds, the only option appeared to be to ask the king to create sufficient sympathetic new peers to secure the passage of the bill. The king, as has been noted, jibbed at the prospect but when the government resigned, and the Duke of Wellington proved unable to form a new administration, he reluctantly acquiesced. In the event, rather than face this prospect, the Tory peers allowed the bill to pass in June 1832.

It was undoubtedly a landmark, but what precisely did it signify? The original drafting committee had been asked to come up with a measure which would 'afford sure ground of resistance to further innovation'. It is evident that the government would have been both surprised and alarmed if it had been portrayed as inaugurating a 'British tradition' by introducing the first in a series of changes in the franchise which would lead, within a hundred years, to every adult man and woman in Britain possessing the 'right to vote'. The claim by the Tory opposition that the Reform Bill was indeed but the first step down a democratic slippery slope was strongly rejected by the government. There was no 'right to vote', it stated, and the franchise still properly rested on a property qualification. The expansion of the electorate in England and Wales after the 1832 Act – there were separate bills for Scotland and Ireland – cannot be stated precisely. Even an increase of around 60 per cent to a figure in excess of half a million still left the electorate a small

---

[9] Wellington cited in M. Bentley, *Politics without Democracy 1815–1914* (London, 1984) p. 80.

minority in the population. An emphasis upon the conservative character and intention of the 'Great Reform Act' is therefore not misplaced.

Even so, it does not do justice to the significance of what had occurred. In the end, it was not so much the matter of what had been passed as the manner. Pressure had clearly moved beyond the formal context of Parliament between October 1831 and May 1832. It would be difficult to put 'the people' back in their place. How close 'revolution' had actually been in these months is necessarily only a matter for speculation but, at least in the eyes of the political elite, it had been too close for comfort. No formal change, however, had occurred in the position either of the Crown or the Lords, although precedents had been established which indicated, though did not define, the limits of their authority. It was, after all, an aristocratic chamber which had in the end, against its better judgement, accepted change. Of course, it did so, as had the Cabinet itself, on the assumption that the old order had been dented but not destroyed. There would remain for some time to come an aristocratic presence, perhaps even an aristocratic dominance, in British government. That presence, however, knew that it rested, in the last resort, on consent, or at least acquiescence, rather than on power which it independently possessed.

Few historians would now argue in a simplistic fashion that 'the middle class' took over the reins of government after 1832. Indeed, it is not easy to decide what the term means or who should be included within such a 'class' – did 'commercial' and 'professional' men, for example, have the same interests and aspirations? Granted this difficulty, however, it remains the case that the Reform Act substantially enlisted groups and communities behind the new political order, even if they did not participate directly in it at the highest levels. By the same token, though, it also highlighted the continued exclusion of the majority of the population from direct political participation.

It was hard to determine what 'philosophical basis', if any, now undergirded the new order. Why some towns and not others had seats in the House of Commons remained puzzling. And, despite attempts at uniformity, the franchise categories were in practice fuzzy. Was there any principle which established a balance between rural and urban seats, or between north and south in England, or between England and the rest of the United Kingdom? If so, it was not readily apparent. It would be difficult, therefore, to resist the notion that 'anomalies' might be tidied up. That, in turn, might cause the entire structure to again look shaky – more speedily than anyone anticipated in 1832.

Crisis of the *ancien régime* (2): the repeal of the Corn Laws

It was not an accident that it had been a Whig government which took up the cause of reform. Notwithstanding the fact that many Tory MPs had come to feel that it had been an 'unrepresentative' House of Commons which had passed the 1829 Catholic Emancipation Act, and which therefore led them to give some sympathetic consideration to the possibility of 'reform', it remained the case that a Tory government would not have introduced the 1832 Act. The social composition of the Whig Cabinet, however, is a reminder that the 'great debate' took place within as much as between social 'classes'. It has also to be noted that British aristocrats were a curious caste, regarded with some disdain by their more punctilious continental counterparts. The fluid entry into its ranks must not be exaggerated, but in comparative terms it was an 'open elite', prepared in some cases to dabble in trade and industry, and marry 'out', without concern for caste rigidities. Espousal of 'reform' by Whig aristocrats was seen as all of a piece with attitudes which they had inherited from their eighteenth-century ancestors. From their perspective, a judicious broadening of 'representation' and the repeated rhetoric of 'liberty' was entirely consonant with the maintenance of social privilege and the possession of substantial wealth. The first great political transition from 'the past' to 'the modern' in Britain did not therefore take the form of a confrontation between 'the aristocracy' and other aspiring and ascendant social groups. The context was a cleavage within a still essentially aristocratic order.

It left open, however, whether this was merely an opening round in a more protracted struggle which would produce a sharper break with the past than 1832 appeared to have done. It was uncertain, for example, whether the 'party system', as it had evolved over the previous century, could survive the transition intact. Issues of political principle, encrusted within the politics of personal or collective advantage, did divide 'parties' both at Westminster and in the country, but they still remained loose agglomerations of opinion and interest. The links between the world of 'high politics' and even the modest expansion of the electorate after 1832 might be more difficult to sustain within the existing political terminology and (by later standards) still rudimentary organizational structures.

It was also an open question, in that context, whether this form of party politics could continue without coming to take on a more pronounced 'class' character; that is to say a system in which 'class identity' and accompanying 'interests' formed the basis of party division in a more clear-cut and transparent fashion than existed in 1832.[10] It was a problem which initially most afflicted the Tories. It was hardly surprising that the first general election after 1832 saw them heavily defeated. It could appear that they would be destined to be pushed to the political margins, out of touch with the 'march of time'. It was a problem addressed by Sir Robert Peel who had awkwardly signalled his realization that something more relevant was required when he refused to serve in the Tory administration which Welling-

---

[10] P. Mandler, *Aristocratic Government in the Age of Reform: Whigs and Liberals, 1830–1852* (Oxford, 1990).

ton tried to form in May 1832. An added spur to his reflection came from his belief that the Whigs were simply wrong in supposing that 1832 constituted a permanent settlement of the franchise. The Whig government formed on Grey's retirement by Lord Melbourne in August 1834 provided confirmation that the Whigs themselves were internally in some disarray. 'Middle-class' men, calling themselves 'radicals', wanted to go further and faster in certain matters than the leadership at Westminster – which remained substantially aristocratic. Taking the rather dramatic view that his government was ineffective, the king decided to dismiss it. No subsequent British monarch has dismissed a government in this manner. To general surprise, Peel formed a short-lived government in December 1834, before Melbourne returned in April 1835 to head an administration which lasted until September 1841. At this point, Sir Robert formed his second administration which lasted until July 1846. Significantly, it was a 'Conservative' rather than a 'Tory' administration.

Of course, in 1832 Wellington and Peel had together proclaimed the need to 'conserve'. After that débâcle, however, Peel gave the idea of 'conserving' what he believed to be more positive content. A 'Conservative Party' might attract into its ranks, at some stage, Whigs for whom their own party might prove too radical and, in Peel's language, 'destructive'. However, it could not survive let alone thrive on the basis of this hope. It had to show by more than administrative competence that there was virtue in 'Conservatism'. The past could not be and should not be blindly jettisoned but equally prudent adaptation was more sensible than unyielding adherence to a status quo. Peel's own background (son of a rich and baroneted cotton manufacturer) appeared in this context to be an advantage. His Oxford academic career and his administrative record at the Home Office in the 1820s showed him to be a man of unusual capacity. Under his leadership, the 'Conservatives' would make good their own emergence from their Tory past – or so it appeared. He also had an unexpected but noteworthy interest in the details of party organization alongside the public attempt to fashion a new 'ideology' as evident in his 'Tamworth Manifesto' (1834).

There was, however, an inherent difficulty in stressing the virtues of 'Conservatism' at a time of increasingly rapid social and economic change. Peel himself, having formerly opposed Catholic Emancipation, had come round to supporting it in 1829. How was the 'permanent' past to be distinguished from the 'pliable past'? The problem came to haunt Peel in 1845–46. The 1815 Corn Law had attempted to protect British agriculture – and the landed interest that lay behind it – by imposing a range of duties on agricultural imports. The recent long period of war was also held up to illustrate the dangers which could result from too much dependence on foreign food supplies. Even at the time, it had aroused vehement opposition. It was only in the early 1840s, however, that a sustained campaign against the Corn Laws came to be mounted.

PUNCH'S PENCILLINGS.—N⁰. LXVIII.

A PLEASANT POSITION.

Sketched in the House of Commons, Friday, February 17th, 1843.

7.3 No nineteenth-century issue was more capable of being painted in simple black and white than the issue of 'bread for the people' in the controversies stimulated by the campaign for the repeal of the Corn Laws. Here, apparently, was the turning point between the old rural agricultural Britain and a new free trade open-to-the-world Britain. The oratory of John Bright created the atmosphere of a crusade. The old order was sitting on a powder keg which was about to explode. (Cartoon in *Punch*, February 1843.)

The Anti-Corn Law League seemed to contemporaries to be an illustration of new post-1832 politics. Ostensibly at least, it was a 'single-issue' rather than a 'catch-all' movement of protest. Its organizational base was in Manchester. Its most prominent spokesmen, Richard Cobden and John Bright, toured the country and made uninhibited use of public platforms to advance their cause and to attack the government. The battle lines were drawn with deceptive clarity. Cobden and Bright stood as middle-class, northern, commercial, practical men who had no nostalgia for the past, little enthusiasm for the present and great anticipation of the future. Their opponents were the landed, aristocratic interest, bent on preserving a social and economic order which deserved to be pushed into the past as speedily as possible. Britain's future, Cobden and Bright argued, would be guaranteed by the adoption of Free Trade, a principle which was not only economically beneficial as the world then stood but which was also likely to prove the highway to international peace. Bright, who was a Quaker in his religious beliefs, lambasted the Established Church and indeed saw the attempt to maintain the Corn Laws as another example of that interlocking network of churchmen, soldiers and diplomats at work trying by any means to keep the past in the present.

Opponents of the Anti-Corn Law League responded to accusations that they were imposing a 'Bread Tax' by suggesting that the manufacturers prominent in the League were in fact only looking for their own narrow economic gain in seeking repeal. Manufacturers treated their workers badly and tried to ease their consciences by talking of the iniquities of this 'Bread Tax'. It is rare to find such a dramatic confrontation between 'past' and 'present' and there were, of course, exaggerations and distortions in these rival presentations, but in the 1840s it seemed the issue of the hour.

This general campaign, coupled with the specific complications caused by the ruin of the potato crop in Ireland in 1845–46, brought the crisis directly to Peel's door. As he himself had said several years earlier, Britain's lot was apparently cast. Corn fields might be preferable to cotton factories and an agricultural population preferable to a manufacturing population, but it was too late to turn back. In this respect, maintenance of the Corn Laws ran counter to the broad thrust of his own economic policy. On the other hand, Conservative MPs, in large numbers, remained wedded to protection. They were sceptical of Peel's claim that the Irish famine rendered the abolition of the Corn Laws necessary. Peel himself was adamant that he had reached his decision on general grounds and he was not bowing to an extra-parliamentary campaign whose very existence he disliked. In any event, in June 1846 sufficient Tory MPs voted against the government, or abstained, to render its continuance impossible.

Peel had done what he conceived to be his duty, but in so acting he had split his party. The 'Conservative' experiment appeared shattered. The episode also illustrated how difficult it might be to act the 'statesman' before the country in the face of fierce party demand for 'accountability', particularly when it was marshalled by someone as eloquent and unscrupulous as Disraeli. 'Peelites' were alarmed that, after all, the Tories would descend into a disgruntled rump in parliament, vainly seeking to defend an agricultural age and its social concomitants, an age which would inexorably fade into the past. It would have come as a great surprise to them in 1846 that it would be Disraeli himself who, twenty years later, would lurch both party and country once more in the direction of Reform.

Chapter 8

Preservation and Progress: Representing the People *c.1845–c.1945*

The queen

In 1837, at the age of eighteen, Queen Victoria, niece of William (who lacked a legitimate heir), came to the throne. The political/constitutional crisis of 1832 was therefore behind her, though the economic/political crisis of the Corn Laws lay ahead. At this critical period of change, therefore, the monarchy was in youthful and inexperienced hands. Few would then have suspected that she would reign until 1901, thus far the longest reign in British history. In his chapter on monarchy in *The English Constitution*, Bagehot argued that of all nations in the world the English were the least a nation of pure philosophers. It would be a very serious matter for them to have to change the visible head of their world every four or five years. Victoria certainly enabled them to escape that fate.

At the personal level, the queen could scarcely fail to be an improvement on her immediate precessors. She had the advantage of youth if not of beauty. She married her German cousin, Albert, in 1840. He brought with him intelligence and a serious approach to public life. It was not possible to think of him as a Regency dandy. Queen Victoria was not physically impressive – she was under five feet tall – but she was a determined lady.

Victoria personified continuity in the extraordinary nineteenth-century decades of change that lay ahead. In her early years, for example in the so-called 'Bedchamber Crisis' of 1839, Victoria had not fully grasped the implications of what had happened over the previous decade. Between 1846 and 1859, however, in a context of considerable party confusion in the Commons, it was possible, indeed necessary, for the queen to exercise considerable political influence. Her views on individuals could prove decisive – as for example in 1851 when Palmerston resigned as Foreign Secretary. In circumstances in which parties, particularly in Opposition, were not sure who their leaders were, the queen had to make choices, within certain limits.

No monarch, however circumspect, can be without likes and dislikes. It is well-known that she preferred Disraeli to Gladstone, but no vast constitutional impropriety was involved in such a preference. The queen certainly had views on appointments, episcopal and other, which could not be ignored. She had a vast network of royal relatives in Europe which gave her a not unjustified sense that she knew more about the mind and mood of Europe than some of her ministers. She was unhappy when Lord Palmerston and Lord John Russell, to name but two, did not share the view that she had some special duty of supervision over their conduct of British foreign policy.

Bagehot's overall assessment was that in the British constitutional monarchy the sovereign had three rights: the right to be consulted, the right to encourage, the right to warn. A monarch of great sense and sagacity would want no others. He also suggested that the people expected to be 'dazzled' by their monarch (perhaps against their reason and their sober judgement). Victoria was not altogether dazzling and the death of Albert in 1861 sent her into protracted and reclusive mourning. Her public appearances were very limited and their paucity caused some political consternation. Critics of the monarchy spoke their minds in the Commons – amongst them Sir Charles Dilke and, for a time, Joseph Chamberlain. They questioned whether the country was getting value for money from the civil list. In the 1860s a republican movement emerged of very modest size, but with some prospects.

However, in the last thirty years of her reign, Victoria made a public return, though she could not be persuaded to dress other than as a mourning widow. After 1870 France again became a republic and the celebrations in Britain which accompanied the queen's jubilees in 1887 and 1897 served to point up the contrast between the two countries. Historians have noted the extent to which, at this juncture, a 'public' monarchy was invented. Victoria played her part satisfactorily. She contrived to stand above party to an acceptable extent, though there was Liberal anxiety that her willingness to become Empress of India played into Disraeli's hands. Except in very isolated quarters, criticism of the monarchy had virtually died out by the end of the century. Britain and its monarchy belonged inseparably together, whatever other changes were taking place. The advent of the postage stamp and its worldwide circulation emphasized the point. This arrogant country, unlike others, did not trouble to identify itself by name. In the age of Gladstone and Disraeli it was deemed sufficient for the queen's head to appear.

Equipoise: Gladstone and Disraeli *c.*1845–1867

Provided that a man's inclusion did not lead to 'sudden or violent, or excessive or intoxicating change', William Gladstone concluded in 1864 that 'every man who is not presumably incapacitated by some consideration of personal unfitness or of political danger is morally entitled to come within the pale of the Constitution'. It had taken him thirty-two years as an MP to reach this conclusion and its precise implications, even yet, were somewhat opaque. The date of Gladstone's conclusion is, however, significant. The 'Age of Equipoise', as Professor W.L. Burn described the years from 1852 to 1867, was coming to an end. How and why a new equilibrium had to be sought is examined predominantly through the minds and actions of two leading figures: Gladstone and Disraeli.

Mr Gladstone's history

In abhorring 'sudden or violent, or excessive or intoxicating change', Gladstone continued to express sentiments which reflected his own deepest anxieties from early manhood. No major politician in the nineteenth century wrestled more profoundly with the relationship between past and present. In his own personal life and his conception of national life, he felt its constant tension. Elements in his ancestry fused with his early environment, upbringing and education to give him an unusually complex perspective on his country and its past. Gladstone felt national dilemmas with a disconcerting intensity and was perhaps unique in the extent to which so many of them were bound up with his own personal experience, decisions and actions. The very span of his life (1809–98) meant that, at its close, he had witnessed a century in which, in so many fields, there had been more change in the history of 'Britain' and in its global outreach than in any previous century.

Gladstone's sense of the past was extensive and comprehensive, refreshed by constant reading from boyhood onwards. It could not be only of the British past. His Christian belief, in its successive phases, necessarily endowed him with a framework which could not be restricted to a horizon that was national. His increasing awareness of the Church as a corporate entity led him to wrestle at length and in print, over many years, with two interrelated problems.[1] In the first place, Gladstone had tried initially in his *The State in its Relations with the Church* (1838 and 1841) to sustain a strong belief in the confessional state. The Church of England represented truth and there was 'a real and not merely suppositious personality of nations, which entails likewise its own religious responsibilities'. If that was the case, could the state, for example, give modest support to Presbyterians and Roman Catholics, both of which bodies were naturally outside the Estab-

---

[1] P. Butler, *Gladstone: Church, State and Tractarianism – A Study of His Religious Ideas and Attitudes 1809–59* (Oxford, 1982); B. Hilton, 'Gladstone's Theological Politics' in M. Bentley and J. Stevenson, eds, *High and Low Politics in Modern Britain* (Oxford, 1983) pp. 28–57.

lished (Anglican) Church of Ireland? 'Nationality' and 'Religion' could not be severed.

Yet, although his own commitment to the Church of England did not waver, he knew at close quarters what it was that led contemporaries to convert to Roman Catholicism. Indeed, on his own first visit to Rome in 1832, while noting his own preference for English Gothic cathedrals and contempt for 'the idea of an ecclesiastical sovereign', he nevertheless felt most deeply 'the pain and shame of the schism which separates us from Rome'. It was, of course, the case that the guilt lay not upon 'the Venerable Fathers of the English Reformed Church, but upon Rome itself'. Even so, he prayed that God would 'bind up the wounds of his bleeding Church'.[2] In subsequent decades, as will be seen, Gladstone's views evolved in particulars but, fundamentally, he did not cease to plead earnestly, as he put it in 1841, 'for those great ethical laws under which we are socially constituted, and which economical speculations and material interests have threatened altogether to subvert'.[3] He feared for the future if Christianity, and particularly the Church of England, were indeed subverted. Such a severance from the past could not but fail to have catastrophic consequences for the nation as Gladstone conceived it.

Gladstone's past was also located in classical antiquity. After Eton, he studied 'Literae Humaniores' and Mathematics at Oxford, culminating in a formidable Double First in December 1831. As has been observed, there was only one set book in Lit.Hum. which had been written after the first century AD. All his ways of thinking at this stage were pre-industrial and were not tainted by Scottish or any other political economy. Gladstone himself, on graduating, was adamant that there was no case for any change in the educational system which he and others of his class had experienced arising 'from the changes which have taken place in military tactics, in popular science, in manufacture'.[4] Homer, Plato and Aristotle remained lifelong companions – of course, in the original Greek. In 1858 Gladstone published his own *Studies in Homer and the Homeric Age*, an accomplishment not now emulated by aspirants to high political office.

By comparison, although always curious about particular facets of British history, Gladstone's immersion in its study was modest. At school he read Clarendon and Burnet and biographical studies of Walpole and Pitt. He found Hume's *History of England* 'delightful' except for the author's scepticism in matters of religion. He read 'Ossian' (James Macpherson) and was addicted to the Scottish novels of Walter Scott. It was perhaps appropriate that his approach to British history should owe so much to Scottish authors because, although born in Liverpool and educated in England, he was by de-

---

[2] H.C.G. Matthew, *Gladstone 1809–1874* (Oxford, 1986) p. 37.
[3] Cited in R. Shannon, *Gladstone 1809–1865* (London, 1983) p. 87.
[4] Cited in Matthew, *Gladstone 1809–1874*, p. 18.

scent a Scot. In schoolboy debates on historical topics, initially he supported the 'Stuarts' with regard to the 1745 rebellion. However, despite certain 'blots' he came to praise the career of Walpole for being 'the bulwark of the Protestant Succession'.

Gladstone's father – Sir John as he became in 1846 – was a 'British' merchant. That is to say, he was born in Leith, the port of Edinburgh, but made his considerable fortune in property, shipping, sugar, cotton and slavery in Liverpool before buying a house and estate on the east coast of Scotland. An understanding of that commercial – though not industrial – background is as vital to understanding William Gladstone as is his academic achievement and scholarly interests. It was this side of his character that Peel successfully harnessed when he placed Gladstone at the Board of Trade in the early 1840s.

Apocalypse?

As an undergraduate, Gladstone had made his name with a speech at the Union against Reform. When he entered the House of Commons at the age of twenty-three in 1832 as MP for Newark, a pocket borough in the hands of the Duke of Newcastle, that fear of 'sudden' and 'violent' change still evident in 1864 had been even more pronounced. He thought then that the signs of the times were appalling. Britain seemed to be 'the main remaining home and hope of the cause of order throughout the world and even this last bulwark is assailed from within as well as without'.[5] The Reform Bill of 1832 was 'monstrous'. Even so, Britain seemed to offer the possibility of a more determined resistance to the general principles of democracy than any other country in the civilized world.[6] That sense of impending cataclysm never entirely departed, though a decade later, serving under Peel, he had become less apocalytic in his views. The opponent of the Reform Act came to support the Repeal of the Corn Laws – an action which cost him his Newark seat. Instead, however, after a short interval, he became one of two MPs for Oxford University, an election which gave him much initial satisfaction but which hardly gave him a constituency which prodded him in a more liberal direction.

The death of Peel in 1850 made a reappraisal of his own career necessary. It also required a fresh assessment of the national mood and circumstances. The Tory split remained profound and it seemed likely that the Peelites would be a dwindling band with their master gone. More than that, however, were not all 'parties' on the brink of dissolution? The confusion in Par-

---

[5] Ibid., p. 25.
[6] Ibid., p. 43.

liament could not be denied and neither Whig/Liberal nor Tory/Conservative could feel confidence in the significance of these labels. For some, as Stanley (Lord Derby) put it, shortly before forming the short-lived Tory administration in 1852, the 'real battle of the Constitution' remained 'whether the preponderance in the legislative power is to rest with the land and those connected with it, or with the manufacturing interests'. For others, that battle had already been lost. The socio-economic balance of the Britain of their childhood was a past that could not be recovered. In the Derby administration – which Gladstone had declined to join – Disraeli was Chancellor of the Exchequer. There could be no return to Protection, but Disraeli had to do his best to rally the landed party while producing a scheme suited to 'the spirit of the age'. Gladstone savaged its technical inadequacies and the government went down to defeat. Preceding him, Disraeli had raised the spectre of a coalition which might follow in such an eventuality. 'Coalitions', he remarked, 'although successful, have always found this, that their triumph has been brief. This too, I know, that England does not love Coalitions.'[7] It was a conviction to be repeated on more than one occasion over the next century and a half.

There had been twenty years since 1832 in which to come to terms with the fact, as Professor Hanham puts it, that 'the constitution had ceased to be based on the principle of prescription and had come to be based on the principle of representation'.[8] Parliament, on an enlarged but still very restricted franchise, required ministers to be answerable in a more direct sense than hitherto. But it was still far from clear what 'representative government' implied – a deficiency which John Stuart Mill, amongst others, was anxious to address. A coalition of Whigs, Peelites and Radicals under the Peelite, Lord Aberdeen, did indeed follow, although it lasted only a little more than two years before collapsing under the strain of the Crimean War (1854–56).

In that ministry, Gladstone came in as Chancellor of the Exchequer and in his budget of 1853 outlined a scheme to abolish income tax gradually over the next seven years. The Crimean War put paid to that. It also put paid to Gladstone's career. Although he had initially supported the war, he

---

[7] Disraeli, 16 December 1852, cited in R. Blake, *Disraeli* (London, 1969) p. 345.
[8] H.J. Hanham, *The Reformed Electoral System in Great Britain, 1832–1914* (London, 1968) p. 8.

8.1 The House of Lords, the Home Rule debate of 1893: oil painting by Dickenson and Foster. In 1893 Gladstone, in his last Liberal government, introduced his second Irish Home Rule Bill. It passed in the Commons by 43 votes but was rejected in the Lords by 419 to 41. Gladstone urged an immediate dissolution of Parliament but his colleagues would not agree. By 1900 466 Conservative peers sat in the Lords but only 69 Liberals, a reflection in part of the collapse of Whiggery. The stage was set for the political crisis of 1910–11 which trimmed the powers of the upper house.

took the view in 1855 that British participation was ceasing to be just. Shortly after Palmerston succeeded Aberdeen as Prime Minister, Gladstone resigned. Quintessentially ministerial, he did not like back-bench politics and the 'irresponsible' criticism which seemed so congenial to Radicals. The Viscount Palmerston of Palmerston, County Dublin, educated at Edinburgh University, was even less congenial. He was, at least externally, just that kind of arrogant, flippant, jaunty Englishman that Gladstone most disliked, though since Gladstone liked aristocrats, he could not hold his rank against Palmerston. Only after the defeat of the second Derby/Disraeli government in 1859 did Gladstone find it in himself to take office, again as Chancellor of the Exchequer. He held this post continuously until July 1866, under Russell after Palmerston's death in 1865. It was a tenure which Gladstone emphatically made his own. His immense industry and grasp of detail largely gave the office its central significance in modern British government.

First principles?

Attention to Treasury issues to an extent enabled Gladstone to take his mind off those issues which had so much bothered him in the later 1850s after his resignation. In an anonymous article in 1856, he spoke of the 'interval between the two parties' as having very greatly narrowed. He found himself on some matters closer to Cobden or even Bright than he did to Palmerston. He might have drifted back to the Conservatives were it not for the prominent presence in their ranks of Disraeli. Was politics simply a matter of personality? From a different perspective, the young Lord Robert Cecil (the later Lord Salisbury) complained subsequently of 'The tacit unanimity with which this generation has laid aside the ingenious network of political first principles which the industry of three centuries of theorists had woven.'[9] Expediency reigned supreme and the past had been jettisoned.

For others, however, the laying aside of 'political first principles', supposing that it had indeed happened, was not without advantage. The narrowing of party 'intervals' and a disposition to coalesce was a sign of maturity and wisdom. The decade which had begun so signally with the splendours of the Great Exhibition at the Crystal Palace had witnessed steady commercial growth. The contrast between it and the 'hungry forties' which had preceded it was marked. The 'feel good' factor, as it would now be expressed, was conspicuous amongst the 'middle classes' where fear and foreboding had previously been evident. To all such generalizations, exceptions can of course be found, but for men of Gladstone's generation there was reassurance in the fact that, unlike what had happened widely on the

---

[9] Cited in W.L. Burn, *The Age of Equipoise* (London, 1968) p. 55.

European mainland, there had been no British revolution in 1848. It was to London that Prince Metternich had fled from Vienna. Objectionable though reform had been in 1832, it could at least be claimed in retrospect that a judicious adjustment had spared the country that drastic rupture between past and present which revolution attempted elsewhere. These facts were more than adequate compensation for the laying aside of the three centuries of theorizing on political first principles so much lamented by Cecil.

Such complacency in the 1850s about the national fabric was buttressed, at least for a time, by the Crimean War. Previously, however, there had been anxious moments. 'Popular' disappointment with the modest adjustments of 1832 remained evident. That gradual and acceptable adjustment from past to present, over which all established politicians and parties believed themselves to be presiding, seemed altogether too sedate and self-interested to sections of the population unable to grasp the profound advantages which the existing social and political order held for them. Protest and discontent, though spasmodic, was still sufficiently widespread to fuel the fears of landed gentlemen or factory owners. Gladstone himself, through his wife's family, now had direct experience, at Hawarden, just over the Welsh border, of a landed estate.

Chartism – the road not taken

From such a perspective, there were various causes of anxiety. Although their titles were somewhat grandiloquent, John Doherty's Grand General Union of Operative Cotton Spinners (1829) and Robert Owen's Grand National Consolidated Trades Union (1834) aspired to weld together the aspirations of previously unorganized workers. William Lovett, the latest in a long line of London Radicals, acted as secretary to the London Working Men's Association and launched a fierce diatribe against the 'robber factions' who controlled *The Rotten House of Commons* (1836). Veteran Radicals – Thomas Attwood and Francis Place among them – resurrected old programmes for radical reform. The New Poor Law (1834) was widely detested and was held to disprove the idea that the middle and labouring classes had much in common. Radical orators conjured with the notion of an 'alternative Parliament' which would be really responsive to the needs of a people weighed down by taxation, inadequately fed and forced to endure the horrors of the factory system.

These grievances lay behind the 'Charter' which was proclaimed in the summer of 1838. It embodied the famous Six Points: manhood suffrage, annual parliaments, secret ballot, equal electoral districts, abolition of property qualifications for MPs and payment of MPs. Here was nothing about the glories of the British constitution. What was being demanded, with increasing vehemence in the midst of a protracted economic depression, was a 'democracy', a political order which claimed no special descent from the British past. In 1838 a strike of Glasgow cotton-spinners caused alarm to those in authority. Between 1839 and 1842, as class tension mounted, it proved extremely difficult to promote any cooperation between Corn-Law Repealers and Chartists in the city. In July 1839 the House of Commons refused to consider the Chartist National Petition, presented by Attwood, which claimed to carry more than a million signatures. In reaction, there was talk of a 'general strike' or a 'run on the banks' and, in more outraged circles, of insurrection. In November 1839 at Newport, in South Wales, there was an attack by armed Chartists which led to some twenty deaths. Rumours of insurrection were rife, but they failed to materialize, though troops were on stand-by. Subsequently, historians have stressed the disparate elements in Chartism, its inadequate leadership and its ambivalent attitude towards the industrial society that was emerging. The difficulty, too, was that the Charter embodied a political programme which, while it might help workers in the long run, offered little by way of immediate alleviation of their economic circumstances. Even so, for several more years, Chartism was perceived to constitute a serious threat to law and order. Parliament again rejected a further petition, which claimed 3 million signatures, in May 1842. The Irishman, Feargus O'Connor, by his oratory and journal *The Northern Star*, kept hopes alight. The year of European revolution, 1848, witnessed the last major effort of Chartism. In April O'Connor threatened a mass procession of Chartists from Kennington Common, where they had assembled, to Parliament in order to present a third petition. Having first dispatched Queen Victoria to the Isle of Wight, the government ensured a substantial presence of troops, police and special constables, amidst other measures, to prevent any such occurrence. Amongst the special constables was William Gladstone. 'May our hearts feel profoundly the mercies of this very remarkable day', he wrote after the collapse of the Chartist challenge.[10]

A decade later, however, although Chartism had fizzled out, it was evident that a new challenge to the post-1832 order was emerging. Reform was back on the agenda. In 1858–59, John Bright, Quaker Radical and opponent of the Crimean War, led a campaign in the country for further franchise reform. It was dubiously successful. Working-class leaders suspected that Bright's proposals would have the effect of shoring up the political power of the 'millocracy'. Yet, without the anxiety their ambitions engendered, Bright could not persuade middle-class audiences that some further change was imperative in the interests of stability. Nevertheless, Bright brought the issue back into debate and both Tory and Whig politicians skirted around it. It was felt that Palmerston's well-known opposition would prevent any change in his lifetime – and he did not die until 1865.

---

[10] Cited in Shannon, *Gladstone*, p. 209.

Democracy – monster or miracle?

The outbreak of the American Civil War gave a new dimension to constitutional debate. For decades, 'American democracy' both in theory and in practice had played a not insignificant part in British debates. For some, it remained a horror to be avoided at all costs. Not so for John Bright. In his home town of Rochdale in 1863 he contrasted America with Britain. In America the working man found a land not cursed with feudalism. Hope prevailed everywhere. Careers were open and a man could rise by his own honest efforts. There was no privileged class. America, he declared on another occasion, was a happy and prosperous land which, somehow, prospered without an emperor, without a king, without a court, without nobles, without state bishops and state priests. He spearheaded further Reform agitation in Britain.

It was scarcely to be expected that Gladstone, who, with Russell, had taken over the 'Liberal' leadership after Palmerston's death, would echo such sentiments. In any event, Bright, a strong supporter of the North, had been infuriated by Gladstone's speech in 1862 in which he had declared that Jefferson Davis and his Southern colleagues had made a nation. Nevertheless, in 1866 Gladstone knew that something had to be done and framed a measure which would stop short of 'household suffrage' – that is to say a vote for all male heads of households. The complex manoeuvres which then ensued, which cannot be detailed here, ended in disaster for the government. Some of its own normal supporters – the 'Adullamites' – believed that the existing franchise maintained that balance between land and commerce which was so essential for the country's welfare. Their objections enabled the Tories to defeat the government's proposals. In turn, Derby again became Prime Minister and, in the view of most reformers, their cause had again ignominiously failed. The surprise, the following year, was that the Tories successfully passed the 'Second Reform Act' which brought to an unexpected end that phase in British political development which supporters of the 1832 Act had supposed would represent a permanent solution. In doing so, Mr Disraeli showed that there was more way than one in which the past could be interpreted for the benefit of the present. He had his own ideas about an equilibrium.

Mr Disraeli's history

The oddest aspect of nineteenth-century British history was that at this critical juncture its political future lay in the hands of one who was an Italian Sephardi Jew by descent. It was perhaps a tribute to the openness of British society that this was the case, though a suspicion of Semites was by no means absent in the circles in which Disraeli moved. For some, he always remained, in Bismarck's words, 'the old Jew' dubiously qualified to lead an ancient and great nation as it grew mightier still and mightier.

That he was in some sense a 'foreigner' was something Disraeli never altogether denied. It made him seem even more mysterious than he already was. Yet, born in 1804, he could never have contemplated a political career as a young man if he had not been baptised a Christian, a little tardily, at the age of thirteen. Later in life he described himself as 'the blank page between the Old Testament and the New'. Reconciling past and present had a particular personal significance. To the British party which prided itself most on its essential Englishness he was to bring a self-consciously exotic and romantic touch which infuriated – until it was found necessary for the party's survival.

In 1817 it remained the case that every MP had to take his oath on the faith of a Christian. While it could be argued that atheists had not found this stipulation an undue impediment, Jews were likely to be more scrupulous. It was not until 1847, ten years after Disraeli had entered the Commons, that Lionel Rothschild was elected as member for the City of London. The House passed a resolution that he could not legally take his seat. For a decade passions ran high on the issue, but in 1858, when the Lords agreed to alter the required oaths, Rothschild became the first Jewish Member of Parliament.[11]

Disraeli had avoided these matters. On his father's side, he was third-generation British and on his mother's side he was fifth-generation British. That enabled him comfortably to lay claim to the British past. His father, amongst his other activities, had some status as a historian, though of Judaism rather than England. The family background was comfortably 'middle class', a secure background from which to criticize the comfortable middle class. Without the burden of a major public school or university education, the young Disraeli launched himself upon disastrous financial speculation, novel-writing and European and Mediterranean travel. After five attempts this dilettante dandy entered the Commons, with a trail of novels insecurely behind him. Two years earlier he had almost exhausted his stock of historical knowledge in a lengthy *Vindication of the English Constitution* which left the reader in no doubt that the Whigs had a lot to answer. Five years later, he loosely led 'Young England', a miscellaneous gathering which seemed devoted to Old England. Disraeli's critique of Peel's compromising Conservatism was developed in further novels, particularly in *Coningsby* (1844) and *Sybil* (1845). The view of present and past which they conveyed emerged from a novelist's imagination but nonetheless created a past that could be used.

---

11 D.S. Katz, *The Jews in the History of England 1485–1850* (Oxford, 1994); D. Feldman, *Englishmen and Jews: Social Relations and Political Culture 1840–1914* (London, 1994).

In the years that immediately followed, he pursued Peel remorselessly and ingeniously until the latter resigned in 1846. The split in the Tory ranks was, in the short term, fatal. Although, as has been noted, Lord Derby was able to form administrations, these were short-lived since the Tories lacked a Commons majority and, indeed, were not able to gain one until 1874. These were not ideal conditions for Disraeli to flesh out the political implications of his alternative Tory vision, a vision which would lead to 'One Nation'. Indeed, to some observers, it looked as though the barren defence of Protection – for Free Trade rapidly and almost universally came to be thought in Britain's interest – had only succeeded in consigning the Tory Party to the margins of British politics. It was a disgruntled rump with a proud past, a precarious present and no future. That was the situation apparently confronting Disraeli in 1866–67.

Equilibrium or oblivion?

Lord Derby was Prime Minister for a third time, but Disraeli's position in the Cabinet was pivotal. The ministry had been formed in an atmosphere of crisis – there had been riots in Hyde Park – and something, it seemed, had to be done about Reform. Then, however, the temperature of the issue dropped and it was not until January 1867 that government plans to extend the household suffrage, with plurality of voting, moved forward. The twists and turns of what followed cannot be elaborated here. In its passage, the measure introduced in March became broader in its scope than Disraeli himself had anticipated. It was with difficulty that he kept his own side on board. In the event, in England and Wales (with subsequent separate and somewhat different measures for Scotland and Ireland) the Representation of the People Act extended the borough franchise to householders with a one-year residential qualification, and to lodgers in premises worth £10 a year, also with a one-year qualification. In the counties, it created an occupation franchise for those occupying lands worth £12 a year and a property qualification for those with lands worth £5 a year. In round terms, the net effect of the changes was to raise the proportion of voters in England and Wales from one in five to one in three and in Scotland from one in eight to one in three. A Redistribution Bill transferred some seats between county and borough constituencies, largely in an attempt to mitigate the consequences for the Conservatives of their triumphal 'success'. Even with the assistance of a helpful Boundary Commission, many Conservatives feared the worst. It was no doubt an achievement to have 'dished the Whigs' but this 'leap in the dark' could well still end in electoral disaster.

In his remaining months in office – and he at last became Prime Minister in February 1868 – Disraeli sought in some measure to make the Tory

Party attractive to some sections of the new electorate. A Factory Act Extension Act, together with an Hours of Labour Regulation Bill, showed a concern for the conditions in which women and children worked. Public health measures not only gave local authorities powers but also prescribed them duties, with penalties if they defaulted. In short, an embryonic 'Social Conservatism' could be discerned which took short steps away from *laissez-faire*, but the ministry did not last long enough for its substance to be tested. In 1868 Gladstone gained a substantial victory in the general election under the new franchise. Disraeli's adventure might have given the country a new plateau of political stability, but, if so, that fresh national equilibrium perhaps also still threatened his party's oblivion.

The franchise framework: *c.*1868–1914

No understanding of political change during this period is possible without a grasp of the underlying franchise framework. In 1872 the introduction of the secret ballot made a significant change in the activity of voting. It had long been opposed on the ground that any man of character should be willing to declare his allegiance publicly. His intentions would be known to those who might seek, by one means or another, to get him to change his mind. While there were indeed benefits for some, it was coming to be thought that voting was a sacred activity, removed so far as possible from either blandishments or coercion as exercised, for example, by some landlords.

The basis of this political system was altered once more in 1884–85 by a further extension of the franchise and constituency redistribution – arrangements which were to last until 1918. In the latter case, there was an attempt to create new seats and thereby introduce some kind of uniformity in the electoral jungle inherited from the past. An attempt was to be made to work to a common population size (50,000) for each constituency. It became clear, however, that this was easier said than done. In any case, the historic principle that 'communities' should be represented rather than abstract units of population still had force and excited feeling. The abolition of two-member constituencies did, however, severely dent the sense in which great cities as coherent entities were represented.

This Third Reform Act created less enthusiasm and controversy than either of its predecessors. There was a grudging admission, even amongst opponents, that further reform was inevitable. Even so, there was no abrupt and comprehensive change from the 1867 franchise to one which accepted the principle of 'one person one vote'. The changes that were introduced, which included making the basis of the franchise more uniform throughout the United Kingdom than it had ever been before, produced a system in which no more than six out of ten adult males could vote in parliamentary elections before 1914. Most of them did so in their capacity as householders, whether owners or tenants. Very wide discrepancies continued to exist between constituencies in their levels of enfranchisement. One further, and arguably anomalous, survival was the university franchise. In addition, the registration requirements reduced considerably the ability to vote of those who were eligible to do so.

A Liberal era?

At first sight, Disraeli's gamble, if such it was, seemed to be a disaster. In the first election under the new franchise in 1868 it was Gladstone, whose party had a majority of 116, to whom the queen turned to form a new government. Disraeli did not even wait for Parliament to meet before resigning. It would be tempting to see in this first fully 'Liberal' government a significant turning point in British nineteenth-century history. It would be an administration whose 'progressive' credentials would push Britain inexorably in the direction of 'democracy'. Such an interpretation ignores the pedigree of the new Prime Minister. It turned out that that category of men who in 1864 were still, in Gladstone's mind, 'a political danger' and who therefore existed outside the pale of the constitution was quite broad. It included those who lacked 'self-command, self-control, respect for order, patience under suffering, confidence in the law, regard for superiors'.[12] Although 'household suffrage' had in the event brought him electoral victory, he had been less than enthusiastic about it.

In 1866 Gladstone still believed that 'England' stood uniquely poised between what he called the feudal institutions under which European states were formed, which had given the country 'her hierarchy of classes', and the United States, where the basis of society rested upon the principles of equality.[13] 'England', by its peculiar historical and geographical position, could still blend past and present distinctively. Worthy working men, liberally endowed with regard for superiors, could be incorporated into political society. There was no reason to suppose, so he argued, that the working classes, if enfranchised, 'would act together as a class'. Voting was not an abstract right, but the privilege of those who possessed appropriate qualities. Since 'regard for order' featured prominently amongst these qualities, Gladstone's Liberalism hardly heralded its radical overthrow.

In confident mood, some Liberals saw themselves as shaping a new era. 'Liberal Britain' would stretch far into the future and establish its defining

---

[12] Matthew, *Gladstone 1809–74*, p. 139.
[13] Ibid., p. 140.

8.2 House party at Haddo House, Aberdeenshire. Mr Gladstone did not altogether forget the fact that, by descent, he was a Scot. It was sensible, he found, for a Scot to manage his investments. He liked Scottish company, particularly when it was aristocratic but also generously inclined (as this photograph of him in 1884 at Haddo House, home of the Earl and Countess of Aberdeen indicates) to give him due prominence. Lord Aberdeen's father, like Gladstone, had begun life as a Conservative but became leader of a Whig-Peelite ministry which fell in 1855 over the management of the Crimean War.

characteristics. After May 1915, however, when the wartime Liberal government broadened into a coalition, there was never again to be a British Liberal administration. A rump Liberal Party contrived to struggle on into the late twentieth century but, despite occasional claims of revival, remained a shadow of its former self. The 'Liberal era' was therefore a mere half century, however much 'Liberalism' subsequently penetrated the outlooks of other parties. Even in this half century, of course, Liberal domination was by no means complete, indeed in aggregate there were Liberal governments in office for only half of this period (1868–74, 1880–85, a few months of 1886, 1892–95, 1905–15). Nevertheless, despite Conservative administrations, Liberals continued to believe, though perhaps with diminishing confidence, that the future was inexorably theirs.

The Liberal mansion (1): Whigs, a wasting asset?

It was essential for Gladstone to be able to demonstrate in 1868 that the motley band of Whigs, Liberals and Radicals who had now been loosely associated for over a decade had indeed come together as 'the Liberal Party'. As such, it attempted both to lay claim to some two centuries of Whiggery and the sacred scrolls of the 1688 Revolution, but also could now countenance elements of that radicalism which had been driven underground a century later. While there could be a sense of fellow-feeling with Abraham Lincoln, the Liberal Party was not an American export, still less was it a transplant from the European mainland where parties with the same name mushroomed. It came from the British past.

Although 'Whig', as a party label, disappeared at this juncture, it was important to Gladstone to be able to incorporate the Whig inheritance, not least because he had not himself shared it, except as a result of matrimony. When Gladstone resigned the party leadership after his election defeat in 1874, it was Lord Hartington, son of the Duke of Devonshire, who succeeded him in the Commons. It was not clear, however, what Whiggery now stood for in any ideological sense. To speak of an 'inheritance' is quite appropriate since, whatever it was, it was something transmitted by aristocratic families who took care in their breeding. From the comfort and security of a great house, a Whig aristocrat demonstrated a certain indifference to the more parochial orthodoxies of squire and parson. What one historian has referred to as their 'gentle rhetoric' and their willingness to evolve a strange commuting existence between national and local levels, still gave Whigs an important mediating role in the equally gentle movement away from aristocratic government.[14]

It comes as no surprise, therefore, that even in 1880 when he formed his second government, Gladstone was happy to find space in a Cabinet of twelve members for a duke, a marquess and five earls. They provided a

---

[14] M. Bentley, *Politics without Democracy 1815–1914* (London, 1984) p. 6; A. Adonis, *Making Aristocracy Work: The Peerage and the Political System in Britain, 1884–1914* (Oxford, 1993); D. Cannadine, *The Decline and Fall of the British Aristocracy* (London, 1990). There are many insights to be gained from Sir John Habakkuk's monumental study, *Marriage, Debt and the Estates System: English Landownership, 1650–1950* (Oxford, 1994).

counter-balance which Gladstone deemed necessary to pushy provincials like Joseph Chamberlain. Whig Liberalism of mind, however, was increasingly accompanied by anxiety about the security of property, particularly for those families – like that of Lord Lansdowne, for example – whose holdings existed on both sides of the Irish Sea. There was satisfaction in the degree of deference Gladstone felt obliged to show, and felt no great hardship in showing, but it was no substitute for the erosion of real power which urban Radicals of the stamp of Joseph Chamberlain or John Bright at least appeared to be threatening. The result was a steady drift away from the Liberal Party, either directly to the Tories or indirectly to the Liberal Unionists who emerged when Irish Home Rule split the Liberal Party in the mid-1880s. Nevertheless, it was an earl (Lord Rosebery) who briefly and unsuccessfully followed Gladstone as Liberal Prime Minister in 1894. Some Whig ornaments still survived in the Liberal Party as the twentieth century opened and gave a fig-leaf of covering to the notion that it was political doctrine rather than class alignment which separated the two major parties in the emerging world of mass politics. There was still an initial place in Asquith's 1908 government for the Marquess of Ripon who had served under Gladstone in 1868. His durability is even more remarkable when it is recalled that he had become a Roman Catholic in the early 1870s – the first to serve in a Liberal administration. Taken in the round, however, the Whigs were a wasting asset, though their passage out of British history was protracted and difficult to pinpoint exactly.

The Liberal mansion (2): men of business

It is sometimes argued that what made the Liberals more of a 'national' party than their rivals was the fact that they embraced much more of commercial and industrial Britain. There is truth in the observation, but the significance of the embrace was problematic. Indeed, in talking of nineteenth-century transitions, nothing is more difficult to summarize than the relationship between men of business and the political scene. The paradoxes puzzled contemporaries, particularly foreigners, as much as they have done subsequent historians. An advanced industrial country, by the standards of the time, whose people lived by commerce, or thought they did, was still governed, at the top, by a political elite whose way of life and personal experience was, in general, remote from this world. Why did 'the middle class' fail to make a more immediate and profound impact? Was the failure to make a more visible and dramatic transition in this period a source of enduring weakness thereafter?

Various answers are possible. 'Business' is itself far from being a homogeneous category with a single objective and outlook. Also, speaking generally, the British landed aristocracy continued to show, by European standards, an unusual degree of interest in industry and commerce. The cultural cleavage, therefore, while it could be profound, was not invariably so. The inter-relationships make the simple categorization of MPs in this period somewhat arbitrary, but in the Liberal Party the percentage engaged in commerce, finance and industry hovered around 40 per cent, with no marked trend emerging. Roughly the same percentage can be described as 'professional', about half of whom were lawyers.

More simply, men of business found their world too engrossing and rewarding to forsake it. Politics was an expensive business and it required formidable energy and stamina to both pursue a political career and remain an active businessman. It is not surprising, therefore, that the two 'businessmen' in Gladstone's government – Chamberlain and Bright – had either taken 'early retirement' or had never in fact been very active. It was also transparently the case that success in business did not guarantee success in national politics. It has been noted, for example, that Samuel Holland, Liberal MP for Merionethshire (1870–85), only rose to his feet in the Commons half a dozen times in twice as many years. Business was business and the affairs of his enterprises remained his most important concern throughout.

Later, in January 1910, after the deadlocked general election, Lloyd George was reported to be toying with the idea of creating a 'government of businessmen', with himself as premier. 'They are very simple people, these Captains of Industry', he remarked, 'I can do what I like with them. I found that out at the Board of Trade.'[15] It is not altogether surprising, therefore, that involvement in local government was often a more feasible proposition. Joseph Chamberlain was exceptional in making the transition from local to national government.[16]

In any case, Gladstone, building on his Peelite training, believed he had established the proper framework which set the parameters for the respective spheres of government and commerce/industry. Central government should not expand inexorably. It was the duty of Parliament to 'balance its accounts as a neutral onlooker, beholden neither to employer nor worker, merely ensuring in the world market–place the cheapest bargain for the British consumer'. It was the duty of what would now be described as the 'voluntary sector'[17] to

---

[15] G. Searle, *Entrepreneurial Politics in Mid-Victorian Britain* (Oxford, 1993) and 'The Edwardian Liberal Party and Business', *English Historical Review* 386 (Jan. 1983) p. 39.
[16] D. Fraser, 'Joseph Chamberlain and the Municipal Ideal' in G. Marsden, ed., *Victorian Values* (London, 1990) pp. 135–46. For weighty considerations of local government in all its complexity see D. Eastwood, *Governing Rural England: Tradition and Transformation in Local Government 1780–1840* (Oxford, 1994) and R. Trainor, *Black Country Elites: The Exercise of Authority in an Industrialized Area, 1830–1900* (Oxford, 1993).
[17] C. Matthew, 'Gladstonian Finance' in Marsden, ed., *Victorian Values*, p. 116.

attend to pauperism and the admitted casualties of a capitalism which lurched in imperfectly understood cycles from periods of great prosperity to periods of great distress.

Such a 'minimalist' concept of central government and the financial system which underpinned it may have been ideal for that particular phase of British development. The difficulty for the Liberal Party lay in the prime ministerial longevity of Gladstone, something which could never have been anticipated when he first became Prime Minister at the age of fifty-nine in 1868. It is persuasively argued that, notwithstanding his own changes of mind, he lacked a sense of flux and the impermanence of all political arrangements. He sought a final settlement of the state and could see little reason, once he believed he had more or less achieved it, why the 1890s should be any different from the 1860s. In being 'unusual among British Prime Ministers in expecting the permanent settlement of some fundamental questions of economic policy',[18] Gladstone greatly complicated the process of transition for his Liberal successors. Younger men, conscious in the 1880s and 1890s of unemployment (a new word), of social deprivation and of apparently rising social tension, believed that if Liberalism was to survive, and the country was to evolve peacefully, a more positive view of the role of the state was required.

Identification as the 'party of business' was therefore somewhat hazardous. Gladstone himself, son of a self-made millionaire, had strong views on the perils of wealth generation and risk-taking. One indication of instability was the collapse of the Savings Bank in Glasgow in 1878. Speaking in the city in the following year as Lord Rector of its university, he lamented the emergence of a new and powerful 'class of hybrid or bastard men of business' drawn from many walks of life. Such people, acting rashly, were united by a desire for gain which went beyond 'the legitimate produce of toil by hand or brain'. His reservations, while no doubt genuine, were to prove increasingly necessary if the party was also to sustain its appeal to the enfranchised working class.

However, speaking in the Commons in May 1900, Campbell-Bannerman, the Liberal leader, uttered an inter-party commonplace when he claimed that Britain had 'happily been free for two or three generations from any imputation of mercenary or corrupt motives on the part of our public men'.[19] The Panama Scandal in France a few years earlier, and the normal assumption that the United States seethed with corruption, led Campbell-Bannerman to the comforting conclusion that his analysis of Britain applied to few other countries. When he became Prime Minister, Campbell-Bannerman revived Gladstone's rule, imposed on his fourth ministry, that ministers

---

[18] H.C.G. Matthew, *Gladstone 1875–1898* (Oxford, 1995) pp. 52–3.
[19] See the discussion of the subject in G.R. Searle, *Corruption in British Politics, 1895–1930* (Oxford, 1987).

had to divest themselves of all their company directorships before taking up office.

The Asquith government, though stiff with lawyers, was not without its business links, and the Prime Minister's second wife was the daughter of Sir Charles Tennant, the multi-millionaire chemicals manufacturer. Lloyd George, as Chancellor of the Exchequer, sailed perilously close to the wind on occasion and was almost sunk by the Marconi Scandal (1912–13). Indeed, one historian rejects altogether a conventional picture of a Liberal Party too divorced from business in this decade for its own good. Rather, he sees the social and commercial connections between leading ministers and their wealthy business supporters as being often 'dangerously tight'.[20] In 1871 Gladstone felt that, from a political view, the 'spirit of plutocracy' required to be vigilantly watched and checked. It would have been difficult to look at the Liberal government in 1914 and believe that this had been effectively done. Campbell-Bannerman, whose own inherited fortune came from Glasgow business, might not have been quite as happy as he was in 1900.

The Liberal mansion (3): a supply of conscience

In comparison with dignified Whig reticence and whatever backstairs activity might have been engaged in by Liberal businessmen and financiers, much public noise and rhetoric emerged from other quarters in this party of precarious unity. In particular, the Liberal Party provided a vehicle for the political re-emergence of a religious Dissent which had been marginalized since the time of Cromwell and which still smarted under certain grievances. It was with consternation that Gladstone had studied the outcome of the 1851 religious census and saw the strength of religious Dissent which it disclosed. Twenty years later, though he still found their lack of a sacramental sense defective, Gladstone found that he shared with Nonconformist leaders that sense of a national mission under God in which he believed. A tea meeting with a 'conclave of Dissenters' led him, somewhat to his surprise, to conclude that their teeth and claws were 'not very terrible'. The number of Nonconformist MPs increased (to sixty-two in 1874, for example) and their alignment with Liberalism was clear.

Things seemed to be going the way of Dissenters as irksome reminders of past exclusions or symbols of second-class status were removed – religious oaths for public office in 1866, church rates in 1868 – and by 1871 Nonconformists were able to take part on almost equal terms in Oxford and Cambridge. There remained, however, many educational matters on which Dissenters felt strongly and on which they embarrassed both Gladstone and

---

[20] Searle, 'Edwardian Liberal Party', p. 39.

his prime ministerial successors from 1870 onwards. The most conspicuous example of their opposition was the 'passive resistance' campaign mounted in opposition to the favours extended to Anglican education under the 1902 Education Act. In 1869 Gladstone disestablished the Anglican Church in Ireland and agitation to achieve the same objective waxed in Wales. The Liberation Society, which saw itself as 'part of the Liberal force in each constituency', believed it saw the prospect of disestablishment in England.[21] Nonconformists spawned many other pressure groups reflecting their concern with education, temperance and peace. Their multiplicity, however, was both a strength and an embarrassment. Prime ministers had to look about for 'single issues' around which disparate enthusiasts might conceivably cohere.

In the opinion of one leading Dissenter, the political changes which Liberalism was effecting meant that as the privileges and ascendancy of the Established Church were removed so there was an opportunity for the Church, as a free collective religious society, to 'become all the more capable of being the social conscience, at once individual and common' of the nation. Here was the 'Nonconformist Conscience' which, for a time, gave Liberalism a distinctive colouring. The relationship could lead to hyperbole, as when one boastful Congregationalist claimed in 1877 that 'the history of Liberalism is identical with the history of English liberty, and it may be said with equal truth that Congregationalism is identical with Liberalism ... '. But, under Gladstone's orchestration, no one could mistake British Liberalism in this era for that European Liberalism which often had a strong anti-religious or at least anticlerical tinge.[22] The moral and religious colouring attaching to British Liberalism, insofar as it permeated British public life as a whole, also gave rise to a strong external perception that what defined the British at this juncture was their capacity for hypocrisy.

Even by 1914, however, some Nonconformist leaders were having second thoughts about this rhetoric. It was no doubt gratifying that after the Liberal election victory of 1906 there were more Nonconformists in the House of Commons than at any time since Cromwell, but had not Nonconformity become too much a 'part of the Liberal force' and lost its essential religious impulse? In addition, as other groups had found in the past, with the removal of the disabilities under which Nonconformity had laboured for centuries, it proved increasingly difficult to sustain a sense of group identity. A specific illustration is provided by H.H. Asquith, Liberal Prime Minister after 1908, whose original Dissenting credentials wilted under the impact of

---

[21] Cited in M. Johnson, *The Dissolution of Dissent, 1850–1918* (London, 1987) p. 56.

[22] S. Koss, *Nonconformity in Modern British Politics* (London, 1975) and D. Bebbington, *The Nonconformist Conscience: Chapel and Politics 1870–1914* (London, 1982) for further discussion.

Balliol College, Oxford, and the Bar, not to mention his second wife. The healing of the past which Liberalism appeared to have achieved was therefore to prove a double-edged sword for both Liberalism and Nonconformity.

Conservative come-back (1): Disraelian apotheosis

Defeat in 1868 inevitably raised questions in Conservative ranks both about Disraeli's maverick style and about the role the party could aspire to play. Disraeli himself, not in good health, reacted calmly to his fate and settled down to write a financially rewarding novel, *Lothair* (1870). In Hatfield House (his home), the new Marquess of Salisbury refurbished his domestic chapel and resumed his writing career, one which was rather different from that of the Prime Minister. In the *Quarterly Review* he took the line that the attempt to outbid the Whigs and appeal to a supposed new constituency in the country – he expressed himself sardonically on the subject of 'the gratitude of the artisans' – was a short-term failure and would prove a long-term disaster. The duty of a Conservative Party was simple: it was to preserve the power of the middle and upper classes. He watched with dismay as Gladstone meddled with the universities, tampered with the army (by abolishing the right to purchase commissions) and emphasized his commitment to opening up the Civil Service to competitive examination. Such interference with institutions which, in Salisbury's eyes, had served the country well over centuries should be firmly resisted. He was infuriated by what he regarded as Disraeli's insouciant conduct. Since the two men did not speak to each other, however, it was not easy to have a useful exchange of views. In other country houses, other Tory notables took to thinking that party prospects would improve under another leader.

From 1872 onwards, perhaps because he felt better, perhaps because he had no other novel to write, perhaps because he sensed that dissatisfaction with his leadership was becoming more serious, perhaps because he sensed the government's growing discomfiture, Disraeli became more active and vocal. He made big speeches, notably in Manchester and at the Crystal Palace. Five minutes at the former occasion on the subject of health legislation have sometimes been seized on, perhaps with some exaggeration, as an indication of a defining thrust for future Conservative policy. He was perhaps happier speaking at the Crystal Palace when he reiterated that the 1867 Reform Act had been based on the belief that the working classes were, in the 'purest and loftiest' sense, Conservative. They were proud to belong to a great and imperial country. They believed 'on the whole' that England's imperial greatness was to be 'attributed to the ancient institutions of the land'. He contrasted the 'national' ideas of the Conservatives with the cosmopolitan or, even worse, continental ideas which had infected the governing party.

8.3 Prepare to serve: Napoleon's characterization of at least the English as 'a nation of shopkeepers' is only a provocative generalization. However, there was a remarkable prodigality in the shops of Britain – ranging from the emerging department store to the corner shop. On both sides of his family, the present author stems from Victorian small shopkeepers. In this family group of 1897, his great–grandparents are posed proprietorially outside their corner-shop general store in Totterdown, Bristol, while his grandfather holds the pony.

Perhaps Lord Salisbury could take comfort from the praise of ancient institutions, but it could hardly be said that Disraeli's reference gave any specific indication as to what might be done, or need to be done, to preserve them in the present. In fact, Disraeli viewed change now with a mellow detachment which contrasted with Salisbury's youthful immobilism. He was also seasoned enough to know that if he were ever to be Prime Minister it would not be because the country would succumb to an enthusiasm for the past as it was perceived from Hatfield House. It was because the Liberal government, debilitatingly enmeshed in the complexities surrounding the university system in Ireland and other matters, would indeed come to constitute that 'range of exhausted volcanoes' Disraeli had so brilliantly identified in his Manchester speech.

So it proved. In March 1873 Disraeli refused to take office prematurely after a Liberal defeat in the Commons. In January 1874 Gladstone called an unexpected election. Helped in particular by the advance of the Irish Home

Rule Party, at the expense of Irish Liberals, Disraeli at last carried the day and formed a majority government, the first Conservative administration for thirty-three years. Put simply, a fall or division in the Liberal vote, as compared with 1868, lies behind the outcome rather than any positive endorsement of whatever Disraelian Conservatism was supposed to be. A playing of the 'Protestant' card helped in certain constituencies. And, given the extent to which the personal rivalry between Gladstone and Disraeli had been a familiar feature of British politics for nearly thirty years, if the electorate had tired of Gladstone then Disraeli was the only conceivable alternative.

Sensing that the mood of the country was conservative, in the sense that it desired a rest from Gladstonian changes, Disraeli certainly saw no virtue in a counter-revolutionary Conservatism. The institutional imprint left by Gladstone could not be reversed. The past could not be recalled. So a new balance had to be struck and, as if symbolically, Disraeli's small Cabinet was made up of six peers and six commoners. Middle-class men of business were there too – Cross as Home Secretary and, in 1877, W.H. Smith, the news-agent, as First Lord of the Admiralty. A significant and growing number of Tory MPs can be categorized as 'business and commerce', though there remained a greater 'landed' element than was to be found on the Liberal benches. Lord Salisbury, with pained expression, accepted first the India Office and, later, the Foreign Office. That gave him ample opportunity to engage himself in external matters and take his mind momentarily off the social deluge that was undoubtedly still approaching.

Disraeli was substantially free to return to the theme of social improvement and reconciliation which had found expression in his early novels and which had fitfully been returned to thereafter. Few historians, however, detect, in the legislation that followed, signs that Disraeli himself had a sequence of detailed proposals to hand which were then systematically implemented. Having said that, however, he did give support to those ministers whose task it was to carry through legislation. There was also a discernible difference in emphasis from comparable Gladstonian measures – an Intoxicating Liquors Act was more sympathetic to brewers and publicans than the Licensing Act of 1872. This was most importantly also displayed in a Conspiracy and Protection of Property Act which legalized peaceful picketing and an Employers and Workmen Act. The language used in the title of the latter act was significantly different from the Liberal 'Master and Servant' and went further in freeing workers from liability to criminal prosecution for breach of contract than Gladstone was prepared to go.

In these measures, it is possible to detect a difference in approach between Liberal individualism and a Conservative acceptance of group interests, but it should not be pushed too far. Neither should there be an absolute contrast between a Liberal permissive approach and a Conservative willingness to develop state compulsion. The 1875 Public Health Act did have a strong whiff of compulsion but the Artisans Dwelling Act was an enabling act empowering local authorities to undertake improvements if they wished, which most, for whatever reason, were slow to do.

It is not plausible to see in these measures, which cannot be discussed in more detail here, the first steps towards a Tory 'Welfare State'. On the other hand, the social legislation was not accidental. To seek to gain the 'lasting affection' of the working classes was perhaps too ambitious an objective but the Conservatives had some reason to suppose that they had forestalled or contained pressure from below which might otherwise have placed Disraeli's prized 'ancient institutions' in jeopardy. For the Tories to go further and seek to outflank the Liberals by becoming the 'party of the working classes' was an impossibility, given the prominence of 'business' within their own ranks. In effect, despite the public rhetoric that divided them, necessary in a competitive struggle for office, the two great parties did not greatly differ in their approach to the task of 'incorporation'.

In any event, after the government's initial display of domestic energy, issues of foreign policy, for both good and ill, came to the fore in the later 1870s and engaged Disraeli's attention. Since they also brought Gladstone back into the political arena after his initial retirement as party leader in 1875, politics again had an appearance of gladiatorial personal conflict. Disraeli himself moved to the House of Lords as Earl of Beaconsfield in 1876. When the election came in 1880 he had sadly to admit that he had failed to give the party continuity in government. 'The People's William', fresh from his oratorical performances in Midlothian, was back in power. A year later Disraeli was dead, still leaving Tory MPs wondering whether he had destroyed their party or rescued it from an impending oblivion.

Conservative come-back (2): gloom and doom

The 3rd Marquess of Salisbury, who now took over the leadership of the Conservative Party in the Lords, with Northcote in the Commons, had a marked tendency to depression from his earliest years. Not even the luxuriant beard which he sported in his maturity could disguise his endemic pessimism. Some expressions of his alarm at the pace of change have already been noted. It had taken nearly 300 years for that Cecil genius, so evident in the reigns of Elizabeth and James I, to manifest itself again, but such a pedigree ensured an acute awareness of the past and a sense of insecurity in the present. Such anxiety, however, was not merely the product of a lugubrious disposition. It reflected the concern of a penetrating mind that the network of families upon whom the governance of Britain had so long rested was about to be swamped. That elite, no doubt, had its own interests, but it also possessed a certain disinterested capacity to judge where the 'national interest' lay. There was something spurious in the notion that 'the people' constituted what he called 'an acting, deciding, accessible authority'. The outcome of a particular general election could turn on how a relatively small number of votes were cast in particular constituencies – and the outcome in 1880 was a case in point. Although MPs pretended otherwise, what 'the people' decided at an election did not necessarily have any close bearing on their feelings on particular issues four or five years later.

It was no accident that the last article Salisbury published in the *Quarterly Review* in 1883 had the title 'Disintegration'. The transition to 'popular government' made inevitable by 1867, and which Salisbury had opposed then, was not some kind of logical adjustment but rather a step towards social disintegration. The Conservative Party and the House of Lords now stood out as the only institutions which could provide effective opposition to a Liberal Party which, in his view, bore scant resemblance to the party of Grey and Palmerston. Salisbury had little inclination to 'trust the people'. Such reflections chimed in well with misgivings being expressed at the time by some Conservative writers. On the other hand, for Disraeli's political heirs, what was being promulgated was a strategy which accepted – gloomily and disastrously – that the Conservatives could not be other than a minority party, committed to the past, unhappy in the present and with no governing future. The best that could be hoped for, it seemed, was a Liberal government which would be in office but which would be too weak for 'violent legislation'. In such a circumstance 'the professional advocates of change find themselves by the force of circumstances retained to defend inaction'.[23]

Despite this prognosis, Salisbury found himself in office as Prime Minister on three occasions (1885, 1886–92, 1895–1902) and, but for the three brief years of Liberal government between 1892 and 1895, it appears to make sense to refer to this period as 'the Conservative Ascendancy'. Such dominance *after* the Third Reform Act would appear to be perplexing. Salisbury's 1885 government was a minority administration following the Liberal government's defeat on a budget amendment. It took office only until the election under the new franchise which was imminent. Queen Victoria could have chosen either Northcote or even Lord Randolph Churchill, both in the Commons, but she was on the watch for 'strong and able and safe men' and only Salisbury seemed able to oblige. He could not oblige with an election victory, however, but within a couple of months of Gladstone's return the Liberal Party split disastrously on the question of Irish Home Rule. In 1886, although the Gladstonians still outpolled the Conservatives, the Conservatives and their Liberal Unionist allies – the most prominent of whom was Joseph Chamberlain – had a substantial majority over the Liberals and Irish Home Rulers. What was in Gladstone's mind when he 'converted' to Irish Home Rule has been much speculated upon and the late-nineteenth-century

---

[23] Cited in P.T. Marsh, *The Discipline of Popular Government* (Hassocks, 1978), p. 37.

'Irish question' will be considered further subsequently. Its consequence, however, so long as Liberal reunion proved impossible, as it did, was that Salisbury could exercise power. The most important sphere in which he could do so was the field, after all, in which he had acquired expertise – foreign affairs. He was his own Foreign Secretary until 1900 when he made way, in his last two years as Prime Minister, for Lord Lansdowne. But the affairs of the greatest empire in the world, if they were to be successfully managed, required a quiescent domestic population so far as possible.

Lord Randolph Churchill was made Chancellor of the Exchequer and the exponent of 'Tory Democracy' and son of the Duke of Marlborough seemed poised to rise even higher. In rhetoric and demeanour there could apparently be no greater political contrast than between Salisbury and himself, scions of English nobility though they both were. Lord Randolph claimed to have no fear of democracy. The people could be trusted. Checks and securities to protect minorities were not worth 'a brass farthing'. However, when Lord Randolph soon resigned on a relatively minor matter, what 'Tory Democracy' might have become in practice was academic. Despite occasional wavering, Joseph Chamberlain remained in support. A.J. Balfour, the Prime Minister's nephew seemed to be a coming man.

It would, of course, be quite misleading to suppose that in his second and third governments Salisbury placed a complete embargo on domestic legislation. The Local Government Act (1888) had profound consequences for rural Britain. It took local government out of the hands of that rural elite which had in effect governed counties for centuries through the quarter sessions. Some individuals from the pre-1888 era did still continue to play major roles in the new elected structures but party politics began to make its mark. In many rural areas, the impact of local government reform was greater than anything that was going on at Westminster. In the creation of a Board of Agriculture (1889) and in passing a Tithes Act (1891) and a Small Holdings Act (1892) the government responded with some success to the problems of a rural economy which, for more than a decade, had been in some distress. In general, it could be argued that the Prime Minister had at least a passing interest in domestic reform. That, however, was not the point. The 'discipline of popular government', to use Professor Marsh's term, required that the electorate should understand that good government should not be confused with endless legislation. Much of the government's time was, of course, spent in trying to tackle Irish issues and discontent. There, too, it believed that good government would calm dissent. The exercise of government, Salisbury came to see, required some adaptation on his part. He recognized that the wheels of the party machine had to be oiled for electoral purposes, though its pretensions had to be curbed. Salisbury had to pretend that he enjoyed speaking at large public meetings. He had to pretend to enjoy visiting Scotland. These were his own modest contributions to social integration.

At another level, the contribution of the Primrose League – the highly structured Conservative organization founded in 1883 to forward the aims of 'Tory Democracy' – was immeasurably greater. Its 'habitations' proved a convenient rampart to the Conservative faith. The Liberal Party could not compete with the champagne luncheon offered to all-comers at Blenheim by the Duke of Marlborough at which the local merchant's wife met the squire's wife and the parish councillor met the Duke of Marlborough himself.

Yet when Salisbury made way for his nephew, Balfour, in 1902, it was not clear either to himself or to contemporaries precisely what he had achieved. From his perspective, it could appear that the skills of party management which he had refined might only, at the end, have achieved but a further period of delay. He had kept the past alive for twenty years. *The Times* commented that his 'half-cynical superiority' had enabled him to lay a strong hand upon popular movements by measuring them and checking their extremes. It concluded, however, that he had only 'more or less' succeeded. To what end if, after him, came the deluge?

Sinister assault?

There were also some who forecast a deluge when Edward VII, the new king-emperor, ascended the throne in 1901 at the age of fifty-nine. The merry monarch stood in distinct contrast to his mother. Mr Gladstone's worst fears concerning the triumph of hedonism were to be realized. In his behaviour the monarch again seemed to personify a shift in the public mood, or at least one section of it, towards greater 'permissiveness'. In this respect there was real meaning to be attached to the change between the 'Victorian' age and the 'Edwardian' age. The king liked to meet the people, though he took a fierce dislike to being 'snap-shotted', whether at racecourses or elsewhere. It would be wrong, however, simply to perceive the Edwardian monarchy through a haze of cigar smoke. The king certainly did not understand himself to be merely a ceremonial figure, even though the ceremonial reached new heights. He was, for a time, variously described as 'Uncle of Europe' and 'Edward the Peacemaker'. His interest in military and naval matters could be serious. He held out, in the end unsuccessfully, against the introduction of khaki uniforms in the British army. In domestic politics, he did not relish the prospect that his Liberal Prime Minister would require him to create sufficient peers to allow the proposed Parliament Bill to pass through the House of Lords. He rather liked the powers the House of Lords still retained. In the event, he did not have to make a decision since he died in May 1910 in the middle of the crisis. His reign, at one level, suggested a mood of self-confidence and assertion. At another, however, there was more than a suspicion that the splendour of his short reign was superficial.

189

The extent to which, at the end of the century, the two major parties with recognizable roots in the past had nonetheless apparently succeeded in adjusting to very different electoral circumstances was thought to be remarkable. No other European country could point to such continuity. In part it was because, although occasionally advocated in some quarters, the British system avoided proportional representation. The franchise was extended, but MPs were still elected on a 'first past the post' basis. The two major parties remained broad churches and the obstacles to the emergence of third parties, or more, were substantial. Latterly, the dispute that had split the Liberal Party arose from disagreement over how to handle Ireland rather than from a more broadly based ideological cleavage. The blatant identification of political parties with specific class or confessional interests, characteristic of some other European countries, was missing. But perhaps for not much longer.

It had not escaped attention that socialist parties, wedded more or less to Marxist doctrine, seemed to be advancing fast – in Germany, for example.[24] In theory at least, such parties were revolutionary in orientation and they rejected as bourgeois, or even worse, the system in which with reluctance they functioned. Such participation was supposedly only temporary, though some 'revisionists' openly accepted that the road to socialism could lie through the existing parliamentary institutions. On mainland Europe there was a widespread, and seemingly justified, assumption that socialism would prove inexorably attractive to the 'industrial proletariat' as that grew in size in different countries.

In this context, the situation in Britain appeared baffling to external observers and infuriating to some internal ones. Basic facts about British social and economic development should have led to the conclusion that Britain would have been in the van in producing a mass working-class party committed, in some sense, to socialism. In contrast to the position in France, for example, the agricultural sector had shrunk drastically. Around the turn of the century, only just over 10 per cent of the British working population was employed in agriculture, with the figure still declining, and around 75 per cent were manual workers. At this juncture, no other nation in the world was more 'working-class', but there was no mass party. There were, however, some indications that there might yet be one.

The trade union movement showed some signs of enlarging its constituency. Although the Trades Union Congress (TUC) had been formed in 1868, it was little more than a pressure group, largely on behalf of unions of skilled workers. In the late 1880s and 1890s, however, as increased bitterness entered some labour disputes, there was a 'New Unionism' which had a strength, although a somewhat fleeting strength, amongst dock, transport

---

[24] S. Berger, *The British Labour Party and the German Social Democrats 1900–1931: A Comparative Study* (Oxford, 1994).

8.4 The Great Dock Strike: The entire labour force of the London docks turned out in August 1889 to demand a rate of sixpence an hour – the "dockers' tanner" – and improved working conditions. Processions through the City of London gained sympathy from the public and press. In this famous photograph the coal heavers' float is shown, basket symbolically hoisted aloft. Despite popular support, dwindling resources made success look doubtful by the fifth week of the strike. A surprise grant of £30,000 from Australian trade unionists bolstered the campaign, however, and in early September the London dock companies were obliged to concede most of the strikers' demands, including the dockers' tanner.

and other general workers. The London Dock Strike (1889) was an illustration of this militancy. Even so, despite this growth, only a quarter of the male workforce was unionized and only a tiny proportion of the female. The issue was whether there was a need to match unionism with a specific political alignment. A few working men had been in the House of Commons since the 1870s, normally under a 'Lib-Lab' banner. Their number increased to nine by the mid-1880s and included three successive secretaries of the TUC among their number. That there were not more such men was a reflection of the difficulty in getting constituency associations to adopt them as candidates. Amongst engineers and railwaymen, in particular, there were moves to break with this tradition and seek political independence.

An Independent Labour Party (ILP) had been formed in Bradford in 1893 and had made some progress in the industrial towns of the north of England, and a little elsewhere, but it was far from being a mass party. In

London, a coterie of intellectuals had formed the Fabian Society in 1884 and had sponsored the publication of pamphlets on social, economic and political issues. The Society took its name from the Roman general Quintus Fabius Maximus whose military success had allegedly come about because of his infinite capacity to delay. Such an inspired title hardly suggested that the Fabian Society wished to jettison the present precipitately. The Social Democratic Federation, led by an ex-stockbroker, H.M. Hyndman, who had studied Marx, was prepared to take more risks. Hyndman and others obtained some prominence as a result of disorders which took place in Trafalgar Square in 1886. The Federation's attack on prevailing capitalism was serious but sectarian. So was the Socialist League under William Morris, poet and art-craftsman. 'Socialism', it was clear already, was a word with many meanings, but it was without difficulty that it was made to sound exotic and unBritish.

It was in 1900 in London that the ILP, the Fabians and some trade unionists came together to form the Labour Representation Committee. Its apparently limited objective was exemplified in its title. Not until six years later was the name 'the Labour Party' adopted and that designation was also significant. The word 'socialist' did not appear, even though the ILP was committed to 'public ownership'. In its new guise, major trade unions were won over, but even so, it was not clear that their members were wholeheartedly in favour. The party began to make some electoral progress – returning forty MPs in 1910 – but in circumstances of ambiguity. Was Labour really a separate body or was it, as an electoral pact of 1903 seemed to suggest, still in some sense aligned to Liberalism? Certainly there was some blurring of the allegiance of individuals. It was the tactic of Winston Churchill and David Lloyd George, then identified as the leading Radical Liberals, to flatter trade unionists while discounting the need for a separate party.

In examining this period, historians have come to very different conclusions about the Liberal/Labour relationship in the period leading up to 1914. For some, the Liberal government was engaged, from 1906 onwards, in a desperate struggle for survival against the burgeoning Labour Party. The measures introduced – from labour exchanges to old age pensions, culminating in Lloyd George's 1909 budget – have been seen as desperate attempts to delay Labour's advance. For others, that is far too simple a picture. The Liberal Party had won three successive elections and might have done so again in 1914–15, had one been held. Although detailed analyses of different parts of the country could produce different conclusions, the 'progressive' Liberal formula was still very attractive and the party was not collapsing on its knees as 'class' politics threatened. A summary cannot do justice to a complex problem. Perhaps one recent detailed study by Duncan Tanner comes close to the heart of the matter as things stood before 1914: 'The Liberals were not an entirely "viable" force, but Labour's capacity to replace them was not so evident that major electoral changes were inevitable. There were areas of Labour growth before 1914, and areas of Liberal success. The political system was an elaborate jigsaw.'[25]

There was no certainty amongst the new Labour leaders – men such as MacDonald, Snowden, Henderson and Hardie – about their precise socialist objectives. MacDonald assumed the mantle of intellectual and books and pamphlets argued the case for an evolutionary socialism which would grow out of existing structures and parties. Parliament would remain central to this process of change. There could be no revolutionary short-cut. When there was a further extension of the franchise and Labour was able to 'deliver' the working-class vote that would be its natural constituency, it would then be able to move Britain forward. Such an accommodating attitude to change, while not without its socialist critics, made the Labour Party an uncomfortable partner for European socialists for whom, whenever it came, socialism would emphatically constitute a clear break and the inauguration of a new era. It was difficult for Arthur Henderson, for example, Methodist, teetotaller, supporter of Newcastle United FC, to approach the past from a rejectionist standpoint.

The arguments about the meaning of, and the path towards, socialism in these years had important long-term consequences, but, in the short term they took place in a context of industrial conflict without parallel. There were individual causes of conflict in particular industries but historians generally agree that there was a pervasive sense of insecurity which is in turn normally linked to a fall in real wages. The total working days lost by stoppages rose from around 2 million in 1907 to 10 million in 1911 and peaked at 40 million in 1912. The year 1911 witnessed a long summer of discontent and fears/hopes that Britain was on the brink of mysterious but engulfing change. The long nineteenth-century process of accommodation and adjustment was at an end. It was being replaced by confrontation and conflict. 'Syndicalism' threatened, some contemporaries believed, at every turn. In South Wales, for example, the pamphlet *The Miners' Next Step* set out an agenda for workers to gain control of, and then administer, their particular industries. In its directness, the language was far removed from the evolutionary parliamentarism of MacDonald. The confluence of 'questions' – the industrial, the Irish, the women's – led contemporaries to feel that something cataclysmic was in the air.

Breaking the domestic mould?

In 1884 the franchise remained restricted to males. The issue, however, had been raised. John Stuart Mill, philosopher and economist, had written on the

---

[25] D. Tanner, *Political Change and the Labour Party 1900–1918* (Cambridge, 1990) p. 420.

subjection of women (1861) and had presented a women's petition to Parliament. Speaking there in 1867, he claimed that there was pervasive feeling
that women had no right 'to care about anything except they may be the
most useful and devoted servants of some man'. His motion lost by a large
majority. Patriarchy, it was clear, was far from being a thing of the past. The
influence of women on British party politics had not been altogether absent,
but it had been in their capacity as wives, mistresses and hostesses that it
had been exercised. That was how most men continued to want it to be. It
was clear in the period under review that a proportion of women, beginning
in the 'middle class', was no longer willing to accept the status which the
past had bequeathed to women. The basis on which women would be 'incorporated' into the positions of power and influence in structures of British
society was as problematic as the 'incorporation' of the 'working class'.

The 1884 Act highlighted the anomaly of their position, as it appeared
to many, though perhaps still not to most women. The Third Reform Act
swept aside the still prevalent assumption amongst reformers in 1867 that
the fitness of working men to vote had to be proved. There were now many
thousands of working men who, by previous criteria, would have been
judged 'unfit' but who could now vote. While some middle-class women in
the past might have been prepared to admit that they were less 'fit' than
middle-class men who had the vote, they certainly did not concede that any
longer. A further corollary was that those working men without the vote
could suppose that at some stage it would come to them – a comfort that
allowed a sense of superiority over the opposite sex to survive. It was therefore inevitable, Martin Pugh argues, that sex was highlighted as the outstanding disqualification and debate centred 'inevitably upon the contrasting
qualities of men and women from a political point view'.[26]

Mary Wollstonecraft's manifesto of a century earlier, *A Vindication of
the Rights of Women* (1792), in a British context, is often taken to launch
the assault on the notions of sexuality and gender roles which had hitherto
largely prevailed. Of course, if they were queens, a certain political capacity
in women had perforce to be conceded, and even, in the case of Queen Boudicca, no mean skill as a charioteer on the battlefield.

The British past, it need scarcely be said, queens apart, had witnessed
the spasmodic public presence of women. Nevertheless, it had been men
who believed themselves to have shaped the country's destiny in every significant public sphere from the churches to commerce, from army and navy to
Parliament and the Foreign Office. The systematic presence of women would
not be welcome. The reconciliation of past and present, in the sphere of gender, therefore could not fail to have the most profound political consequences. What was a man? What was a woman? Perusal of the Book of Genesis,

---

[26] M. Pugh, *'Women's Suffrage in Britain 1867–1928* (London, 1980) p. 8.

to name only one book of the Bible, disclosed to contemporaries that these questions were not entirely new, though perhaps the answers given there were ceasing to have the authority they had once possessed.

That there were separate spheres still seemed axiomatic to most contemporaries, but the boundaries of these spheres were becoming blurred. In the 1860s and 1870s, for example, Elizabeth Blackwell, Elizabeth Garrett Anderson and Sophia Jex-Blake broke down the barriers to women in the profession of medicine, though it still remained the case that among learned medical men were to be found some of the strongest expressions of the belief that the physiological make-up of women and its psychological consequences should debar them from major public roles. Various Married Women's Property Acts (1870, 1874, 1882), by allowing women to retain their property on and in marriage, gave some recognition to the notion that women had some independent status. Middle-class female education burgeoned and, by the end of the century, some progress had been made in sapping such male citadels as the universities of Oxford and Cambridge. Even so, all the major institutions in British society remained firmly under the control of men. It had not escaped their notice that there were more women than men in the population. If women became the majority in the electorate, and voted primarly as women, men feared that the priorities inherited from the past might be drastically overturned. That was precisely what ardent feminists – the word came into general use in the 1890s – desired.

In a more narrowly defined sense of the word politics, however, at the level of Westminster nothing appeared to have changed. In local government, on the other hand, certain breaches in male bastions were made, and although it was something of a legal puzzle it was established early in the new century that women could not only vote for but also sit on the county councils which had been established in 1888. Slightly earlier, school boards and Poor Law boards had also been seen as acceptable spheres of activity for propertied women – an extension, it was thought, of their proper concern for education, health and welfare. The real business of politics, like the real politics of business, remained beyond them.

In these circumstances, women were divided as to the best way forward. Some believed that they could enhance their professional and social roles without directly addressing the franchise issue. The vote would come in due course once their abilities could not be gainsaid. Others believed, on the contrary, that both symbolically and practically the vote was the key to the enhancement they sought. Historians have noted, however, that 'feminist' activity fluctuated quite sharply. At the turn of the century, perhaps because it coincided with reviving Liberal optimism, as Brian Harrison has pointed out, campaigning revived after a period in the doldrums.

The formation of the Women's Social and Political Union in 1903 under Mrs Pankhurst was the signal for 'suffragette' militancy. The contemporary publicity which it attracted, and the attention it has received from

8.5 'Keep the home fires burning' was a nostalgic sentimental song of the First World War. It kept before the men an image of domestic bliss which may, or may not, have accorded with their memories of home. What was important, however, was that it was women who now had the unexpected task of keeping the home wheels turning in a variety of occupations. Here we see group of women railway workers in 1915. After the war, in terms of stereotyping, work could never be quite gendered in the pre-war mode, though it was not for want of trying on the part of returning men.

historians, should not detract from the solid work that suffragists had been engaged in for decades. Yet whatever tactics or strategy were employed, it was far from clear how an all-male Parliament could be persuaded to cease to be so – if most of its members were content with that position. By the Edwardian period, the issue had also become inextricably bound up with party advantage. Who would benefit most electorally if a change were made? And if it were contemplated, should it be on a basis of equality with men as the franchise existed, or should any measure for women await a further extension of the franchise for men? The difficulties lay not so much in principle as in the detail of what might be proposed.

Although many prominent Liberals, such as Churchill, Grey and Lloyd George, supported some kind of votes for women, Prime Minister Asquith's opposition was very apparent. The rift, in other words, was not absolutely on party lines. While most Tories were opposed, there were some who were favourable. The view is generally held that the militant tactics adopted by the suffragettes were counter-productive. They served, indeed, to confirm some men in the belief that the women involved exhibited signs of mental instability in their passionate commitment to 'the Cause'.

Some Conservative spokesmen also continued to affirm without reservation that nature had distinguished between men and women. As Austen Chamberlain put it, the sex of a woman was a disqualification in fact; it should remain so in law. Lord Curzon was devoted to women, though, as Elinor Glyn pointed out, he liked them 'rather in the spirit in which other men like fine horses or good wine'.[27] They could not be equal souls worthy of being seriously considered or trusted. F.E. Smith summoned up all his knowledge of biology, perhaps with a little aid from H.G. Wells, to argue that the entire trend of evolutionary forces had been towards differentiation. It was, he believed, indisputable that the education and mental disposition of a woman reeked of sex. It was not her task to ignore it by seeking to enter the world of men, but rather to 'refine and put a point to it'. From his gaze, a woman's costume was 'clamorous with the distinctive elements of her form' and he would not have it otherwise. Misogyny, it was certain, did not come into it. By one means or another, therefore, arguments with this degree of subtlety, together with Liberal divisions, ensured in 1914 the male political order was still intact.

Strange death and constitutional crisis

George V had grown to manhood in the expectation that he would never be king. It was only the death of his elder brother in 1892 that brought him into the direct line of succession. The Prince of Wales, as he became in 1901, was reputed to be one of the best shots in the country but his other talents

---

[27] Cited in B.H. Harrison, *Separate Spheres: The Opposition to Women's Suffrage in Britain* (London, 1978) p. 97. See also his 'Women's Suffrage at Westminster, 1866–1928' in Bentley and Stevenson, *High and Low Politics*, pp. 80–122; B. Caine, *Victorian Feminists* (Oxford, 1992); A. Taylor, *Annie Besant: A Biography* (Oxford, 1992); P. Hollis, *Ladies Elect: Women in English Local Government 1865–1914* (Oxford, 1987); J. Rendall, ed., *Equal or Different: Women's Politics 1800–1914* (Oxford, 1987).

were not widely known. He was, however, made aware from an early age of the fact that the British monarchy now reached around the world. He opened the first Parliament of the new Commonwealth of Australia. His conscientious observation of elephants at work in Burmese timber yards was applauded. He liked this British Empire rather better than he liked 'being abroad' in mainland Europe. 'Abroad is awful', he commented, 'I know. I have been.' In Coronation year, 1911, some 3 million people visited London. In the same year, the king-emperor held the great Delhi Durbar, an event which proved to be the apotheosis of British imperial display in the Indian sub-continent.

Back home, however, he inherited the constitutional crisis of 1910. Like his father, he resented the path of duty pointed out to him by Asquith and it was only with reluctance that he agreed that, if need be, he would create sufficient peers to enable the legislation to pass. In the event, he was not called upon to do so, though he continued to resent the pressure exerted by Asquith. This crisis, together with the linked issue of Irish Home Rule, illustrated the difficulty of monarchy as a symbol 'above party'. The king knew that the country was deeply divided and he would be likely to upset roughly half of the population. The consequence of the Parliament Act was that the monarchy had to relate increasingly to an undifferentiated 'people' rather than to the aristocracy which had hitherto buttressed its position. Of course, such a shift was neither complete nor immediate.

Some historians have been persuaded that the multiple problems of the period were not discrete but rather were manifestations of a single deep-seated crisis. Some interwar writers looked back to the immediate prewar years and described them as 'a nightmare of passion and paradox'. The authority of the state seemed to be collapsing. One writer was clever enough to call his best-selling book *The Strange Death of Liberal England*.[28] More recently, Michael Bentley, while conceding that 'almost everyone within the parliamentary world seems to have sensed some acceleration in the rate of social change', notes that there was no agreement on what it portended and how it could be tackled. He further adds percipiently that the greatest difficulty in estimating the extent to which the 'Edwardian Age' marked a turning point of great significance lies in 'overcoming the certainty, unknown and implausible to contemporaries, that the period constitutes a terminus.' The politicians of the time were under no particular compulsion to 'solve' all their problems 'before the chiming of some midnight hour in August 1914'.[29]

There were indeed outstanding issues still awaiting 'solution' in 1914 but *the* specific cause of division in 1909–11 could in the end be represented as another 'logical' corollary of nineteenth-century constitutional change.

---

[28] Dangerfield's book with this title was first published in London in 1936.
[29] Bentley, *Politics without Democracy*, pp. 345–6.

Even before 1886, the Liberals were in a permanent minority in the House of Lords – by a substantial margin. Judicious creations after 1906 had not seriously altered this position and the power of the Upper House to thwart the work of the Campbell-Bannerman ministry had become apparent. Was it constitutionally tolerable that the supremacy of the Commons was obscure? The Lords rejected Lloyd George's first budget of 1909. The government denounced this move as unconstitutional. To Tory peers the budget was a piece of social engineering rather than a budget. It had not been put to the people. In the background was their awareness, or so they believed, that the electorate did not want Home Rule for Ireland. The House of Lords, therefore, was not an obscurantist citadel but a safeguard against the bogus claims of the Liberal majority in the Commons to interpret the mind of the people, or at least the electorate, on all issues. Both Tories and Liberals could claim to be vindicated by the outcome of the January 1910 election.

Charge and counter-charge echoed through the Commons in sessions which strained the normal capacity of MPs to maintain personal friendships and social relations across the party divide. There was talk of a referendum – something in turn denounced as unBritish. There was talk of abolishing the House of Lords or of reforming its composition and/or amending its power to veto legislation passed in the Commons. The discomfiture of Edward VII and George V has already been noted. There was an uncomfortable sense in which pillorying the aristocracy edged near to the throne itself. Die-hard Tory peers contemplated the last ditch. In the event, without elaborating further the twists and turns of the debate, the Parliament Act went through the Lords.

Their lordships accepted that henceforth they would have no power over money bills (certified by the Speaker) and could only impose a delay for two years on other measures. The supremacy of the Commons, it seemed, had been triumphantly asserted. Disgruntled peers and their Tory friends in the Commons felt that a still necessary dyke against a potentially tyrannical populist assembly had been removed. The outcome, however, ensured that, at least on the surface, king, Lords and Commons still endured into the twentieth century. Once again, Britain had reformed that it might preserve.

Britain is best

In 1945 Britain appeared well-placed to be 'tutor' to a continent in dire need of reconstruction. The extraordinary fact was that unlike practically every other European country Britain maintained a continuity with its past. It had not undergone revolution or occupation. In 1928 an English writer on *The New Democratic Constitutions of Europe* (and the problems they encountered), basing her views on the belief that the English system of parliamentary government was 'a natural product of the English character', concluded that the system clearly did not work well amongst other nations with different national characteristics. Agnes Headlam-Morley was fearful that failure on the Continent of what she called 'an imperfect imitation of our constitution' might lead would-be reformers at home to press for ill-considered adoption of institutions which other nations, unable to make 'the English system' work, had devised out of their own genius. But that did not appear to have happened.[30] The makers of a new round of European democratic constitutions after 1945 would surely wish to reflect on thirty years of British history.

Kings

The Crown was still intact, although from the First World War it had undergone significant changes and one period of personal crisis. After the bitter domestic disputes of the early years of his reign, King George V had demonstrated that he could be 'father of his people' at a time of national crisis. It could not be disguised, however, that the ruling house was German/British at a time when all things German were reviled. It seemed appropriate, therefore, to create the 'House of Windsor' in 1917. The king himself was considered to have behaved in an exemplary manner, diligently visiting ships and army units as requested. The war had securely 'indigenized' the British monarchy. Nevertheless, the ending of monarchy in Germany and Russia, together with the fact that most of the new states in Europe after 1919 were republics, produced a significantly different world from that of 1914.

George V accommodated himself to the first Labour government in 1924 and Labour ministers found him straightforward. The king's disapproval of the 1926 General Strike was not in doubt, but the monarchy stayed aloof. The king's voice was first heard by his people in April 1924 when he broadcast at the opening of the British Empire Exhibition at Wembley in 1924. In 1932 he gave a Christmas broadcast – something which became an annual event. By 1935, the year of his Silver Jubilee, it became apparent that this rather ordinary man had achieved considerable personal popularity. Until his death in January 1936, he seemed to offer personal reassurance that in a still troubled world the British Empire was a rock of stability.

Stability was not what the new king provided. Edward VIII reigned only from January to December 1936. It became apparent that he wanted to marry a divorced American woman, Mrs Wallis Simpson. Such a step was

---

[30] A. Headlam-Morley, *The New Democratic Constitutions of Europe* (London, 1928) pp. 8–9. Professor Headlam-Morley subsequently supervised this author's doctoral thesis.

unacceptable to the government and most leading members of the opposition parties. There were certain things a king could not do without falling foul of the prevalent conception of monarchy. The Duke of Windsor, as Edward became, left the country and married Wallis in June 1937.

His younger brother, Bertie, came to the throne as George VI, fortunately already equipped with a wife, the daughter of a Scottish earl. It was evident that she was a charming and determined woman who gave confidence to her rather reserved and nervous husband. The couple were early dispatched on visits to countries where it was felt that the presence of the British royal family would be politically beneficial – France in 1938 and Canada and the United States in 1939. As had happened in 1914, the advent of a major war helped the monarchy to re-establish itself after its uncomfortable recent past. The king and queen, and their young daughters, successfully served as the focus of a national effort which transcended internal political and social divisions. Winston Churchill maintained a proper respect for his monarch, though did not let it interfere unduly with his own sense of his indispensability. Even though, elsewhere in Europe, many erstwhile monarchies rapidly disappeared, there was no serious suggestion that the British monarchy was obsolete. The Labour victory of 1945 carried no such imputation.

Parties

After 1919, all of Europe had seen the rise both of communism and fascism in circumstances of considerable political instability. In comparison, though both communists and fascists were active in interwar Britain, they remained marginal. The political system seemed able to contain both extremes within its customary structures. The electoral system with its emphasis on 'first past the post' remained the same. It continued to be a mechanism designed, it was claimed, to ensure governmental stability rather than to provide an accurate reflection of opinion in the country. The notion that it rested on two major parties, each capable of forming either government or the opposition, seemed again confirmed. In fact this was as incomplete a picture in the interwar period as it was in the nineteenth century. In the 1920s it was the case that three parties – Conservative, Liberal and Labour – were all in serious contention.

Immediately after the First World War, when it became clear that Labour was seriously challenging for office (a minority administration was formed in 1923), there was talk of a different kind of coalition designed to ward off the rise of Labour. That party's rise and the decline of Liberalism has been much debated. Some writers have seen this change as an inevitable consequence of the further democratic extension of the franchise in 1918. (It should be noted that this franchise reform included provision for women over thirty to vote. A decade later, women obtained the vote on the same basis as men. It remained the case, however, with only a few exceptions, that men continued to dominate national politics. In this respect, 'votes for women' proved far less of a break with the past in its political impact than many had supposed likely.)

Other writers have argued that the decline of Liberalism owed more to the personality clashes and problems caused by the First World War than to deep-seated social factors. However it is explained, the rise of Labour certainly seemed to constitute a break with the past. The two other major parties claimed that the divisions between them arose from issues of principle and policy. Neither the Conservatives nor the Liberals explicitly appealed to class and claimed to draw support from all sections of society. However, a 'Labour Party' rather than a 'Socialist Party' suggested an appeal to a class solidarity rather than an ideological principle. Of course, many Labour supporters saw themselves as 'socialists' and some as Marxists, but the emphasis of the party as a whole was upon 'evolutionary' rather than 'revolutionary' progress.

In other respects, however, Labour can be seen as an heir of Radicalism and many ex-Liberals came into the party. Other Liberals, however, despairing somewhat of the revival or even survival of their party, drifted into supporting the Conservative Party. The need to compete for the Liberal inheritance arguably made it necessary for the other parties to curb 'extremism' either on the Left or the Right in their ranks. In both parties, there were individuals and groups who wanted more radical action, but they failed to get it. 'What I am beginning to doubt', wrote Beatrice Webb in 1932, after the fall of the Labour government, 'is the inevitability of gradualness.' She saw no sign of any political leader who had thought out *how* to make the *transition* without upsetting the apple cart'. She did not altogether share her husband's comforting belief that the transition would 'make itself' and that Britain would 'slip into the equalitarian state' as it had done into political democracy.[31]

In their different ways, Ramsay MacDonald (Labour and National Prime Minister) and Stanley Baldwin (Conservative and National Prime Minister) personified an apparently comfortable sense of continuity. Bald-

---

[31] 'What I am beginning to doubt' Beatrice Webb wrote in 1932 'is the inevitability of gradualness. ... Anyway no leader in our country has thought out *how* to make the *transition* without upsetting the apple cart. Sidney, however, thought that Britain would "slip into the equalitarian state" as it did into political democracy'. (Seymour–Jones, *Beatrice Webb: War of Conflict* (London, 1993) p. 306. She also recorded in her diary in September 1931 that Britain would have to 'follow suit' by adopting either American capitalism or Soviet communism when it became clear 'in the course of a decade' which system yielded the better life for the bulk of the people. N. Mackenzie, ed., *The Diary of Beatrice Webb* iv. (London, 1985).

win, in particular, fell easily into ruminating on the past. Peering over a Worcestershire gate, the pig-loving, pipe-smoking premier saw the past spread before him and spoke *On England* with moving effect. To him, 'England is the country, and the country is England'. He wondered what England would stand for in the minds of generations to come if her fields continued to be converted into towns. His message was reassuring, if nostalgic, in an era of industrial conflict and General Strike.[32]

It was undeniable that there was social and class tension in Britain, yet, in comparison with its sharp edges on the Continent British class boundaries were blurred. Conflict within the country was solved or at least contained, not by the actions of extra-parliamentary militias, but within a House of Commons which had a continuing confidence in its place in British society. It was symptomatic that some MPs, seeing threats to democracy and individual freedom in cross-channel Europe, believed that the time was ripe for a many-volumed *History of Parliament* which would emphasize the antiquity of the institution. It was a project directed by a man who had begun life as a Polish Jew, Lewis Namier, but had become enamoured of British history. Namier detected a 'very special trout-stream' in the House of Commons which had been vigorous in the eighteenth century but which was perhaps now dying out.[33] As things stood, however, Parliament was not in serious danger of losing its central place as the fulcrum of British political life.

Even so, there was something odd about the pattern of British government between 1931 and 1945. The disintegration of the Labour government in 1931 under the pressure of the financial crisis removed the widespread assumption that the Labour movement was on the brink of a protracted period of office. Instead, what had been initially cobbled together as a short-term 'national' response to the crisis showed every sign of becoming normal. The scale of the Labour defeat in 1931, and the still decisive defeat in 1935, reduced the party to a marginal role. Conservative ascendancy within the National governments was undoubted but the presence of some National Liberals and even, initially, National Labour, gave a veneer of plausibility to the claim that the administrations put 'country' ahead of 'party'. A nation that was supposed not to love coalitions saddled itself with a rather exiguous one for nearly a decade.

And, under Churchill after 1940, a more far-reaching coalition was formed with the involvement of prominent Labour politicians. There was an electoral truce between the established parties for the duration of the war. In most respects, at least until the latter phase of the war, party differences were subordinated to the overwhelming need to win the war. In addition,

---

[32] D. Cannadine, 'Politics, Propaganda and Art: The Case of the Two "Worcestershire Lads"' *Midlands History* (1977) (Baldwin is one of the lads). S. Baldwin, *On England* (Harmondsworth, 1937).
[33] J. Namier, *Lewis Namier: A Biography* (Oxford, 1971) p. 200.

8.6 London Pride: The scale of Labour's victory in 1945 was a surprise. Attlee, the Labour leader, himself, (seen here speaking at the party's celebratory meeting in London on 11 August 1945) represented a London constituency and Herbert Morrison and other prominent Labour figures took pride in the extent to which they had 'delivered' the capital for the party. The bomb-damaged, ravaged city was to be transformed, as was the country as a whole, into a 'New Jerusalem'. In the exhaustion and euphoria at the end of the war it was difficult to resist such a tantalizing prospect.

Churchill brought into his administration men without formal party affiliation to do specific jobs. There were some suggestions that this rather curious 'national' government was in fact the best way of handling fundamental problems, but the mood was shifting strongly in favour of the resumption of 'normal' British politics, that is to say with a government of one colour being confronted by an opposition of another. By 1945 there had not been a general election for a decade and it was time for normal service to be resumed.

The scale of Labour's sweeping victory in 1945 came as a surprise, but spirits amongst Labour supporters were high.[34] The defeat of Churchill apparently showed that the country wanted to draw a line under the past. It

[34] S. Brooke, *Labour's War: The Labour Party and the Second World War* (Oxford, 1994).

was time to translate the wartime rhetoric of partnership and progress into reality. It was certainly not the moment to go back to the party allegedly responsible for the unemployment and social deprivation of the 1930s. Even if it could be argued that the seeds of the 'Welfare State' had been sown before the First World War, it was novelty and not continuity which Labour sought to emphasize. Similarly, the programme of nationalization was presented as the beginning of a new socialist Britain. What Labour sought was 'New Jerusalem' not a return to the social equilibrium of interwar Britain.

Even so, in pressing forwards, the Labour leadership which had itself been in wartime coalition in the common national cause still possessed a strong self-confidence in the national past. Britain had a great deal to teach the world as it apparently did slip into Beatrice Webb's 'equalitarian state'. It was not the Soviet Union which offered the world a new civilization but Britain as it successfully married its old institutions and conventions with socialism. It showed that there was a third way between what was widely regarded as the obnoxious character of American capitalism and the tyranny of Soviet communism. Writing in 1943 when he was in America, the British economist James Meade recorded the admiration for Britain which he encountered amongst radical young Americans. The United Kingdom, he was convinced, had 'an absolutely unique opportunity of taking the moral lead in the matter of building the new society, if it will only cling on to, and develop' what it had started during the war.[35] In the decades that followed 1945, it was to become evident that, for Britain, 'taking the moral lead' was not a straightforward matter.[36]

---

[35] S. Howson and D. Moggridge, eds, *The Wartime Diaries of Robbins and Meade* (London, 1991) p. 131.

[36] The volumes by W.H. Greenleaf under the title *The British Political Tradition* offer a wealth of information on and critical assessment of matters summarily treated in this and the preceding chapter: Vol. 1: *The Rise of Collectivism* (London, 1983), Vol. 2: *The Ideological Heritage* (London, 1983), Vol. 3: *Parts 1 & 2 A Much Governed Nation* (London, 1987).

Chapter 9 ....

Pax Britannica: Domination and Decline: *c.1745–c.1945*

For some two centuries there was an 'Empire' that was 'British' and, for some minds, it was not possible to conceive of 'Great Britain' without thinking of 'Greater Britain'. It was an enterprise on a truly world scale. Never before had a single country – its soldiers, sailors, traders, administrators, missionaries – extended its power and influence across the globe in such diverse contexts. The establishment and consolidation of this empire, particularly in the nineteenth century, was celebrated in propaganda and myth. The British, it seemed, were intrepid pioneers, establishing what they conceived to be the virtues of their civilization in the most remote and unlikely places. The maps of empire, glowing red, reinforced that sense of possession and achievement. They still contrived to confirm the centrality of the islands off the coast of mainland Europe to the viability of the project empire.

Even to speak in such language, however, begs questions. The empire, as it unfolded, was certainly extensive but it was the diversity rather than the coherence of the territories which it embraced which was most striking. To refer to 'project empire' would appear to suggest deliberate planning at the highest political levels informed by clear and consistent notions concerning its management and structure. Paul Langford, for example, suggests that even to speak of colonial policy before the Seven Years War is somewhat misleading.[1] It is certainly an exaggeration to suppose that the empire was acquired simply in a fit of absence of mind. Even so, it lacked that uniformity of administrative method and metropolitan oversight to which other European colonial powers at least aspired. There were, of course, some who found this untidiness irksome and alarming. They urged greater emphasis on formal unity. Unless 'Greater Britain' could be drawn more tightly together, constitutionally and politically, it was likely to fall apart.

---

[1] P. Langford, *A Polite and Commercial People: England 1727–1783* (Oxford, 1989) p. 171.

The sense that this ramshackle and far-flung collection of territories was a fragile 'empire' was never wholly absent, even during periods in the nineteenth century when expansion seemed easy and 'natural'. Each generation went through a crisis, great or small, which exposed some weakness and peril.

The tie that binds?

There was, too, an underlying anxiety about the identity of this 'British' Empire. In what sense was it 'British'? It was a question to be posed in many different contexts throughout the imperial centuries. It has already been noted that the colonies of North America had, from the outset, their own distinct ethos.[2] Their local legislative assemblies had significant power. They were not mere 'provinces' of a British state, indeed their foundation antedated its formation, though Scotsmen were increasingly to be found in the Americas – an estimated 35,000 before 1775 and some 5 per cent of whites by 1790. Other European nationalities were also coming to the American colonies. Thus, though few perceived the imminence of a grand crisis, there was more to the Seven Years War which began in 1756 than simply another round in the struggle between Britain and France for global predominance.

That war naturally also had its European dimension. Even if it was news of battles in Bengal or Canada which excited most interest, the reality of Britain's geographical position could not be ignored. There was a reluctance to see the commitment of major British forces to the Continent, but some presence was necessary, in addition to financial subsidy, to support Frederick II of Prussia against France, Austria, Russia and Sweden. The Prussian/British success at the Battle of Minden (August 1759) not only safeguarded Hanover, it also made a French victory in Central Europe unlikely. It was Pitt who had overall responsibility for the deployment of British resources. His position was bolstered by the success of British commanders in the field – Clive in India at Plassey in 1757 over Siraj-ud-Daula, and Wolfe in Quebec in 1759 over the French. A certain megalomania overcame Pitt at this point, but his enthusiasm to 'fight to the finish' was not universally shared. After various false starts, it fell not to Pitt but to Lord Bute to conclude the Peace of Paris (1763) on terms which Pitt described as 'totally inadmissable'.

Historical interpretation has swung against the view that this peace settlement constituted an undiluted British triumph. Perhaps only in India was

---

[2] P. Marshall and G. Williams, eds, *The British Atlantic Empire Before the American Revolution* (London, 1980); R. Middleton, *Colonial America: A History, 1607–1760* (Oxford, 1992); P.D. Morgan, ed., *Diversity and Unity in Early North America* (London, 1993).

this the case. The surrender of Guadeloupe and Martinique, in the Caribbean, back to France in exchange for French acceptance of British mastery in Canada was intensely controversial, as was the surrender back to Spain of Havana in Cuba and Manila in the Philippines in exchange for swampy Florida. Britain was indeed dominant in North America, but there is general agreement that France still had the capacity to revive commercially – and indeed was to do just that. In the nineteenth century, in particular, British historians often argued that if Pitt had indeed been able to 'fight to the finish' British mastery would have been secure beyond any doubt. In fact, in the heady atmosphere of the 1760s, most contemporaries did indeed believe that this mastery had been obtained. However, if Pitt had been able to continue, despite the growing economic strain on Britain, there was the risk (though no certainty) that all the major European powers would have united against Britain – this maritime monster that threatened to throttle Europe from the periphery of the continent.

In 1776, when the new American Congress issued a Declaration of Independence, 'Britain' in North America looked rather different. After seven years more of war against Britain, a war in which French assistance to the rebels was invaluable, perhaps decisive, 'Americans' were free. It was only to the north in 'Canada' that 'Loyalists' remained determinedly and obstinately 'British'.[3]

This is not the place to rehearse in detail the sequence of events that led to the American War of Independence. Even at this distance of time, there is an element in its interpretation which goes beyond the normal differences of emphasis between historians and includes issues which touch on both 'British' and 'American' identity. There are, indeed, some grounds for suggesting that increasing use of the term 'American' in mid-century was not a deliberate revocation of an 'English/British' identity but rather a product of the need to distinguish the colonists from the 'British' of the Caribbean. We might suggest that an 'American identity' had to be forged after 1775, every bit as much as British identity had to be forged after 1707. In neither case are we dealing with something fixed and solid. These are complex issues and are now normally discussed as 'American history'. The question to be asked, however, is whether it is premature to bifurcate 'British' and 'American' history at this point. To do so is perhaps to assume that the war was simply between 'Britain' and 'America', a war which Britain lost. Was it not also a kind of British civil war, another kind of religious war?

Since the United States has never lost its independence it would be foolish to suppose in any formal sense that the subsequent history of the

---

[3] For a more extensive discussion of the extent to which the ensuing empire was 'British' see C. Bridge, P. Marshall and G. Williams, 'A "British" Empire', *International History Review* 12 (1990); P. Buckner, *English Canada – The Founding Generations: British Migration to British North America 1815–1865* (London, 1993).

United States is 'British history'. On the other hand, there is too ready an acceptance, particularly in Britain, that the pre-independence history of the thirteen colonies is 'American history' rather than 'British history'. The point at which an erstwhile common history separates into distinct streams is always problematic for historians. It is particularly the case when writing on the histories of 'Britain' and 'America'. The 'parting of the ways' may obviously be identified in the 1770/80s, but in senses other than constitutional it is not possible to pinpoint a date when the past vanishes. In language and common law, to name only two areas, it still identifiably flows into the American present, notwithstanding the vast changes in the United States over subsequent centuries.[4]

And, of course, migration from Britain continued after independence. By 1820, for example, Americans of English stock constituted some 60 per cent of the white population. Between 1820 and 1900 around 2 million English arrived, some 350,000 Scots and 43,000 Welsh. In the first half of the twentieth century roughly the same number of Scots and Welsh arrived, though only around 1 million English. These 'national' figures should be treated with some caution because additionally between 1820 and 1900 some 750,000 immigrants simply described themselves as 'British'. Even at the end of the twentieth century the 'British stock' in the United States can be estimated at some 25–35 per cent, the largest US ethnic group. In short, despite the fact that 'Britain' and 'America' had been at war, and were to be so again in 1812, the United States was as popular, often more popular, a destination for British emigration as the 'British' Empire.

There are other matters to be considered as well as 'ethnicity'. In the eighteenth century, the Atlantic had not proved a barrier to the passage of individuals or ideas. John Wesley, for example, had ministered, not very agreeably, in Georgia before returning to England. Transatlantic religious revivalism was a reality and in religious circles George Whitfield was as well known in America as he was in Britain.[5]

The major ports on the west coast of England – Bristol and, increasingly, Liverpool – were bound into an Atlantic commerce. In Scotland, the rise of Glasgow, particularly after 1750, to pivotal importance in the tobacco trade was of great importance. More generally, for Scots merchants, the creation of a united British state had had as a corollary access to 'English' North America. It was increasingly the case that these major ports on the

---

[4] R.A. Burchell, ed., *The End of Anglo-America: Historical Essays in the Study of Cultural Divergence* (Manchester, 1991); R. Tucker and D. Hendrickson, *The Fall of the First British Empire: Origins of the War of American Independence* (Baltimore, 1982); I. Christie, *Crisis of Empire: Great Britain and the American Colonies, 1754–1783* (London, 1966).
[5] W.R. Ward, *The Protestant Evangelical Awakening* (Cambridge, 1992); S. O'Brien, 'A Transatlantic Community of States: The Great Awakening and the First Evangelical Network, 1735–1755', *American Historical Review* 91 (1986).

western seaboard had direct bilateral relationships across the Atlantic which may be described as 'inter-provincial' in the sense that no direct intervention from London was necessary to make them flourish.[6]

It cannot be denied, however, that great profit in these ports and elsewhere was derived from the slave trade, that is to say from the triangular voyages from Europe to Europe via Africa and America. The first African slaves had been brought to Virginia in 1619. Perhaps a quarter of a million had been brought in by 1775. The plantations in the West Indies were also expanding on the backs of black slave labour. One contemporary suggestion was that there were some 15,000 black people living in London in 1772, though it is not possible to confirm this figure. Slavery was thus an aspect of the British/American world – though so also was the opposition to it which was to mount steadily over subsequent decades.[7]

The British/American world was arguably a reality in another important respect. In all the controversies which started with the imposition of the 1765 Stamp Act and which were summed up in the cry 'No Taxation without Representation', some suggest that the colonists behaved as certain kinds of Briton would behave in the circumstances. They fought their way out of the British world because they were 'the best kind of British'. On the other hand, some historians are keen to stress that there was indeed an American *Revolution* which took a new direction, whatever its origins. Certainly, the Declaration of Independence stressed rights allegedly possessed by all men and opened up a national future which did not rest upon the long historical identities of Europe. This American vision was attractive to many Britons, particularly to Dissenters, many of whom had considerable sympathy with the American 'rebels'. George III, depicted in the Declaration of Independence as a prince whose every act marked him in the character of a tyrant, unfit to be the ruler of a free people, was, in this interpretation, Charles I writ large. It was, however, an interpretation which was not fair to George, who believed himself to be fighting on behalf of the rights of Parliament as well as his own.

The rupture therefore left in its wake loose ends and unsevered contacts and connections. There was an enduring relationship which, while not

---

[6] N.C. Landsman, 'The Provinces and the Empire: Scotland, the American Colonies and the Development of British Provincial Identity' in L. Stone, ed., *An Imperial State at War: Britain from 1689 to 1815* (London, 1994); I. Graham, *Colonists from Scotland: Emigration to North America 1707–1783* (Ithaca, N.Y., 1956); T. Devine, *The Tobacco Lords: A Study of the Tobacco Merchants of Glasgow and their Trading Activities c.1740–90* (Edinburgh, 1975).

[7] P. Hair, *The Atlantic Slave Trade and Black Africa* (London, 1978); J. Walvin, *The Black Presence: A Documentary History of the Negro in England* (London, 1971); D. Killingray, ed., *Africans in Britain* (London, 1994) – various essays cover some two hundred years; J.R. Oldfield, *Popular Politics and British Anti-Slavery* (Manchester, 1994).

without disagreement and the possibility of conflict, nevertheless had a specially intimate quality. In the short term, however, the successful revolution was most often treated as a disaster for Britain. At the beginning of the crisis, in 1775, George III wrote to Lord Dartmouth, Secretary for America, that 'with firmness and perseverance America will be brought to submission. If not, old England will ... perhaps not appear so formidable in the eyes of Europe.' Six years later, Lord Shelburne was in lugubrious mood. 'The sun of Great Britain is set', he wrote on hearing the news of the British surrender at Yorktown in 1781, 'and we shall no longer be powerful or respectable.' Britain could not defeat the American colonists and two years later, in the Treaty of Versailles, recognized their independence. British troops sailed out of New York in November 1783.[8]

Shelburne's pessimism, however, proved at least premature. The notion of a 'Greater Britain' still had much life in it, and indeed in territorial extent, the 'new' British Empire of the nineteenth century far exceeded the old. It was commonplace to look at a map of the world and declare that the sun never set on the British Empire. The 'Land of Hope and Glory' (1902) could be mightier yet.

Great Britain: world state?

This successful further expansion, therefore, seemed to confirm that 'imperialism' was not a dead end. Sir John Seeley, Regius Professor of Modern History at Cambridge, endeavoured in the early 1880s to discern what he called 'Tendency in English History'. In what direction and towards what goal had the English state been advancing? He accepted that there was a tendency towards 'democracy', a process which has been considered in the previous chapters. However, looking back, he placed more emphasis on what he called 'the simple obvious fact of the extension of the English name into other countries of the globe, the foundation of Greater Britain'. 'Greater Britain' had survived whereas 'Greater Holland', 'Greater Spain' and 'Greater Portugal' had all failed. Of course, he was not ignorant of the American Revolution, but believed it quite wrong to infer that all colonies necessarily fell from the tree as soon as they ripened. Indeed, the greatness of the United States was proof that a state might become immensely large and yet prosper. The old colonial system had clearly been an error but he was

---

[8] P. Thomas, 'George III and the American Revolution', *History* (Feb. 1985) pp. 30–1; J. Bradley, *Religion, Revolution, and English Radicalism: Nonconformity in Eighteenth-century Politics and Society* (Cambridge, 1990) pp. 410–11; Shelburne cited in M. Chamberlain, *'Pax Britannica'? British Foreign Policy 1789–1914* (London, 1988) p. 22.

optimistic that the right lessons had been learnt. He could not believe that state-builders overseas from the British Isles would have the heart 'to sever themselves from English history, from all traditions and memories of the island where their fathers lived for a thousand years'. It was quite wrong to suppose that 'all development has ceased in English history'. England, he argued, had not arrived at a permanent condition of security and prosperity. On the contrary, large struggles and changes certainly lay ahead and 'when the crisis arrives, it will throw a wonderful light back upon our past history'. Only then would it really be possible to say whether Britain had produced 'a great and solid World-State' or 'an ephemeral trade-empire, like that of Old Spain'.[9]

The past, in other words, could point in contrary directions but it at least made Seeley's vision of 'Greater Britain' a real possibility. From his perspective, the country in the nineteenth century faced no greater challenge. He was by no means sanguine that it would respond adequately because, as he put it, 'We seem, as it were, to have conquered and peopled half the world in a fit of absence of mind'. In making this famous statement, Seeley himself seems to have been somewhat absent-minded about the extent to which deliberate policy did in fact inform successive British acts of aggression. The 'British Empire' was the empire of a sea power whose influence spread out from its original coastal trading posts and stations. It was also, in part, an empire of settlement from Britain itself.

The map of the world in the late nineteenth century might show large areas of Asia, Africa, the Antipodes and North America painted red but in what sense, if any, was the whole 'Greater Britain'? Seeley conceded that even in the 1880s the British had not ceased 'to think of ourselves as simply a race inhabiting an island off the northern coast of the Continent of Europe'. It did not occur to people to count the population of Canada and Australia in the 'English population'. Historians had been partly to blame for this failing because they had not grasped that in the eighteenth century 'the history of England is not in England but in America and Asia'. The future of Britain as a 'World-State' required a fundamental change of perspective.

It was a change advocated with increasing enthusiasm but also with a certain despair in the late nineteenth century and into the twentieth. In *Imperial Federation: The Problem of National Unity* (1893), George Parkin was only one of a number of authors who forecast that 'in mere mass of

---

[9] J. Seeley, *The Expansion of England* (London, 1891), pp. 151, 169. The literature on British imperial expansion is considerable – for example R. Symonds, *Oxford and Empire: The Last Lost Cause?* (Oxford, 1992); A. Godlewska and N. Smith, eds, *Geography and Empire* (Oxford, 1994); M. Bell, R. Butlin and M. Heffernan, eds, *Geography and Imperialism, 1820 to 1920* (Manchester, 1995); R. MacDonald, *The Language of Empire* (Manchester, 1995); P. Rich, *Race and Empire in British Politics* (Cambridge, 1990); J. Mackenzie, *Propaganda and Empire* (Manchester, 1986); J. Mackenzie, ed., *Imperialism and Popular Culture* (Manchester, 1987); J.A. Mangan, ed., *The Cultural Bond: Sport, Empire, Society* (London, 1993).

numbers English-speaking people are destined at no distant date to surpass any other branch of the human stock'. It was vital to devise structures and institutions in 'Greater Britain' which would prevent another 'great schism of the Anglo-Saxon race'. The problem of 'British unity' could be satisfactorily resolved – to mutual benefit. In 1913 Lord Milner, lately High Commissioner in South Africa, was another to address himself to the problem of *The Nation and the Empire*. The wide dispersion of the British race had given Britons 'a unique range of experience, and the control of an unrivalled wealth and variety of material resources'. But that very dispersion was also a source of weakness because it made the problem of maintaining British unity so difficult. To fail to find a solution would be incredible folly and a huge disaster. The *Pax Britannica* was essential to the maintenance of civilized conditions of existence among one-fifth of the human race. He talked without reservation about the importance of the 'racial bond'. 'It is the British race which built the Empire, and it is the undivided British race which can alone uphold it.' Within the 'British race' he included all the stocks of the British Isles. Empire had another significance – for it was their 'common work' and, as such, held a foremost place in forging the national unity of Britain itself.[10]

Colonial British?

Such writers believed that, given time, their views would prevail, but feared that time would not be granted them. On the other hand, in mid-century, views had been expressed with equal conviction that separation and dissolution were inevitable and not necessarily disastrous. 'Greater Britain' was an unrealizable dream. Distance and individual cultural and economic development would ensure the emergence of distinctive identities and lead to *de facto* autonomy if not *de jure* independence in the British colonial world. So long as existing patterns of migration prevailed, 'Britishness' would be an inescapable part of the inheritance of those who settled in the Antipodes or in Canada but it would become something more than merely a variation on the mixture which made up 'Great Britain' itself. The sense of identity would inevitably be different, though it would not be possible to say with what speed and completeness it would crystallize.

There was, indeed, one final paradox. The colonies of settlement were, in a sense, more genuinely British than Great Britain because there the various peoples of Britain lived more closely alongside each other than they did at home. To some extent they participated in cultural and social activities from which, in Britain itself, they would have felt excluded or which they

---

[10] G. Parkin, *Imperial Federation: The Problem of National Unity* (London, 1893) pp. 4–5; Lord Milner, *The Nation and the Empire* (London, 1913) pp. xxxi–v.

never came across. In Natal, for example, the young Alan Paton, son of a Scots father, found himself participating in what was admittedly an English-language *Eisteddfod*. Such 'Britishness' should not be taken too far but it was undoubtedly a unifying response in an environment which was still fraught with uncertainty, not least concerning relationships either with indigenous peoples or with French-speakers or Afrikaans-speakers who were living, reluctantly, in territory which was advertised as 'British'. Moreover, Canada and Australia were more 'Celtic' than was Britain itself – though there was as great a difference between the Scots-Irish Orangemen of Ontario and the Irish Catholics of Melbourne as there was within Ireland itself. In 1901, for example, Scots formed 15 per cent of the British-born in Australia, 21 per cent in Canada and 23 per cent in New Zealand, whereas Scots constituted some 10 per cent of the United Kingdom population.[11]

Some Victorians therefore watched the development of New Zealand, the Australian states, the 'British' colonies in South Africa, and British North America/Canada with admiration but with a certain amount of anxiety as the century progressed. At its close, the formation of the Commonwealth of Australia, on a federal basis, was a further sign that 'colonial nationalism' was a reality, though its full import was not clear.

Earlier, the creation of the Dominion of Canada in 1867, also on a federal basis, had been a step of great importance. The belief that 'the British North American possessions will become one great and independent Country' had gained ground in the 1860s – initially to the dismay of some British observers – in the context of the Civil War in the United States. Some mid-Victorian writers at home, however, believed that 'Canada' was a nonsense. Sir Charles Dilke in his *Greater Britain* (1868) condemned 'the narrowness of mind that has led us to see in Canada a piece of England, and in America a hostile country'. He urged the position 'that we are no more fellow-countrymen of the Canadians than of the Americans of the North or West'. The Canadians and the Americans should then be made to sort out their own relations with each other. Twelve thousand British troops and a royal standard hoisted at Ottawa could not protect a frontier which was 2,000 miles in length.

Anglo-Saxons all?

Dilke and other writers were very conscious of the United States. It was there, after all, that a greater proportion of the 'British race' went rather

---

[11] W.S. Reid, ed., *The Scottish Tradition in Canada* (Toronto, 1976); T. Devine, ed., *Scottish Emigration and Scottish Society* (Edinburgh, 1992); M.D. Pentis, *The Scottish in Australia* (Melbourne, 1987); J.M. Bumsted, *A History of the Peoples of Canada* (2 vols, Toronto, 1993).

than to any settlement within the bounds of the British Empire. 'For purposes of commerce and civilisation', Dilke wrote, 'America is a truer colony of Britain than is Canada.' Just what the British-American relationship should be was indeed of fundamental importance in the nineteenth century. Inevitably, after the War of Independence, bitterness and suspicion remained on both sides of the Atlantic. Yet their commercial relationships were of great importance to both countries and may be held to be an underlying factor which promoted peace. Even so, Anglophobia on the one side and fears of growing American power on the other caused friction which issued again in war in 1812. Boundary disputes between the United States and Britain (in respect of 'Canada') were not resolved until the 1840s, whilst those over fishing continued. The United States believed it faced a hostile Britain in the West Indies. The British were fearful of American expansion in the south and west. The outbreak of the American Civil War again exacerbated relations and a third British-American war seemed a possibility. There were those in Britain who believed that 'the South' had created a nation – and who were also not unmindful of the benefit that might be gained if 'America' became permanently fragmented. A victorious North did not forget. Even so, speaking generally, relations between the two countries began to improve, though as late as 1895 there was talk of war arising out of the boundary dispute between British Guiana and Venezuela.

By the new century, however, not least owing to the work of British scholars and politicians, particularly James Bryce, who explained *The American Commonwealth* to British readers, a different climate had been created. British-American marriages amongst the political and social elite were a sign that a rapprochement had been reached – for example Joseph Chamberlain, William Harcourt, Lord Randolph Churchill and George Curzon all had American wives. No one was so foolish as to suppose that the United States could be re-enlisted in 'Greater Britain', but another concept was to hand, that of 'Anglo-Saxon patriotism' or of 'the English-speaking peoples'. It was the product of a British-American union, Winston Churchill, who was to seek to write the history of the latter in the new century. 'We have a domestic patriotism as Scotchmen or as Englishmen or as Irishmen, or what you will', declared Arthur Balfour in 1895. The future Prime Minister continued, 'We have an Imperial patriotism as citizens of the British Empire. But surely, in addition to that, we have also an Anglo-Saxon patriotism ... '.[12]

This healing of the 'schism in the Anglo-Saxon race' was a reflection of social and ethnic forces then in the ascendancy on both sides of the Atlantic. The process was still uncertain in its implications. The past could continue to throw up awkward perceptions and conflicts of interest. Nevertheless, not least in the ease of communication made possible by a common language,

---

[12] Cited in C.S. Campbell, *From Revolution to Rapprochement: The United States and Great Britain, 1783–1900* (London, 1974) p. 204.

the past also brought a particular intensity and intimacy to the British-American relationship. America, in short, was not simply a fading aspect of the British past. Indeed, its present was so vibrant and dynamic that it threatened to become a more significant element in the twentieth-century British present than the British past itself.

India: British?

Before Clive's victories in Bengal, the notion that 'India' would in any sense be thought 'British' would have seemed a fantastic and possibly undesirable vision. Even then, but a small part of the sub-continent was under the control of the East India Company and whether that company was subordinate to government was a vexed issue over subsequent decades. The India Act (1784) in theory set up a dual system between the company and the government with each party knowing its respectives roles. In practice, the position was not as clear, partly because the company was itself a formidable factor in domestic British politics. Therefore, so far as the position in India was concerned, 'the British' did not present a monolithic appearance in dealings with 'Indians'. By the 1780s, however, the British seemed to be gaining the upper hand over their European rivals, the French. That position was not settled, even so, until after the conclusion of the protracted Revolutionary and Napoleonic Wars. In 1798 the Marquess Wellesley arrived in India as Governor-General, determined upon a 'forward' policy. He was assisted by his younger brother Arthur (later the Duke of Wellington), the victor at Waterloo in 1815 when he brought Napoleon's 'Hundred days' to an end. Over the next half a century, British control was extended in area after area of the sub-continent. Sometimes territory was directly annexed as 'British India', sometimes treaties were made with native rulers which allowed them a certain independence but which nevertheless ensured that British interests were protected. Although there were some disasters, notably the failure of the advance into Afghanistan in 1842, the British military campaigns were generally successful. One thing, it seemed, simply led to another, but as the magnitude of British involvement became evident questions as to its long-term significance could not be avoided. By any standards, this was a conquest on a scale beyond anything any British government had previously contemplated.[13]

---

[13] C. Bayley, *Imperial Meridian: The British Empire and the World 1780–1830* (London, 1989); M. Fisher, ed., *The Politics of the British Annexation of India 1757–1857* (Oxford, 1994); T.A. Heathcote, *The Military in British India* (Manchester, 1994); P. Marshall, *Problems of Empire: Britain and India, 1757–1813* (London, 1968); P. Marshall, *Bengal, the British Bridgehead* (Cambridge, 1988).

It was apparent that India would not be a country of settlement. How could a huge sub-continent containing an extraordinary mosaic of languages, peoples and religions be governed? It would certainly require a network of Indian subordinates and clients, amongst them soldiers. In this sense, as the inheritors of a Mogul empire which had decayed, the British were but the latest in a long series of conquerors who had shaped 'India' to their liking. But that was not enough either for Evangelicals or Utilitarians. Before addressing himself to his *History of England*, Macaulay turned his historical mind to the problem which India now presented. He confessed – and he was not unique in this – that the destinies of British India seemed to him covered with thick darkness. In 1833, in the House of Commons, he preached a different message for India from that which applied in 1832 in Britain itself. In India, Britain should not reform that it might preserve but reform that it might, one day, become redundant. He foresaw the possibility that 'by good government we may educate our subjects into a capacity for better government, that, having become instructed in European knowledge, they may, in some future age, demand European institutions ... The sceptre may pass away from us.' It would be 'the proudest day in English history'. To achieve this transformation, however, it was necessary to be unsentimental: 'a single shelf of a good European library was worth the whole native literature of India and Arabia'. Macaulay was, perhaps, not as familiar with that literature as some British scholars who did interest themselves in it, notably Sir William Jones. Nevertheless, he was strong in his belief that what India needed at this juncture was a class, inevitably an elite, who were 'Indian in blood and colour, but English in taste, opinions, in morals, and in intellect'. Macaulay did not add 'in religion', but English and Scottish missionaries, now allowed more scope, believed that Christianity would also be an important element in this process of transformation.[14]

The notion of an elevating and unimpeded production of brown Britons received a setback in 1857 (100 years after Clive's victory at Plassey). A mutiny began at a small military station some 40 miles from Delhi. Whether now perceived as local in its origins and significance or seen as a national rebellion, it shattered British complacency. If it happened once, it might happen again. Although the mutiny was successfully put down, it was necessary to think hard about military resources. The mutiny also dealt a blow to assumptions that social intercourse between rulers and ruled could be uncomplicated. The British – soldiers, merchants, missionaries, administrators – were all aware that they were a small minority in a large country. It would be safer to keep themselves to themselves. For such people, enduring the rigours of Hindustan was not a universally attractive prospect. 'Anglo-Indians' (i.e. the British in India) felt themselves somewhat despised by the British at

---

[14] Macaulay, 10 July 1833, cited in G. Bennett, ed., *The Concept of Empire: Burke to Attlee* (London, 1953) p. 74.

home. It was felt in the British army, for example, that those officers who sought service in India did so for financial reasons, a very base motive. It was only there that they could afford to pay for the sport and social life they enjoyed. They were not sufficiently well off to enjoy these things at home. The Victorian military hero Lord Wolseley found the British officers he encountered in India in the 1850s wanting in good breeding and badly educated. The small 'Anglo-Indian' (Eurasian) community that emerged suffered from similar disdain. It identified with the British but the British did not reciprocate.

It was evident, after the mutiny was suppressed, that new structures for British rule in India were required. The East India Company was abolished and 'dual control' disappeared. India, however, could not be simply incorporated into 'Great Britain' and governed from London as though it were Scotland. A new kind of dual system came in. In India, at the apex, stood the Viceroy with his advisers in the Government of India. In London, the Secretary of State for India was a member of the British Cabinet and was responsible to Parliament. He had a Council to advise him. The successful government of 'British India' depended on a satisfactory working relationship between these two men and their officials. The pomp and ceremony surrounding a Viceroy was a sight to behold. British officials in India placed the scale of their responsibilities above those of their counterparts in the small states (by comparison) of Europe.[15]

It was this extraordinary position in India which went a long way to convincing the British political and administrative elite that they too were extraordinary. The 'Raj' made Britain special. No European state had anything like it. As the mutiny slipped into the past, there was renewed optimism and a fresh stress upon 'good government' and 'efficiency'. That, in turn, required a massive improvement in the country's roads and railways. No one doubted that the British position in India rested still on the possession of

---

[15] A.T. Embree, ed., *1857 in India: Mutiny or War of Independence?* (Boston, 1963); T. Metcalf, *The Aftermath of Revolt: India, 1857–1870* (Princeton, 1964); R.K. Renford, *The Non-official British in India to 1920* (Delhi, 1987); S. Gopal, *British Policy in India, 1858–1905* (Cambridge, 1965); R.J. Moore, *Liberalism and Indian Politics, 1872–1922* (London, 1966,); F. Hutchins, *The Illusion of Permanence: British Imperialism in India* (Princeton, 1967); D. Dilks, *Curzon in India* (2 vols, London, 1969, 1970); B. Parry, *Delusions and Discoveries: Studies on India in the British Imagination 1880–1930* (London, 1972).

9.1 Depot Picnic: Darjeeling, 1876. The British in late-Victorian India were conscious at every turn of time and space in the country they governed. The shock of the Indian Mutiny was behind them but, even when clustered together as one big happy family for the camera, it could not be forgotten that they constituted a meagre ruling elite grouped together against a background full of strange gods and incomprehensible structures. The imposing later edifices of imperial British New Delhi were, from this perspective, only pimples on alien terrain.

power but the rulers allowed themselves the feeling that they exercised it, in general, with unusual benevolence. Queen Victoria, as has been noted, allowed herself to become an empress in 1876. It is important to grasp, however, that she was only an empress in respect of India where she was queen/empress. Great Britain itself had not been turned into an empire. As Empress of India, she received the obeisance of a galaxy of Indian princes, some of whom in turn came to London.

At the end of the century, Lord Curzon, as Viceroy, continued to express the view that the symbiosis which 'British India' had come to represent was remarkable. He deceived himself about its permanence and was himself to encounter growing problems in Bengal. Even so, it was by no means clear that 'British India' was doomed. The Liberal government did institute modest reforms (the Morley-Minto Reforms) in 1909 as a measured response to the demands of the Indian National Congress for self-government, but it did not suppose that 'the proudest day in English history was at hand'. Sir Arthur Hirzel, one of the architects of the reforms, remained convinced that the British Empire had been given to the British to make it Christian: 'This is to be Britain's contribution to the redemption of mankind'.[16] Lofty aspirations of this kind abounded. 'If we are judged', wrote G.K. Chesterton, 'it will not be for the merely intellectual transgression of failing to appreciate other nations, but for the supreme spiritual transgression of failing to appreciate ourselves.'[17]

Other more jaundiced commentators felt that there was little danger of that happening. They saw rather an enormous gap between these lofty aspirations and the reality of British rule not only in India but in Malaya and elsewhere in South-East Asia. The French were present in Indo-China, the Dutch and Portuguese in the East Indies, the Spaniards (followed by the Americans) in the Philippines, but Britain's presence in the 'Greater India' which extended from the Arabian Gulf to the Malay States was pre-dominant. In this region, as Dilke put it, 'England in the East is not the England that we know. Flousy Britannia, with her anchor and ship, becomes a mysterious Oriental despotism, ruling a sixth of the human race ... '. The means by which she did so did not altogether accord with the rhetoric of Liberal England in 1868. Were the fortunes to be made out of Hong Kong (obtained from China in the Treaty of Nanjing in 1842) and Singapore (developed by Raffles after 1819) exemplary? Indeed, was it not more likely that Britain would be 'corrupted' by India than that India would be won for 'Liberty'? Early on, when Warren Hastings (Governor and Governor-General of Bengal, 1772–85) had been impeached by the House of Commons (1788–95),

---

[16] Cited in G. Studdert-Kennedy, *British Christians, Indian Nationalists and the Raj* (Delhi, 1991) p. 47.

[17] See the discussion of Chesterton's views in J. Grainger, *Patriotisms: Britain: 1900–1939* (London, 1986) pp. 104–12.

Edmund Burke spoke scornfully against what he called 'geographical morality'. There was no dual standard. Behaviour was either right or wrong. The location of that behaviour was not relevant. He feared that the people of England would be turned into 'a people of *Banyans*' (Hindu traders). The national character would be lost in a fraudulent conspiracy which extended from Cheltenham to Calcutta. Despite Burke's strictures, however, Hastings was acquitted. The British presence in India, based as it was on conquest, required an improving mission to sustain it over the long term, but for the time being it made sense, some believed, to do in India what the Indians did.[18]

However, the central tension of 'British India' would not go away. The transition to 'democracy' in Britain itself, as has been noted, rested on the notion that government depended upon consent for its legitimacy. The British Empire did not presuppose any such principle. It is perhaps appropriate to speak of this issue in terms of an unresolved tension rather than an admitted contradiction. British Radicals, like John Bright, rued the day Britain had got itself mixed up in India but, having done so, it was impossible simply to withdraw. The inconsistencies would be resolved sooner or later. Some European and American observers, however, were not persuaded by such justification. Victorian Britain, in their eyes, was shot through with hypocrisy. Britain, this paragon of constitutional development, busied itself at the same time in creating or consolidating in its empire the greatest overseas extension of itself that the world had ever seen. It joined with zest in the 'Scramble for Africa' and in the late nineteenth century added huge tracts of West, East, Central and South Africa to its domain. The capitals of Europe rang with denunciations as the might of the British Empire was pitted against the 'gallant little Boers' in South Africa in the war that ended the century. After so much pride, they said, there would surely come a fall. And, despite the glories of Elgar's *Pomp and Circumstance*, there were some in the land of hope and glory who were fearful of the future. Was the titan getting weary?

In the nineteenth century, therefore, it was scarcely possible to avoid the notion of Britain's imperial destiny. New lands in far corners of the world caught the popular imagination. Their products featured in advertisements, a reflection of the degree to which Britain was now at the heart of a global economic system. Wool came to be identified with 'Australia' or New Zealand, wheat and timber with Canada. There were dramas – the death of Gordon in the Sudan or the relief of Mafeking in the Boer War – to satisfy newspaper correspondents and writers of adventure stories. This 'propaganda' of empire was ubiquitous but it did not encounter substantial opposition. True, it was pointed out that the sun which never set on the British Empire never penetrated the dark and squalid corners of British cities, but even the

---

[18] P. Marshall, *The Impeachment of Warren Hastings* (Oxford, 1965); Burke's speech of 7 May 1789 in Bennett, ed., *Concept of Empire*, pp. 56–7.

deprived might sense that they were superior to the subordinate races of the empire.

The overseas challenge reinforced a certain conception of national character. Mad dogs and Englishmen went out in the mid-day sun – perhaps Scotsmen were a little more circumspect. Englishmen of the solid middle class distrusted arid intellectualism, for they knew that they would be called upon to face physical danger in exotic surroundings. They had to pull together and 'team spirit' was a necessary aspect of the imperial enterprise. It was cultivated in the newly codified games which were vigorously encouraged on the playing fields of public schools. Englishmen who emerged from these pavilions of applause had an arrogant dignity about them which impressed even as it repelled those 'lesser breeds' with whom they later came into contact. The City of London which had risen to become the leading world financial centre depended upon an intricate network of personal relationships and implicit codes of conduct. In the eyes of some later historians, it flourished as the distinctive hive of gentlemen capitalists.

There was, however, an unresolved paradox. It was a commercial orthodoxy that Britain benefited from peace, but empire, in the last analysis, depended upon the capacity to exercise force. Bright and Cobden in mid-century disliked formal empire because it necessarily entailed conquest and a military machine to sustain control. Their views were influential but not decisive. The world was not a peaceful place. Informal empire – a position of influence without direct annexation or control – might be preferable but it could not be sustained if other powers, chiefly European, were bent on annexation. It was necessary for Britain to maintain garrisons across the globe, modest in size though they were, and, above all, to maintain naval supremacy.

'More an Asiatic power than a European'?

These preoccupations, and the social and cultural assumptions which flowed from them, were natural in a global power. Yet, despite this evidence of 'exceptionalism', Great Britain was necessarily and inescapably European. Geography could not be ignored. A position of 'isolation' – in the sense of complete detachment from the political, military and economic developments of the European mainland – was neither feasible nor desirable for British governments or commercial companies. Even so, from 1815 to 1914, the British position was one of great caution. British forces had played their part in the final defeat of Napoleon in 1815 but then, for a century, they were not seen in Western Europe. British forces did take part, however, in the war against Russia in the Crimea in the mid-1850s.

Britain was not invaded, though in the 1860s Palmerston prompted the construction of a series of forts to defend the country's main ports and arsenals against attack. The enemy might be France, or possibly even Russia or the United States. Invasion scares recurred at regular intervals, climaxing again in the years before 1914 when Germany was popularly supposed to be contemplating an attack. The emphasis remained upon naval supremacy. Britain's security would be best maintained by deterring a potential invader rather than by seeking to develop a large standing army to match the military might of other European powers. Given the increasing pace of change in naval engineering as the century developed, it was generally thought that it would be quite impossible to do both. In the first decade of the new century, however, a campaign for 'National Service', that is to say for military conscription, was unsuccessfully mounted. A Liberal government remained suspicious of such a force. It smacked of that 'militarism' which Britain had thus far largely escaped but which afflicted other European countries. It followed that Britain did not take part in the significant wars that did take place – in the Italian peninsula, between Prussia and Austria, and between Prussia and France.

Britain's lack of military might to some extent restricted its diplomatic role in Europe. Naturally, Britain was represented (by Wellington and Castlereagh) at the Congress of Vienna (1814–15) but in the eyes of the other major conservative European powers Britain did not fully share their aim to preserve the old European order through a 'congress system'. It had not escaped notice that in the peace settlement Britain had been most anxious to secure extra-European territory (Malta, Heligoland, Ceylon, Tobago, St Lucia and Mauritius). Castlereagh rejected the right of the powers to interfere in the affairs of neighbouring states. Britain would be found in its place, he wrote in 1820, when an actual danger menaced the System of Europe, but it would not 'act upon abstract and speculative principles of precaution'. The 'System of Europe', over subsequent decades, proved rather frail, and the British perception of 'actual danger' was rather restricted. Alongside a rather general enthusiasm for peoples rightly struggling to be free (Greeks or Italians) and a certain predisposition towards 'constitutional' movements, there was a recognition, certainly by mid-century, of the delicate position in which Britain found itself. During the Prussian-Austrian war of 1866, for example, Disraeli claimed that 'England is no longer a mere European Power; she is the metropolis of a great maritime empire ... she interferes in Asia, because she is really more an Asiatic power than a European'.[19] At the same time, in convoluted language, he reiterated that there could nonetheless be occasions when it might be England's duty to interfere in European wars.

By the last quarter of the century, in the absence of such interference, 'Europe' had come to assume a rather different appearance. The unification of Germany and Italy had both taken place, and the power of the former

---

[19] Disraeli cited in W. Monypenny and G. Buckle, *The Life of Benjamin Disraeli* iv (London, 1916) p. 467.

was apparent. There had been some observers in 1870 who had supposed that the Franco-Prussian war was indeed one in which Britain should 'interfere' but they did not prevail. Thereafter, as a system of alliances and alignments crystallized on the Continent, the British position became increasingly difficult. Gladstone, in his prime, had still remained attached to the notion of a 'Concert of Europe' in which Britain should play its part, but that era now appeared to be passing. Should Britain align with France and Russia or with Germany and Austria-Hungary plus Italy, or with neither? Of course, in particular situations the choices which had to be made were more subtle than this bold statement suggests. In addition, the blocs that have been mentioned were themselves to some extent fluid. Nevertheless, in essence, that was the problem which confronted British diplomacy in Europe into the twentieth century.

In 1904 an *entente* was signed with France which resolved some colonial issues between the two countries and, although it entailed no military commitment, it could be held to tilt Britain in the direction of France. In 1907 an agreement was also signed with Russia, again specifically dealing with an 'imperial' issue (Persia/Iran), but which might have broader implications. At the same time, the Foreign Secretary, Grey, endeavoured to keep his options open and indicate that Britain had not aligned itself with an 'anti-German' camp. Britain, it seemed, had evolved into a semi-detached position. No one in Paris or Berlin knew with certainty how London might react in the event of a European conflagration. Perhaps the British did not know themselves. In what circumstances did they really have to give 'Europe' the priority which they had been reluctant to assign it during their century of empire?

Perhaps inevitably, statecraft exists on a level of its own. Beneath the calculations and communications of diplomats were a range of popular prejudices and attitudes which sometimes coexisted very uneasily with their preoccupations. British greatness seemed self-evident. There was no call to probe more deeply the nature of Britain's European identity. By the last decades of the century, however, one underlying issue was coming to the surface – the relationship between Britain and a now united Germany. We have noted earlier the extent to which 'Britishness' in the eighteenth century had been forged with France, first Catholic and then for a time Atheist, as 'the Other'. Now, while there were still colonial flashpoints with France, the 'threat' which it had allegedly posed for so many decades had all but disappeared. Was 'Germany' the new threat against which 'Britain' defined itself?

There was no straightforward answer. From one point of view, Britain and Germany were both 'Protestant' and 'Teutonic' countries whose royal families had intermarried – though of course there was a substantial German Roman Catholic population. From Handel to Mendelssohn, Germany had apparently remedied Britain's musical deficiencies. German scholarship in many fields was widely admired. On balance, British sympathies favoured

Prussia rather than France in 1870. Preaching before the German Kaiser at Sandringham in 1899, the Bishop of London had no hesitation in stating that 'the Teutonic race has the same fundamental ideas'.

Yet, in the new century, a more negative picture emerged. It stemmed in Britain from alarm at the pace of German industrial and economic development – apparently challenging the position Britain had come to assume for herself. At another level, the zeal to create 'English music' perhaps responded to a wish to escape from German musical domination and link up with an earlier English musical past. When the 'naval race' between the two countries intensified in the early twentieth century, negative images began to replace positive ones. Perhaps it was time to bury that common 'Saxon' past which had been so gloried in by an earlier generation of historians. It appeared that Germany was no longer content with the hegemonic role in Europe which could be hers but was challenging for a 'place in the sun', in the process seeking to be the 'World-State' that Britain considered itself to be. Perhaps this was the challenge that Seeley had forecast in 1883. The outcome would determine whether Britain was indeed the 'great and solid World-State' which he desired. It would be in Europe, after all, that the fate of the Empire would be settled.[20]

'Fundamental instincts'

Participation in a major European war had taken millions of Britons to a continent which would otherwise have remained unknown to them. Of course, British travellers of a certain class, had long made themselves felt in various European countries. It was often when they were abroad that they had become conspicuously aware of the merits of their native land. 'I think being far away', wrote the Victorian historian J.R. Green, 'makes one fairer to England when one is at home and worried with all the pettiness and ignorance.'[21] There was a consensus, too, that the English were acute observers of foreign scenes because they never succumbed to foreign ways. Expatriates made a virtue of national segregation and distinctiveness. The novelist Rider Haggard, familiar with the empire, speculated that this persistent refusal to be overwhelmed by any surrounding people was the mark of a ruling race. It was the coolness of an Englishman's manner, when confronted by continental bluster and gesticulation, which invariably carried the

---

[20] R. Ashton, *The German Idea: Four English Writers and the Reception of German Thought 1800–1860* (Cambridge, 1960); K. Robbins, *Protestant Germany through British Eyes: A Complex Victorian Encounter* (London, 1993).
[21] Cited in J. Premble, *The Mediterranean Passion: Victorians and Edwardians in the South* (Oxford, 1987) pp. 270, 271, 269.

day. In no way should Englishmen seek to be anonymous in an alien climate. Users of Murray's *Handbook to Greece* were urged to make sure that their dress should at all times 'be obviously that of an Englishman'.

The Great War, however, had brought a very different set of visitors – dressed in mud-stained, blood-spattered khaki uniforms. There were corners of many foreign fields which would remain for ever 'England'. But was this eruption into Europe merely a temporary aberration? 'The great fault of the English', one English scholar wrote in 1897, 'is their insularity, and insistence on the English ideal as the only possible.'[22] Had anything changed as a result of the recent past?

Clemenceau and Lloyd George (not an Englishman) had been allies in the Great War. Neither had been slow to claim credit for victory. After his retirement, the former came to Oxford in 1921 to receive an honorary degree from the university. 'I have to tell you', the French 'Tiger' declared to the British Prime Minister during his visit, 'that from the very day after the Armistice I found you an enemy of France.' 'Well', replied Lloyd George, 'was it not always our traditional policy?'

According to Lloyd George's private secretary, Philip Kerr (an Anglicized Scotsman), Britain had another 'traditional policy'. It was, he believed, 'a fundamental instinct with the British people to avoid intervention in Europe except in crises which threatened their own security'. It was better to 'leave Europe to itself' and he advised Lloyd George to turn his 'whole attention to the problems of Great Britain and the British Empire'. As the previous section in this chapter reveals, that there were sufficient problems to engage his full attention was indisputable, but it was far from clear that 'traditional policies' and 'fundamental instincts' constituted infallible guides for the future.[23]

---

[22] L. Creighton, *Life and Letters of Mandell Creighton* (London, 1913) p. 499.
[23] Cited in A. Sharp, 'Standard-Bearers in a Tangle: British Perceptions of France After the First World War' in D. Dutton, ed., *Statecraft and Diplomacy in the Twentieth century* (Liverpool, 1995) pp. 56–8; A. Orde, *British Policy and European Reconstruction after the First World War* (Cambridge, 1990).

9.2 Securely anchored: British naval vessels in Valetta Harbour, 1860. The Malta of the Knights of St John came to an end when Nelson took the island in 1799 after the brief French occupation. It came formally under the Colonial Office in 1836 and during the remainder of the century it became one of the most important naval fortresses of the British Empire. Malta came to have great strategic and sentimental importance. During the Second World War, it withstood aerial bombardment and naval blockade. The entire island was awarded the George Cross by George VI for its bravery. Although there was intermittent talk, in the era of decolonization, that Malta might buck the trend and be 'integrated' with Britain, it became independent in 1964 and the Royal Navy withdrew from its bases. Malta's long history is complex but the island's continuing use of the English language in many contexts still makes it seem like an unusually sunny part of the British Isles for British holidaymakers.

Britain had entered the twentieth century with insular pride still intact. 'You English boys', declared a naval captain, 'often do not realize the great privileges, the great heritage, you possess simply though being born in this little island.' For Englishmen, a late-Victorian anthologist wrote, the sea had been both a dread and wonder, but so far as was known, 'no peoples have loved it as in these latter days it is loved by us'.[24] It was as 'the Island Race' that the British defined themselves. The sea which surrounded the islands of Britain had made the quality of their civilization possible. The Royal Navy was their vital protection. British travellers in the Mediterranean saw the Union Jack flying in Gibraltar, Malta and Cyprus. A writer in Malta in 1882, standing upon the Barecca of Valetta, looked down with pride upon the great forts and British ironclads which slept securely beneath their walls. It was a sentiment expressed in many parts of the world. Britain's security was safe so long as it controlled 'Blue Water'. A certain hysteria was apparent when a German Fleet, at the beginning of the century, appeared to be a challenge to that supremacy.

Then, in 1906, the *Daily Mail* put a shocking interpretation upon the tentative advances in the ability of men to fly. 'England is no longer an island', it announced. The chariots of a foe would descend on British soil in a future war – which came, indeed, within a decade. Something fundamental was happening. The psychological barrier which the sea had represented over so many centuries was being challenged.[25]

There was even renewed talk of constructing a Channel Tunnel after the end of the war. The Foreign Office addressed the threat which this represented in a memorandum in May 1920. It conceded that there could be real advantages in such a project if Britain and France would maintain a perpetual friendship and never quarrel. However, such an assumption could not be made. Real friendship had 'always' been difficult because of 'differences of language, mentality and national character'. There were no grounds for supposing that these differences would decrease. Britain would never be liked in France and nothing could justify the loss of security which 'our insular position' continued to bestow, scientific and mechanical developments notwithstanding. By 1925, the French ambassador in London was writing that the British would not make more commitments in foreign policy. Britain's detachment from the Continent was all the more strong because it represented the thinking not just of an oligarchy, but of the new democracy. Talented writers were quite unable to convince the British people that the Rhine was

---

[24] Cited in C.F. Behrman, *Victorian Myths of the Sea* (Athens, Ohio, 1977), p. 151; B. Semmel, *Liberalism and Naval Strategy: Ideology, Interest and Sea Power during the Pax Britannica* (Boston, 1986).
[25] See the two books by A. Gollin, *No Longer an Island: Britain and the Wright Brothers 1902–1909* (London, 1984) and *The Impact of Air Power on the British people and their Government, 1909–14* (London, 1989).

their frontier.[26] The past, as taught in school, still showed that it was the sea which made Britain what it was. The historian Ramsay Muir had compiled his very successful *New School Atlas of Modern History* (1911 and many subsequent editions) which was 'intended to be used by young people of the greatest colonising nation in history'. Such works perpetuated a framework for thinking of Britain into the postwar world.

At the Royal Academy Banquet in May 1912 the Archbishop of Canterbury contrasted the drab and uninspiring surroundings in which the officials of His Majesty's Government had to work with the artistic achieve-ments adorning the walls of public buildings abroad. A mural artist who was present, troubled by this example of British exceptionalism, promptly offered his services at no public expense. His scheme for the Foreign Office met with the approval of Sir Edward Grey, the Foreign Secretary, and work commenced, unfortunately interrupted by war. The murals were fixed in place at its conclusion, having taken the artist seven years. The paintings were to depict 'the origin, education, development, expansion and triumph of the British Empire … '.[27]

Britannia Sponsa represented 'the seafarers or successive waves of overseas tribes landing to obtain possession of Britannia, conceived as a wild, fair-haired shepherd girl, and the withdrawal of an earlier and ruder race'. Between the two groups stood the vision of an angel holding the chalice (an echo of the Glastonbury legend). Thus the spirit of Christianity was represented. The Roman occupation was hinted at in the broken fragments of classical architecture amongst the irises. *Britannia Nutrix* has the bride becoming the mother. The rearing of 'a sturdy race of children and the mother's devotion are emphasised – Britain the Motherland'. *Britannia Bellatrix* has Britannia teaching her sons those bodily exercises and manly sports which would fit them for war, should it come. *Britannia Mater Colonorum* conveys the spirit of the expansion of the race overseas. Finally, *Britannia Pacificatrix* was inspired by Great Britain and the United States, 'the two great English-speaking races' concluding a general Arbitration Treaty. The main idea was that, having won her position in the world, Britain's influence was for peace. 'Happily', the artist noted, 'the diplomatic re-grouping of the nations did not cause serious artistic difficulties.' The 're-grouping of the nations', it has to be admitted, has proceeded apace since 1919.

---

[26] Cited in M. Cennick, ' "The Myth of Perfidious Albion" and French National Identity' in Dutton, ed., *Statecraft and Diplomacy*, pp. 27–8; A. Sharp, 'Britain and the Channel Tunnel, 1919–1920', *Australian Journal of Politics and History* 25 (1979).

[27] The artist's descriptive account of the 'Mural Decorations at the Foreign Office' was kindly made available to me by the Foreign and Commonwealth Office. See also the publication *Foreign and Commonwealth Office* (London, 1994).

An old-fashioned island fortress?

Amongst the 'talented writers' who argued that the war had made a fundamental difference, there were some historians. In a paper read before the British Academy in 1919, G.M. Trevelyan lamented 'that insular ignorance of recent continental history' which was one of the hallmarks of English education. It was time to end the notion that Britain was simply some kind of old-fashioned island fortress. 'Since the war', he concluded, 'we are, whether we like it or not, a part of the Continent.' The tragedy, he supposed, was that the British were quite untrained to mix with their neighbours, or even talk to them.[28] There were other writers of similar views, but they did not predominate. The war was as often seen as an aberration, though perhaps a necessary one. It did not foreshadow any national redefinition as 'European', in a fundamental sense.

Indeed, the past that was most immediately present after 1919 was the horror of the Great War itself. The scale of the suffering touched practically every household in Britain. It has been calculated that around 3 million Britons lost a close relative in the war, though there were many more among the 'secondary bereaved'. Somewhere in the region of 5 million served and survived, though they were never quite the same again. Of these, perhaps some 3 million had experienced the nightmare of trench warfare on the western front. A way had to be found – from Cenotaph in Whitehall to village memorial – to cope with such loss. The rituals that evolved embedded themselves in British culture. The losses that had been suffered extended across England, Scotland, Wales – and Ireland – in an army that was British. 'To wear a poppy in November', one historian writes, 'or to glance at a war memorial in a church, chapel or school, is to look back on an extraordinary moment in British history, when this country joined the rest of Europe in embarking on a new era of warfare.'[29]

There was a widespread consensus, however, that 'this country' should not do so again. Mourning was something which the British shared with all other belligerent European nations, but the battlefields on which they died were distant. The memorials that sprung up all over the country testified to a devastating past that was both present and absent. England's green and pleasant land had not been turned into a muddy wilderness but the minds of Britain's soldiers had been churned up, in some cases beyond repair. 'Joining

---

[28] G.M. Trevelyan, 'Englishmen and Italians' in *Recreations of an Historian* (London, 1919) pp. 240–2; K. Robbins, ' "British History" and European Integration' in *History, Religion and Identity in Modern Britain* (London, 1993) pp. 45–57.
[29] J.M. Winter, *The Great War and the British People* (London, 1985) p. 305 and also his *Sites of Memory, Sites of Mourning The Great War in European Cultural Memory* (Cambridge, 1995); A. Gregory, *The Silence of Memory: Armistice Day, 1919–1946* (Oxford, 1994); J. Bourne, *Britain and the Great War, 1914–1918* (London, 1989).

9.3 Mourning Heroes/Galar am yr Arwyr: A bilingual caption is appropriate for a war which had special complexities in Wales. It was David Lloyd George, a Welsh-speaking Welshman, the only such British Prime Minister, who had led Great Britain and the British Empire to victory. Wales joined Belgium and Serbia in his litany of great little nations fighting on the side of freedom. Welsh-speaking recruits from rural Wales, however, could find themselves lost and bewildered in the English-speaking world of the British army. The war, too, came just at the moment when Welsh Non-conformity thought that it had triumphed, but the triumph was bitter-sweet and post-war Wales had a different flavour. This photograph shows the dedication of the War Memorial at Llanfair Caereinion, near Welshpool in mid-Wales.

Europe' appeared tantamount to participation in a continuing 'new era of warfare' and therefore had little to be said for it.

Talking of Castlereagh ...

Of course, at the level of foreign policy, Britain's detachment is not to be equated with indifference or isolation. Successive Foreign Secretaries in the interwar period engaged, as their nineteenth-century predecessors had done, in the traditional activities of 'old diplomacy', but they did so now within a context that was at least formally more democratic. The new League of Nations purported to provide a new framework for the conduct of international affairs. It was an institution and an idea which attracted more popular enthusiasm in Britain than in any other country. In one sense, 'collective security', if taken seriously, implied the end of a British foreign policy which had as its objective the defence of 'British interests', however they were conceived. The Covenant of the League embodied the notion that any member resorting to war in disregard of its obligations should be deemed to have committed an act of war against all other members. Sanctions would follow and, conceivably, British forces – greatly reduced though they were – would enforce a collective peace.

Within these constraints, by the mid-1920s British foreign policy sought to promote Franco-German reconciliation with minimum direct British involvement in whatever structures and agreements might emerge. The agreements concluded at Locarno in 1925 seemed at the time to be a high spot in this process and Britain did appear to be committed (simultaneously) to securing France against Germany and vice versa. It was never clear how this was going to be done, but perhaps that did not matter.

Austen Chamberlain, then Foreign Secretary, did devote considerable attention to Britain's place in Europe, but it did not imply an enduring, deepening and reorientating engagement. Trained himself as a historian, he looked instinctively to the past. 'I was called to face a situation comparable to that which faced Castlereagh after the fall of Napoleon', he wrote to his sister in November 1925. Chamberlain had come into office with clear ideas as to what should be done. Later, reading the historian Webster on 'Castlereagh's foreign policy', he found that he had been 'talking Castlereagh (adapted to the XXth century) without knowing it. And I like to think that there is a continuity of British foreign policy ... '. The past apparently still remained an excellent guide.[30]

'Continuity of British foreign policy' precluded possible British participation in the kind of puzzling European 'federation' which momentarily emerged in French minds in late 1929. It could be dismissed as 'M. Briand's pan-European claptrap', unlikely to see fruit, or alternatively as a sinister design for economic Franco-German cooperation which might have serious implications for British interests. In the event, in this decade, such schemes came to nothing.[31] In part, British anxiety stemmed from the belief that the 'continental' countries still lived in the old world of alliances and the balance of power. There was a supposition, widely shared by the British public, that the League of Nations had put an end to such things.[32]

---

[30] R. Self, ed., *The Austen Chamberlain Diary Letters* (Cambridge, 1995) p. 285.

[31] R. White, ' "Through a glass darkly": The Foreign Office Investigation of French Federalism, January-May 1930' in Dutton, ed., *Statecraft and Diplomacy* pp. 75–95; P.M.R. Stirk, ed., *European Unity in Context: The Interwar Period* (London, 1989).

[32] G. Egerton, *Great Britain and the Creation of the League of Nations* (Chapel Hill, 1978); D.S. Birn, *The League of Nations Union 1918–1945* (Oxford, 1981).

Ideology and nation

A decade later, when Britain again went to war in a conflict which originated on the mainland, there was no room for such comforting assumptions.
After 1933, when Hitler came to power in Germany, a new complexion entered European politics. Until that point, and indeed for some years after,
British preferences in Europe were still substantially driven by inherited perceptions of the national characteristics of other states. Such perceptions remained deeply entrenched, but now jostled uneasily with the increasingly
'ideological' issues which in turn divided British opinion to a degree that had
not been the case since the era of the French Revolution. In one sense, the
ideological/national cleavage had begun earlier than 1933 with the Bolshevik
Revolution in Russia in 1917. The fears and hopes engendered by that event
had reverberated through British public life thereafter. The appeal of 'communism', for some, lay in the fact that it transcended national boundaries. It
rendered obsolete 'national identity', as traditionally conceived, and the
emotions and loyalties bound up with it. In the Soviet Union lay a new civilization whose values and performance were superior to the fossilized structures of a decaying capitalist/imperialist Britain. It was no treason to jettison
'old Britain' confronted by such a tantalizing prospect.

On the other hand, 'fascism', as it operated in Italy after 1922, also
had some admirers. In such a divided Europe, the civil war in Spain which
began in 1936 was frequently seen as an event which foreshadowed a pan-
European struggle between 'fascism' and 'socialism/communism'. British volunteers were eager to join the coming struggle for power. The ideological
conflicts which divided most European states, to greater or lesser degree, in
the 1930s were not absent from Britain but, in general, advocates of communism or fascism existed on the margins of political life, however much
they occasionally occupied the headlines. Viewed from the parliamentary
consensus of London, with only modest variation, the ideologies which
dominated in Europe, whether of Left or Right, were unattractive.[33]

There was sufficient division of opinion, however, to make it difficult
to determine what 'continuity of foreign policy' now required. The past was
coming to seem an uncertain guide in a present in which desire to avoid war
at almost any cost mingled with sympathy/hostility towards fascism/com-
munism, a mingling which in turn rested upon older national perceptions of
France, Germany, Italy or Russia. It seemed that only in Britain, of those
countries which had gone to war in 1914, was there both continuity with the
past and an unforced unity that was 'national' in the present. The debates
which were sparked off by 'Appeasement' in the late 1930s revolved around
the extent to which that individuality was best maintained, either by an active

---

[33] A. Thorpe, ed., *The Failure of Political Extremism in Inter-War Britain* (Exeter,
1989).

alliance policy in Europe, even with unpalatable partners, or by detachment, even if it involved indifference to the fate of small nations in the process. It was the judgement of Neville Chamberlain, Prime Minister after 1937, that Britain had to go to extravagant lengths in the search for peace. Win or lose, a war in which Britain was again involved in Europe would be likely to be disastrous. Only very late in the day could military and political thinking adjust to the fact that, after all, Britain might have to fight another war on the mainland, a war in which the country was not equipped to take the offensive.[34]

Our tight little island

The year 1940 came to have enormous significance. The European war which began in September 1939 remained of uncertain quality for many months. Britain and France were thrown uneasily together. Both countries retained ambiguous memories of their past collaboration in the Great War. It was not easy to be sure that each was not fundamentally concerned with its own survival to the detriment of their prospects against the common enemy. And was that enemy 'Germany' or 'fascism'? Were there still the makings of some kind of deal which would end the war before it properly began? The catastrophic British performance in the North Sea in the spring brought Churchill to power in London. The catastrophic defeat in France and Belgium at the same time threatened to make his time in office short-lived. Churchill summoned up the past, in brilliant oratory, to the rescue of the perilous present. No other person in British public life saw history so clearly and had such a strong sense of his own part in its unfolding. Voices who felt, and sometimes said in private, that the British game was up, and that the only thing that could be done was to seek terms, were brushed aside. The island story lived again at a time of impending disaster. The 'miracle of Dunkirk' seemed an encouraging omen, regardless of the fact that from a sullen France it could appear one more example of scuttle and perfidy.

'We are at bay on our tight little island', broadcast the novelist J.B. Priestley to the Americans, but he felt that there was a marvellous spirit abroad. Britons had no one else to depend on but themselves. It was a sentiment shared by King George VI who found, with some relief, that he no longer had to worry about the French. Every helpful and encouraging aspect of the British past was dredged into the present. Later in the war, after the tide had turned, Laurence Olivier foreshadowed the Normandy landings with his brilliant film of Shakespeare's *Henry V* in which the hero carried the day. T.S. Eliot, naturalized British poet, meditated at moving length on

---

[34] K. Robbins, *Appeasement* (Oxford, 1997 edn).

time past and time present in his wartime *Four Quartets*. The rhetoric of freedom was in full swing, but it was a freedom which did not rest in a particular ideology but rather in the institutions and mores of the British people themselves. It was a war, in a broad sense, for 'Christian civilization' but particularly for the form that civilization took in Britain itself.[35] No society is ever spontaneously and completely 'at one' and beneath the public face there was discord and some tension, particularly as the war drew to an end in Europe and the future had to be considered. Nevertheless, past and present did seem for a time to be fused to an extraordinary degree. In itself that fusion could not take the country to 'victory', but without it, defeat, in the dark years, might have been more likely.

---

[35] P. Maillaud, *The English Way* (London, 1945). Maillaud, a Frenchman who broadcast to France five times a week on the French service of the BBC from June 1940 onwards, wrote 'The English struggle was clearly, whether intentionally or not, the defence of the West and of England's Western self. The German struggle was for the annihilation of the West', p. 259.

Chapter 10

Churches and Chapels: Believing *in Britain* *c.*1745–*c.*1945

Providential integration

Amongst the justifications advanced for British imperialism was the belief in the intrinsic merits of 'British civilization'. The capacity of that civilization to preserve and yet to reform its political institutions has already been noted, but its merits went deeper. British civilization, it was frequently claimed, was a distinctive manifestation of the Christian civilization of Europe. That note, struck in the eighteenth century, was still heard in some surprising quarters in the dark days of 1940.[1] The spectacle of troops from the British Empire assembling together then in defence of freedom reminded the Canadian High Commissioner in London of 'the warfare against the infidel, when Christian men from every part of Europe were gathered together to fight for the deliverance of the Holy Sepulchre'.[2] Similarly, in 1939, when Lord Lloyd advocated *The British Case*, he took the view that British national endeavour should be 'shaped and determined by the requirements of Christian morality'.[3] Belief in a providential mission was certainly not confined to pulpits. *The Times*, for example, continued to assert 'we are a Christian people still'. The newspaper found it odd that Britain, a country which was apparently staking its all in defence of Christian principles, should nevertheless have a national education system which allowed the citizens of the future to have a purely heathen upbringing. The exciting prospect that 'Christendom' might be restored engaged both intellectuals and clergymen. It was understandable, in the prevailing dire circumstances, that somewhat exaggerated claims for Christian Britain should have been made. They had a long pedigree.

---

[1] K. Robbins, 'Britain, 1940 and "Christian Civilization"' K. Robbins, *History, Religion and Identity in Modern Britain* (London, 1993) pp. 195–213.
[2] V. Massey, *The Sword of Lionheart* (London, 1943) p. 25.
[3] Lord Lloyd, *Leadership in Democracy* (Oxford, 1939) pp. 16–17.

At the beginning of the eighteenth century the formation of the British state was widely seen as a providential act. 'England', declared a Welsh preacher, Daniel Williams, in the course of his thanksgiving sermon in London on 1 May 1707, 'is agrandized by the ingrafture of a Nation, so famous for Warriors and men of Sense; and which is more, a people noted among Foreign Churches for Purity of Religion, eminent for Glorious Martyrs, and for Men enjoying the most intimate Communion with God.' He had every expectation that, unless prevented by future backslidings, further marks of Divine Providence might be expected in 'Britain United'.[4]

There was, however, a paradox. It remained the case that it was in their religious convictions and the ecclesiastical structures which expressed them that the diversity of the nations of 'Britain United' was most apparent in 1745. It was a diversity which became even wider in the nineteenth century. Britain came to contain a multiplicity and variety of religious denominations without parallel elsewhere in Europe. Not all of these bodies possessed equal status, either legally or socially, but acceptance of diversity was becoming a marked feature of British life. Even so, the principle of Establishment remained: Church and state mutually reinforced each other. Those outside the ranks of the Established Churches were in a sense still not fully part of conceived national communities – English or Scottish. And two hundred years later both the Church *of* England and the Church *of* Scotland continued to exist as two (rather different) 'Established' Churches within the British state – significantly no 'Church of Britain' had ever come into existence.

In the interval, however, much had changed. 'Establishment' was no longer what it had once been. In particular, in 1945 it was no longer possible, as it had still been a century earlier, to equate 'Britishness' with 'Protestantism'. Roman Catholicism had come to be a significant element in British life, though still somewhat on the margins of public life. 'Dissent' or 'Nonconformity', negative in original stance, now presented itself positively as 'Free Church'. The changing pattern of religious allegiance, therefore, had significant implications for a national identity forged with different assumptions from those which had come to prevail.

Established pattern: England, Scotland and Wales c.1745–c.1845

The interpenetration of late-eighteenth-century Church and state can scarcely be disputed. In the absence of the Convocations, suspended in 1717, Parliament in effect governed the Church of England. 'King, Church and Country' stood together against the insidious influences of the French Revolution. The

---

[4] Cited in Robbins, *History, Religion and Identity*, p. 173.

disasters that had befallen there were a terrible warning of what could happen to a nation if it abandoned its Christian heritage. The Evangelical clergy of the Church of England were, on the whole, strongly Tory in disposition. Bishops were at home in the House of Lords. The beginning of the nineteenth century did not necessarily suggest that this beneficial connection was on the brink of dissolution. Dissent, though important, was not rampant. Yet, within thirty years, as has already been noted in the political sphere, the *ancien régime* was substantially undermined. Indeed, arguably, the repeal of the Test Act and the Corporation Acts in 1828, followed by Catholic mancipation in the following year, had implications even more profound than the Reform Act of 1832. Taken together, the measures shook past assumptions severely. Of course, in 1828–29, the Reform Act could not have been precisely forecast and indeed some supporters of the 'Protestant Constitution' were so aghast at what an unreformed Parliament had done that, for them, a reformed one could scarcely be worse. Yet the measures of 1828–29 were not so much a concession to a strident campaign as a supposed recognition that Dissent, even Roman Catholic Dissent, was ripe for accommodation. It was the extent to which Dissent, or at least some of its leaders, saw the measures as a launching pad for a wider assault on 'privilege', ecclesiastical and social, which occasioned dismay. The intention of Dissenting leaders to seek remedies for discrete grievances might cause 'Establishment' to wither away before anyone quite realized what had happened. And many sensible Church of England men in Parliament and beyond believed that the Church did stand in need of reform.

John Keble, Oxford don, clergyman and poet, however, attacked the Whig government's plans for reforming the structures of the established but minority Church of Ireland, sister church of the Church of England. In a famous Assize Sermon in 1833 he denounced what he termed *National Apostasy*. The 'Oxford' or 'Tractarian' movement is generally held to have had its origins in this sermon, though other influences fed into its development. What was at issue was the nature of the Church of England in the new circumstances with which it was confronted. What did it mean to claim that it was 'holy, catholic and apostolic' after so many centuries of English Erastianism (the belief that the state should control the church)?[5]

It was a debate which engaged many minds. For John Henry Newman and Henry Manning, for example, their reflection on these matters led them out of the complicated nexus of politics and religion, which they judged the Church of England to be, into the unadulterated and non-national Catholic Church. Newman was received in 1845 and Manning six years later. Such departures notwithstanding, the Church of England remained in a central

---

[5] O. Chadwick, *The Spirit of the Oxford Movement: Tractarian Essays* (Cambridge, 1990); P. Nockles, *The Oxford Movement in Context: Anglican High Churchmanship 1760–1857* (Cambridge, 1994).

position in English society. How it should stand in relation to the state remained a problem. William Gladstone was one who wrestled long with this issue but it became clear to him, even as he wrote, that he was arguing as the sands shifted beneath him. The past was ceasing to offer a firm foundation in these matters but how they should be properly ordered was not yet plain.

It had already become apparent, however, that just as all Englishman could not automatically be assumed to be 'Anglicans' so not all Anglicans were English/British. The American Revolution had had a devastating impact on the Church, with a considerable number of Anglican clergy leaving the new United States. Samuel Seabury, eager to reconstitute the Church, arrived in England seeking consecration, but did not receive it. How could the English state Church consecrate bishops for 'foreigners' as the Americans had now become. Seabury was fortunately able to get the consecration he wanted from Scotland where the Episcopalians obliged.

British imperial expansion also meant that the issue was no longer confined to the British Isles. Enlightenment opinions and Evangelical fervour had fused in the campaign against the slave trade which culminated in 1833 in the abolition of slavery in British dominions. According to the Bampton Lecturer at Oxford University in 1843, the expansion of the empire meant that it was 'no longer a question whether the heathen shall be left to themselves. Our colonies are already planted in the midst of them; they are our fellow-subjects; *we must* as a nation, exercise untold influence upon them.'[6] It was not, of course, a novel idea. Anglican missionaries were already active in India and elsewhere. Some of them became aware, in the process, of the extent to which the gospel they preached was rather a 'British' gospel. Their experience abroad also in some cases made them wonder how 'Christian' Britain really was. Certainly, it led them to behave in unusual ways. Reginald Heber, for example, Bishop of Calcutta, disliked attaching any status to his office. His habit – which had few parallels in England – was to enter the station he was visiting on a pony, with an Indian cork hat to shelter his head from the sun, and an umbrella in his hand. Moreover, the Indian context gave a different perspective on the ecclesiastical position at home. Heber wrote warmly to the nearby Baptist missionaries, Carey and Marshman, saying that 'if a reunion of our churches could be effected, the harvest of the heathen would ere long be reaped'.[7] That was not a message which the churches at home wished to hear.

The crisis of the Church of England's cultural identity had an additional complexity in Wales. Dissent in Wales capitalized on cultural and social grievances and pilloried the Established Church as 'English', largely guided by bishops who were not Welsh and who, in many cases, seemed to regard

---

[6] Cited in W.L. Sachs, *The Transformation of Anglicanism: From State Church to Global Communion* (Cambridge, 1993) pp. 110–11.
[7] S. Neill, *A History of Christian Missions* (Harmondsworth, 1986 edn) p. 228.

tenure of an impecunious Welsh see as a temporary penance only to be endured until English preferment was offered. There was sufficient reality in this picture to allow the generation of potent legend. Establishment was coming under siege and church and chapel marshalled their flocks to the best of their ability in a great contest that apparently could not be avoided. There was some uncertainty, however, as to whether Dissent should concentrate on overthrowing Establishment in Wales or whether this was a *British* matter to be addressed by Dissenters in all three countries as a single struggle.

A difficulty with a *British* campaign was that Scotland was different. The main bodies of English/Welsh Dissent – Baptists, Independents, Quakers – had made little impact in Scotland. Nor had Methodism. In the year of Wesley's death, there were only some thousand Methodists in Scotland. It was difficult for these Anglo-Welsh bodies to identify with schismatic Presbyterian bodies and the great rupture of 1843 was difficult to understand south of the Border. There was even some continuing if distant admiration among English Dissenters for the Church of Scotland and the 'Establishment' that it possessed. Conversely, the Church of England did not see the Church of Scotland as a sister church with which it shared a common interest in upholding 'Establishment' as a general principle. Scottish ecclesiastical politics and polities seemed so distinctive that in practice it was within England/Wales that alliances and alignments were meaningful.

Dissenting accommodation: England, Scotland and Wales c.1745–c.1845

In the mid-eighteenth century, the restrictions to which Dissenters were subjected were irksome rather than oppressive. By the 1770s, a Dissenting lobby was hard at work to relieve Dissenting ministers and schoolmasters of the necessity to subscribe to the Thirty-Nine Articles of the Church of England – something still required under the Toleration Act. In 1779 Parliament agreed that such Dissenters should only be required to declare that they were Protestants and accept the Scriptures. It was in this decade, partly under the impact of events in America and partly because Baptists and Independents (Congregationalists) were again growing in numbers, that Dissenters became more assertive in pursuit of what they believed to be their rights.

This reinvigoration of Old Dissent also owed something to the example of 'Methodism', a new force in English religious life. Methodism, in turn, was an expression of a wider 'Evangelical Revival'. The fact that there were only some 30,000 Methodists at the time of the American Revolution hardly suggests that the decades between 1740 and 1790 constitute the 'Age of Wesley'. Yet Wesley was remarkable in the scope and scale of his itinerant preaching – 'I must be on horse-back for life, if I would be healthy'. He had been ordained to the ministry of the Church of England but, step by step, he put himself beyond the ecclesiastical pale, protesting all the while that he had no intention of initiating a formal rupture with the Established Church. Wesley's work has been interpreted as a piece of private enterprise, made necessary by the fact that the machinery of the Church of England was not equal to its missionary task and the state would not assume responsibility for bringing salvation to the people. What was distinctive about Wesley's message, and which marked him off from the Calvinism of Old Dissent, was his Arminianism – the belief that Christ died for all. 'No single voice touched so many hearts', declared an early-twentieth-century British Cabinet minister, and no other figure influenced so many minds.[8]

Even if this is fair comment, there has been much dispute about the wider significance of Methodism. Some argue that it conditioned the proletariat to accept the demands of the nascent industrial capitalism. Others suggest, on the contrary, that it 'empowered' workers by giving them practical organizational experience arising out of the essentially societal character of Methodism. It is well-known, on the other hand, that Wesley himself was Tory by inclination. He took the view that the greater share the people had in government, the less liberty, civil or righteous, a nation enjoyed. Even so, the Duchess of Buckingham was not alone in detecting something subversive in Methodist sermons. Their preaching, she believed, was 'strongly tinctured with impertinence and disrespect towards their superiors'. She was also not alone in thinking it quite monstrous to be told that she had a heart as sinful as that of the commonest wretches who crawled on the earth.

Any overall assessment of Methodism, therefore, has to recognize that it appeared to face in two directions. The main body of Methodists, the Wesleyans, grew rapidly in the period 1800–30, approaching 2 per cent of the population of England. Revival movements, splits and constitutional differences, however, led to the creation of other Methodist bodies – Primitive Methodists, Bible Christians, Independents and a Methodist 'New Connexion'. One of the issues which proved divisive was whether Methodist preachers should administer sacraments. There was, in turn, much debate on whether Methodism was essentially a religious society, still closely linked to the Church of England, or whether it was in the process of becoming a separate Church. The tendency was in the latter direction, but for the moment it stood uneasily poised between Old Dissent and the Church of England, capable, perhaps, of bridging the gap between church and chapel which was so much a feature of the Victorian Age to come.[9]

---

[8] A. Birrell, *Essays and Reviews* (London, 1922) p. 15.
[9] E.P. Thompson, *The Making of the English Working Class* (Harmondsworth, 1968); H.D. Rack, *Reasonable Enthusiast: John Wesley and the Rise of Methodism* (London, 1989); D.N. Hempton, *Methodism and Politics in British Society 1750–1850* (London, 1984); W.R. Ward, 'The Evangelical Revival in Eighteenth-Century Britain' in S. Gilley and W. Sheils, eds, *A History of Religion in Britain* (Oxford, 1994) pp. 252–72; W.R. Ward, *The Protestant Evangelical Awakening* (Cambridge, 1992).

Dissent in Scotland was not the same as it was in England. In the eyes of the Church of Scotland it was Episcopalians – the counterparts of the Established Church south of the Border – who dissented from the Presbyterian majority. Indeed, earlier in the century, leading Scottish Presbyterians had resented the Act for the Toleration of Episcopacy (1712), claiming that it was something they would never have done if they had retained a Scottish Parliament. They claimed that it was a measure imposed on Scotland by English Tories in the new *British* Parliament, though in fact most of the Scottish MPs and peers at Westminster supported the measure. Particularly in the Scottish Highlands, the Church of Scotland took energetic steps to prise Episcopalians out of parishes. Much was made of the extent to which Episcopalians sympathized with Jacobitism. Over time, however, Episcopalian Dissent came to be grudgingly recognized in Scotland – as Protestant Dissent came to be grudgingly recognized in England. There was even more resentment in Scotland against the Patronage Act, also of 1712, which restored to patrons, except such as were Non-Jurors or Catholics, the right to present ministers to parishes. Here was an issue with a long past and a lively future.

Episcopalians, however, were not the only Dissenters. The Church of Scotland had a considerable capacity for generating schism on grounds of theology or church government. By 1800, for example, while the Church of Scotland was still clearly the largest single Church in Scotland, perhaps a fifth of the population in the Lowlands belonged to Presbyterian Dissenting bodies. The issue of patronage, and the social and economic tensions surrounding its exercise, became steadily more divisive. In the 1830s attempts were made by the Evangelical wing of the Church of Scotland to insist that no minister be 'intruded' on any congregation against its wishes. Matters came to a head in the early 1840s. Did the General Assembly of the Church have the power to support such a congregational veto? Amidst much talk of spiritual freedom, speakers found it intolerable that the state, particularly the *British* state, might be required to reach a decision on this matter. Was not Christ the Head of the Church? When about a third of its ministers solemnly walked out of the General Assembly in May 1843, the Church, and Scotland, was rent in twain. It was an upheaval which had no substantial parallel in England. However, Thomas Chalmers, the leader of the Dissenting ministers, who set about organizing a new Free Church throughout the country, insisted that he was not a 'voluntarist'. It was desirable that there should be some connection between Church and state – what mattered was that it should be reached on an acceptable basis. Chalmers himself died in 1847 but the 'Dissenting' Free Church sprang up alongside the Established Church throughout Scotland.[10]

---

[10] K. Robbins, 'Religion and Community in Scotland and Wales since 1800' in Gilley and Sheils, *Religion in Britain*, pp. 363–80; A. Fawcett, *The Cambuslang Revival* (London, 1977); A.J. Hayes and D. Gowland, *Scottish Methodism in the Early Victorian Period* (Edinburgh, 1981); C. Brown, *The Social History of Religion in Scotland since 1730* (London, 1987).

In the mid-eighteenth century Wales was by no means a Dissenting paradise. Dissenters were probably even weaker, numerically, than they were in England. In the north, for example, probably fewer than 1 per cent of the population were Dissenters at this time. Independents and Baptists, where they existed, did so on the margins of society, both literally and metaphorically. Differences amongst Dissenters were very evident, initially about baptism but later the doctrine of the Trinity proved divisive. There were, however, evangelical stirrings within the Established Church which Wales shared with England. Men such as Howell Harris, William Williams and Daniel Rowland initially sought ordination in its service. At this time such 'revivalists' occupied a kind of border country between Church and Dissent. However, although Wesley came to Wales to preach on many occasions, 'Methodism' in Wales was predominantly Calvinist rather than Arminian. Welsh Methodists came to adopt a Presbyterian form of Church government and formally separated from the Church. Welsh was overwhelmingly the predominant language amongst non-Wesleyan Methodists and further contributed to giving Welsh Dissent, even amongst Baptists and Congregationalists, a flavour distinct from English Dissent. Its numerical growth was remarkable, though by no means uniform, denominationally, throughout Wales.

Such expansion of Dissent throughout the three countries of Britain, diverse in its impact though it was, inevitably raised the issue of 'Establishment'. It was in 1844 that the British Anti-State-Church Association (later the Liberation Society) was founded. It urged that 'in matters of religion man is responsible to God alone'. It was not the business of the state to favour one ecclesiastical body rather than another. It was argued that it was the state's partiality, perhaps now subdued, which made it impossible for the 'favoured' and the 'degraded' sects to cooperate together. It was significant that the Anti-State-Church Association described itself as *British*. Its attack was directed as much north as south of the Border. It is important to stress, also, that its fire was not directed against religion as such – unlike the situation in other European countries which lacked British religious pluralism. Rather, there was a notion that Christian belief and practice would be more likely to be pervasive without, rather than with, state recognition.

Protestant Britain and the Catholic question *c.1745–c.1845*

In the late eighteenth century, Catholic Dissent had remained under greater disability than Protestant Dissent. Catholic proprietors had to pay a supplementary land tax; there was no legal form of Catholic marriage; Catholics in the armed forces had to attend Protestant worship; Catholics could only hold office under the Crown in the unlikely event that they were willing to deny the spiritual and temporal authority of the Pope and the doctrine of

Transubstantiation. This position reflected the continuing sense that Britain's national destiny had to be conceived in a Protestant/Evangelical framework.

Even so, a Catholic community in England had survived, probably numbering around 80,000 at the time of the first significant measure of Catholic relief in 1778. Catholicism survived in Wales too, but only in small pockets. In the Scottish Highlands and Islands, but not to any substantial extent elsewhere, some Catholic communities resisted the sustained attention of the Church of Scotland, but it was difficult to maintain the continuity of their parochial life. Earlier in that decade, priests were still being prosecuted in London for saying Mass. Henceforth, however, Catholics were allowed to conduct schools, and hindrances to their transmission and acquisition of property were removed. In London, Bishop Challoner gave effective leadership for many decades after his consecration in 1741. Outside traditional areas of recusancy, such as Lancashire (where a third of the Catholic population lived), some new congregations were formed in English provincial towns. Challoner himself wrote *Britannia Sancta* (Holy Britain) in an attempt to reassure his flock that it had a legitimate place in the history of *Britain*. As the Jacobite threat faded into the past in the decades after 1745, restrictions on Catholics seemed increasingly unnecessary.

Even so, anti-Catholic riots in the Scottish Lowlands in 1778 and, above all, the Gordon Riots in London in 1780 showed how a mob could still be mobilized by the prospect of Catholic relief. Pillaging, burning and destruction terrified the authorities in the capital as they watched the excesses that followed the Protestant Association's presentation of its petition. However, Professor Colley is right to stress that the Gordon Riots should not be dismissed as merely an atavistic survival from an earlier age. The 'Catholic menace' had for long served to unite English, Welsh and Scottish Protestantism, in all its diversity, as *British*. Could Protestantism continue to do so with the advent of 'Catholic Emancipation'? And, if it could not sustain a British identity, what, if anything, could replace it to buttress the state? That was still a long-term issue, but perhaps it was one that could not ultimately be avoided."[11]

Via media?: The Church of England *c.*1845–*c.*1945

'It is quite impossible', wrote Mandell Creighton, the Bishop of London, from Fulham Palace in 1898, 'that any considerable number of Englishmen

[11] J. Bossy, *The English Catholic Community, 1570–1850* (London, 1975); E. Duffy, *Peter and Jack: Roman Catholics and Dissent in Eighteenth-Century England* (London, 1982) and *Challoner and his Church: A Catholic Bishop in Georgian England* (London, 1981); S. Gilley, 'Catholic Revival in the Eighteenth Century' in K. Robbins, ed., *Protestant Evangelicalism: Britain, Ireland, Germany and America c.1750–c.1950: Essays in Honour of W.R. Ward* (Oxford, 1990).

should be Roman Catholics.' In his opinion, to join that church was simply to stand on one side 'and cut yourself off from your part in striving to do your duty for the religious future of your country'.[12] The Church of England remained central to England's self-understanding. A distinguished ecclesiastical historian, he wrestled with the past as he grappled with the conflicting tendencies in the Church of England in his day. He summed up that understanding in a sequence of axioms: the Church of England had to maintain truth held according to liberty yet with order; the Church of Rome cared for truth and order, but subordinated truth; Nonconformists cared for truth and liberty, but truth was dissolved into opinion. It was hard indeed to maintain truth, liberty and order but that constituted 'England's work'. It was a task at once 'national' and 'ecclesiastical'.

It was inescapable that the Church of England was a complex entity. It was conventional to think of it as being divided into three camps, camps which were themselves broad in scope – Evangelical, Broad Church and Anglo-Catholic. A powerful stream of publications, learned and unlearned, together with a periodical press, supported the contending groups. There were constant prophecies that the Church would be rent asunder as controversies – and some spectacularly unsuccessful litigation – multiplied.

It was the Evangelical wing which seemed most dispirited in the latter part of the nineteenth century as compared with the earlier half. Its leadership came from the older generation. Between 1865 and 1900, for example, only six clear Evangelicals were promoted to the episcopal bench. It was the spread of 'Ritualism' which provoked bellicose exchanges. Various groupings monitored the arrival of 'Mass', vestments, choral music and incense with militant vigilance. One ritualist vicar even issued his flock with brass knuckle-dusters, the more adequately to repel the defenders of England's Protestant heritage. On the other hand, however, into the new century, some Evangelicals became more comfortable with certain forms of ritualism and found them compatible with what they understood to be 'the English Church'. At the same time, however, they firmly resisted attempts to bring back from the past 'medieval and sacerdotal pretensions' which had no place in English life.

In the interwar period, however, Evangelicals were in disarray. The disagreements about particular doctrines, which had been long present, came to a head. Put simply, the conflict was between 'conservatives' and 'liberals' concerning 'fundamentals', specifically the status of the Bible. Was the Bible free from error, or at any rate 'substantially' so? What right had scholars to 'contextualize' the Gospel? It had been delivered at a particular point in the past but was valid for all time. It would outlive the passing assumptions of England in the 1920s. 'Fundamentalism' was a major controversy in the United States in the 1920s and it afflicted the Church of England also. The

---

[12] L. Creighton, *The Life of Mandell Creighton* (London, 1913) p. 349.

wording of a statement concerning the authority of Scripture occasioned a split which ruptured the Church Missionary Society. Such conflict was debilitating. It encouraged, too, a 'fortress' mood and mentality. It was necessary to hold fast to the past, to what had once and for all time been delivered. The only 'victory' which could be accorded Evangelicals, though there was no single mind even on this issue, was the part they played in the parliamentary defeat of the Revised Prayer Book which was mooted in the Church of England in the 1920s. Evangelicals were troubled by the proposed order of holy communion and the question of the reservation of the sacrament. After protracted internal discussion the measure was presented to the House of Lords which approved it. On two separate subsequent occasions, however, the measure was defeated in the Commons where Sir William Joynson-Hicks, an Evangelical layman, played a prominent part. While Evangelicals were gratified by the outcome, they could see the dangers inherent in a situation in which Parliament, composed of members of many churches and of none, could determine what the Church of England could legally do in the revision of its Prayer Book.

The Broad Church approached the challenges of these decades from almost the opposite perspective. By definition, however, it lacked coherence and a strong party spirit. The instinct of a man such as A.P. Stanley (1815–91), for example, prolific writer and traveller, was to be inclusive rather than exclusive. An admiring pupil at Rugby School of Dr Arnold, who likewise had a comprehensive vision, it was fitting that as Dean of Westminster from 1864 he sought to make the abbey truly a national shrine and to admit to its pulpit churchmen of all denominations. At Oxford, Benjamin Jowett, later Master of Balliol, had contributed contentiously to *Essays and Reviews* (1860). Scholars asked again what was the authority of Scripture, the nature of revelation and the meaning of traditional orthodox doctrine. Influential German scholarship, though reaching no unanimous conclusion, pointed to the layers and levels within Scripture itself. The past, it seemed, could not simply be accepted, it had to be assimilated into the present. Leading products of Balliol College followed their Master in believing that the life and death of Christ had to be 'worked out without mysticism in society and in the daily routine of life'. So did a great many other Englishmen. As Jowett himself expressed it: 'Religion is not dependent upon historical events, the report of which we cannot altogether trust. Holiness has its sources elsewhere than in history.'[13] It was an uncomfortable conclusion for historians.

In the twentieth century, this approach in the Church of England continued to be influential, manifesting itself in a 'liberalism' to be found in universities and amongst some members of the episcopate itself. It would be difficult to define the content of this liberalism with any precision since by its very nature it emphasized an openness to change and development – and

---

[13] P. Hinchliff, *Benjamin Jowett and the Christian Religion* (Oxford, 1987) pp. 196–7.

development to a degree and in a direction not envisaged by John Henry Newman when he had earlier worked out an idea of development in Christian history. 'Modern Churchmen', to their critics, however, were playing fast and loose with the past as they reformulated their Christian understanding in the light of contemporary science and philosophy.

The 'Broad Church' turned a sceptical mind both to notions of biblical inerrancy and to ecclesiastical exclusiveness and authority. In this sense, therefore, both Evangelicals and 'Anglo-Catholics' tended to a common temper, even when most vehemently opposed to each other. Once again, however, we are dealing with broad categories, and it is a matter of mystery where Tractarian/Anglo-Catholic/Anglo-Papalist shade into one another. From the mid-nineteenth century until after the First World War, some clergy had gone across to France and Italy and succeeded in erecting statues, pictures and candlesticks in some profusion on their return. Rituals associated with the Mass were also imported. Some Anglican priests took pleasure in being thought more Roman than Rome in their liturgical practices. They could be identified in the street by the wearing of a Latin cassock, with a cape or *soutane* over the shoulders. They were to be found introducing alien beauty in slum churches. In some cases, too, rejection of Protestantism also entailed the rejection of its alleged progeny, capitalism. Cultivation of the 'religious life' blossomed in convents and monasteries within the Church of England. Anglo-Catholics were thought popularly to be characterized by an enthusiasm for smells and bells as they busily and and often spikily set about restoring the past, or so they believed. The English Church Union – founded in 1860 with only 200 members but claiming 39,000 members in 1901 – published church guides to enable potential worshippers to locate those churches where 'Catholic privileges' were to be found.[14] The generalization may be risked that Anglo-Catholicism made most progress in south-east England – as Protestantism had done 400 years earlier. Many Anglo-Catholic priests felt that it was most unfortunate to be separated from the Pope and the sooner this separation could be ended the better. Yet they were also Englishmen (women could only be 'associate members'), and there remained an ambiguity at the heart of Anglo-Catholicism. The Church of England might need to be 'Romanized' but most Catholics still retained some 'Anglo' elements in their bones.

In fact, though the 'Catholic tradition' within the Church of England was significantly rediscovered in the century after 1845, the Church as a whole was not 'Romanized'. It was noted in some quarters that continental Protestants were turning in admiration to the Church of England to learn the secret of an organization which treasured the past, understood the present and aspired to serve the future. Hensley Henson, recipient of one such letter,

---

[14] W.S.F. Pickering, *Anglo-Catholicism: A Study in Religious Ambiguity* (London, 1989) p. 93..

was impressed, but did not recognize the Church of England in this description! Many Anglicans, however, had little interest in continental Protestants. Rather, they took satisfaction in the extent to which 'Anglicanism' was becoming anchored as a world rather than an English/British phenomenon. The process identified earlier in this chapter continued. The first Lambeth Conference was held in 1867, the year of the Second Reform Act. It brought together bishops from across the world who were certainly not English and who had certainly not been appointed to their offices by the Crown. It met at regular intervals thereafter. It would be a mistake, however, to exaggerate the 'internationalization' of the Church of England. Of the 1930 Lambeth Conference, Hensley Henson noted that mainly, 'the business of the Conference has been in the hands of the English bishops'. He thought the Scottish bishops counted for nothing and the Welsh had hardly uttered a word.[15]

At home, it remained the case, as a sermon on 'Anglican Comprehensiveness' had noted in 1917, that 'there is hardly any doctrine that you hear in one church which you may not hear denied in another, and all of them Church of England'. The preacher J.N. Figgis argued that the party divisions of the Church corresponded to real differences in human nature – institutional, intellectual, mystical – and they would subsist, however much an attempt might be made to secure a rigid uniformity. Figgis, no mean political thinker, was attracted at this time to 'pluralism' as a fundamental aspect of social organization. The Church could no longer embrace all, but neither should its members be coerced, in practice, by a state which might seek to impose its own 'secular' uniformity. There was a case for the recognition and protection of 'groups' within society. It was argued elsewhere that the acceptance of diversity was the glory of the Church of England, irritating and anomalous to tidy minds though it might appear. It contributed to (and also reflected) the principle of toleration in English society as a whole.[16]

The Church of England was also still 'Established'. Under the Enabling Act of 1919, a new Church Assembly, with modest administrative functions, met first in June 1920 but it fell far short of the 'Life and Liberty' for the

---

[15] H.H. Henson, *Retrospect of an Unimportant Life: Vol. II 1920–1939* (London, 1943) p. 277.
[16] J.N. Figgis, *Hopes for English Religion* (London, 1919) pp. 82–8; D. Nicholls, *The Pluralist State: The Political Ideas of J.N. Figgis and his Contemporaries* (London, 1994 edn); J. Wolffe, *God & Greater Britain: Religion and National Life in Britain and Ireland 1843–1945* (London, 1994).

10.1 St Giles's, Cheadle: Pugin's church (1840–46), the gift of a munificent patron, the Earl of Shrewsbury, was an expression of his belief that the Gothic style of architecture was *the* style for churches. It came to be used extensively by almost all denominations in the later nineteenth century and spread throughout the English-speaking world. It was suggested that medieval masons and craftsmen expressed in their work a profound spirituality which the nineteenth century needed to recapture.

Church pressed for by William Temple and others. The Revised Prayer Book débâcle of the late 1920s raised again the question of 'church freedom'. 'Men', wrote Bishop Hensley Henson of Durham in 1929, 'especially religious and patriotic men, cling to their causes long after they know them to be hopeless.' However, contrary to his own earlier opinion, it now seemed absolutely certain: 'there is no future for the Establishment'.[17] He argued that in the relatively small electorate before 1914 the Church was a considerable, even a dominating factor, but that was no longer the case. The Church was a minor element and might easily become a negligible quantity. A commission established in 1930 by the archbishops enquired into the relationship of Church and state. Reporting in 1935, it concluded that what had been done in Scotland six years earlier could not be done in England since 'the history and conditions of the two countries and Churches are not the same'. While recommending some modifications, from the standpoint of the Church, it continued to argue that 'the history of Church and nation is, in England, so closely intertwined that the separation could not be effected without injury to both of a kind impossible to forecast or to forestall … '.[18]

Dissent – progressive dissolution: England, Scotland, Wales c.1845–c.1945

The intertwining Church and state, though indeed close, was far from complete. The 1851 census produced detailed information concerning Church allegiance in England and Wales; it was rather less complete for Scotland. The plurality of British religious life was confirmed: no less than thirty-five different religious bodies were identified. No quick summary can do justice to the complexity revealed by the census and even at the time there was debate about whether the day concerned was 'typical' and whether one religious body or another 'cheated'. The significance of the outcome can be read in various ways. It can be argued that the Church of England was still shown to be clearly the most 'popular' Church in England, with the Methodists in second place, followed by Congregationalists, then Baptists, and then small bodies like Unitarians and Quakers. On the other hand, Nonconformists were keen to point out that the number worshipping outside the Church of England approximately equalled those worshipping inside. Supporters of the Church, on the other hand, stressed its individual supremacy and the extent to which Nonconformity could not be considered a homogeneous entity. The Methodists remained divided between various bodies and could not be

---

[17] H.H. Henson, *Disestablishment* (London, 1929) p. 77.
[18] *Church & State: Report of the Archbishops' Commission on the Relations between Church and State 1935* (London, 1935) p. 49.

considered a single denomination. The national aggregates, too, are mislead-ing insofar as more detailed examination discloses the considerable variation across the country in the strength of the Dissenting congregations.

Dissenters, however, took heart from the results and pressed on with their campaign to remove the surviving 'disabilities' from which they suf-fered. The institution of civil marriage in 1837 had made it possible to per-form marriages in Nonconformist chapels. In the same year, registration of births, deaths and marriages ceased to be an Anglican monopoly. The pay-ment of church rates, however, was still enforced and a number of politi-cians – for example the Quaker Radical, John Bright – began their careers by campaigning against payment. It was not until 1868 that church rates were abolished by the incoming Liberal government. Religious tests at Oxford and Cambridge were removed in 1871. The Burials Act (1880) largely set-tled the vexed question of whether Nonconformists could be buried in parish churchyards. One by one, therefore, the exclusions were removed. Even so, Establishment, as such, was not removed, though the Liberation Society still struggled to achieve this goal.[19]

By the last decades of the century, therefore, Nonconformity was enter-ing an awkward phase. Unacceptable though the 'second-class' status had been, it nevertheless served to maintain the solidarity of the various Noncon-formist bodies. They were able collectively to rehearse their sense of continuity with a past in which persecution had been a reality. Could that continue? R.W. Dale of Birmingham, perhaps the leading Congregationalist in this period, doubted it. Nonconformists had to find a new identity. In his *Culture and Anarchy* (1869) the poet and critic Matthew Arnold had painted an unflattering picture of Nonconformity. It possessed a self-contained culture entailing 'a life of jealousy of the Establishment, disputes, tea-meetings, openings of chapels, sermons'.[20] Hence the desire amongst some to make a fresh start. 'We are like men who have been asleep for the past hundred years, and persist in wearing the garb and clinging to the customs of last cen-tury', one Congregationalist speaker declared in 1877.[21] One answer was to move close to the heart of the erstwhile Anglican university. In advocating what became Mansfield College at Oxford, one speaker argued that there were 'aids to culture' at Oxford which could not be provided in an institu-tion as limited as a denominational college. But what kind of culture? Others feared that Mansfield would become in time virtually another pillar of the Church of England. There lay the difficulty. How could equality be seized without succumbing to assimilation? Public schools presented the same dilemma. It was noted with dismay that boys sent to them by their Noncon-

---

[19] F. Knight, *The Nineteenth-Century Church and English Society* (Cambridge, 1995).
[20] M. Arnold, *Culture and Anarchy* [1864] ed. J. Dover Wilson (Cambridge, 1935) p. 58.
[21] M.D. Johnson, *The Dissolution of Dissent, 1850–1918* (London, 1987) p. 155.

formist fathers seemed to pass 'naturally and inevitably into the Establishment'. The formation of some Nonconformist public schools was an attempt to stem the tide.

The erosion of the past was therefore a gnawing anxiety amongst perceptive Nonconformists but it seemed to contrast with public signs of their waxing collective strength. In local politics Nonconformist influences were increasingly observable and the number of Nonconformist MPs steadily grew. Mr Gladstone took great care to have regular meetings with leading Nonconformist ministers. He had to take note of the dictum enunciated by the great Wesleyan, Hugh Price Hughes, that what was morally wrong could not be politically right. The 'Nonconformist Conscience' was a force to be reckoned with. Moreover, the various churches had taken steps to make themselves more coherent nationally. Both Baptists and Congregationalists continued to stress the importance of the local church but had nevertheless formed national 'Unions'. Hugh Price Hughes urged Wesleyans to overcome their ecclesiastical ambiguity and think of themselves unequivocally as a Free Church. At the same time, he urged Wesleyans to come closer to the historic Dissenting bodies. They should stand 'shoulder to shoulder with our true ecclesiastical kinsmen, the Congregationalists, the Baptists, and the Presbyterian Churches, throughout the English-speaking world'. His frame of reference is significant. It was in that wider world that he believed that Dissent was in fact in the majority. He was convinced that both at home and in the diaspora 'God has committed to the Anglo-Celtic people the defence of human freedom, the vindication of the race's conscience, the protection of the weak and the propagation of Scriptural Christianity'.[22] A National Council of the Evangelical Free Churches, formed in 1896, offered some further evidence of the forward march of the Free Churches.

The general election victory for the Liberals in 1906 was taken in some quarters as solid evidence that the new century would belong to the Free Churches. It was remarked that there were more Nonconformists in the House of Commons than at any time since Cromwell. The past was coming alive again. The government was more conspicuously non-Anglican than any previous administration in the history of the British state. In reality, however, the scale of this representation proved to be a Dissenting climax rather than the harbinger of the future. In Asquith and Lloyd George, to take only two examples, the erosion of their pasts had long set in. It is generally agreed that the membership of the leading Free Churches peaked in the years just before 1914. Between 1914 and 1939 their average decline in England and Wales was 6 per cent. And in terms of public influence during this period, Nonconformity suffered from the sharp decline of the Liberal Party through which its influence had largely been exercised, a decline which shared some common causes.

---

[22] Hugh Price Hughes in July 1898.

The reaction of the Free Churches to the First World War constitutes another key illustration of their accelerating 'nationalization'. From the mid-nineteenth century onwards there had been a general support for such bodies as the Peace Society and hostility to what was described as 'militarism'. In the crisis of 1914, however, only relatively few Nonconformists were pacifists in an absolutist sense, though among the small number of such pacifists overall there were considerably more Nonconformists than Anglicans. More satisfaction was taken in the appointment, for the first time, of Free Church chaplains to the armed forces, and it did not escape notice that the man who was apparently winning the war was a Welsh Nonconformist. Immediately after the war a Federal Council of the Free Churches was formed and it was clear that the consolidation of a loose 'Free Church' constituency in English life was taking place. It was, moreover, a consolidation which no longer had the achievement of Disestablishment as a primary objective. The Baptist leader M.E. Aubrey gave the opinion in 1935 that it would not be possible to stir up a vigorous Nonconformist campaign on the issue. In another related development, Methodist reunion was achieved in 1932. To some extent, but not to an entire extent, such processes were a response to decline in numbers and to the financial burdens which stemmed from perhaps over-ambitious chapel-building. There was also, however, an increasing awareness that Nonconformists had not sufficiently focused on the long Christian past. *Our Catholic Heritage* (c.1927), written by a Methodist, was not a title which would readily have been used thirty years earlier. 'The past', he claimed, 'with all its conquests, its fragrance, its saints, its immortal splendour, is ours.' However, more generally, although the process of Nonconformist erosion still had decades to run, it is sufficient to note that the signs were already apparent. Its pace, however, should not be prematurely exaggerated. A faultline between 'church' and 'chapel' still ran deep through English society. Given the Gothic enthusiasms of some latter-day architects employed within Nonconformity, the visual contrast between 'church' and 'chapel' throughout England/Wales was not as complete as it had been, but the symbolic contrasts still pointed to long-generated and deeply-felt differences of emphasis and understanding within Christian tradition.[23]

It was in England that the incipient Free Church crisis was most detectable, at any rate in the interwar period. By contrast, in the last half of the nineteenth century the Nonconformity of Wales appeared incontestable. Supposedly, some 80 per cent of the population was Nonconformist. Chapels sprinkled the landscape in rich profusion. They were centres not only of religious life, narrowly defined, but also of vigorous social and cultural activity, frequently using the Welsh language. The battle against Establishment was truly joined with a degree of vituperation, in some cases, that was not altogether charitable. Both 'church' and 'chapel' deployed their strengths

---

[23] C. Driver, *A Future for the Free Churches?* (London, 1962).

10.2 Fresh Start: Baptism at New Tredegar, 1843. Nonconformity in mid-nine-teenth century Wales seemed to be expanding inexorably. Baptists stood out from other denominations by their emphasis on the baptism not of infants but of believers who had come to a conscious decision. The symbolism of total immersion was potent and, in many instances, far from private. A stream or river could be used and the ceremony could be watched by large crowds on nearby banks or bridges. One bapt-ism at Llandeilo in the Teifi valley reputedly attracted 10,000 people eager to witness new beginnings.

and accused the other side of inventing figures of attendance and even more serious offences against truth and justice. Welsh Liberal/Nonconformity, strong after 1868, took the cause to the Commons but, after some twenty years of debate, it was not until the eve of 1914 that legislation disestablish-ing the Church was passed, and even then it was suspended until hostilities ended. The significance of the measure lay in the extent to which it con-stituted a specific legislative recognition of the distinctiveness of Wales. It became the only part of Britain where the state recognized no Church as having a position of pre-eminence.

The outcome, in the interwar period, was paradoxical. It was widely supposed that the new 'Church in Wales' would struggle to survive, deprived of considerable resource, in the face of Nonconformist dominance. In prac-tice, after diocesan reorganization, the obituaries proved premature. The Church in fact continued to have a certain self-confidence and Noncon-formists found it difficult to know what Nonconformity was supposed to mean when there was no Church to which anyone was expected to conform.

In general, therefore, it proved to be Nonconformity which had more difficulty in adjusting to the new situation and which was reduced to rehearsing particular denominational shibboleths submerged in the crusade against Anglicanism. It was partly because its ministers in a number of cases found it tedious to return to ordinary pastoral duties after the excitement of the public platform they had enjoyed for the decades of the struggle. It was also because, by the time it was achieved, disestablishment no longer seemed as vital an issue in a Wales beset by social and industrial problems. Additionally, as it became apparent that the Welsh language was in decline, many chapel-goers seemed more concerned to see chapels as bastions in its defence than to open their doors to an increasingly Anglophone population. These trends, however, did not seriously damage the image, held elsewhere in Britain and beyond, that Wales was Nonconformist territory. Such an image was reinforced by the fact that Wales regularly exported ministers to England and other parts of the English-speaking world. Hugh Price Hughes was only the most prominent example in the late nineteenth century.

By 1945, however, another modest but not insignificant trend could be discerned. Some intellectuals and writers of Nonconformist heritage, the most well-known being Saunders Lewis, converted to Roman Catholicism and in the process asserted, as was to happen in the other countries of Britain, that his nation could not rediscover its true identity unless it returned to the old faith. However much Nonconformity had come to seem typically Welsh, it was argued, Protestantism was essentially Anglo-Saxon in spirit and had led Wales down the wrong path into the present.

These developments had certainly established Welsh ecclesiastical exceptionalism in a manner never previously achieved. Scottish exceptionalism – viewed from England – remained strong. After the 1843 Disruption the new Free Church engaged in a vigorous programme of church-building across Scotland to establish itself as a national presence alongside the Church of Scotland. In addition, in 1847 other smaller Presbyterian groupings came together to form the United Presbyterian Church, a denomination whose more 'democratic' polity had considerable appeal in Edinburgh and Glasgow. Nevertheless, by the 1880s and 1890s the strains which this kind of competition entailed were evident. At the turn of the century, the two major 'Dissenting' Presbyterian groupings came together – with the exception of some dissidents – to form the United Free Church. Logic also seemed to point in the direction of reunion with the Church of Scotland. After protracted negotiations, this was eventually achieved in 1929. It had been necessary to find a formula which both entailed some element of state recognition as the national Church and recognition of its spiritual freedom – an issue which had proved so divisive over a long past in Scotland. Now the only Dissenters, Roman Catholics apart, were Episcopalians, Baptists and Methodists, and their memberships were small. A past littered with Presbyterian schism appeared largely to have been overcome.

Protestant Britain and the Catholic question *c.*1845–*c.*1945

In 1850 Rome restored the Catholic hierarchy in England. 'Catholic England has been restored to its orbit in the ecclesiastical firmament', declared Cardinal Wiseman. Parliamentary Westminster, however, still found it difficult to accept an Archbishop of Westminster in whose appointment it had no say. Here was the spiritual leader of English Catholics who had not been appointed by the Crown, as bishops of the Church of England were. Demonstrations against the restored hierarchy were got up all over the country. 'No Popery' lingered on and the prospect of 'papal aggression' proved very alarming. Pope Pius X professed himself puzzled, remarking 'So you English imagine I meant to insult Queen Victoria and violate the laws of your country. You are a very strange people. You seem to me to understand nothing thoroughly but commerce.'[24] For his part, Wiseman did his best, in a rather Italianate way, to show that Roman Catholics in England were not lacking in patriotism. 'Never in the history of nations', he declared in 1850, 'was any people advanced beyond ours, at the present time, in all that constitutes social and intellectual greatness.'[25] It was a fundamental task, thereafter, for English Catholics to sever that 'social and intellectual greatness,' from its foundations, as Protestants supposed, in the ethos and spirit of Protestantism itself.

Ample scope remained for suspicion and confusion in the decades that followed. Some English men and women who converted to Catholicism did so from a deliberate wish to 'write off' the Reformation and all its consequences, subsequently, in the life of England. They were joining a Church which was incontrovertibly supranational. It had a far longer past than the merely English Church which, they argued, had really been created only in the sixteenth century. A 'Second Spring' would return England to the historic faith. Such a conversion would again anchor England in Europe and shatter the insular Protestantism which had triumphed for 300 years. In their minds they were rediscovering an English identity which had been compromised over this period.

John Henry Newman himself, however, although not wavering in his Roman allegiance, contrived to profess it in a rather English way. To become a Catholic did not mean that an Englishman changed his identity and became an Italian, although some converts seem, on the contrary, to have been definitely attracted by such a prospect! To Newman's critic, Charles Kingsley, however, the drift to Rome was alarming, not least because of the effect he supposed it would have on what he thought English character to be. His ideal Englishman, it seems, from an article he contributed to the

---

[24] Cited in E. Norman, *The English Catholic Church in the Nineteenth Century* (Oxford, 1984) p. 105.
[25] Cited in Norman, *English Catholic Church*, p. 113.

Saturday Review in 1857, was 'a man who fears God and can walk a thousand miles in a thousand hours'.[26] Catholics did not seem to him, in general, to be very muscular.

In fact, the very substantial increase in the Catholic population of England which had occurred by 1914 stemmed from Irish immigration rather than the conversion of the English, unmuscular or otherwise. Indeed, the reconciliation of the perspectives of 'old' English Catholics, recent English converts, and Irish settlers in England, put the Catholic claim to catholicity sorely to the test. Some Irish-born priests in England were as concerned to maintain the Irishness of the Irish Catholic community as they were to extend the Catholic community in England. The number of Catholic priests in England rose from 392 in 1771 to 3,298 in 1901. The Society of Jesus, restored to England in 1829, likewise expanded. The Catholic community grew steadily, perhaps aided by intense use of the churches it erected – there had been a reluctance to muster resources in building too many churches. In Liverpool, for example, although additional Catholic churches were built, it was still the case that non-Catholics had proportionately more churches in relation to church-goers than Catholics had.[27] This Catholic growth did not pass unremarked. In Liverpool in 1909–10, for example, the setting up of a street altar for a public Catholic procession provoked spectacular rioting. It seemed indeed that Liverpool was an 'Irish' city in the extent and nature of its religious cleavages. Protestant Unionism in Ireland could look for some support in Britain in the tense years before 1914. The Easter Rising of 1916 and the vision of a Gaelic Catholic Ireland offered by republican revolutionaries made many Englishmen unexpectedly aware of the extent to which, however loose their church commitment, they felt themselves to be Protestants.

By 1920, however, the Catholic community in England/Wales (the Church made no distinction between the two countries) stood at around 2 million with an institutional infrastructure which had grown steadily. Largely because Irish immigrants started at the bottom of the social ladder in England, Catholics could legimately claim to embrace a wider social range than any other Church. Notwithstanding the growing self-confidence of the Catholic community, however, it remained set apart from the main English churches whose Christian legitimacy was still for the most part rejected. Conversion was the only possible objective and in the interwar period significant 'names' were enrolled, such as the writers Evelyn Waugh and Graham Greene. There was a strong disposition amongst intellectuals to see Roman Catholicism as the only available rampart in a dissolving world. If the Church could not reclaim cathedrals from the Church of England it could at

---

[26] Cited in Chadwick, *Spirit of the Oxford Movement*, p. 129; see also D.E. Hall, ed., *Muscular Christianity: Embodying the Victorian Age* (Cambridge, 1994) for insights into 'muscular Christianity' and national identity.

[27] R. Gill, *The Myth of the Empty Church* (London, 1993) pp. 155–61.

least show that it could itself build the medieval past in the present – as in the case of Buckfast Abbey in Devon. In some Catholic quarters, too, there was also sympathy in the 1930s for the clerico-fascist regimes that were emerging in some European countries, and even for Mussolini himself. Distaste for the Protestant aberration in English history could even extend to its supposed offspring, democracy. In the somewhat fevered atmosphere of 1940 in England there was therefore some suspicion that, in the event of an invasion, some elements in the Church might be prepared to 'do a Vichy'. Yet that was only one side of a complicated Catholic picture. Hinsley, Archbishop of Westminster after 1935, undoubtedly English, was prepared to countenance some cooperation with Anglicans and to recognize that in the battle for 'Christian civilization', if that was what the war was about, it was undesirable to man the barricades against other churches with the rigidity which the Vatican would have desired.

Much, though not all, of what has been said about the Catholic revival in England applied also in Scotland. It is important to remember that in 1850 it was not to *Britain* that the Roman hierarchy was restored. It was not until 1878 that it was restored in Scotland. Rome therefore recognized that ecclesiastically Britain remained two distinct countries. As in England, Irish immigration into Glasgow and other Scottish cities was changing their 'national' character considerably. The basis was being laid for a substantial Catholic population in Scotland, though whether and when it would see itself and be perceived as a *Scottish* Catholic population was another matter.[28] The Irish influx – though it was not only Catholic – challenged the fundamental notion that Scotland was Presbyterian to its core. The need to maintain the country's Protestant identity was asserted in strong language, even in the highest Presbyterian circles. Arguably, concern about Catholic growth played a subsidiary role in the process of Presbyterian reunification. There was also alarm at the conversion of a number of Scottish writers and intellectuals. Such converts, as in the case of their English and Welsh counterparts, dismissed Scotland's post-Reformation past and urged that it was necessary to find Scotland's real identity in the centuries before that 'disaster' occurred. It was the 'Irish Catholic' presence, however, which was still widely seen in Presbyterian circles as an alien wedge up to and during the Second World War. In October 1939 Winston Churchill, who was admittedly not a Presbyterian, wrote that there were 'plenty of traitors in the Glasgow area' who would be supplying the German embassy in Dublin with details of shipping movements on the Clyde. In such an atmosphere, Lord Lloyd's *British Case* still appeared in Scotland to be a strongly Protestant one.

---

[28] B. Aspinwall, 'Scots and Irish Clergy Ministering to Immigrants, 1830–1878', *Innes Review* XLVII (Spring 1996).

Community and commitment

When contemporaries considered the 1851 religious census, they were interested in the distribution of allegiance between the churches we have identified, and in how that allegiance subsequently shifted, as has been considered in this chapter. Churchmen of all denominations, however, were concerned and indeed alarmed by that half of the population which was not present on the Sunday concerned, whether in cathedral or conventicle. Subsequent work by historians suggests, however, that the level of attendance achieved in 1851 was high, not only in relation to the future but also to the past. Contemporary disappointment was rather a measure of the earnest endeavours and high expectations of mid-Victorian Britain.

Why did 5¼ million people not attend worship in church or chapel on a particular Sunday in 1851? There is no simple answer. In the decades that followed there was much speculation, inside the churches and outside, about the reasons for 'non-church-going' and its regional and social incidence. The churches, on the whole, had responded vigorously to the challenges posed by dramatic population growth and urban expansion. Even so, there remained many millions only tenuously in contact with what the churches claimed Christianity to be.

All sorts of reasons, both at the time and subsequently, were given for this state of affairs. At an intellectual level, men and women came to state more openly, and in some cases enthusiastically, that they did not believe in God and rejected the entire framework of Christian understanding. Alternatively, in a word newly coined by T.H. Huxley in 1869, they expressed themselves as incurably 'agnostic' about issues of faith and belief. It was Sir Leslie Stephen, son of an Evangelical household, founder and editor of the *Dictionary of National Biography*, who as it were 'established' agnosticism. Such positions could be reached for different reasons. Some thought the Christian notions of 'heaven' and 'hell' (whatever they pointed to) were themselves a hindrance to moral conduct. Others continued to be troubled by discoveries in geology or biology. How could 'natural selection' be reconciled with the Book of Genesis?

Britain, in other words, was not set apart from the 'secularization of the European mind' in the nineteenth century. The secular high-priests of the pre-1914 'Bloomsbury Group' knew that they had abolished religion. In *Eminent Victorians* (1918) one of their number, Lytton Strachey, wittily unpicked the pretensions of the past. Virginia Woolf, Leslie Stephen's daughter, detected a change in human nature taking place in December 1910. She based this opinion on an exhibition put on by Roger Fry on 'Manet and the Post-Impressionists'. She herself had appeared at the subsequent Post-Impressionist Ball in March 1911 as a Gauguin-like savage, draped in African cloth. That was not normal for an English lady. Such was the impact of the exhibition, she believed, that all human relations shifted in these few months

– between masters and servants, men and women, children and parents. And when human relations changed, there was, amongst other things, necessarily a change in religion.

What is nevertheless notable, over previous decades, when Britain is compared with other European countries in the same era, is the virtual absence of strong and enduring anticlerical or secularist movements. In the 1880s Charles Bradlaugh, a radical politician, certainly made his atheism a matter of public controversy when he refused to take the oath in the House of Commons on being elected an MP in 1880. It was not until 1886, after having been three times re-elected, that he was allowed merely to affirm allegiance and then take his seat. However, 'secularism' as such did not make organized headway in the decades thereafter. In the interwar period it may be that there was little need for a specific movement for 'secularization' to progress, a view often taken by historians who see 'secularization' as an inexorable and corrosive process in the twentieth century.[29]

Beneath the still intimate relationship with the British past which the British churches still possessed at one level, the 'intertwining' of Church and nation, of past and present, was a more puzzling phenomenon than the outward continuities suggested. Even more is this the case when, throughout Britain, the official/clerical world of all the churches, and its corresponding links with the state, with only slight exceptions, remained male. It is arguable, however, though even the most basic facts about sex ratios in Church membership and active participation are unclear, that in the pew and at prayer there were more women than men. Most men, lay or ordained, did not envisage any more substantial role for them in the life of any of the main-line churches. Reflecting on the campaign for 'Votes for Women', the *Church Times*, within a week of the outbreak of the First World War, declared: 'The monstrous regiment of women in politics would be bad enough but the monstrous regiment of priestesses would be a thousandfold worse'. After 1919, some women, notably Maude Royden, breached certain outlying ecclesiastical citadels, but the patriarchy of the past remained firmly in control in 1945. There was some recognition, however, as Henson put it in 1930, that 'The triumph of Feminism in the political sphere cannot be without effect on the status of women within the Church'.[30]

In addition, the millions who had little contact with the life of the churches, and who may not have done so for generations, might nevertheless resist the notion that they were not Christians, or believers of some kind. Historians, eager for supposedly hard evidence in the form of attendance records or 'membership' statistics, can only go a certain way in penetrating

---

[29] W.L. Arnstein, *The Bradlaugh Case: Atheism, Sex and Politics among the Late Victorians* (Columbia, 1983 edn).
[30] S. Fletcher, *Maude Royden* (Oxford, 1989); Henson, *Retrospect*, p. 263.

the undisclosed and perhaps inchoate assumptions both of church-goers and of non-church-goers, of those who *believed* in Britain and those who believed in *Britain*.

Chapter 11

Communities and Countries: *Believing in* Britain *c.1745–c.1945*

Identifying the issue

To believe in *Britain* entailed allegiance to a protean entity over some two centuries. 'It is in the interest of the United Kingdom', wrote Sir John Sinclair of Ubster in the 1790s, 'to keep alive those national, *or what, perhaps, may now be properly called local distinctions* of English, Scotch, Irish and Welsh.'[1] His language, with its uncertainty about what was 'national' and what was 'local', is revealing. It was a fundamental issue in *Britain*, though by no means invariably considered as such. Were its inhabitants after 1707 'British', or in the process of becoming 'British', or did they remain fundamentally – insofar as they reflected on the matter – English, Scotch and Welsh respectively? Was there a conflict between the acceptance of a 'British' identity and continuing identity as English, Scottish or Welsh? Was it a matter of choice? Were the contexts in which the question of identity might be asked all-important? Within Britain its inhabitants might identify themselves primarily as 'English' or 'Scottish' but in relation to 'foreigners' they were British.

Sir John, like many of his contemporaries, experienced these tensions in the everyday aspects of his life. His great claim to fame is that he inspired a 21-volume *Statistical Account of Scotland* (1791–98). With the cooperation of the General Assembly of the Church of Scotland, ministers inquired in great detail into the basic facts of parochial life throughout Scotland. He had an acute sense of what was 'local', what was also 'Scottish national' and what was 'British' national. He possessed an intimate knowledge of the peculiarities of the north of Scotland but he was an MP at Westminster for over thirty years. His father had been educated at Stoke Newington, London,

---

[1] Cited in L. Colley, *Britons: Forging the Nation 1707–1837* (London, 1992) pp. 373–4.

by Isaac Watts, the English Dissenter. Sir John sent his son to Harrow.[2] The Sinclair family – in a manner which was to continue, in the event, over many generations – had an acute sense of both the local and the national. The difficulty both of 'keeping alive' the local, while cultivating the national, and of maintaining a balance between the two, ran all through British life. In the two centuries that followed the failure of the 1745 rebellion, however, it did appear that 'local distinctions' could still exist – though perhaps under threat – without endangering the unity of a united kingdom that was a world power. After 1945, in changed circumstances, the stability of that balance ceased to be axiomatic.

England and Scotland in Britain

In Scotland in 1707 there was naturally much debate about what the new unitary state of Britain would mean. The union between England and Wales had now existed for nearly 200 years but the model it provided did not figure prominently in Scottish debates. Indeed, 'Wales' as an entity scarcely troubled the minds of lawyers and *literati* in Edinburgh. In contrast to Wales, at the very least Scotland would secure within the new union its ecclesiastical, legal and educational system. Some Scottish writers, however, had hoped for a different kind of union from that which did emerge. Andrew Fletcher of Saltoun, for example, unsuccessfully argued for the continued existence of a separate Scottish Parliament and militia. His concept of union was federal. It was important that Scotland should not be considered merely as an appendage in a Britain which was, in effect, an 'English empire'.[3] It could not be denied that contemporary Edinburgh had a population only a tenth of London but it should still remain a functioning capital. He dreamed not of the Great Britain that did emerge but of a United Provinces of Great Britain with the provinces acting together for certain purposes but in other respects continuing to give life to their own distinctive historical traditions.[4]

Such an approach would have preserved the pasts of both countries, both Scottish and English. Some advocates of union, however, found such an approach too restrictive. In seeking to preserve pasts it neglected the new possibilities inherent in Britain. Instead of looking backwards, where their histories had been at times conflicting, the peoples of Britain should look

---

[2] J. Grant, *Memoirs of Sir George Sinclair* (London, 1870) pp. 3–4.
[3] D. Daiches, ed., *Andrew Fletcher of Saltoun: Selected Political Writings and Speeches* (Edinburgh, 1979).
[4] J. Robertson, 'Union, State and Empire: the Britain of 1707 in its European setting' in L. Stone, ed., *An Imperial State at War: Britain from 1689 to 1815* (London, 1994) pp. 224–57.

forward. They would free themselves from the vagaries of dynastic inheritance and royal confessional allegiances. A single, sovereign Parliament would in future determine the royal succession and ultimately regulate the religious life of both countries. It would have authority over all of Britain. In short, this would be a new state and its ethos would evolve over time in a British sense.

In general, Scottish constitutional thinking at this juncture was more sophisticated and reflective than English consideration of these matters. That was understandable. A junior partner in any merger is always more likely to think that its adherence will make a difference. A senior partner is more likely to consider that the junior partner is signing up to a going concern and keep things largely as they were before. The English political elite had little doubt that it was the senior partner in this new relationship.

Union, therefore, could not be other than difficult. It was not even as though long-held stereotypes and prejudices, entertained by both parties of each other, had been abandoned. Clarendon's classic *History of the Rebellion and Civil Wars in England*, first published in 1702–4, did not refrain from describing the Scots of half a century earlier as 'vermin'. Their numerous proud and indigent nobility, he wrote, had strangely submitted to their ignorant and insolent clergy: that was Scottish life in a nutshell. Clarendon thought it a fault in Charles I that he had what he termed an immoderate love for Scots. It would not be difficult, in turn, to find Scots who expressed themselves less than favourably about the English. Turning a state into a nation-state evidently had certain inherited perceptions to overcome.

English inability, or unwillingness, to grasp the *novelty* which the new Britain represented, is easily understood. The British Parliament was the old English Parliament – to which Welsh MPs had been added in the sixteenth century. The Scots were merely the latest to be added. English MPs felt under no special obligation to understand the peculiarities of Scotland. Their indifference, in this respect, was in a sense reinforced by the very success of the Scots, under the Act of Union, in 'ring-fencing', as they believed, the cardinal expressions of their distinctiveness – education, Church and law. Putting it perhaps too boldly, the English had little incentive to understand Scotland but the Scots had little alternative but to understand England if they were to play an effective part in a Britain moulded by England.

Some historians, in such a context, have identified in Scotland what might be called a post-Union identity crisis which cast into doubt the very possibility of a continuing Scottish historiography. Such elements can indeed be seen, but Scottish historiography retained an important polemical and political function for at least half a century after 1707.[5] To continue to stress the distinctiveness of the Scottish past was a way of asserting that

---

[5] C. Kidd, *Subverting Scotland's Past: Scottish Whig Historians and the Creation of an Anglo-British Identity* (Cambridge, 1993).

'Scotland' could not simply be obliterated in the new structure. Scotland was not Wales. It had proud and ancient universities and urban cultures. It was true that 'pan-British Protestantism' underpinned unity, but the previous chapter has demonstrated that it was itself a somewhat frail concept.[6]

The legacy of the 1745 rebellion was awkward. It still remains difficult to find the right language to use in describing the mass-reprisals carried out by 'Butcher' Cumberland's troops in the aftermath of the Battle of Culloden. Professor Lynch, for example, writing in Scotland, speaks of this bloodletting as coming 'after forty years of frustration and failure in dealing with a Celtic people. It was one more act in the long drama of the consolidation of an English Empire.' Dr Langford, writing in England, concedes that the campaign of terror in the Highlands was harrowing but adds that it is 'often exaggerated'.[7] Certainly, the immediate repression was followed by measures which at length did strike at the heart of Highland peculiarity; the abolition of military tenures and of heritable jurisdictions. Forfeiture of estates was effectively carried out. Bagpipes and tartans were banished. In one sense, such measures were indeed 'the consolidation of an English Empire' but that is not the complete picture. The victory at Culloden was not merely English. The number of Scots in Cumberland's army at the battle approximately equalled the number in the army of Charles Edward. It had been the throne of Britain that Charles Edward had sought. The father of the great Victorian sage, Thomas Carlyle, indubitably a Scot, watched the earlier Battle of Prestonpans, when the Jacobites were victorious, from the steeple of its kirk. '*We* were completely defeated', he told his son. In addition to other elements, therefore, the 1745 rebellion had the aspect of a Scottish civil war: Highlander against Lowlander, Presbyterian against Episcopalian/Catholic, town against country, 'progressive' against 'conservative'. Later, it was one of Sir Walter Scott's achievements in his *Waverley* novels (1814–32) to draw together the discordant elements in Scottish history. Such an achievement was perhaps only possible because it then seemed that the Scottish past was firmly anchored in the British present.

It was in the midst of this cultural uncertainty that James Macpherson claimed to have recovered and published (1761–62) a third-century 'Scottish' epic which he attributed to Ossian, a Celtic bard. This 'discovery' caused a sensation and electrified not only literary Edinburgh, but also painters and writers across Europe over subsequent decades. How far Macpherson was or was not a charlatan need not detain us here. What he was determined to achieve, however, was the revelation of an authentic Highland past which

---

[6] Colley, *Britons*, p. 6; K. Robbins, 'An Imperial and Multinational Polity, 1832–1922' in A. Grant and K. Stringer, eds, *Uniting the Kingdom? The Making of British History* (London, 1995) pp. 252–3.

[7] M. Lynch, *Scotland: A New History* (London, 1991) p. 339; P. Langford, *A Polite and Commercial People: England 1727–1783* (Oxford, 1989) p. 199.

was 'civilized' rather than 'barbarian'. He claimed to be able to demonstrate that 'British liberty' was not simply an English creation. In the midst of 'barbarity', the Celtic peoples formed 'as just notions of liberty as other free nations have done in the most cultivated times'.[8]

In general, the 'local distinctions' of the Highlands did not seem particularly admirable amongst some intellectuals in Glasgow and Edinburgh. There was some agreement that the 'Highland problem' stemmed from the failure to develop legal authority there. Its 'barbarity' needed a drastic cure. These dramatic events had brought home the extent of cultural cleavage in 'Scotland'. It is not altogether surprising, therefore, that we see in the work of historians and 'sociologists' in Scotland in the later eighteenth century some realignment of identities. It was unprofitable to hark back. It was time, with Adam Smith, to consider *The Wealth of Nations*. The 'Scottish Enlightenment' charted a course towards what was conceived to be 'the modern'. One recent historian suggests that at this time the history to which the Scots had been admitted by the Union was more relevant to a general understanding of institutions, politics and society. Since England appeared to be in the van of commercial progress it was England's past which, as it were, came to stand proxy for Scotland's.[9]

It is at this point, for example, that the historian and philosopher David Hume substituted the title *History of England* for his earlier *History of Britain*. That was not simply because it was easier to write the history of England than the history of Britain – a view which can be readily understood! – but because it was *English* virtues and achievements which would henceforth inform the history of *Britain*. Scots could also take advantage of the fact that the ill-educated English did not themselves fully understand the significance of their own history. Scots could help them realize how odd/distinctive the English were, because they came to that history at a tangent. They might even be able to inject a wider European perspective into English/British history.

Such developments, however, would take time to work through into a British consciousness. In mid-century, there still remained much uncertainty about how relations between the two countries would develop. 'By all I can judge', declared the 3rd Duke of Atholl in 1766, 'publick affairs never was in such confusion since Britain was a country, nor do I see how those who are, or may be, at the helm will be able to mend them'. It was fortunate for him that he was able find solace amongst the 'peaceable rocks and mountains' of Scotland, far from 'the distant voice of faction and licentiousness' which emanated from London.[10]

---

[8] Cited in Kidd, *Subverting Scotland's Past*, p. 234; R. Craik, *James Boswell (1740–1795): The Scottish Perspective* (London, 1994).

[9] Kidd, *Subverting Scotland's Past*, p. 210.

[10] Cited in A. Murdoch, 'Lord Bute, James Stuart Mackenzie and the Government of Scotland' in K. Schweitzer, ed., *Lord Bute: Essays in Re-interpretation* (Leicester, 1988) p. 136.

11.1 Back to Basics: Stereotypes and caricatures designed to highlight 'charac-teristic' deficiencies in the peoples of Britain as perceived by their neighbours can be found over many centuries. Naturally, in the past, they found particular expression at points of tension. In this instance, *Sawney in the Boghouse*, published on 17 June 1745, during the 1745 rebellion, the 'typical' Scot is seen as the rude warrior of the seventeenth century who had unfavourably impressed English opinion.

It may be misleading to describe the defeat of the 1715 and 1745 rebel-lions as a defeat for 'the Scots' but there were many in England who saw it this way. Satirical prints were to be found circulating in England whose basic aim was to show that the Scots remained bloodthirsty warriors, ignor-ant of the basics of civilization. One such print, for example, has a certain

'Sawney' established, kilt and all, in a boghouse.[11] English poets, preachers and historians remained content with their notions of the sophistication and superiority of England. The Scots would have to find their own way without special treatment. In this there was arrogance but also an acceptance of the fact that the English past was itself a mixed affair to which many influences and peoples had contributed. Daniel Defoe expressed this sense earlier in his *The True-Born Englishman* (1701):

> We have been *Europe's* sink, the *Jakes* where she
> Voids all her Offal Out-Cast Progeny[12]

Such lines clearly offered King William III the possibility that he might become a true-born Englishman after all! The English, Defoe reiterated, were the 'mix'd relics' of 'all the nations under heaven'. In such a context, one more mixture mattered little.

Other writers, however, were less accommodating. Dr Johnson, whose great dictionary did so much to 'nationalize' English, engaged in sustained banter with his companion, James Boswell. 'Seeing Scotland, Madam, is only seeing a worse England' is only one of his remarks to encapsulate a sense of superiority. Boswell, of course, had begun life as a Scot but had become a 'Briton', that is to say someone who, by residence and mode of life, could not readily be classified as fully English or fully Scottish. A transition from Scot into Briton was inevitably much more frequently made than the transition from Englishman into Briton. Scottish 'infiltration' into English life attracted unfavourable comment, in much the same vein as it had done after the accession of James I. Lord Shelburne found the Scots 'a sad set of innate, cold-hearted, impudent rogues'. He addressed this opinion to Richard Price, radical economist, philosopher and minister, clearly supposing that no Welshman would have difficulty in endorsing it.[13]

It was the radical John Wilkes, however, who uninhibitedly played on English anxiety.[14] The Scots, in his vision, were alien and would always be so. He feared the ambitions of the periphery and proudly proclaimed that English liberty was not for the taking. Lord Bute, who rose so high in contemporary politics, was pilloried as a Scot. Wilkes exaggerated the incomprehensibility of Scottish speech to the English and stridently contrasted his own plain English with pretentious 'Scotticisms'. Ironically, however, although offence was taken in Scotland at the crude nature of the attacks,

---

[11] M. Duffy, *The Englishman and the Foreigner* (Cambridge, 1986), p. 151.

[12] Cited in J. Lucas, *England and Englishness: Ideas of Nationhood in English Poetry* (London, 1991) p. 18; Kidd, *Subverting Scotland's Past*, pp. 48–9.

[13] J. Black, 'Ideology, History, Xenophobia and the World of Print in Eighteenth-Century England' in J. Black and J. Gregory, eds, *Culture, Politics and Society in Britain, 1660–1800* (Manchester, 1991); Langford, *Polite and Commercial People*, p. 328.

[14] P.D.G. Thomas, *John Wilkes: A Friend of Liberty* (Oxford, 1996).

Scots themselves were sensitive throughout the century about these very 'Scotticisms' in their speech. There was an increasing division between the 'Scots' used in informal context and the 'English' used in formal. Scottish gentlemen had a particular interest in the purchase of dictionaries which told them of the 'Scotticisms' which they should now avoid. Some scholars have subsequently argued that English English was 'psycholinguistically alien' to eighteenth-century Scots. It was a kind of foreign tongue: hence, perhaps, the overelaborations and pedantry of speech which could occasion mirth or irritation in England.[15]

New Britain therefore confronted ambitious Scots with a dilemma. Its possibilities could only be exploited if their 'local distinctions' of speech could be abandoned or at least modified. And many were anxious to move beyond Scotland, within England and overseas, to take advantage of empire. Englishmen, however, despite John Wilkes, were not 'losing' their country, even though some anxious minds still supposed that Britain, taken seriously, would undermine the English past. In any event, during the first century of unified British history it is clear that making one present out of two pasts was not a straightforward process. Nevertheless, by the time Queen Victoria came to the throne in 1837 it is arguable that Scotland had come to terms with what had happened. Linda Colley, for example, takes the view that by this juncture Scotland certainly continued to retain many of the characteristics of a distinct nation, but she believes that it was 'comfortably contained within a bigger nation'.[16] Such an accommodation is partly attributable simply to the passage of time. New generations knew no other reality than 'Scotland in Britain'. More positively, Scotland was experiencing a degree of unusual internal stability within the larger framework, was sharing in lucrative imperial and commercial enterprises and was content with what may be described as Protestant warfare.

The extension of the franchise and the gradual democratization of British politics brought fresh stresses and strains. It was then no longer possible to 'manage' Scottish affairs within an Anglo-Scottish political elite which was largely aristocratic. There were periodic attempts, as with the mid-century Association for the Vindication of Scottish Rights, to express discontent with the way Scotland was being governed. Leading English politicians found it increasingly necessary to pay visits north of the Border and such figures as Melbourne, Peel, Russell and Aberdeen had unusually strong Scottish links. Until the mid-nineteenth century, it could be said that the interaction between the two countries had been relatively limited. From this point on, however, the traffic increased substantially. The 'railway age' opened up

---

[15] Kidd, *Subverting Scotland's Past*, pp. 112–13; see also his later article 'Teutonist Ethnology and Scottish Nationalist Inhibition, 1780–1880', *Scottish Historical Review* 197 (1995).
[16] Colley, *Britons*, p. 113.

Scotland to England and vice versa on a new scale. In 1848, when the first railway link to England was completed, London could be reached from Edinburgh in twelve hours. The 'tyranny of distance' which had hitherto preserved Scotland in a kind of semi-independence was diminishing.

It was in 1885 that Lord Salisbury established the post of Secretary for Scotland, the holder of this office becoming a member of the British Cabinet in 1892. Salisbury hoped that such an office would 'redress the wounded dignities of the Scottish people'. In Liberal circles there was talk of 'Home Rule', an aspiration which fluctuated in its appeal over the next couple of decades. It was never achieved. Indeed, at least at the level of high politics, the government of Britain became a conspicuously Anglo-Scottish enterprise. William Gladstone himself could in a sense be accounted a Scot and came latterly to represent Midlothian at Westminster. Lord Rosebery was another Anglo-Scottish Liberal Prime Minister. Later, when the fateful decision to go to war was made in 1914, it was taken by a Liberal government and a House of Commons with a strong Scottish presence. The Prime Minister, Asquith, though indubitably an English Liberal, sat for a Scottish consti- tuency, as did Winston Churchill, the First Lord of the Admiralty. Lord Hal- dane, though a Scot, was Lord Chancellor. Bonar Law, Leader of the Opposition, grew to manhood on Clydeside, though he now sat for an Eng- lish constituency. James Ramsay MacDonald and Arthur Henderson, leaders of the Labour Party, were also English MPs, while Keir Hardie represented a Welsh constituency – all Scots of a kind. Asquith's predecessor as Prime Minister, Sir Henry Campbell-Bannerman, was the first unambiguously Scottish commoner to hold that office. A.J. Balfour, his predecessor as (Con- servative) Prime Minister, was half a Scot. One could go on. Such interpene- tration suggests that at a certain level Britain had 'come of age' politically.[17]

The Great War turned out to offer ample scope for the heroic qualities of 'the Scottish soldier' and the image of a martial race of men: Scotland the Brave. In the person of Douglas Haig, Scotland provided an English-edu- cated Commander-in-Chief of the British Expeditionary Force in France. Scottish regiments had their proud place in the British army, even though re- cruiting imperatives sometimes meant that their Scottishness was somewhat diluted. In a war for 'King and Country' it was difficult to disentangle whether that country was Scotland, Britain or the British Empire. For decades, Glasgow, Scotland's largest city, had projected itself (in competition with Birmingham) as 'the second city of the Empire'.[18]

---

17 K. Robbins, *Nineteenth-Century Britain: Integration and Diversity* (Oxford, 1988); K. Robbins, 'Core and Periphery in Modern British History'; in K. Robbins, *History, Religion and Identity in Modern Britain* (London, 1993) pp. 239–59; I.G.C. Hutchison, *A Political History of Scotland, 1832–1924: Parties, Elections and Issues* (Edinburgh, 1985).
18 K. Robbins, 'The Imperial City' [Glasgow], *History Today* 40, (May 1990) pp. 48–54.

Such an identity, so carefully fostered and cultivated, was an early casualty of peace. Scottish heavy industry was never quite the same again after the war and 'new' industry was difficult to attract north. 'Red Clydesiders' drew necessary attention to bad health and bad housing but their rhetoric deterred investment. It was in this increasingly gloomy economic climate that debate began again on Scottish identity and prospects. The author of *Caledonia or the Future of the Scots* (1927) spoke starkly of the Scots as a 'dying race'.[19] In the same year, the Scottish National War Memorial was officially opened in Edinburgh. 'Scotland', wrote Ian Hay, 'is small enough to know all her sons by heart.'[20] The memorial named every one of her 100,000 dead. On the other hand, one Unionist MP felt that little was achieved by grieving as a small country. Scotland, he suggested, had passed the stage of nationhood, having been absorbed into a wider area. It was that claim, however, which was resisted by the National Party of Scotland (1928) – but the party's appeal remained limited. The achievements of Hugh MacDiarmid and the 'literary renaissance' were trumpeted in some quarters but in others such a recycling of archaic Scottish words was a pathetic search for an irrecoverable past.

In one sense, what was coming to a head was a reflection of a demographic balance in Britain which was shifting inexorably southwards. The proportion of the British population which lived in England grew steadily through the nineteenth century. At least several hundred thousand 'Scots' and their descendants were becoming 'English' as they settled south of the Border. By 1901, over 30 million people lived in England as compared with 4.5 million in Scotland. By 1931, over 37 million lived in England and 4,842,000 in Scotland – 40,000 less than in 1921, the first recorded decline. The Scottish birth-rate was higher than the English, but it was a population, it appeared, being bred for emigration. John Buchan, novelist and Unionist politician, was among those who urged that Scotland should save its national identity while there was still time. He did not want to see Scotland become 'merely a Northern Province of England'. Yet these sentiments were expressed from the comfort of his Oxfordshire home, far removed from the Glasgow of his youth.

Industrialists complained that business after business was being bought up by 'English money' and if the process of 'English absorption' was not stopped, Scotland would drop to a position of industrial insignificance. Columnist after columnist complained of 'the fundamentally false policy of centralizing everything on London'. Partly as a response to such criticism, the

---

[19] G.M. Thomson, the author, also wrote *Scotland, that Distressed Area* (Edinburgh, 1935); T. Devine, *Clanship to Crofters' War: The Social Transformation of the Highlands* (Manchester, 1994) deals with an earlier 'distressed area'.
[20] Ian Hay, *Their Name Liveth: The Scottish National War Memorial* (London, 1931) p. 6.

Scottish Office was transferred from London to Edinburgh in 1932 and a major new building planned to cater for a degree of administrative devolution for Scotland. On the other hand, were there really grounds for believing that a 'Home Rule Parliament' would be able to cure Scotland's ills? Robert Boothby, MP for East Aberdeenshire, painted a picture of his fellow-countrymen – certainly not educated as he had been at Eton and Magdalen College, Oxford – as a pack of miserable savages before 1707, whereas afterwards they had been 'partners in the greatest undertaking the world had ever seen'.[21] For others, 'Home Rule' would only create fresh friction and make 'the English' even more inclined to wash their hands of Scotland's difficulties. And was it not the case that Scotland needed, and received, 'English money' to pay for Scottish unemployment benefit? The prospect, for some, that Scotsmen and Scotswomen would be shut out from 'taking the biggest positions in the Empire', as they allegedly did, was too dreadful to contemplate. The Empire Exhibition held in Glasgow in 1938 attempted, a little despairingly, to keep the imperial fires burning.[22]

The years immediately before 1939 brought re-armament and injected fresh orders for Scottish heavy industry. It could seem, momentarily, as though the clouds had lifted. Scotland could recover its pride by its part in a new war. In the interwar period, the 'problem of Scotland' had frequently been defined as how to reconcile Scottish aspirations and sentiments with the maintenance of its position as an integral part of a Britain which had its political life centred on what was still most frequently referred to as the 'Imperial Parliament'. That political life in the 1930s had been in turn dominated by a National government which alienated large sections of the Scottish working class. During the war, however, different circumstances obtained. Under a Labour Secretary of State, Thomas Johnston, a distinctive mode of government emerged. A 'Scottish Advisory Council of ex-Secretaries' was formed and Johnston largely succeeded in persuading Churchill that London should look sympathetically on any proposal about which Scotland was unanimous. Johnston himself claimed that Scotland's wishes had been respected during the war to a greater degree than at any time since the Union. In 1945, 200 years after Bonnie Prince Charlie landed, it could appear that Great Britain was working properly.

[21] R. Finlay, 'National Identity in Crisis: Politicians, Intellectuals and the "End of Scotland"', 1920–1939', *History* (June 1994) cites both Buchan and Boothby; R. Campbell, *The Rise and Fall of Scottish Industry, 1707–1939* (Edinburgh, 1980); C. Lee, *Scotland and the U.K.: The Economics of the Union* (Manchester, 1994) – covers a long span.
[22] B. Crampsey, *The British Empire Exhibition of 1938* (Edinburgh, 1988).

England, Wales and Britain

In the sixteenth century, certain Welsh Catholic exiles in Rome kept up their spirits by entertaining fantasies. 'My lord', declared one of their number, Owen Lewis, to a Scottish envoy from Mary, Queen of Scots, 'let us [the Welsh and the Scots] stick together, for we are the old and true inhabitors of the isle of Brittany [Britain]. These others [the English] are but usurpers and mere possessors.'[23] Two hundred years later, there was little prospect that the possessors would be dispossessed. Was it the case, therefore, that 'Wales' was losing its distinctiveness after two centuries of union with England?

In one sense, the answer was yes. Welsh bards lamented that their traditional services were no longer required. The literary, historical and musical functions which they had once performed were in process of becoming redundant. This was not the result of any particular English malevolence. It rather reflected the fact that, by 1700, Welsh people at particular social levels were catching up with styles of living and behaviour fashionable in England perhaps a century earlier. It was increasingly the case that Welshmen settled on a fixed surname rather than use a string of patronymics joined by *ap* (son of).[24] Yet, though some English satirists mocked the 'gibberish' of 'Taphydom', it was still the case around 1700 that 90 per cent of people in Wales spoke Welsh.[25] What is more difficult to estimate, is how many people in Wales also spoke English at this time. Increasingly, however, the country came to be divided between bilingual and monoglot Welsh areas.[26] The Welsh people were being inexorably drawn into the English-speaking Atlantic British Empire.

Nevertheless, there was a strong desire, particularly among the London Welsh, to ensure that some kind of distinctive Wales survived. After the Society of Ancient Britons (1715) came the Honourable Society of Cymmrodorion (1751). Both titles reflect the claim that in Britain it was the Welsh who were the original Britons. Later, in 1770, came the Gwyneddigion (men from North-West Wales) and it was with their assistance that in the 1780s *eisteddfodau* (gatherings for poetry, prose and music) were revived. In Wales itself there was an upsurge of publishing (and printing) in the Welsh language, largely on religious themes. The Morris brothers of Anglesey sought out

---

[23] Cited in P.R. Roberts, 'The Welsh Language, English Law and Tudor Legislation' in *Transactions of the Honourable Society of Cymmrodorion* [1989] (London, 1990), pp. 68–9.

[24] T.J. and P.T.J. Morgan, *Welsh Surnames* (Cardiff, 1985).

[25] P. Morgan 'From a Hunt to View: The Hunt for the Welsh Past in the Romantic Period' in E.J. Hobsbawm and T.O. Ranger, eds, *The Invention of Tradition* (Cambridge, 1983) pp. 48–9; C. Harvie, 'The Folk and the *Gwerin*: The Myth and the Reality of Popular Culture in 19th Century Scotland and Wales', *Proceedings of the British Academy* 80 (1993) helpfully compares the two societies.

[26] P. Jenkins, *A History of Modern Wales 1536–1990* (London, 1992) p. 128.

examples of Welsh poetry and music. There were vigorous efforts, by means of fresh grammars, to give the Welsh language stability and to prevent it from collapsing into mutually incomprehensible dialects.

Edward Williams, 'Iolo Morganwg', claimed to have confirmed what others had only suspected: that the Welsh bards were the successors of the ancient Druids. He staged a *Gorsedd*, with suitable prayers and chants, on Primrose Hill in London in 1792. What was particularly striking, amongst many things that were striking about Iolo, was that he did not spring from the gentry or clergy who had often delighted to dabble in antiquarian pursuits.[27] He was a consistently penniless stonemason. The enthusiasm for a long-gone past was not confined to Iolo Morganwg. Lewis Morris, for example, came across the sixth-century Welsh poem *Gododdin* in 1758 and thought it might qualify as the work of a 'Celtic Homer'. This enthusiasm for a long Celtic past paralleled the concerns of Macpherson in Scotland. A new mixture of language and culture, religion and politics, was emerging in Wales at the end of the eighteenth century. A 'Druidic' past, if it could be suitably dressed up in appropriate robes, might give a new twist to the future.

The population of Wales grew from 587,000 in 1801 to over 2 million in 1911. Some 80 per cent of the Welsh population lived in rural areas at the beginning of the century, but only 20 per cent by the end. The increase in the population of Wales in the first decade of the twentieth century was roughly equal to the total population of Wales in 1700. Glamorgan became the county in which more than half of the population of Wales lived. It became the magnet not only for populations from rural West Wales and even North Wales, but also for workers from counties across the English border. It was industrial expansion which enabled Wales to retain its native population. Welsh overseas emigration to North America or the British Empire was modest compared with that of the Irish or the Scots. Workers in industrial Wales were frequently able to maintain their links with their villages of origin and, at least for a time, sustain their cultural and linguistic heritage in new surroundings, in the Rhondda, for example.

But perhaps this was only a temporary stage and in due course Welsh would decline in the 'melting pot' that existed in the valleys. The 1911 census disclosed that only 44 per cent of the population of Wales could speak Welsh, a drop from 54 per cent in 1891. The absolute number of those able to speak the language began to fall. Until this point, the increase in the number of Welsh speakers as the population grew had enabled a flourishing Welsh periodical press to develop. The close association between cultural life and chapel has already been noted. What then did the future hold?

The complexities of language, culture and identity became steadily more apparent in the twentieth century. Was 'Welshness' something for chapel and 'culture' and 'Englishness' for school and business? The English language

---

[27] P. Morgan, *Iolo Morganwg* (Cardiff, 1975).

11.2 Cardiff Civic Centre: Cardiff, a nineteenth-century coal metropolis, demanded status for the twentieth century. The Marquess of Bute paid attention to Cardiff Castle, amongst other things, but that was not enough. Hence the planned creation of Cathays Park and imposing embodiments of civic pride. In what sense, however – if any – these public buildings epitomized Welshness was another matter. They were the creations, in a sense, of capital but, not yet at least, the creation of a capital.

had been imposed educationally as a necessary prelude to the 'modernization' of Wales. There was undoubtedly coercion in this process but there was also a substantial acceptance by parents that English did indeed offer the path to the future. So, perhaps, the surviving bilingualism was merely a phase before Wales became a monolingual English-speaking country. Such a prospect seemed in the eyes of some commentators to entail the end of all that was significant and important about 'Wales'. Their concerns were summed up in the expression *Heb Iaith, heb Genedl* (No language, no nation). Other writers, however, thought themselves no less Welsh for writing in English. The fact was that there was no single 'Wales' but rather a plurality: an 'English' Wales, a 'Welsh' Wales and a 'British' Wales, not to mention that parts of South Wales seemed almost 'American' in atmosphere.

The role of the city of Cardiff – as it became in 1907 – in the life of Wales symbolized many of these uncertainties. The laying out of splendid Edwardian civic buildings in Cathays Park, among them the *National* Museum of Wales, showed how far Cardiff had come over a century from a community of a mere 2,000 people in 1801. But it was not the capital city of Wales. Indeed, Wales had no such thing. Whether Cardiff could be or should be such a city was a matter of contentious discussion. The Earl of Bute, George III's Prime Minister, safely buried at Rothesay on his Scottish isle, would have been amazed by the scale of the activities of his descendants, the Marquesses of Bute, in Cardiff. It was the Marchioness of Bute who featured as a rather unlikely 'Dame Wales' in a distinctly aristocratic 'National Pageant of Wales' held in 1909 in Cardiff Castle, a building on which the Marquess had lavished a good deal of the wealth he had obtained from coal and property in South Wales. Such Cardiffian antics did not seem authentically Welsh in the rural fastnesses. In their eyes, Cardiff did not seem a very Welsh place. It was better to have no capital at all than to have Cardiff. In the pre-1914 decades deliberate attempts had been made to develop significant institutions outside the south-east. University colleges were founded in the north and west – federalized with Cardiff as a national university in 1893 – and a grand National Library was erected at Aberystwyth. Such developments were testimony to a new if ambiguous national institutional maturity.

The advent to power of David Lloyd George as British Prime Minister in 1916 could also be taken to be a sign of a new Welsh political maturity in a British context. As Chancellor of the Exchequer before the war and a Welsh MP he had gained a unique status in Welsh life. He had given encouragement and support to the developments which have just been mentioned. Although he happened to have been born in England, he was Welsh-speaking and represented the Caernarfon boroughs in the heart of Welsh-speaking Wales. He had shown some youthful enthusiasm for 'Home Rule' for Wales – a campaign which foundered to a considerable extent because of the tensions between Liberals in North and South Wales. Yet it is clear that almost from the beginning of his career he aspired to a greater role than any that a 'Home Rule' Wales could have offered. To be Prime Minister of Great Britain and to preside over the destiny of the British Empire was something no Welsh-speaking politician had ever previously done. His wartime rhetoric drew upon the traditions of chapel to inspire victory. There is a certain irony in the fact that Adolf Hitler was later to write in praise of 'the towering political ability' during the war of 'this Englishman' [*sic*]. A due recognition of 'Welshness' did not require the break-up of Britain and, in private, Lloyd George found irksome many of those facets of Welsh Nonconformity with which he was publicly identified.

Lloyd George's domination of the British political scene proved transient. The pulsating expansion of the Welsh economy between 1870 and 1914 also did not endure. As in Scotland, the price would be paid over the next two decades for a reliance on particular industries, a reliance deemed excessive when overseas markets disappeared. In the case of Wales it was above all the coal industry and the technologies based upon it. By the early 1930s unemployment was high across the principality, in Anglesey as much as in Glamorgan or Monmouthshire (Gwent). Merthyr Tydfil, for example, the boom borough of the nineteenth century, was a blackspot, full of unemployed miners and steelworkers. It lost a quarter of its population between 1913 and 1939. Men moved out to the English Midlands and elsewhere in search of jobs to be found in 'new' industries there – some 450,000 between 1921 and 1939. It was depressing to realize that the location of many mining communities had little advantage once it was no longer profitable to exploit the natural resources which had brought people into them in the first place. Poverty and malnutrition were rife and, with them, psychological depression and alcoholism. 'Something must be done for these people', declared the Prince of Wales on a visit to Dowlais, by Merthyr, in 1936, but no one knew quite what. Industrial Wales, so recently teeming with life, seemed on the brink of becoming 'Gwalia Deserta'.

The socio-economic crisis of these decades was accompanied by prolonged cultural and political debate. In the 1890s there was some talk that Wales should have a Secretary of State on the Scottish model but nothing came of the idea nor of resurrected proposals for Home Rule. The Liberal Party which had claimed to 'speak for Wales' since 1868 was in an acute condition. The decline in the use of Welsh appeared to be accelerating. It was largely on this account that *Plaid Genedlaethol Cymru* (National Party of Wales) was formed in 1925. There was a tendency to argue that the industrial crisis could be solved by deindustrialization. Although influential intellectual figures were associated with the movement, it made little headway outside strongly Welsh-speaking areas, partly because it was not even sure that it wanted to appeal to Anglicized Wales. As in Scotland, a common theme in Plaid circles was that Wales was poor because it had to live under an alien imperialist government. It was such thinking, coupled in some cases with pacifism and in others with a certain sympathy for fascist ideas, which led to some opposition to the militarization of Wales and participation in the Second World War. It would be wrong, however, to suppose that these strands represented majority opinion. 'British' voices still predominated in Wales and took pride in Welsh participation in a war that was British.[28]

Irish in Britain and British in Ireland

The Act of Union, passed in 1800, which united the British and Irish Parliaments from January 1801 inaugurated the United Kingdom of Great Britain and Ireland, a state that was to exist until 1922. At that date, two separate

---

[28] D. Smith, ed., *A People and a Proletariat: Essays in the History of Wales 1780–1980* (London, 1980); C. Williams, *Democratic Rhondda: Politics and Society 1885–1951* (Cardiff, 1996); I.G. Jones, *Explorations and Explanations: Essays in the Social History of Victorian Wales* (Llandysul, 1981); M.J. Daunton, *Coal Metropolis: Cardiff 1870–1914* (Leicester, 1977); M. Cragoe, *An Anglican Aristocracy: The Moral Economy of the Landed Estate in Carmarthenshire 1832–1895* (Oxford, 1996); K.O. Morgan, *Modern Wales: Politics, Places and People* (Cardiff, 1995); D.H. Davies, *The Welsh Nationalist Party 1925–1945: A Call to Nationhood* (Cardiff, 1983).

entities came into existence within the island of Ireland – the Irish Free State which had Dominion status and Northern Ireland which had internal self-government as a continuing constituent part of the United Kingdom. Acceptance of Dominion status led to a bitter civil war in the new Free State. In 1932, after Eamon de Valera came to power, steps were steadily taken to distance the new state from Britain and the British Empire/Commonwealth – for example, the abolition of the oath of allegiance to the Crown. A new constitution in 1937 changed the country's name to Eire. On the outbreak of the Second World War, Eire remained neutral. The country's history between 1922 and 1945 cannot be considered to be *British* and therefore has no place in this account, even though there remained central legacies of a British past which formed part of that Irish present. It looked likely, for example, notwithstanding official enthusiasm for the re-Gaelicization of Ireland, that the Irish Free State/Eire was likely to be English-speaking.

The extent to which Irish history between 1801 and 1922 was also British history was and remains contentious. From one perspective, this period of union was the logical corollary of the unity of Britain. For centuries, as has been fitfully noted in this book, English/Scottish/British involvement in Irish affairs had been almost constant. Arguably, however, those who intervened on behalf of the English/British Crown had never been able to decide their ultimate objectives in a country which was itself fractured in structure and identity. After 1801 it seemed, at last, that Ireland should in some sense be fully 'British' and be fully integrated into a United Kingdom which was itself a diverse entity. There were indeed some elements in Irish society which were not averse to a role as 'West Britons' within such a framework. They were, however, a minority, and over subsequent decades it soon became clear that this assimilationist path was unacceptable to the country as a whole. From mid-century onwards, the call for Irish Home Rule grew steadily under the leadership of Parnell. The growth of such a parliamentary party which came to dominate Irish representation at Westminster thrust the 'Irish question' back to the British government and parties. One response, to which Gladstone became attached, was to recognize the strength of Irish feeling and propose measures of Irish Home Rule. In the course of the debates which raged around this proposal – which split the Liberal Party – it became clear that it was by no means easy to find a structure which both gave the desired autonomy and also preserved unity. How was revenue to be apportioned? Was foreign and defence policy to remain 'Imperial'? Were Irish MPs to remain at Westminster and if so in reduced numbers? Could they vote on domestic British issues whilst British MPs would be precluded from voting on domestic Irish issues? Supporters of Home Rule in its various forms up to 1914 remained convinced that it would be an enduring solution which would preserve the essentials of a 'British Isles state'. Critics supposed it to be a solution built on sand which would lead to the break-up of the state.

What were the alternatives? Opponents of Home Rule argued that it could be avoided by a judicious mixture of kindness and coercion. If Ireland's economic problems could be satisfactorily addressed then Home Rule would lose its attraction. In the meantime, it was necessary to maintain law and order with vigour, even if that risked alienating the Irish population further. It was assumed that the maintenance of the Irish/ British state was in fact a British interest. A firm grip of Ireland was necessary for the security of Britain itself. There might come a point, however, when the costs associated with 'Britain in Ireland' would become too onerous. The Easter Rising in 1916 was a warning of what might come. After the end of the Great War, the methods used in Ireland by the 'Black and Tans' and others sullied the good name of Britain. In the end, it was clear in Britain that the authority of the United Kingdom could not be upheld indefinitely by such means.

If, at this juncture, it had been a simple matter of two coherent entities – 'Ireland' and 'Britain' – dissolving a union which had only existed for a little over a century then it might have been done relatively straightforwardly. It was not, however, a simple matter. The religious dimensions of the problem have already been touched on in the previous chapter. Chiefly in the south of Ireland 'Anglo-Irish' aristocratic and gentry families, predominantly Protestant, cherished the British link and were reluctant to see it severed. It was incontestable that Irishmen, at a certain social level, had moved freely between the two islands and had felt that no chasm separated the two. In the eighteenth century, the fact that his father was an Irish barrister had not prevented Edmund Burke from making a name for himself in British politics and satisfying the electors of Bristol. Many other people moved happily back and forth across the Irish Sea. Dublin was a great city of the British Isles, not only of Ireland.

In 'Ulster' the maintenance of the Union appealed to a much broader section of society: Belfast would not yield hegemony to Dublin, and Protestant would not yield to Catholic. It was perfectly possible to be Irish and British, many Protestants argued, just as it seemed apparently perfectly possible to be Scottish and British. In the stormy years before 1914, 'Ulster will fight and Ulster will be right' was a powerful cry. Ireland was on the brink of a civil war with issues of identity and self-definition at its heart and, arguably, Britain itself was close to that point. For the British Unionist Opposition, to ignore the right of the majority in Ulster to remain 'British', if that was what it wanted, was a kind of treason against the very idea of Britain itself. Undoubtedly, in playing the 'Orange card', some hoped to scuttle Irish Home Rule altogether, but when that came to seem an impossible objective partition appeared the only way out. In Ireland there would be one 'Irish/Catholic' state and one 'Irish/British/Protestant' statelet.

Such a division would naturally leave communities in each entity who felt themselves to be spiritually at home in the other and who resented the extent to which either explicitly or implicitly they were 'second-class citizens'. To give the statelet some degree of territorial viability, it was necessary to include a Catholic/Irish Nationalist minority in Northern Ireland, a minority which turned out to be proportionately larger than the Protestant/Irish-British minority in the Irish Free State. Of course, these labels are misleading and inexact in particular cases. Some individuals might choose to stress their religious rather than their ethnic/political allegiance and vice versa. There were Protestants in the south who accepted the Irish Free State with good grace just as there were Protestants in the north who had supported Home Rule and regretted partition.

The creation of a Government of Northern Ireland with defined devolved powers alongside some continuing representation of Ulster at Westminster had a paradoxical consequence. It was an outcome which had not been extensively desired or foreseen from any perspective. In the very act of embodying 'Britishness' in Northern Ireland in the shape of the Stormont Parliament with its administrative substructure, the British government and Parliament distanced itself from the internal affairs of the 'province'. The party political cleavages were not the cleavages of 'mainland' Britain. The majority suspected that the minority had only one purpose – to subvert the legitimacy of the statelet. The minority resented its *de facto* exclusion from political power. British politicians at Westminster did not intervene in the internal affairs of the province. There were very few individuals who were simultaneously at home in the political networks of London and Belfast. In short, those in Ulster who thought of themselves as British, to a greater or lesser extent, did so at this time in a more deliberate fashion than did the 'mainland British' themselves. Northern Ireland, as a part of the United Kingdom, was necessarily at war in 1939, a fact that highlighted the neutrality of Eire. The suspicion that there might be a British/American deal to bring Eire into the war by offering to end partition was never far below the surface, but it was warded off. Northern Ireland's facilities became of crucial importance after the United States came into the war. In 1945 the survival of the 'province' as a kind of 'Britain in Ireland' seemed secure. However, little had been done – indeed, perhaps little could be done – to end the hostility of the minority community for whom the British army, in which Ulstermen had served with such distinction in the Second World War, was an 'army of occupation'.

At one level, therefore, the picture appears to show the abject failure of the Act of Union. No British/Irish state was consolidated in the nineteenth century which could be equally 'owned' on both sides of the Irish Sea. In the twentieth century, the picture thus far in our account appears to be one of a determined elimination of 'half-way houses' – the replacement of lingering 'Britishness' in the Irish Free State/Eire and the assertion of an established but somewhat marginalized 'Britishness' in Northern Ireland. In each case, though in different ways and to different degrees, Ireland was a country apart.

Paradoxically, however, this same period saw Irish immigration into Britain on a scale without previous parallel. It had begun before the disaster of the mid-century famine but thereafter became a flood. The Irish-born population of England and Wales rose from 291,000 in 1841 to 520,000 in 1851 and peaked at 602,000 in 1861, some 3 per cent of the total population. Thereafter, although the Irish-born section of the population did not remain at this level, there was necessarily a large English-born but Irish-descended population in England. It is scarcely necessary to add that the Irish-born/Irish-descended population was not equally distributed across England and Wales. In mid-century, 22 per cent of the population of Liverpool was born in Ireland and 13 per cent of Manchester/Salford's. It was a population which started at the bottom of the social and economic scale. The Irish presence was also substantial in Scotland. In the 1841 census there were some 125,000 Irish-born persons in Scotland. In 1848, after the failure of the Irish potato crop, Irish people were coming into Glasgow at the rate of a thousand a week. In 1851 there were some 207,000 Irish-born residents in Scotland, some 7 per cent of the Scottish population. Glasgow, Paisley and Kilmarnock all had over 10 per cent of their population Irish-born. In Dundee the figure reached over 19 per cent. Seasonal migration from Ireland had long been familiar, but what was now happening was something new. The Irish were not going to go 'home'.

Were the Irish in Britain indelibly 'foreigners' or were they only another British element in the diversity that was the United Kingdom? One section of Victorian opinion quickly formed the impression that the Irish were a race of unskilled paupers much given to drinking and fighting. Friedrich Engels, in his examination of working-class Manchester in mid-century, considered the Irish as a whole to be a feckless people. They had no sense of decent living conditions and corrupted English workers by their very presence. Images to be found in the pages of *Punch* and elsewhere fed fears that Britain was being threatened by an anarchic presence. As late as the 1880s, Keir Hardie, Scottish socialist pioneer, spoke scathingly of the Irish collier who had 'a big shovel, a strong back and a weak brain' and who came straight from 'a peat bog or a tattie field'.[29] Later, he found Irish colliers in Merthyr Tydfil too. Irish people lived often in what were tantamount to ghettoes in English and Scottish cities.

Yet, as decades passed, a kind of integration took place, mocking the stereotypes that had once done duty. Although priests and others who saw themselves as community leaders tried very hard to maintain a cohesive Irish community, thousands melted into the mainstream of British life. They intermarried, became socially mobile, and became active in British politics,

---

[29] Cited in D. Howell, *British Workers and the Independent Labour Party, 1886–1906* (Manchester, 1983) p. 142; T. Gallagher, *Glasgow: The Uneasy Peace: Religious Tension in modern Scotland* (Manchester, 1987).

particularly the Labour Party. Even so, a sense of Irishness was still sustained through the continued reinforcement of fresh immigrants over the generations and by the geographical proximity of Ireland itself. The events of 1916–22 could not but have a legacy of mixed emotions, but Irish migration continued after 1922. And, as had been the case in 1914–18, there were volunteers from Eire who were very willing to serve in the British army. Continuing relationships of some intimacy at various social and cultural levels have to be set alongside the considerable hostility that existed between the governments of Britain and Eire on commercial and defence matters in the 1930s.

It was in Scotland that the Irish presence triggered most suspicion and hostility. There was a long background to this tension. Whereas, prior to the 1800 Act of Union, Scotland, with roughly three times the population of Wales, stood indubitably next to England ('the two Kingdoms'), that second place was usurped by Ireland. The population of Ireland in 1841 stood at around 8,200,000, some three times that of Scotland. However, as a result of the catastrophe that was about to overtake the island, the Irish population drastically dropped. It was in the 1911 census that the population of Scotland was first recorded as exceeding – by 370,000 – that of Ireland. Scotland was again the second kingdom, but perhaps only by virtue of the fact that it now had its own Irish population. If, in the twentieth century, the Scots were indeed 'a dying race', it was because 'the Irish' (rather than the English) were outbreeding them at home. It was in Scotland, too, where some of that Irish population was 'Orange', that there was most sympathy for the Ulster cause. Here was a pan-Presbyterian identity which occasionally drew upon a long past to emphasize the extent to which north-east Ireland and the west of Scotland were 'one'. The internal self-government in Northern Ireland might profitably be repeated in Scotland. Indeed, in some quarters, there was talk that Scotland and Northern Ireland might become a kind of joint statelet within Britain or even outside it. Belfast and Glasgow were much more akin to each other than Belfast and Dublin.

The ingredients of Britain, in short, shifted substantially over two centuries. To speak in such a context of a 'Celtic fringe' or even of 'the Celtic nations' standing starkly against 'England' oversimplifies a much more complex set of identities and relationships. It is nonetheless the fact that it was

---

11.3 Wild Court: In the mid–1850s, the editor of *The Builder* sketched very poor workers' dwellings in London. Wild Court, near Drury Lane, consisted of thirteen ten-room houses in which more than a thousand people lived. It was taken over in 1854 by Lord Shaftesbury's Society for Improving the Conditions of the Labouring Classes. Four years later, however, the presence of 'a good many low Irish' was said to keep respectable English away. However, although in parts of London there were streets which were 'Irish Territory' or 'Little Dublins', Irish migrants had to and did mix with the English for many purposes. Total segregation was neither desired nor resulted. The same point applies broadly in other British cities.

'England' which both set the pace within Britain over two centuries and yet also found the concept of 'Britain' difficult to handle. As has already been noted, England drew unto itself substantial populations from Ireland, Scotland and Wales at different periods over two centuries. In terms of this admixture England was more 'British' than Ireland, Scotland or Wales. In these circumstances would there always be an England and, if so, what was it?[30]

England in Britain

In the United Kingdom outside England, 'Britishness', whatever it was precisely taken to mean, entailed a kind of dual identity. There was rarely any such sense in England itself. England offered hospitality, as it were, to institutions identified as 'British' or 'National' – the British Museum or the National Gallery – and took them to be its own. There were 'national' museums or libraries of Scotland and Wales but not of England. In many contexts, no doubt ignorantly, the union flag was taken to be the flag of England and use of the cross of St George was almost antiquarian. Comparatively speaking, it was only in the smaller countries of Britain that some felt it necessary to seek to protect individual identity against the tide of 'Anglicization'. The English were under no such necessity, though from time to time, in the nineteenth century and beyond, there were complaints about what was regarded as an excessive influence being exerted by the 'Celtic fringe'.[31] Such sentiments surfaced during periods of Liberal government. It was in England that the Conservative Party enjoyed the greatest proportion-

---

[30] S. Gilley and R. Swift, *The Irish in the Victorian City* (London, 1985); J.E. Handley, *The Irish in Modern Scotland* (Cork, 1947); L. Lees, *Exiles of Erin: Irish Migrants in Victorian London* (Manchester, 1979); M.A.G. O'Tuathaigh, 'The Irish in Nineteenth-Century Britain: Problems of Integration', *Transactions of the Royal Historical Society* Fifth Series 31 (1981); D.G. Boyce, *The Irish Question & British Politics 1868–1986* (London, 1988); B. Collins, 'The Irish in Britain, 1780–1921' in B. Graham and L. Proudfoot, *Historical Geography of Ireland* (London, 1993) pp. 338–98; R.F. Forster, *Modern Ireland 1600–1972* (London, 1988); P. Jalland, *The Liberals and Ireland: The Ulster Question in British Politics to 1914* (Brighton, 1980); P. Bew, *Ideology and the Irish Question: Ulster Unionism and Irish Nationalism, 1912–1916* (Oxford, 1994); J.J. Lee, *Ireland 1912–1985: Politics and Society* (Cambridge, 1989).
[31] F.M.L. Thompson, ed., *The Cambridge Social History of Britain 1750–1950: Vol. 1 Regions and Communities* (Cambridge, 1990) p. 2; P. Hudson, ed., *Regions and Industries: A Perspective on the Industrial Revolution in Britain* (Cambridge, 1989); P. O'Brien and R. Quinault, eds, *The Industrial Revolution and British Society* (Cambridge, 1993); E.A. Wrigley, *Continuity, Chance and Change: The Character of the Industrial Revolution in England* (Cambridge, 1990).

ate strength and it was therefore sometimes thought unacceptable that Liberal government in Britain should be made possible by Liberal strength outside England. There were jibes before 1914, for example, about the small number of Englishmen in the government. The very size of the English population militated against the creation of a 'national voice' which had happened, to an extent, in Scotland and Wales. Indeed, noting the plethora of local war memorials after 1919 and the absence of an English National War Memorial, Ian Hay argued that for the Englishman 'The county is the unit, not the country'. An Englishman born in Lancashire would not be very interested in Middlesex, and vice versa.

There was exaggeration but also an element of truth in this perspective. England did remain a country of considerable diversity into the twentieth century. The English village and the 'peasant civilization' that it encompassed and expressed had evolved roughly over the two centuries between 1570 and 1770. The character of such villages, as expressed in vernacular buildings, reflected realities of craftsmanship, design and materials which remained essentially local – the Lake District was not the Cotswolds. The refining of 'local history' as a discipline after 1945 has resulted in an emphasis on the local for its own sake and in its own terms. It was emphasized that each English place had its own long past. There was a sense in which it was 'the local' which formed the context of experience and identity rather than 'England' or 'Britain'. It was local government rather than central government which most people experienced. It was the vigour or lack of it shown at a local level which determined the quality and variety of provision. There was a continuing attachment to a sense of 'county community' with a long past and an elected 'county council' seemed an entirely appropriate solution when in 1888 the Conservatives decided to break with the non-elected landowner predominance which had hitherto prevailed. The Justices of the Peace were reduced to considering judicial matters.

Yet, though a sense of place remained strong, it was challenged from a number of quarters from the mid-nineteenth century onwards. It would be wrong, even before 'the railway age', to suppose that there was no mobility between county and county. Nevertheless, England was 'opened up' by rail transport on a scale never before achieved, although such mobility did not necessarily entail the immediate erosion of 'small differences' across England.

In the second place, London, already with a population of around 1 million in 1801, continued to expand rapidly through the century. The 1891 census revealed a population of more than 5.5 million – it contained some 20 per cent of the population of England/Wales at this time. It was then the largest city the world had ever known. It 'overspilled' into the adjoining counties at a great rate. 'Greater London' seemed capable of almost infinite expansion. This was a metropolis on a frightening if exciting scale. How could such a monster be governed? As 'the capital', its pivotal importance in

English/British life was undeniable. No single county could hope to compete with it in influence and power.[32]

In the third place, notwithstanding the extent to which mid-century governments remained committed to a limited role for the state, circumstances appeared to be changing. In public health, housing and education, to name only three areas, the central state appeared bent on an increased role in regulating and supervising and, if necessary, intervening. Choice as left in the hands of local authorities naturally entailed the risk that some would perform better than others. Was it not the job of the state to identify and endorse national standards? 'Centralization' seemed the obvious answer. Steadily, into the twentieth century, there were cries for the abolition of old ways of handling social issues as no longer efficient. 'National' Insurance began. The extent of 'national' regulation during the First World War seemed to support the point of view that a modern society required standards and services that could not rest on the whim of local provision.

Local government, in short, was supposed to need a drastic overhaul. In 1929, as Minister of Health, Neville Chamberlain introduced a Local Government Act which abolished the Boards of Guardians who had been responsible for the provision of poor relief since 1834. The duty now fell upon county and borough councils. By the 1930s, however, there was considerable though unresolved debate about the respective spheres of local and national government. Was local government merely there to oversee the local implementation of national decisions taken by central government or could it make its own decisions? Financial issues were inevitably at stake in this debate. For some writers local government was becoming virtually redundant, while for others it remained central to their understanding of the English past. Continental writers lavished praise on English local democracy at the beginning of the twentieth century, just at the point when it appeared to have lost its way. Government during the Second World War contributed further to the erosion of a distinctive local sphere of decision-making.

One further factor deserves emphasis. The shires and counties of the 1880s were not what they had been even a century earlier. There was an element of glorious English continuity stretching back a thousand years but urbanization and industrialization had played havoc with boundaries and the balance of populations. The scale of London has already been noted but the expansion of major provincial cities through the nineteenth century rendered redundant many ancient divisions. In the 1820s only Liverpool, Manchester and Birmingham, besides London, possessed 100,000 inhabitants. By 1901, there were twenty-eight such towns and their number was still rising steadily in the first half of the twentieth century. Over two centuries the scale of this transformation has been profound. The urban cultures that have surfaced,

---

[32] H.J. Dyos and M. Wolff, eds, *The Victorian City: Images and Reality* (2 vols, London, 1978) provides an introduction.

diverse in some measure though they have been, have supplanted old allegiances and loyalties. It was in the census of 1851 that 'the rural' became a minority when 50.1 per cent of the population of England/Wales and 51.8 of the population of Scotland were recorded as 'urban'. Needless to say, what is 'town' and what is 'country' needs to be subjected to endless qualification and refinement. When all that has been done, however, Professor F.M.L. Thompson is right to argue that 'Urbanisation has been so thoroughgoing in the two centuries since 1750 that it has in effect liquidated what was a social region, by turning it into the nation'.[33]

This development arguably creates a greater rupture with 'the past' than any that has been hitherto considered. Writing of Manchester, but in terms which he believed could be applied to Birmingham or Leeds, Engels shuddered at the consequences of the feverish activity he observed. It was crazy that such a social and economic structure should survive at all. Pessimists believed that cities could not last for long. Optimists believed that they could bring culture and enlightenment, even to the masses, in a way never achieved before. Certainly the new cities sought public buildings of appropriate splendour. Leeds Town Hall, a local paper declared, had no superior in England and very few in Europe.[34]

For a time, too, in mid-century, it was supposed by some commentators that these northern cities signified a dramatic shift in the balance of 'England'. Notwithstanding the importance of London, it was 'the north' which, perhaps for the first time in English history, led the way into the future. London was despised and alleged to be economically secondary, despite its social and cultural pretensions. Whether it was indeed 'parasitic' to the degree suggested would now be contested. However, it was in 'the north' that men understood the new processes of manufacturing and made their fortunes. It was there that the challenge to the 'agricultural south' was mounted – exemplified by the attack on the Corn Laws from Manchester. Civic pride was to be found in abundance but a real and enduring shift was not obtained. It was in large measure because 'provincial England', almost by definition, had no unity other than the fact that it was not London. The new major cities did not emerge as leaders of definable 'regions' with a coherent identity. They were in many ways more interested in competition with each other – Liverpool/ Manchester, Leeds/Bradford/Sheffield etc. – than in heading

---

[33] J.E. Kendle, *Federal Britain: A History* (London, 1997) offers the most comprehensive treatment of this theme.

[34] J. Stevenson, ed., *London in the Age of Reform* (Oxford, 1977); R. Colls and P. Dodd, eds, *Englishness: Politics and Culture 1880–1920* (London, 1986); R. Stradling and M. Hughes, *The English Musical Renaissance 1860–1940: Construction and Deconstruction* (London, 1993); F.H.W. Sheppard, *London 1808–1870: The Infernal Wen* (London, 1971); P.L. Garside, 'London and the Home Counties' in Thompson, ed., *Cambridge Social History* pp. 471–539; C. Fox, ed., *London – World City 1800–1840* (London, 1992).

11.4 Well-suited: a tailor's workshop in Manchester's Jewish community, *c.* 1910. Jewish newly-immigrant communities established themselves in major British cities and specialized, at least initially, in trades and occupations where they deployed traditional skills in a close-knit structure and context. That their arrival led to some anti-Semitism cannot be disputed but in comparative perspective it is perhaps the ability of British society to accommodate incomers which is more striking. The significance of 'assimilation' was as much contentious within the Jewish community as it was between the Jewish and Gentile communities.

---

discrete regions. Indeed, it was scarcely possible to speak of English 'regions' at all – administrative, diocesan, industrial boundaries overlapped in an incoherent fashion. The past was there in the shape of the counties and the present in the shape of the cities but the 'region' was without form and void.

It is symptomatic that when the pre-1914 Liberal governments toyed with the idea of 'Home-Rule-All-Round' as a way both of dealing with Irish aspirations and to some extent those of Scotland and Wales, the problem of 'England' was a major reason why the scheme faltered. It was sometimes suggested that the Anglo-Saxon heptarchy might be revived as a way of regionalizing England but, not unexpectedly, that turned out to be a past too far. But unless England was in some way 'regionalized' it was not easy to see how a federal or quasi-federal Britain/United Kingdom could be produced.

This section has been concerned with England, but the phenomenon of urbanization was British. Between 1801 and 1911 the population of the Edinburgh region grew from 224,000 to 843,000 and that of Glasgow from 341,000 to 2.191 million. Taking Aberdeen and Dundee into the reckoning, the bulk of the Scottish population lived in four city-regions. Perth and Stirling, two towns of great significance in Scottish history, did not grow to any extent. The population of the Highlands only increased from 303,000 to 342,000 over this same period. The northern counties, where more than half of the Scottish population lived in the mid-eighteenth century, diminished in comparison with the central belt where most of the population now lived.[35] The urbanization of much of South Wales and the consequential demographic lop-sidedness of Wales has already been noted.

The dislocations which accompanied the urbanization of Britain were therefore profound. The England, Scotland and Wales of 1745 seem in this respect very different societies from what they were two centuries later. It might be argued that the major cities of Britain now shared much in common with each other and were in important respects set apart from their hinterlands. They all contained, to greater or lesser degree, 'minorities' from elsewhere in the British Isles and were in this sense more 'British Isles' in composition and ethos than the countryside around them. In addition, it was largely to the cities that immigrants from continental Europe came in considerable numbers. Germans came as political refugees, merchants, bankers and industrialists – about a half settling in London. The novelist J.B. Priestley claimed that in the Bradford of his youth a Londoner was a stranger sight than a German. Between 1870 and 1914 perhaps around 120,000 Jews arrived from Eastern Europe, settling particularly in Leeds, Manchester, the East End of London and Glasgow. It was the appearance of such 'aliens' – around 300,000 in Britain as a whole in 1911 – which gave rise to legislation designed to restrict their entry.

A touch of class

Urbanization and industrialization were distinct but overlapping developments. It was their combined impact which made these two centuries so disturbing to contemporaries. Once upon a time, 'the Industrial Revolution' in the three countries of Britain – classically located *c.*1760–1820/40 – would have been seen as a clear marker which separated the early nineteenth century from 'the past'. Britain, it is popularly supposed, became 'the first industrial

---

[35] T.C. Smout, *A Century of the Scottish People 1830–1950* (London, 1986).

nation' – or perhaps nations, for the chronology, location and nature of change was not exactly the same in England, Scotland and Wales. However, historians have become uncomfortable with the term 'Industrial Revolution'. What counts as 'industry'? What is meant by 'revolution'? Are we to think of an industrial revolution as separate from an agrarian revolution, or are the two linked? What counts as 'technological innovation'? How important in the British 'take-off' was transport as opposed to finance? These questions cannot be answered here in the complexity that they demand, and indeed, having attempted to do so elsewhere, some scholars feel unable to do more than advance multi-factor explanations. They stress the need to look at the problem industry by industry and area by area. It is no doubt necessary to avoid simplification, but it seems perverse to deny that far-reaching changes were indeed taking place in Britain in spinning, smelting and the supply of power, even if the timing and degree of the impact was patchy and heavily regional/local in incidence.

It may not make sense to speak of a single uniform Industrial Revolution but there was a pattern of change which altered the landscape of Britain profoundly. In South Wales, for example, the output of coal increased from 4.5 million tons in 1854 to 56 million tons in 1913. The valleys were no longer green. The 'industrial regions' of Britain, different in the precise pattern of their activity though they were, nevertheless came to share an identity that was often work-based. The feelings they evoked often came to seem more significant than older county or national loyalties. Keir Hardie, a Scot, could be more at home amongst the miners of Merthyr Tydfil whom he represented at Westminster than he was in non-mining areas of Scotland – to give only one example.

In effect, therefore, industrialization, however it is precisely defined, created the possibility, indeed to some observers the probability, that among the working population 'identity' was conceived as a matter of 'class' or 'occupation' rather than 'nation'. E.P. Thompson's *The Making of the English Working Class* (1963) attempted to pinpoint a time when that sense of class-consciousness was 'made' – in England but, analogously, in Wales and Scotland also. Much attention ever since has been devoted to analyses of the language of 'class' and the industrial structures in which it evolved. Considerable doubt, however, has been cast on the notion that a working class was 'made' at a specific moment. The new world of industrial work threw up multiple alignments and allegiances. The socio-economic situation of industrial workers was fractured and disjointed, making generalization hazardous about cultural perceptions and identities. Even so, as with the 'Industrial Revolution', some sense of class did emerge and was seen by some workers as fundamental and defining. From the earliest attempts at a grand national consolidated trade union, to involvement in the European Socialist International in the decades before 1914, some were indeed attracted to the notion that workers of the world should unite and shake off national shackles.

British workers had more in common with German workers than they did with their British capitalist employers. The myths and legends of past British history served merely to cement a structure of oppression and control. It was time to bury that 'Britain' or at least only to highlight those episodes in the past, notably in the mid-seventeenth century, when a different road could have been taken.

In one form or another, therefore, in the century up to 1945 'class' and 'nation' existed in tension, although the emerging Labour Party did not, for the most part, seek to disown 'Britain'. And indeed, notwithstanding some flirtation occasionally with notions of 'Home Rule', its predominant emphasis in the period between the wars was on the need to organize effectively across Britain as a whole. Labour could advance the interests of a 'working class' that was British. It was only in the context of Labour's powerlessness in the 1930s that some intellectuals in particular emphasized their disenchantment with the institutions of Britain and supposed that the class interests of British workers would be better served by copying the models offered by that new civilization, the Soviet Union. And for the latter part of the war that followed, when Britain was in alliance with the Soviet Union against Hitler's Germany, dreams of a 'new Britain' which would be in continuing postwar socialist/communist partnership were attractive.

But there was another side to the picture. Nicholas Montserrat, author of the best-selling novel *The Cruel Sea* (1951), had nearly become a communist in the 1930s, but the novel pays tribute to 'Englishness'. Pour any Englishmen into a ship, he wrote, and 'they made that ship work and fight as if they had been doing it all their lives, catching up, overtaking, and leaving behind the professionals of any other nation. It was the basic virtue of living on an island.'[36] This was a refinement of the claim made by Ellis Ashmead Bartlett in 1884: 'The true English working man is proud of his country, is proud of its great past, is proud of its splendid and beneficent empire … '.[37]

Remembrance and the future

Believing in *Britain* and *believing* in Britain came together a little uneasily in remembrance as the future was contemplated. Over previous centuries, like

---

[36] N. Montserrat, *The Cruel Sea* (London, 1951) p. 259. Variations on class, community and culture can be found in P. Joyce, *Visions of the People: Industrial England and the Question of Class c.1848–1914* (Cambridge, 1991); G. Kearns and C. Withers, *Urbanising Britain: Essays on Class and Community in the Nineteenth Century* (Cambridge, 1991); D. Gilbert, *Class, Community and Collective Action: Social Change in Two British Coalfields, 1850–1926* (Oxford, 1992) compares mining communities in Nottinghamshire and South Wales.

[37] Cited in H. Cunningham, 'The Conservative Party and Patriotism' in Colls and Dodd, *Englishness*, p. 286.

other peoples, the British had erected statues or monuments to commemorate their great war heroes. Nelson's column, for example, towered above Trafalgar Square, reminding Whitehall that its plans succeeded or failed at sea as real men fought. It was a universal assumption that it did the nation good to be reminded of what had been done in the past and what might need to be done again in the future. In the event, two world wars were to hang heavily over twentieth-century British history.

In 1918, after the Great War, a different order of remembrance was called for. An uncomplicated celebration of admirals and generals would be an inadequate recognition of the national experience of the late war. Even before it was over, steps were being taken in schools, workplaces and churches to erect some testimony to the dead. In London, the anonymous Cenotaph, unveiled on 11 November 1920, originally conceived as a temporary centrepiece for a victory marchpast, became the permanent memorial to the dead. It became a focus for British/British Imperial mourning on an unprecedented scale.

There were, too, other conclusions which could be drawn from the mathematical austerity of the design by Lutyens. Contrary to some expectation, the memorial was without Christian, patriotic or romantic symbolism. Such restraint could be taken to indicate that the immensity of the suffering which the war had entailed brought a particular past to an end. Now, at last, was shattered the notion that war in the twentieth century was but a continuation of medieval chivalry indulged in by perfect and gentle Christian knights. *Dulce et decorum est pro patria mori* was obscene. So, in Britain between the wars, annually as it turned out, royalty, politicians, the armed services and church leaders called to mind the very recent and very savage past. It was to be hoped that a line had indeed been drawn under a long past in British history. Never again.

The Great War is too vast an event for its significance in British history to be captured in a few paragraphs. Some historians have argued that it accelerated, if it did not produce, the 'Modernist' wave in European culture, a wave present in Britain, though less strikingly than elsewhere in Europe. Poets and artists in Britain in the 1920s looked to the future from 'The Waste Land' of a present which survived on an exhausted past. The symbols of loyalty and identity which had done duty for centuries were now bereft of meaning. Some such mood can indeed be detected but it has been persuasively argued recently by Jay Winter that it was still the case that the gaze of many writers, artists, politicians, soldiers and 'ordinary people' was backward. The 'sites of memory' still evoked the past; the caesura was not complete.[38]

---

[38] J. Winter, *Sites of Memory, Sites of Mourning: The Great War in European Cultural History* (Cambridge, 1995); C. Harrison, *English Art and Modernism, 1900–1939* (London, 1994, edn).

In 1939 another war came. In the twenty preceding years individuals had been pulled in contrary directions by their experiences of war. On one side was cynicism and despair. 'Our island story' was bankrupt. On the other hand, there remained ringing assertions from pulpit and platform that, despite all the loss of life, it had been right for Britain to go to war in 1914. England's sons, as the Bishop of Bradford explained at a service in 1921, had been called to save the world from tyranny and the domination of material force.[39] A decade later, however, such convictions were not so readily expressed. The bishop had indeed been prepared to concede that there were blots on the British escutcheon, as he put it, but in the 1930s the blots came to be thought rather substantial. Church leaders were anxious not to be thought endorsing a 'patriotic war'. In the 1930s some of them tried to establish, via the emerging World Council of Churches, links with German Lutheran, French Calvinist and Serbian Orthodox Christians. It was necessary to try to build a new and rather different Christendom. Some, indeed, declared themselves to be absolute pacifists, convinced that 'British militarism' was no more justifiable in the present than Prussian had been in the past. Canon Dick Sheppard persuaded tens of thousands to pledge that they would never fight in or support another war. Undergraduates at Oxford University voted that they would not fight for 'King and Country'. Such a concept was obsolete. What should one believe in?[40]

In the event, when Britain did go to war, it was, after all, not too difficult to make the defence of 'Christian Civilization' meaningful. Believing in *Britain* and *believing* in Britain could still be reconciled. Even so, the Britons who went to war did so with resignation rather than joy. The days of easy glorification of war were indeed over. The men who marched away in 1914 did belong to a different era. Victory might be as difficult as defeat. 'Some day, perhaps', wrote the anonymous wartime author of *Ourselves in Wartime*, 'the human race, having attained to a happy, prosperous and continuously peaceful federation of the world will look back on the story of how the inhabitants of Great Britain boldly faced and surmounted the ordeal that made the general survival possible – and will pay its tribute to the people … who kept the flame of freedom burning in mankind's darkest hour.' It was comforting to believe in such a possibility.[41]

---

[39] Cited in A. Gregory, *The Silence of Memory: Armistice Day 1919–1946* (Oxford, 1994) p. 36.
[40] A. Wilkinson, *Dissent or Conform? War, Peace and the English Churches 1900–1945* (London, 1986).
[41] *Ourselves in Wartime* (London, n.d.) p. 12; J.D. Cantwell, *Images of War: British Posters 1919–45* (London, 1989).

Epilogue

Chapter 12 ....

Fragile Bearings 1945–

British victory?

When the Home Office came to reflect on the 'Armistice Day' which would fall on 11 November 1945, it was in a difficulty. Was the 'Second World War' simply to be bolted onto well-established ceremonies and new names carved, eventually, on old memorials, or was the conflict that had just ended something other than a continuation, at an interval, of the war of 1914–18? It was not easy to decide then and it has not proved easy for historians ever since.[1] It did seem self-evident, however, that the outcome had been a British victory. Fifty years later, when the mood of 1945 was again recalled in public ceremonies in London and elsewhere in Britain, past and present were again fused momentarily. The queen who had stood beside the king on the balcony of Buckingham Palace was still alive. The princess who had mingled with the crowd was now queen. Dame Vera Lynn sang songs which she had sung in 1945. Veterans paraded. Fireworks were let off. There was an atmosphere of celebration, even among the young who had no memory of the Second World War. A present was temporarily suspended in favour of a past which seemed to be uncomplicatedly a source of British satisfaction and pride.

Some historians, however, sensing that ambiguity was being over-looked in the atmosphere of celebration, did not hasten to the party. Gripping bouts of nostalgia, they thought, were no substitute for historical scrutiny. They suspected that behind the euphoria of 1995 a wake was taking place, though possibly only off stage. The best of Britain was past. For

---

[1] K. Robbins, 'Commemorating the Second World War in Britain: Problems of Definition', *The History Teacher* [USA] 29, no. 2 (Feb. 1996) pp. 155–62; A. Gregory, *The Silence of Memory: Armistice Day, 1919–1946* (Oxford, 1994); D. Morgan and M. Evans, *The Battle for Britain: Citizenship and Ideology in the Second World War* (London, 1992).

12.1 Street party in Corn Street, Liverpool, 1995. Fifty years on from the end of the Second World War the street celebration parties of 1945 were re-enacted in many British cities. A new generation was baptized into the memories of their parents or grandparents. Much of the emotion then generated was unforced and deeply-felt but there were those who criticized both official and unofficial events as manipulative. It was not the Union Jack that was being flown high but the Union Flag which was being hi-jacked for contemporary purposes.

decades since 1945 it had seemed to be downhill all the way. While it was true that the British defiance of 1940 was indeed heroic, and that more was at stake for humanity as a whole, rather than simply for Britain itself, in the struggle of 'the few', it was self-deception to suppose that the victory of 1945 was in any major sense 'British'.

The outcome of the war which began in 1939 depended fundamentally on the struggle between the Soviet Union and Germany in Eastern Europe and on the involvement of the United States from 1941 onwards in a war that had become global. In part, at least, it had the form of a 'War of British Succession' in many areas of the world. The *Pax Britannica* was in the process of being replaced by *Pax Americana*. In that further postwar struggle which became known as the 'Cold War', Britain was a subordinate player. To some historians, it was by no means clear that this status was an unavoidable consequence of the war that began in 1939. It might even have been possible to obtain some kind of settlement with Hitler which would have permitted an enduring 'division of spheres'.

Some have argued in this vein that the very past which Churchill conjured up seduced him into policy error and into an intransigence which was heroic but futile for Britain in the long run. He was insufficiently tough and clear-sighted in his dealings with the Americans and allowed his own attachment to the 'English-speaking peoples' to obscure the reality of American ambition. He could have played his hand much better if he had not been in love with the past. It is an assessment which is by no means convincing but the fact that it has been aired widely in Britain is an indication that 'the past' is no longer quite what it was. The half-century after 1945 has not been kind to even those aspects of Britain's past which were a source of sustenance and pride in the dark days of the struggle.[2]

Some twenty years after the end of the war it was a Labour Prime Minister, Harold Wilson, who proclaimed on coming into office: 'We are a world power or a world influence or we are nothing'.[3] The history of the subsequent decades demonstrated the very severe limitations on Britain as a 'world power'. Using one form of words or another, successive British Foreign Secretaries have continued nevertheless to assert that Britain 'punched above its weight'. The weight, even so, has diminished. Reconciling the gap between Britain's status – as epitomized in its possession of nuclear weapons and in continuing permanent membership of the United Nations Security Council – and its capacity to act effectively, has been a necessary preoccupation of the Foreign and Commonwealth Office. 'Power' in international relations is always difficult to define and some writers may indeed have dismissed Britain's role too swiftly in an international context which is itself always in flux. The history of two decades after 1945, however, showed that that role could no longer be imperial.

End of empire

Even at the moment of independence in 1947, the India that Britain had ruled was divided into two – India and Pakistan – and the following year Burma went its own way outside the Commonwealth. Some Indians argued

---

[2] J. Charmley, *Churchill: The End of Glory* (London, 1993) and *Churchill's Grand Alliance: The Anglo-American Special Relationship, 1940–57* (London, 1995). See also R. Blake and W.R. Louis, ed, *Churchill* (Oxford, 1993); K. Robbins, *Churchill* (London, 1992). I am grateful for sight of an unpublished paper by Dr. R.W. Butler 'Images of Empire: Britain and the Characterization of Nazism, 1936–1939'.
[3] K. Robbins, *The Eclipse of a Great Power: Modern Britain 1870–1992* (London, 1994) pp. 272–3.

that the British strategy of 'divide and rule' had reached its climax – 'divide and quit' – and showed the British to be Machiavellian to the last. Other writers have stressed the weakness rather than the strength of the latter-day British position: it was Indians themselves who made partition inevitable. There has also been a tendency recently in some quarters to play down the significance of the year 1947. The more 'British India' has been looked at 'from below' the more it has become clear that 'the British' had only scratched the multifarious surfaces of India. 'Before' and 'After' the British epoch were not so very different. Other writers have argued that it would have been better if British governments had dispossessed themselves earlier of an India which had become a burden. The handover of 1947 was a belated act of realism after so many decades in which the 'special relationship' between Britain and India had been proclaimed and exhausted by successive Viceroys. There were, clearly, many factors at work as the Raj came to an end and their complexity cannot be fully explored here.

As the last British troops sailed back to their distant insular destination in 1947, was India slipping altogether out of the British past, and if so what did the ending of a relationship which had lasted for two centuries mean for Britain itself? Even at the end, there were unexpected links. 'A moment comes', declared the first Indian Prime Minister, Jawaharlal Nehru in August 1947, 'which comes but rarely in history, when we step out from the old to the new, when an age ends, and when the soul of a nation long-suppressed, finds utterance.' In his own case, however, it was a soul which owed not a little to English institutions, to Harrow and Cambridge, where he had been educated. Clement Attlee, the Labour Prime Minister in 1947, also had an educational link with the sub-continent, having been educated at Haileybury, the institution founded by the East India Company in 1805 to prepare young men for service in India. He had also had first-hand personal experience of India as a member of the Simon Commission of Inquiry. Even at the moment of parting, therefore, the leading actors had 'British India' deep in their respective experiences.

However, the Foreign Secretary in 1947, Ernest Bevin, had not been educated in any such school and he took a more robust view of developments. In a New Year message to Attlee in 1947 he warned – unavailingly – that if Labour appeared to be advocating 'scuttle' in India it would, in the eyes of the British people, lose support and lose it irrevocably. It was a stance not so far removed from Churchill's sentiments in the mid-1930s. He had tried to ram home his message that 'Britain in India' was not some tangential branch office of the main enterprise. To hold on to India, he had then believed, indicated to the world that Britain itself was not finished. 'If we lose faith in ourselves', he declared in a broadcast St George's Day speech in 1933, 'in our capacity to guide and govern, if we lose our will to live, then indeed our story is told.' In the following year, he told Linlithgow: 'I think we differ principally in this, that you assume the future is a mere extension of the past whereas I find history full of unexpected turns and retrogressions'.[4]

End of empire: Africa

It was in South Africa in 1947 that Princess Elizabeth celebrated her 21st birthday and pledged herself to the service of a Commonwealth that was still, in some sense, British. Few, even then, would have forecast that fourteen years later South Africa would withdraw from the Commonwealth. In 1952 the princess was in British East Africa when her father died and she became queen. Within little more than a decade all these three territories were independent. In 1957 Ghana became the first British African territory to become independent, followed by Nigeria (1961), Sierra Leone (1962) and Gambia (1965). In East Africa, Tanganyika (Tanzania) led the way in 1961. Such a simple sequence suggests that British withdrawal from formal power in Africa was a straightforward matter. The reality was more complicated.

Some historians have stressed the extent to which policy in these years was motivated by international factors, particularly by a desire not to offend the United States as a relationship was rebuilt after the 1956 Suez Crisis. The failure of the British attempt to impose a solution in Egypt by force had revealed the limitations of British power if the United States was hostile to any such action. Both countries had an interest in maintaining a common front in Africa to prevent Soviet penetration. It seemed that British withdrawal from Africa would be the best way to ensure a pro-Western or neutral Africa.

In 1957, on becoming Prime Minister, Macmillan asked for something like a 'profit and loss' account on British Africa. Economic considerations, it was concluded, tended to be evenly matched and could not themselves be decisive in determining policy. Overall, there was no case for artificial delay in moves towards independence but Britain would gain no credit from launching immature, unstable and impoverished units along this path. There remained the conviction, expressed at the time, that only British authority and administration enabled peoples of different racial or tribal loyalties to live in peace with one another. States of emergency in Kenya and in Nyasaland (Malawi), however, indicated that in East and Central Africa urgent decisions had to be taken. In 1959 Enoch Powell attacked his own government in the Commons for appearing to countenance the view that different standards of conduct could apply in Africa and Britain itself. 'We cannot', he declared, in an echo of Burke on Warren Hastings, ' ... in Africa of all places,

---

[4] M. Gilbert, *Churchill: A Life* (London, 1991) pp. 518–20.

fall below our own highest standards in the acceptance of responsibility.'[5] Any action was complicated by the presence of 'British' settlers in Kenya and Southern Rhodesia (Zimbabwe), the latter possessing substantial internal self-government. It was difficult to see how the rights of minorities could be entrenched permanently. Fear that this was the case led the white minority to declare independence unilaterally in 1965, a rebellion which did not formally end until 1980 when Zimbabwe became independent. In a very short space of time, therefore, the British monarch had ceased to be an African queen.

End of empire: east of Suez

Independence for the Indian sub-continent had not seen the end of British influence in parts of Asia. Hong Kong proved to be a dynamic commercial centre but a 'return by' label was attached to territory vital for its functioning. Insurgency in Malaya was defeated and Malaysia made the transition to independence in 1957. British forces were, however, again active in the ensuing confrontation with Indonesia. British influence in the Arabian Gulf remained paramount and in 1961 British troops were successfully sent to defend the fledgling independence of Kuwait. A rearguard action was fought in Aden until 1967. In that year, however, after review, it was announced that British forces would withdraw east of Suez by 1971. It was not a decision which was reversed by the Conservative government which came to power in 1970. The legions were indeed coming home.

Let bygones be bygones?

The transitions to independence which have been briefly discussed were matched elsewhere – from Fiji to Jamaica, from Guyana to Malta. With only small exceptions, an empire which had spanned the globe came to an end within thirty years after 1945. The length and intensity of the British connection in the above cases and other instances varied very considerably, but the winding down of such an empire in such a short time represented a sharp rupture with the past. An imperial project which appeared to have been at the heart of national identity was simply no longer there. It was inconceivable either that an enterprise should disappear without trace or that its disappearance would not leave in its wake a formidable 'crisis of identity'.

---

[5] A. Porter and A. Stockwell, *British Imperial Policy and Decolonization 1938–64: Vol. 2 1951–64* (London, 1989) p. 513.

Or was it? How was such a 'collapse of the past' handled during these dramatic postwar decades?

In some other European countries, during approximately the same period, 'decolonization' was accompanied by domestic political instability and revolution. In France, for example, the Algerian crisis precipitated the end of the Fourth Republic and the return of de Gaulle in 1958. In Portugal, the colonial crisis brought about a change of regime. In Britain no such dislocation occurred. Why?[6]

Firstly, Britain had no equivalent of Algeria, a territory with a substantial French population, supposedly part of metropolitan France. Neither Rhodesia nor even South Africa filled a comparable role in national sentiment or attention, though in the former case 'kith and kin' appeals were not without impact and to some extent constrained government reactions.

Secondly, although it was Labour which, in a sense, had set the precedent in the Indian sub-continent in 1947, it was Conservative governments which were in office during the crucial period from 1951 to 1964. Party ideology had long presented the Conservative Party as the pre-eminent party of empire. In the period between the wars, Conservative critics of policy in India talked in terms of a betrayal, something which the party leadership attempted to deny. If Labour had remained in office after 1951, it is arguable, though cannot be proved, that the official Conservative opposition would have been fiercely critical of at least certain aspects of the policies which they in fact carried out in office. Even so, when it came to the point, their reading of the world situation, their consciousness of economic and military strain, coupled with assessments of the degree of economic and political influence and connection which could be maintained after independence, combined to make the Conservative leadership feel that there was no alternative. Churchill, after 1951, had to conduct a pragmatic withdrawal, however much it went against his instincts. In his case, the responsibility of governing disciplined emotions.

It was left to external bodies like the ephemeral, as it proved, League of Empire Loyalists to seek to turn an element of popular unease into effective opposition. Further, the opponents of change in the Conservative Party

---

[6]   M. Kahler, *Decolonization in Britain & France* (Princeton, 1984); M.E. Chamberlain, *Decolonization: The Fall of the European Empires* (London, 1985); F. Ansprenger, *The Dissolution of the Colonial Empires* (London, 1989); D.A. Low, *Eclipse of Empire* (Cambridge, 1991); G. Balfour-Paul, *The End of Empire in the Middle East* (Cambridge, 1991); P. Gifford and W.R. Louis, *The Transfer of Power in Africa 1940–1960* (London, 1982); J. Darwin, *Britain and Decolonisation: The Retreat from Empire in the Postwar World* (London, 1988); J.A. Cross, *Whitehall and the Commonwealth* (London, 1967); R. Holland, *The Pursuit of Greatness 1900–1970: Britain and the World Role* (London, 1993); G. Prakash, ed., *After Colonialism: Imperial Histories and Postcolonial Displacements* (Princeton, 1995); S. Howe, *Anti-Colonialism in British Politics: The Left and the End of Empire, 1918–1964* (Oxford, 1993).

found themselves in a weak bargaining position. They were chiefly to be found among the parliamentary backbenchers and the party rank and file. They could not mount a concerted challenge. There was no leader among them with the oratorical power that Churchill himself had possessed in the 1930s. In 1956 Lord Salisbury did resign in protest at the release of Archbishop Makarios of Cyprus, but this step had little consequence. Who, after all, was Lord Salisbury?

Thirdly, as we have noted, the 'Empire' was in reality a collection of empires. That diversity touched different elements in Britain, governmental and non-governmental, in different ways. People who worried about loss of economic stature in the Arabian Gulf tended to be rather different from those who worried about 'kith and kin' in Rhodesia. People who wrote to their cousins in Toronto did not necessarily worry about the internal politics of Guyana. In this sense, *the* British Empire did not dissolve as a single entity because it never was a single entity.

Once these political and psychological aspects have been taken into account, however, there remain deeper and more difficult questions. For some writers, the fact that there was no political upheaval is an indication that in reality, despite decades of imperial propaganda (Empire days, Empire Exhibitions, Empire Medals, Empire parades), the empire's appeal to the British people as a whole was only skin-deep, and insofar as it did have appeal it was only white skin-deep at that. The speed with which the (British) Commonwealth over subsequent decades became the rather specialist interest of a relatively small number of people rather than a substantial focal point of national policy can be taken to support that view.

In 1947–49, however, it had seemed crucial to the Labour government that India and Pakistan should stay within the Commonwealth. Independent India swiftly made it clear that it would become a republic, but it was found possible to accomodate such a constitutional change. Over the decades that followed, either on reaching independence or subsequently, the new countries of the Commonwealth ceased to have the queen as head of state. It was agreed that the British monarch should be accepted as 'Head of the Commonwealth' but it was a headship with a somewhat obscure significance. South Africa became the first 'old dominion' to dispense with the British Crown – a step which then did lead to South Africa's withdrawal from the Commonwealth.

The concept of a 'multiracial Commonwealth' was attractive to some sections of British opinion but that attraction was not, and perhaps could not be, a substitute for the sentiment which had formerly attached itself to a *British* empire. Commonwealth conferences, particularly during the later 1960s and 1970s when Britain found itself frequently 'in the dock', chiefly over Rhodesian and South African policy, led to disenchantment.

In addition, the 'Britishness' of Australia, Canada and, to a lesser extent, New Zealand was itself changing rapidly during these decades as the former two countries in particular espoused 'multiculturalism' and agonized over their own identities. The teaching of 'British history' as 'our history' came increasingly into question. This change reflected, on the one hand, the more diverse pattern of immigration into those countries and, on the other, the enhanced recognition of the place of Aborigines, North American Indians and Maoris in their own pasts. There were various points, too, when tensions between English-speaking and French-speaking Canada threatened the country's very existence. Cumulatively, these changes reduced the sense in which the 'old dominions' – to use a term which itself was becoming increasingly anachronistic – formed a 'British bloc' within the Commonwealth.

It did remain the case, however, that post-1945 emigration from Britain continued to constitute a major or the major element in their new populations and thereby, to an extent, reinforced once again old ties with the mother country. Even so, in the case of Australia, for example, in foreign policy strenuous efforts were being made by the government in the 1990s to emphasize that, whatever the country's cultural allegiance, geopolitics required that it should be perceived and perhaps even perceive itself as 'Asian'.

Structurally, in any case, the Commonwealth ceased to be serviced and organized by Britain. Civil war and political instability, particularly in Africa, confirmed old Africa hands in their belief that independence had been precipitate, but it had happened and could not be reversed. Wars could even occur between Commonwealth countries. It would be wrong, however, to dismiss the Commonwealth altogether and to ignore the ways in which it continued to provide an effective forum for educational and technical co-operation. Sporting ties were also not without continuing importance. The appearance of cricket teams in Britain from Australia, New Zealand, Pakistan, India, Sri Lanka, the West Indies and, for a time, South Africa, constituted a continuing imperial echo. No team from one of Britain's 'European partners' came to play a Test Match at Lord's.[7]

However, the notion, still widely held in the postwar decade, that the Commonwealth would somehow still perpetuate the past, albeit with new elements, proved disappointing. Even the attempt to make the 'Commonwealth family' some kind of political reality was in some quarters considered to be a mistake. 'The Tory Party', declared Enoch Powell in 1957, 'must be

---

[7] D. Dilks, *Communications, the Commonwealth and the Future* (Hull, 1994); J. Brown, *Winds of Change* (Oxford, 1991); T. Mockaitis, *British Counterinsurgency in the Post-Imperial Era* (Manchester, 1995); M. Templeton, *Ties of Blood and Empire: New Zealand's Involvement in Middle East Defence and the Suez Crisis 1947–57* (Auckland, 1994); C. Doran and E. Babby, eds, *Being and Becoming Canadian* (London, 1995); P. Philips, *Britain's Past in Canada: The Teaching and Writing of British History* (Vancouver, 1989); J.D.B. Miller, ed., *Australians and British: Social and Political Connections* (Methuen, Australia, 1987); T.B. Millar, ed., *The Australian Contribution to Britain* (London, 1988); J. Wilton and R. Bosworth *Old Worlds and New Australia* (Melbourne, 1984).

cured of the British Empire, of the pitiful yearning to cling to relics of a by-gone system.'[8] Analysis of the election addresses of Conservative candidates in the 1959 general election showed that half of them said nothing about the Commonwealth. In reality, however, the legacy which the Commonwealth represented could not be dismissed so swiftly from the memory. At the very point at which, in one sense, Empire/Commonwealth was fading yearly away, some of its most important peoples – their languages, cultures and religions – became realities in the post-imperial present of Britain to an extent that they had never done in the imperial past. Here was one of those 'unexpected turns and retrogressions' which Churchill, despite his gloom about the fall of the empire in the years before his death in 1965, might have recognized as a vindication of his theory of history. It will be considered further in the next chapter.

Clearly, even though the loss of empire has dimished its world status, Britain is not the 'nothing' extravagantly envisaged by Harold Wilson as the stark alternative in the year before Churchill died. Yet, whatever mental and cultural 'space' has been shaped for its inhabitants by the centuries in which, in one form or another, the British Empire existed, the actual geographical space Britain occupies cannot be shifted from the periphery of Europe. This awkward fact has made a 'usable' reconciliation of past and present in the second half of the twentieth century, at a time when other developments have undermined central elements of British life, an arduous and still unresolved enterprise. In the eyes of influential commentators, though their observations are fiercely controverted, the post-imperial 'island story' has come to an end. Its long past, with all its twists and turns, has run into the sands. 'Britain' still has a present but it has no future.

Mere historians, of course, cannot predict the future, but they can put present controversies in context. The protracted and intractable relationship between 'Britain' and 'Europe', it scarcely needs to be said at this juncture, emerges from a long past, but after 1945 it has moved to the centre of British life. Its centrality, taken together with domestic developments considered in the final chapter, explains that disjuncture between the British past and the British present, experienced widely, though neither completely nor universally, in the present. The elaborate and moving ceremonies which followed the death of Sir Winston Churchill in 1965 made that disjuncture very apparent. Heads of state from across the world came to the service in St Paul's Cathedral. London was again momentarily at the hub of the world. The occasion offered a reminder of a great past, but it was a fleeting reminder. It was a world which could not come back, but sentiment nevertheless remained strong. The emotions of an old country could only be realigned with difficulty and pain.

---

[8] Cited in J. Ramsden, *The Making of Conservative Party Policy* (London, 1980) p. 213.

It was easy to recognize that 'Britain' existed at the intersection of the American/Atlantic/English-speaking 'world' and the European 'world', but extraordinarily difficult to disentangle and prioritize the relationships which stemmed from that fact. It was often the case that what appeared to be geopolitical logic existed in conflict with historical memory, with long-established patterns of trade, and with contemporary cultural preferences. These cross-cutting connections give late-twentieth-century British history its peculiar character. They explain why the British self-image has been such a matter of protracted debate, even to the point of wondering whether the 'Britain' of nearly three hundred years will survive into the twenty-first century.

British Europeans?: The bus is waiting 1940–1957

In 1994, after considerable delay, the Channel Tunnel was formally opened by Queen Elizabeth and President Mitterrand of France. At last, the objections to such a project which were still being raised after the Second World War were silenced. Britain had a land link to 'Europe' for the first time since the Ice Age. The psychological anxieties, however, which lay behind the objections, were still far from being resolved. The sense in which Britain was a 'European' country and its past 'essentially' a 'European' past ran like a fault-line through its postwar history in almost every respect and runs on still.[9]

In 1940 the possibility of an 'Anglo-French Union' had appeared briefly on the horizon in the context of the desperate position in which both countries then found themselves. Even to moot such a possibility caused incredulity and even apoplexy in some British circles. Perhaps, the idea was only advanced because its chances of success were minimal. Indeed, events moved on.[10]

In 1944–45 Britain stood at a turning point in relation to 'Europe'. How far could or should Britain exercise 'leadership' in Europe? Inevitably, the diplomacy of the subsequent decade has been subjected to close scrutiny as the documents have become available. The negotiations cannot be fol-

---

[9] J.W. Young, *Britain and European Unity, 1945–1992* (London, 1993); S. George, *Britain and European Integration since 1945* (Oxford, 1991); G. Radice, *Offshore: Britain & the European Idea* (London, 1992); G. Schmidt, 'Grossbritannien, die Grundung der Europäischen Wirtschaftsgemeinschaft und die Sicherheits des Westens: "The American Connection" ' in M. Salewski, ed., *Nationale Identität und die Europäische Einigung* (Göttingen, 1991); J. Stephenson, 'Britain and Europe in the Later Twentieth Centry' in M. Fulbrook, ed., *National Histories and European History* (London, 1993); D. Reynolds, 'Britain and the New Europe: The Search for Identity since 1940', *Historical Journal* 31, 1 (1988).
[10] D. Johnson, 'Britain and France in 1940', *Transactions of the Royal Historical Society* Fifth Series 22 (1972); D. Dilks, *De Gaulle and the British* and *Rights, Wrongs and Rivalries: Britain and France in 1945* (Hull, 1995, 1996) takes the story forward.

lowed in detail here, but there are certain episodes which must necessarily be highlighted. However, behind the diplomacy, as always, lie assumptions, both spoken and unspoken. In general terms, the British people did not emerge from the war with an enhanced sense of their European identity. Of course, the presence of exiled European governments and some troops gave 'Europe' in Britain a quite unusual profile. They were not present, however, as equals. The most prickly aspirant to status, Charles de Gaulle, was kept, with difficulty, in the subordinate position the British government believed he ought to occupy. The British felt themselves to occupy significantly higher ground in all their dealings with 'the Europeans'. The economist Lionel Robbins, conscious in America of the inevitable postwar power of Washington, entered some thoughts on 'the Europeans' in his diary in 1943. They constituted both a complication and a problem but one which Britain might turn to some use 'if it does not lure us too far in the direction of regionalism. Pan-Europa? No, that dream, splendid though it was, recedes; it was always a little difficult to reconcile with the Commonwealth. But calling the old world back into existence to redress the balance of the new ... has an attraction ... '.[11]

'Regionalism' had indeed lured some British minds. Sir Ivor Jennings, the constitutional lawyer, for example, was only one of a number of wartime writers to sketch 'A Federation for Western Europe'. By the end of the war, however, advocates of 'Federal Union' existed only in small numbers in both major political parties. The difficulty was that 'federalism' had infected European minds to a significantly greater degree than it had the postwar British Labour Cabinet which instinctively shied away from any grandiose conceptions of this kind. Bevin, the Labour Foreign Secretary, naturally had policies for Western Europe which entailed closer economic and military cooperation. Britain and France signed a historic peacetime alliance, the Treaty of Dunkirk, in March 1947. A year later, the Brussels Pact bound Britain, France and the Benelux countries in military arrangements but it also had economic and cultural aspects. Bevin, however, had neither aptitude nor inclination to indulge in more fundamental questioning about the significance of the British past in an evolving Western Europe whose reviving states found the notion of British tutelage increasingly irksome.

It was substantially left to Churchill, in Opposition, to play the 'United Europe' card and to utter profundities. He did so to considerable effect in various European cities and then presided over a non-party 'United Europe Movement' founded in January 1947. Its statement of policy argued that Britain had special obligations and ties with the other nations of the 'British Commonwealth'. Nevertheless, it continued, 'Britain is part of Europe and must be prepared to make her full contribution to European unity'. 'Leaders in almost every sphere of British public life' assembled for the inaugural

---

[11] S. Howson and D. Moggridge, eds, *The Wartime Diaries of Robbins and Meade* (London, 1991) p. 55.

meeting in the Royal Albert Hall in May 1947 under a large banner bearing the words 'EUROPE ARISE'. In his speech, Churchill declared that 'If Europe united is to be a living force, Britain will have to play her full part as a member of the European family'.[12] Part of the impetus behind this movement stemmed from anxiety about the Soviet Union in the unfolding 'Cold War'.

Four years later, however, when he again became Prime Minister, his earlier rhetoric was not translated into a major change of policy. The reasons for this are complex, not least being Churchill's latter-day preoccupation with East–West relations and the conviction that he had a major role to play in lessening international tension. In any case, by the early 1950s it had become necessary to move beyond the general aspiration to 'unity' to the consideration of specific propositions. In 1950 Britain had declined to become a member of the European Coal and Steel Community, a decision which has been widely taken to be the point at which Britain lost the opportunity to shape the pattern of European political and economic integration. The tired Labour government resented the temerity of the French government in pressing the plan and the support given it by the Americans. British officialdom took comfort, not for the last time, in the belief that this European initiative would fail. There was objection to the element of supranationality in the Community's 'High Authority' and the insidious threat to 'sovereignty' which it posed. On coming into government, Churchill accepted the outcome. Indeed, there remained considerable continuity of tone in the government's attitude towards the new Council of Europe and towards the mooted European Defence Community. Eden, the Foreign Secretary, made no secret of the fact that his bones told him that Britain could not join a European federation.

There was much picking over British bones in the years that followed. France, Federal Germany, Italy and the Benelux countries signed the Treaty of Rome in March 1957. Britain decided not to participate to any significant extent in the negotiations which led to this signature. The Prime Minister declared that Britain could not contemplate joining a customs union with a common external tariff. In a much-quoted article in December 1957, the German magazine *Der Spiegel* described the British as the 'eccentrics of Europe' to such a point that they could scarcely be considered Europeans at all.[13] Viewing the 'Common Market' with a mixture of scorn and suspicion, the British government orchestrated an European Free Trade Association as an alternative and watched the gathering intimacy between Germany and France with dismay.

---

[12] United Europe: Speeches at the Royal Albert Hall 14th May 1947, p. 11. Lord Beloff, 'Churchill and Europe' in Blake and Louis, *Churchill*, pp. 443–56 gives a rather different emphasis. W.S. Churchill, *Speeches 1947 & 1948: Europe Unite* (London, 1950).
[13] *Der Spiegel* 25 December 1957. See G. Niedhart, *Das kontinentale Europa und die britischen Inseln* (Mannheim, 1993) pp. 205–13.

British Americans?: Over here and over there, 1942–1957

The notion that Britain was 'essentially' a European country might have been more palatable in British public life if the United States had not loomed larger in British consciousness than it had ever done in the past. The entry of the United States into the First World War had often been seen in Britain as belated. There had been anxiety that President Wilson would hijack the peace settlement. He had kept his distance by insisting that the United States be an 'Associate' rather than an 'Allied' power. When he attended the victory banquet at Buckingham Palace in December 1918, he made it clear in his speech that the American people were not 'Anglo-Saxons': 'You must not speak of us who come over here as cousins, still less as brothers; we are neither'.[14] He downplayed even the fact of a common language. Close relations, he argued, depended upon a community of ideals and interests.

In the postwar period, despite American 'isolation', a 'community of ideals' had some resonance in the continuing mutual attachment to democratic systems. Nevertheless, it was by no means clear that there was a 'community of interests'. Indeed, there was considerable resentment at the American challenge to British naval supremacy and continued hostility to the British Empire. Even the Anglo-American Churchill told his Cabinet colleagues in 1927 that war with the United States was not 'unthinkable'. Britain should take steps to ensure that she was not put in the power of the United States. In the same year, Bertrand Russell wrote in the *New York Times* that 'The dislike of America which has grown up in England is due to the fact that world empire has now passed from Lombard Street to Wall Street. The British Navy ... is still nominally ours, but we dare not use it in any way displeasing to Washington.'[15] By the 1930s, it became a working assumption of British policy-makers that nothing more could be expected from the United States, as the European situation deteriorated, than long words and plenty of them.

At a more popular level, in films and music, 'America' was beginning to have a substantial impact – an impact which such guardians of 'British culture' as the *Daily Express* regarded with some alarm. It complained in 1927 that 'the bulk of our picture-goers are Americanised ... They talk America, think America, and dream America. We have several million people, mostly women, who, to all intent and purpose, are temporary American citizens.'[16] 'Britain' stood in some danger of becoming a segment

---

[14] Cited in D. Reynolds, *Rich Relations: The American Occupation of Britain 1942–1945* (London, 1995) p. 6; D. Cameron Watt, *Succeeding John Bull: America in Britain's Place, 1900–1975* (Cambridge, 1984).
[15] B. Russell, 'The New Life That Is America', *New York Times*, 22 May 1927.
[16] But see also D. Reynolds, *The Creation of the American Alliance, 1937–1941: A Study in Competitive Co-operation* (London, 1981). A volume which conveys the

of America. It was manifest, however, that for the young, celluloid America was an attractive magnet and its attractions could not be easily countered. The *Morning Post* took the view that the film was to America what the flag was once to Britain. Since Hollywood was alleged to be undermining national character, the British government took steps to limit the number of imported American films. Even so, it was not possible to eradicate the sense that the America of skyscrapers, jazz and the cinema constituted 'the driving force of the world'. The United States was the land of mechanization and materialism: Britain was a tired old country. Britain was even ceasing to own the world copyright on the English language.[17]

Few of those who pontificated on this matter could have anticipated that between 1942 and 1945 some 3 million young Americans would pass through the United Kingdom. Hundreds of thousands of them, indeed, spent considerable periods in the country. The interaction between the British and the 'occupiers' was on a scale without precedent in modern British history. All sorts of stereotypes were put to the test in the process. It became evident that a serious process of education for mutual understanding was necessary, though it did not prevent many misunderstandings. This complex interaction has been explored by a recent historian in illuminating detail. He demonstrates that it became clear during the war that the 'Brits' and the 'Yanks' did have many things in common, but equally had important differences. For both sides, the perception that the other did regard them as 'different' helped in turn to solidify the respective national self-images. It remained, however, a puzzling relationship, explained by Mass-Observation in terms of 'cousinhood'. 'British people', it claimed, 'have never regarded Americans as on all fours with other foreigners'.[18] Other surveys, however, concluded that as many millions of British people got to know Americans, sometimes as their lodgers, the 'cousin' image declined and British people increasingly recognized America as a foreign country rather than as a former colony. Even so, by the end of the war, it was a foreign country which more British people felt they knew at first hand, with all its defects and attractions, than they did any other foreign country.[19]

The precedent of 1918–19 suggested that this American invasion would not endure beyond the end of the war. It took some time after 1945 to adjust to a different circumstance. From the British perspective, much

---

sentiment of the period is P. Gibbs, ed., *Bridging the Atlantic: Anglo-American Fellowship as the Way to World Peace* (London, n.d.).

[17] F. Costigliola, *Awkward Dominion: American Political, Economic and Cultural Relations with Europe, 1919–1933* (London, 1984) pp. 176–8.

[18] Reynolds, *Rich Relations* p. 42; R.M. Hathaway, *Ambiguous Partnership: Britain and America, 1944–1947* (New York, 1981); C.J. Bartlett, *'The Special Relationship' A Political History of Anglo-American Relations since 1945* (London, 1992).

[19] R. Edmonds, *Setting the Mould: The United States and Britain 1945–1950* (Oxford, 1986) pp. 6–7.

could and should be made of a 'special relationship'. Despite the inevitable frictions between individuals, both military and civilian, the organization of the war effort could reasonably be portrayed as remarkably intimate and successful. There were official whispers that if Britain had to federate with any other state it was better to federate with the United States than with 'Europe' – an echo of a prewar view that it would be better to be an American state than a German *Gau*.

It was undoubtedly the case, however, that Britain was the junior partner. Deeply worried by the prospects for West European security in the face of uncertain Soviet intentions, only America could provide adequate support. Britain could and should be the vital bridge between 'Europe' and the United States. It was against this background that Britain became a founder-member of the North Atlantic Treaty Organization (NATO) on its formation in 1949. There appeared to be no objection to the loss of 'sovereignty' that the alliance entailed. Britain was prepared to undertake to fight, in the event of aggression against any of the signatories, and to accept the preponderating power and presence of the United States within the alliance. The 'Yanks' again came to Britain, particularly to air bases in eastern England. 'To withstand the great concentration of power now stretching from China to the Oder', wrote the Foreign Secretary in a Cabinet paper in early 1950, 'the United Kingdom and Western Europe must be able to rely on the full support of the English-speaking democracies of the western hemisphere; and for the original conception of the Western Union we must now begin to substitute the wider conception of the Atlantic community'.[20] History again seemed to suggest that Britain was specially equipped to play that role.

Expectations of a 'special relationship' seem in retrospect to be exaggerated, but there was initially more mutual benefit for both Britain and the United States than has sometimes latterly been allowed. The early years of NATO were smoothed by the mutual understandings derived from wartime. However, insofar as the 'special relationship' was inevitably a relationship between unequals, the United States had also to entertain other partnerships and irritation in Washington grew with the British reluctance to take part in

---

[20] General discussions of Bevin's foreign policy are to be found in A. Bullock, *Ernest Bevin: Foreign Secretary 1945–1951* (London, 1983); M. Dockrill and J. Young, eds, *British Foreign Policy, 1945–56* (London, 1989); and R. Ovendale, ed., *The Foreign Policy of the British Labour Governments 1945–1951* (Leicester, 1984); E. Dell, *The Schuman Plan and the British Abdication of Leadership in Europe* (Oxford, 1995).

12.2 Cinema-goers, *c.* 1945. In the view of some commentators, the war was accelerating the transition of Britons into Americans, at least as far as popular culture was concerned. Although legislation had consciously tried to preserve a British film industry, the allure of Hollywood was apparently overwhelming. In queuing for 'Gone with the Wind' with such devotion, young Britain in particular was swimming with an irresistible American tide.

the 'uniting' of Europe which it had come to see as desirable. Increasingly, Americans found incomprehensible the way in which the British, on paper and in speech, continued to refer to 'the Europeans', since when they looked at a map it seemed to Americans that the British were Europeans too. Contrariwise, on the mainland of Europe, an Atlantic community was one thing, American hegemony another. From the perspective of Paris, Britain could appear to be a Trojan horse for the interests of Washington. In addition, issues of commercial and economic policy threatened Britain's capacity to exercise that role as 'bridge' which history had seemingly bequeathed. Bevin had perceived the potential dilemma back in 1946 when he realized that the evident wish of some European countries to embark on a process of economic union, in stages, might conflict with the British commitment not to engage in commercial discrimination against the United States. In the 1950s it was becoming apparent that the reviving European countries did not need Britain to be their interlocutor with the United States on commercial matters.

Then, in 1956, came the shock for Britain of the American opposition which scuppered the Suez expedition. It shattered for a time the easy assumptions of Anglo-American amity and required sedulous attention from Eden's successor, Harold Macmillan, to restore. It gave rise, for a time, to some fierce anti-American sentiment, incongruously uniting both extreme Right and extreme Left. Macmillan proved adept at this time in developing Anglo-American defence intimacy, strong in his conviction that Britain should remain a nuclear power – the first British hydrogen bomb was successfully exploded in May 1957. Over the years immediately following, Macmillan tried his hand at world diplomacy, convinced, as his predecessors had been, that Britain still possessed a unique position in the international politics of the Cold War. His own ancestry, it is relevant to note, stood as a kind of classical illustration of what 'Britishness' at this level could entail, mingling as it did Scottish, English and American elements.

The notion that the British were the 'Greeks' in the American/Roman Empire had a conceited and reassuring appeal to a young man who had studied Classics at Oxford. The British, he supposed, could bring their inherited wisdom and sophistication to advise their brash 'cousin' in his exercise of power. Such a notion was congenial to a man of Macmillan's background and education. Some observers, however, wondered what sophistication Britain still had to offer. Back in 1947, the historian G.M. Trevelyan thought he lived in Britain in an age which had no real culture except American films and football pools. In his opinion, the advent of real democracy, coinciding with two world wars, had cooked the goose of civilization – or at any rate of the kind he admired. It seemed increasingly likely that the Americans would stir the pot of civilization on their own.

British Europeans? If at first … 1961–1975

In July 1961, having earlier sadly concluded that the 'Common Market' was 'here to stay' and that his efforts to disrupt it had failed, Macmillan told the House of Commons that the government wished to join, something which had previously been deemed impossible. A substantial negotiation was envisaged as a means of safeguarding British, Commonwealth and European Free Trade Association interests. It had not been easy to bring his party round to the idea and, not for the last time, there was talk that 'Europe' could divide the Conservatives as the Corn Laws had divided them in 1846. Duncan Sandys, extraordinary emissary to the Commonwealth, endeavoured to persuade its suspicious prime ministers that Britain would fight hard to safeguard their interests. In Australia and New Zealand, in particular, it looked as though the very bases of their economies, so tightly related to Britain over so long a period, were now threatened. The *Daily Express* prepared to do battle on their behalf. Its special coronation issue, a decade earlier, had also celebrated the climbing of Mount Everest by 'a Briton' – no less a person than the New Zealander, Edmund Hillary. Some things, in its view, never changed.

Macmillan himself still insisted in private conversation that Britain had to try to 'preserve its position as a great nation with world-wide responsibilities'. The desire to develop a supra-national European organization he attributed to 'the Jews, the planners and the old cosmopolitan element' among European politicians.[21] There were was, indeed, virtual unanimity that British entry, should it be successful, should not cause any perturbation in British self-perception. The Labour Party's National Executive Committee reiterated in September 1962, after negotiations had been dragging on for nearly a year, that historically and actually Britain's interests and connections lay as much outside the Community as inside. It warned that membership of the Community would decisively change Britain's world position. Britain was the centre of the Commonwealth, deemed to be 'a much larger and still more important group'. The following month, the party leader, Gaitskell, emotionally envisaged the end of British history – Britain would become like the states of Australia or of the United States in a new Europe. Such sentiments made it difficult to accept the claim by Edward Heath, the chief negotiator, that the British people were anxious to become 'full, whole-hearted and active members of the European Community'.

President de Gaulle, however, acutely observed in January 1963 that this was not the case and gave it as the pretext for the veto he then exercised. The outcome was devastating for Macmillan since membership was intimately bound up with a programme for the 'modernization' of Britain. Even those who rejoiced in the failure were paradoxically outraged by the national humiliation which they took it to represent. More widely, in Australasia in

---

[21] Cited in J. Turner, *Macmillan* (London, 1994) p. 217.

particular, the writing on the wall began to be read. Britain would surely try again. Australia and New Zealand would have to look elsewhere for commerce and other links.

It was a Labour government which made the next attempt. Following extensive lobbying in the capitals of Western Europe in the winter of 1966 and the spring of 1967, a further application was made. It met with the same fate, though this time de Gaulle laid stress on Britain's immediate economic and financial difficulties as the impediment to entry. There had been a hope that the other members of the Community would press Britain's case with de Gaulle but they were not inclined to do so to any significant extent. Britain might still be highly regarded in the Netherlands, for example, but it was a measure of the change that had occurred since 1945, even more since 1957, that the sentimental attitudes of wartime had been replaced by a more hard-headed attitude on the part of those politicians who saw themselves as 'building Europe'.

When Edward Heath became Conservative Prime Minister in 1970 there was little doubt that he would resume the quest for membership. His experiences as negotiator under Macmillan had not dimmed his enthusiasm. He was the first British Prime Minister to believe in the validity, indeed the necessity, of Britain playing an active part in the European enterprise. Helped by the resignation of de Gaulle, the British application was eventually pressed to a successful conclusion. British entry was fixed for 1 January 1973. Certain transitional arrangements were made but that was all they were. Commonwealth countries would have to make the best of what they considered a bad job. It was equally clear that Britain itself could not pick and choose. There was no alternative but to accept the Common Agricultural Policy and the common external tariff. Hardly had the transition begun, however, when the western economies as a whole were threatened by the dramatic oil price rise. The incoming Labour government declared that continued British membership depended upon renegotiation of the entry terms. Some modest adjustments were made, sufficient for the government to declare itself satisfied.

The outcome was put to the British people in a referendum. Nearly two-thirds of the electorate voted, two-thirds of whom supported continued membership. It was an issue which divided even the Cabinet – several of its leading members campaigned to withdraw – but at last it appeared to be settled. In reality, however, the long British past could not be disposed of so easily. 'Our traditions are safe', the 'Britain in Europe' campaign literature declared. It was quite possible to work together in the Community 'and still stay British'. Those who voted to stay in would be doing their duty to the world and expressing their hope 'for the new greatness of Britain'.

British Europeans: staying British, 1975–

Members of 'Britain in Europe' in 1975 promised that membership of the Community would not entail dull uniformity. It would not make the French eat German food or the Dutch drink Italian beer. It would not damage 'our British traditions and way of life'. Such a claim was inherently implausible at the time, although no one could have accurately forecast the evolution of the Community over twenty years. Participation in its evolution has necessarily 'damaged' the traditions and ways of life of all the participating states, to greater or lesser degree, because the Community could not have functioned unless it did so. By the mid-1990s there was scarcely any area of British life which was not affected, to some extent, by directives and regulations emanating from 'Europe'. Nevertheless, no 'traditional' British institution has been 'formally eliminated'. Parliament still makes laws, judges make judgements, and professional bodies give rulings, and so on, seemingly as they have done throughout the modern centuries of British history. In reality, however, many of their decisions must operate within a context which is European.[22]

In the twenty years since membership, no British government has sought to accelerate this *de facto* and sometimes *de jure* incorporation of Britain into a European framework. In opposition or in government, both Conservative and Labour parties have shown continuity on the issue of 'Britain in Europe' only in their changes of mind. The Conservatives, for a period, took pride in having been the party which took Britain 'into' Europe. It was not impossible for the speeches of Geoffrey Rippon, the entry negotiator, to appear under the title *Our European Future*.[23] In the 1980s, however, under the Thatcher governments, a much more sceptical tone predominated. Britain had to get back 'its' money. The Prime Minister displayed great reluctance to be drawn into schemes and proposals which pointed in the direction of monetary union. On the other hand, she was a strong advocate of the Single European Market. Her attitude caused extreme irritation at times in other European capitals. It highlighted that suspicion of 'federalism' which was deeply entrenched in substantial sections of British opinion. 'Federalism' was

---

[22] W. Wallace, ed., *Britain's Bilateral Links within Western Europe* (London, 1984); S. George, *An Awkward Partner: Britain in the European Community* (Oxford, 1990); A. Milward, *The European Rescue of the Nation-State* (London, 1992); A. Milward, F. Lynch, F. Fomero and V. Sorensen, *The Frontier of National Sovereignty: History and Theory, 1945–1992* (London, 1993); W. Carlsnaes and S. Smith, *European Foreign Policy: The EC and Changing Perspectives in Europe* (London, 1994); E. Meehan, *Citizenship and the European Community* (London, 1993); V. Goddard, J. Llobera and C. Hope, eds, *The Anthropology of Europe: Identities and Boundaries in Conflict* (Oxford, 1995); N. Davies, *Europe* (Oxford, 1996).
[23] G. Rippon, *Our European Future* (London, 1978) cf. M. Thatcher, *Britain and Europe: Text of the speech delivered in Bruges ...* (London, 1988); R. Meier-Walser, 'Britain in Search of a Place "at the Heart of Europe" ', *Aussenpolitik* 1 (1994).

taken to imply a European 'super-state', though many mainland Europeans did not so understand 'federalism'. Britain could never belong to such an entity. That this view was not a personal whim of Mrs Thatcher could be seen from the turmoil in the Conservative Party which followed her departure from office and which continues.

The Maastricht Agreement, concluded in December 1991, was only ratified in the British Parliament with extreme difficulty. Britain had insisted on achieving 'opt-outs' in relation to the 'Social Chapter' which attempted to establish uniform provisions on a whole range of social and industrial issues across the Community. Britain had also reserved the right to postpone making a decision on a single European currency and Central Bank. In the years that followed, important sections of the Conservative Party, cheered on by *The Times*, excoriated the Maastricht Agreement as a treaty too far. A bitter struggle for dominance ensued both within the Cabinet and the party at large, with advantage swinging back and forwards. The 'Eurosceptics' seemed in reality to be 'Europhobes'. The survival of the government was in doubt in the mid-1990s.

'Brussels', for some prominent critics, took on a demonic hue and Conservative opponents of the Community directed their efforts towards 'regaining' British control of Britain's affairs. Opposition to a single currency for the 'Union' increased and in certain quarters it became fashionable to conceive of 'Europe' as the 'enemy'. It was vital to maintain every aspect of what was described as 'sovereignty'. There was also hostility to what was perceived as 'German domination', a fear which grew after the ending of the division of Germany. Old attitudes from the past resurfaced and indeed, for a time, it appeared that the rivalries and antipathies of 'old Europe', dormant since 1945, were resurfacing. The activities of Spanish fishermen even evoked memories of the 'Armada' and in disputes between Spain/the European Union and Canada, the British public's sympathies on fishing matters appeared to be with Canada. 'European Unity', as it had been forged for some thirty years, seemed in danger, not least because the cement provided by fear of the Soviet Union had crumbled with the collapse of Communism. Some British spokesmen deplored the 'new nationalism' which they discerned in Europe, but from a mainland perspective this appeared to be a case of the pot calling the kettle black. As Prime Minister, John Major tried to take a relatively consistent line while dissent swirled around him. He continued to reiterate that Britain would not go down what he called the 'centralizing route'. The nation-state – that is to say Britain – remained a bulwark of comfort and stability in a changing world. On the other hand he dismissed notions that Britain could with impunity withdraw.

The Labour Party, by contrast, moved from a position of outright hostility – expressed in the 1983 general election pledge to take Britain out of the Community within the lifetime of a Labour government – to one of firm support. Although coy about accepting a 'federalist' label, the party nevertheless spoke much more positively not only about the 'Social Chapter', which was only to be expected, but also about a single currency and an integrative agenda in general. Of course, these were only positions adopted by the party in opposition. In government, a rather different stance and tone might be adopted. Even so, in 1997, it appeared that 'Europe' might once again be the great divide between the parties – though there still remained both in the government and in the Labour Party groups who dissented from the party line. Inescapably, various British 'pasts' were being deployed by the adversaries in their struggle for the hearts and minds of the British people at this critical juncture.

In the predominant Conservative version, Britain could only be itself within a 'minimalist' Europe. Experience had supposedly shown that Britain could never be comfortable in the kind of union on which France and Germany, at least, were bent. Britain had a distinctive past and could not be straitjacketed to fit into a European grand design. 'Common foreign' or 'common defence' policies could not be contemplated, certainly if they were determined on the basis of majority voting. They would really mean that 'Britain' had ceased to exist. Also, particularly during the years of the Thatcher administrations, the United States was a greater magnet than 'Europe'. The personal relationship which the Prime Minister established with President Reagan enabled her to believe that there was still great resilience in the 'special relationship'. She contrasted the support which she extracted from the United States in the re-conquest of the Falkland Islands in 1982 with the indifference and even hostility which she encountered within the Community on the issue.

In the predominant Labour version, these conceptions of Britain's 'special' character were not entirely discounted but were felt to be no longer adequate. Britain needed not so much to dwell upon its legacy from an imperial or 'Atlantic' past but rather on the 'failure' of its recent past, stretching back for half a century, in Europe. There had to be a sustained and effective 'engagement' with the European enterprise. It was as vital that this should prosper and succeed as that the special interests of Britain should be protected. It was not altogether clear how this should be done, but there needed to be a new attitude of mind. Sometimes the past suffocated the present. Perhaps that was what had happened to Britain.

Open to the world?

If Britain is now a 'world power' only in a restricted sense of that term, if at all, a case can nevertheless be made that it remains a 'world influence' – an equally imprecise concept. That is to say, Britain possesses an outreach into the world as a whole not matched by other states of similar population and economic stature. It is an influence, of course, which has been made possible by the past. There is scarcely a corner of the world where British connections and contacts do not exist, and where, in consequence, some kind of 'influence' can be shown still to be at work. In turn such networks still bear on the way in which British governments and people conceive their past. On occasion, however, these assets have been seen as inexorably diminishing with the flux of time. Such a doctrine of inevitability has been replaced, however, in some instances in the mid-1990s by attempts to infuse new life (and new images) into old relationships – for example between Britain and Australia – not least because of their contemporary commercial possibilities. The fact that English has become *the* world language, even though Britain no longer has exclusive rights over it, does make possible an extraordinary flow of communication into and out of Britain. It is sometimes suggested in consequence that Britain is at once insular and global – a condition which makes the growth of a continental sense difficult to achieve.

It is, therefore, not possible to say with any confidence whether or not British traditions are indeed 'safe'. The factors which have produced this uncertainty as discussed in this chapter are external, though it has become increasingly difficult to make a sharp distinction between what is external and what is internal. The factors which have combined to undermine self-images of Britain, as they have been held over three centuries, have also occurred within many other contemporary countries. At one level, global communications have had a corrosive impact on indigenous traditions worldwide. Few of them are safe from outside influences. Social, cultural and economic change appears endemic. Most societies in the late twentieth century are therefore inevitably engaged in a dialogue with their past. What to discard and what to conserve? Political and cultural elites are no longer sure what to make of their past. They seem increasingly doubtful whether 'the past' can offer anything to the present because it seems to make itself so remote so quickly. Nevertheless, they also feel, mysteriously, that it cannot be left to fade away, that it is still in the deep structure of the present.

It is, on the other hand, the pervasive uncertainty of the contemporary world, with its built-in assumption of constant obsolescence, which gives rise to a yearning for the past. The past is seen, by contrast, as firm and fixed, reassuringly embellished by tradition and myth, and serenaded by compliant historians. The 'global village' and 'virtual reality' offer wide horizons but do not help the individual to feel at home in any particular space.

Such technological developments have profound consequences worldwide. Britain has not escaped their impact. Individuals and groups confess that they 'communicate' electronically with other individuals and groups worldwide as frequently, and perhaps with more benefit, than they do with their 'fellow nationals'. However, with the destruction or erosion of many of those 'identifiers' which in former centuries have been used as talismans of

'Britishness', it has become increasingly difficult to discern what bearing past traditions have on the late-twentieth-century present. In the final chapter that follows, the domestic ramifications of this upheaval are discussed.

In treating these themes, however, historians often no longer themselves share the confidence of their predecessors in previous centuries that they can extrapolate a particular destiny from the patterns of the past. It is also the case, in contrast to previous centuries, that modern British politicians, with their vast array of supposedly more pressing tasks, no longer, for the most part, share that easy acquaintance with British history which their predecessors could in general assume. Historical analogy drawn from the British past rarely appears in contemporary rhetoric, or what passes for it. British history has largely ceased to be a school for modern British statesmen – but it may be as perilous to be ignorant of the past as it is to be obsessed by it.

Chapter 13 ....

Losing (Domestic) Bearings? 1945–

Return match?

In the immediate aftermath of the Second World War there was much concern about the future of 'the British people'. It led to the establishment of a Royal Commission on Population since it was believed, by analysis of demographic patterns, that there was a real threat of the 'fading-out of the British people'. Eva Hubback, author of a respected Pelican book *The Population of Britain* (1947), speculated on trends which she believed would lead to a British nation which had shrunk to a third of its existing size. It was conceivable that 'an emptying Britain would be largely occupied by people from nations with very different traditions and ideas from our own'. She took the view that it would be a 'world calamity' if the British people in the home islands and in the white Dominions were to become very much reduced or to die out completely. It seemed quite likely that Britain in the future would consist of 'a mixture of our present British stock with that of peoples mostly from Eastern Europe or Asia'. Such peoples had many virtues and qualities but their 'outlook and ideas are likely to be very different from ours today, and whom we should find it extremely difficult to assimilate'.[1] In short, it would be a future which might have only a tenuous connection with what had been believed to be the basic ingredients of Britishness over many centuries.

Half a century earlier, setting sail from Bombay for 'home' in June 1896, Winston Churchill wrote to his mother asking her to try to arrange political meetings for him in Bradford. It was a constituency in the north of England which he might one day represent in Parliament. There were, as noted earlier, 'foreigners' in Bradford, chiefly Germans, but Indians were not amongst them. Wealthy maharajahs and elegant cricketers from the sub-continent sometimes appeared in England but, between the wars, the notion

---

[1] E. Hubback, *The Population of Britain* (West Drayton, 1947) pp. 270–1.

that there would ever be substantial settlement in Britain from the Indian sub-continent would have seemed absurd. It was indeed an 'unexpected turn' that from the moment when it appeared that 'British India' was fading into the past, Indians came to Britain in increasing numbers. One of the cities to which immigrants from the sub-continent went in substantial numbers was Bradford. Urdu signs advertising 'Halal Fish and Chips' and a proliferation of mosques were not in Churchill's mind when he considered visiting in 1896. Southall, west of London, became a mini-Punjab. Hindus and Moslems, Indians, Pakistanis and Bangladeshis of varying linguistic backgrounds became established in major British cities, for example Leicester and Glasgow. 'Indian restaurants' became commonplace in urban and not so urban Britain. Asians from East Africa, themselves originally encouraged there under British rule, fell foul of African governments and many of their number, on coming to Britain in 1968, formed a distinct new section of the Asian population, a population which was in any case diverse in language, geographical origin and skills.[2]

Alongside populations derived from the Indian sub-continent were communities of West Indians whose pattern of settlement was also substantially urban. They settled, for example, in particular districts of Bristol, Birmingham, London or Nottingham. There were also Chinese populations, largely from Hong Kong, Malaysia and Singapore. Chinese restaurants spread throughout the country. Nigerians, Tamils and Vietnamese added to the ethnic complexity. In consequence, to a greater or lesser degree, parts of urban Britain had become 'multi-ethnic'. A phenomenon which had hitherto been largely restricted to port cities such as Cardiff or Liverpool now became much more general.

Immigrants, of course, did not only arrive from the 'new Commonwealth' during this period, nor were they only non-white. White Commonwealth immigrants arrived from Australia and New Zealand, in particular, in steady numbers, but in popular parlance 'Commonwealth Immigration' was talked about in colour terms. It was colour which made the new immigrant stand out and be perceived as 'different', whereas in the nineteenth century and first half of the twentieth century, immigrants from elsewhere in Europe – Jews from Eastern Europe, Belgians, Germans, Italians, Czechs, Hungarians and other nationalities – had not appeared so conspicuous.[3]

Above all, there continued to be a strong Irish presence. Unlike some of the nationalities mentioned above whose arrival as refugees was occasioned

---

[2] V. Robinson, *Transients, Settlers and Refugees: Asians in Britain* (Oxford, 1986) and *Ethnicity and Nationalism in Post-Imperial Britain* (Cambridge, 1991).
[3] C. Holmes, *Immigrants and Minorities in British Society* (London, 1978) and *John Bull's Island: Immigration and British Society 1871–1971* (Basingstoke, 1988); K. Lunn, *Hosts, Immigrants and Minorities: Historical Responses to Newcomers in British Society 1870–1914* (London, 1980).

by a particular event, the Irish population was easily and constantly reinforced. In the 1971 census, 615,820 British residents were born in the Republic of Ireland. Taken in the context of Irish immigration into Britain over
the entire period when it was part of the United Kingdom, and which subsequently became 'British', such a figure is a strong indication of the significance of the Irish element in Britain. In total numbers, one might say that
Britain was now more Irish than the Republic. Whether that population is
'foreign' continues to be part of the problem of British-Irish relations.[4]

Such 'aliens' had by no means been greeted with enthusiasm in the districts in which they settled. Over time, however, as with Poles after 1945 –
the 1951 census returned a figure of 162,376 Polish-born – they intermarried
and appeared to be assimilated as 'British'. Often through their churches or
synagogues, and various cultural societies, immigrants from elsewhere in
Europe maintained an awareness of their heritage – though it was by no
means, in every case, a topic of continuing interest. Of course, there was
always the possibility of ostracism or even incarceration if relations between
their country of origin and Britain were poor, as 'Germans' were to find in
both world wars. In general, 'foreigners' kept some link with 'home' but it
did not stand in the way of 'becoming British'. Strictly speaking, the 'British
past', as mediated in school and in the rituals and institutions of British society, was 'alien', but it was a past that could be adopted without undue difficulty. Indeed, some 'new British' became more British than the 'old British'
themselves. Nevertheless, in Jewish communities, there could be serious
tension between those hostile to Zionism and anxious to stress their Britishness, thereby avoiding the accusation that they had 'dual allegiances', and
Zionists. After 1948, ardent supporters of the state of Israel had to risk that
charge.[5]

---

[4] P.J. Drudy, 'Migration beween Britain and Ireland since Independence' in P.J. Drudy,
Ireland and Britain since 1922 (Cambridge, 1986); J. Jackson, *The Irish in Britain*
(London, 1963).
[5] A. and R. Cowen, *Victorian Jews through British Eyes* (Oxford, 1986); C. Holmes,
Anti-Semitism in British Society 1876–1939 (London, 1979); D. Cesarani, ed., *The
Making of Modern Anglo-Jewry* (London, 1989); M. Berghahn, *Continental Britons:
German-Jewish Refugees from Nazi Germany* (Oxford, 1988); A. Sherman, *Island
Refuge: Britain and Refugees from the Third Reich, 1933–1939* (London, 1994 edn);
G. Alderman, *Modern British Jewry* (Oxford, 1992).

13.1 Pushing forwards: This casual street scene in inner-city Southampton could
have been taken in many British cities. Although 'race riots' sometimes occupied
media headlines, there was also evidence of a symbiosis that was uncomplicated.
Even so, issues of identity remained to worry – perhaps to worry the children in their
pushchairs as they grew up rather more than their parents. Were they 'just' British, or
was their Caribbean, Asian or other heritage to be treasured, preserved and perhaps
even rediscovered and re-emphasized?

There was, therefore, a case for arguing that the British were among the most ethnically composite of the Europeans. Yet, despite the strong presence of foreign-born or foreign-born-descended populations in late-twentieth-century Britain in particular locations, the overall proportion remained small. It is this combination of circumstances which has made the reconciliation of past and present of particular difficulty.

The twentieth century has not seen British governments, and those who voted for them, sympathetic to the notion that Britain could offer an 'Open Door' to all who wished to come. Between 1826 and 1905, no controls over alien immigration existed. However, legislation in 1905, 1914 and 1919, and the associated Orders in Council, introduced a firm system of control over entry, movement and deportation, maintained subsequently by governments of all political complexions. After the Second World War, the Labour government passed the British Nationality Act (1948). It reflected a view of 'Britishness' anchored in the world of the 'old dominions'. Citizens of self-governing Commonwealth countries were guaranteed freedom of entry. Whatever restrictions those countries might themselves have implemented or be contemplating, the British government regarded them as 'British citizens'. 'Citizens of the UK and Colonies' from the remainder of the Commonwealth also had free entry.

A quarter of a century later, that conception was dead. As the scale of coloured immigration mounted during the 1950s, so did public anxiety. 'Race Riots' in Notting Hill, London, in 1958 were interpreted as a sign of things to come unless restrictions were introduced. The 1962 Commonwealth Immigration Act introduced an entry system based on employment vouchers. A further measure, this time introduced by a Labour government in 1968, laid down further restrictions. Enoch Powell's speeches on immigration, which forecast 'rivers of blood' and advocated repatriation, evoked strong support in some quarters. They also led to his dismissal from the Opposition Shadow Cabinet. It seemed on the whole that public opinion, while not subscribing to the direst of prophecies, supported further restriction. From 1973, when the 1971 Immigration Act came into force, primary immigration into the UK from the Commonwealth depended upon the possession of 'patrial' status – a close connection through birth, descent or settlement. Commonwealth citizens without these connections were henceforth treated as aliens. Citizens of the Irish Republic were treated as a special case. The last curtain fell on 'Greater Britain'.

The restrictive measures of the 1960s were accompanied by Race Relations Acts. Their purpose was to influence behaviour and attitudes so that 'everyone in Britain will henceforth be treated on the basis of individual merit, regardless of colour or race'. Discrimination, initially in public places or on public transport but later in employment and housing, was declared unlawful. A Race Relations Board had power to investigate and its work was complemented later by the Community Relations Commission whose task was to promote harmony. A third Race Relations Act, passed by Labour in 1976, replaced both bodies by the Commission for Racial Equality. This activity was attacked from opposite directions. On the one hand, the work of the 'race relations industry' was criticized as an interference with personal liberty. On the other hand, its efforts were seen in other quarters as 'tokenism' which did little to alter the continuing underlying social reality of discrimination and exclusion. Notwithstanding strenuous efforts made to promote mutual understanding, periodic outbreaks of violence still occurred – in Brixton, in Liverpool, in Bristol, for example – which testified to a sense of alienation and frustration on the part of inner-city immigrant communities who remained, in general, at the bottom of the social ladder. But it also became clear that there were significant differences within and between different sections of the immigrant community so that, by the 1990s, a simple contrast between 'natives' and 'immigrants' was scarcely possible. Even from the beginning, East African Asians, expelled by African governments, could not identify with 'blacks'. In addition, it was also becoming apparent that there were serious tensions between the generations, particularly within Asian communities. 'The past' was again a problem.

Debates in Britain from the 1960s onwards now contained an ironic echo of British debates in India in the 1830s. Then Macaulay had argued that the English language was vital if India was to be modernized. Now the question was whether the languages of the Indian sub-continent should find a place on the shelves of public libraries in Southall or Blackburn. Should there be an enduring future in Britain for Urdu? It was pointed out that English as spoken and used in the Caribbean was not quite the same English as used in England. Should West Indian schoolchildren in England be drilled in 'standard English'? A host of other examples of such cross-cultural issues could be given. Looking in the other direction, how far was it desirable or feasible to 'acculturate' the 'native' British themselves into accepting that 'their own' society had suddenly become 'multicultural'?

It was an issue which divided and divides. No reading of the 'British past' as presented in this book can ignore the manifest 'multiculturalism' of certain earlier epochs. 'Britishness', protean though it was, came about through the intermingling, under a supremacy that was 'English', of all the elements that have been described in earlier chapters. In the nineteenth and first half of the twentieth centuries, continuing immigrants, largely from the European mainland, had been required to assimilate without benefit of a Race Relations Board. For the most part, they had been willing, if not eager, to do so, accepting in the process the self-confident images of a country which was indubitably a world power. In short, 'Britain' was a historic society, not a 'nation of immigrants' as the United States, Canada or Australia might be conceived to be. Even in these countries, however, 'multiculturalism' was problematic in the eyes of linguistic, social or ethnic groups who had dominated in the past, and perhaps still did so in an attenuated form in the present.

It is not surprising, therefore, that there have remained both articulate and inarticulate sections of British society who have resisted its multicultural transformation. It is a resistance which reflects the fact that immigration has not directly affected many areas of the country to a significant degree. The past that matters remains a British past – a source, predominantly of pride and satisfaction. It is a past which still needs to be actively transmitted for the benefit of future generations. It provides a cohesion which is national. Britain is for the British – a sentiment which, in extreme form, has been espoused by successive far right, neo-fascist organizations, such as the National Front or the British National Party. 'Britishness' can, however, be inclusive rather than exclusive. It has been argued that immigrants should show themselves willing to respect and accept British institutions, values and behaviour, as these things have been bequeathed by the past. The toleration which was won in the British past must of course also extend to different beliefs and values in the present, but that is not to say that what has been handed down from the past and become 'normative' in Britain must be jettisoned. But the British past, as this volume makes very evident, has rarely been sealed within secure caskets.

Such a perspective has, however, been repeatedly challenged. Roy Jenkins, as Labour Home Secretary in the mid-1960s, described assimilation as a 'flattening process'. It was no longer appropriate to think in such terms. He looked, rather, to 'integration' which he defined as 'equal opportunity, accompanied by cultural diversity in an atmosphere of mutual tolerance'.[6] It was further argued by other writers, particularly in the 1960s, but with enduring echoes ever since, that such diversity was not only inevitable, it was positively exciting and beneficial. It enabled British life to escape from constricting conventions. The past was not a treasure house but a prison from which it was time to break out and forge a new future. Churchill's belief that Britain had a peculiar capacity to 'guide and govern' reflected an arrogance as much outmoded in the cultural as in the political sphere. The British Empire was something to be ashamed of, even to apologize for. The notion that in some way Britain had a mission under Providence was a ludicrous piece of national self-deception fostered by the twin evils of Christian evangelism and classical education. It was a 'mission' which masked exploitation and repression. If Providence was at work, it was in the way in which an opportunity had now remarkably been provided to atone for the racial and cultural arrogance of the past by creating a new Britain in which it was absent.

---

[6] K. Robbins, *The Eclipse of a Great Power: Modern Britain 1870–1992* (2nd edn, London 1994) pp. 286–7; D. Goldberg, *Multiculturalism: A Critical Reader* (Oxford, 1994) offers a global perspective while Z. Layton-Henry, *The Politics of Immigration: 'Race' and 'Race' Relations in Postwar Britain* (Oxford, 1992) and P. Panayi, *Immigration, Ethnicity and Racism in Britain 1815–1945* (Manchester, 1994) offer a domestic angle.

New Britain? New Jerusalem?

The issues raised by immigration must certainly be related to the external pressures considered in the previous chapter, but they must also be seen in the context of a wider questioning of the institutions which had hitherto been thought to be self-defining as British. Such sceptical probing took time to emerge. The election of a Labour government in 1945 was widely and correctly seen at the time as a determined attempt to break with 'the past' in the shape of a 1930s identified primarily as a decade of unemployment, failure and deprivation. 'New Britain' should bear a strong resemblance to a 'new Jerusalem' – at least in England's green and pleasant land. The defeat of Churchill in the general election was taken to show a surprising and refreshing maturity on the part of a democratic electorate which had now 'come of age'. Churchill may have saved the nation but the electorate had concluded that he was not the man to take it into the future. It was time, rather, to translate wartime rhetoric into reality and the support Labour had gained was impressive. 'The people' had at last spoken.

In developing the 'welfare state' it was novelty and progress which Labour sought to emphasize as the National Health Service was unveiled. The coal industry and the railways were nationalized and the debate began as to how far 'nationalization' should be extended in what would probably be an irreversibly socialist Britain. Initially, there was a good deal of confidence in this British way of socialism. Once again it seemed that Britain had successfully married its old institutions with the demands of the age. There was a third way, exemplified in Britain, between what many Labour MPs regarded as the obnoxious character both of American capitalism and Soviet communism. In 1943, when he was working in the United States, the British economist James Meade wrote that amongst radical young Americans there was agreement that Britain had 'an absolutely unique opportunity of taking the moral lead in the matter of building the new society' if it developed and extended the planning which the Second World War had necessitated.[7]

This self-conscious commitment to 'building the new society' in Britain proved rather more complicated than Labour enthusiasts supposed likely. It remained a deep conviction, however, that 'new Britain' both could and should be created on the foundations laid in the five difficult postwar years. A glow of approval has normally been extended to the achievements of the Attlee government. It is a consensus which has been attacked by Corelli Barnett in particular – though his thesis has in turn been found unconvincing in detail.[8] Caught fatally between seductive images inherited from the past and

---

[7] S. Howson and D. Moggridge, eds, *The Wartime Diaries of Meade and Robbins* (London, 1991) p. 131.

[8] C. Barnett, *The Audit of War: The Illusion and Reality of Britain as a Great Nation* (London, 1986) and *The Lost Victory: British Dreams, British Realities 1945–1950*

13.2 A pocket guide to central London: Familiar soaring spires, tremulous towers and dominating domes jostle with new and sometimes evanescent arrivals on this Festival of Britain souvenir handkerchief (1951). Who is being taken for a ride on this metropolitan merry-go-round?

illusory dreams of a new future, he argues, the British government (in its widest sense) and the British people failed to take true stock of their domestic position. Basking in their proven capacity to 'adapt' and the evident stability of their institutions, as it seemed, Britain failed to change in

(London, 1995); J. Harris, 'Enterprise and Welfare States: A Comparative Perspective' *Transactions of the Royal Historical Society* Fifth Series 40 (1990); B. Brivati and H. Jones, eds, *What Difference Did the War Make?* (Leicester, 1993); P. Hennessy, *Never Again* (London, 1992); W.D. Rubinstein, *Capitalism, Culture and Decline in Britain 1750–1990* (London, 1993).

appropriate directions. It was necessary to strip out the past ruthlessly in order to make a success of the present. On mainland Europe, its peoples had no option but to start afresh since in almost every respect the immediate past was 'bad'. The British people certainly wanted change but did not need to banish the past.

The 'Festival of Britain' in 1951 neatly encapsulates this uncomfortable condition. It emerged from a suggestion from the Royal Society of Arts that there should be another Great Exhibition 100 years after that held in 1851. In this sense, it was anchored in the past, but it was also supposed to celebrate the 'modern' in architecture and design as victorious Britain reconstructed itself. Critics ever since have been divided in their evaluation of its success in this regard. Some, not very convincingly, argue that the Festival was the point at which Britain gave up living in the present, where it could not compete, and decided that it was more agreeable to live off the past if sufficient tourists could be persuaded to come and see the time warp in which the British people quaintly lived.[9]

'Socialist Britain' came to a speedy end in 1951. The return of a Conservative government under the aged Mr Churchill was hardly likely to stimulate an assault on ancient shibboleths. Electors in 1950 had been urged by the Conservatives to 'make Britain great again' by voting for them. Britain, it seemed, was to be 'set free' from the restrictions and controls which were synonymous with socialism and resume a path of development which accorded more with the genius of her people, or so it was alleged. In practice, however, the Conservatives accepted that there could be no simple return to a prewar past when they had last dominated government. Although the concept of 'consensus' has perhaps been overworked, it did appear that there was substantial common ground between the two main parties as Britain emerged from postwar austerity into greater prosperity. The Liberal Party seemed on a path to extinction and most of the former voters for the party came over to the Conservatives. Never had the 'two-party' system appeared more complete. Conservative electoral successes both in 1955 and 1959 gave the lie to the assumption, widely made in 1945, that the party could not adjust to the needs of a modern electorate. In power, as it turned out, from 1951 to 1964, under three different leaders, Churchill, Eden and Macmillan, the Conservatives set their stamp on the 1950s. They did not preside over a return to the past but once again showed pragmatism and adaptability. They were able to derive maximum benefit from a pervasive sense of returning prosperity. The contrast between the stability of British government and the volatility of French government under the Fourth Republic, for example, was frequently remarked upon by contemporary commentators. The virtues of continuity stood out.

[9] M. Banham and B. Hillier, *A Tonic to the Nation: The Festival of Britain 1951* (London, 1976).

Tired wreck of old glories?

By the early 1960s, however, as the memory of the war faded, a sense of pride in the past was frequently replaced in Britain by an iconoclastic temper. In part, this was a matter of generation. 'Angry young men' punctured what they saw as the seedy hypocrisies of British public life. The long imperial retreat could not happen fast enough for them. There was, they believed, another Britain eager to escape from the Britain of its institutions – Church, monarchy, *The Times*, the BBC, Oxford and Cambridge – all of which were held to constitute 'the Establishment'. Macmillan, as Prime Minister, occupied himself in sophisticated exercises in the 'management of decline' against a battery of witty assaults from youthful performers on stage and television who railed against the notions of Britain's greatness instilled in Spartan wartime classrooms. It was also the period when the inadequacies and inefficiencies of British industry could no longer be glossed over by pious reference to 'the splendid traditions of British workmanship'. The notion that Britain's pioneering industrialization somehow entitled her staple industries to a perpetual place in world commerce could scarcely be sustained.

Cumulatively, it was a mood which contributed to Labour's election victory in 1964. Harold Wilson appeared to offer 'modernity'. The sense had grown that, despite the achievements of British postwar reconstruction, the country had somehow failed to equip itself for the competitive world which existed twenty years after the end of the war. In market after market, with product after product, British exporters and manufacturers seemed to be losing ground to European and Asian competitors. It became increasingly apparent that excessive reliance had continued to be placed on the 'old' industries which had been the staple of Britain's past as a pioneering industrial country.

Not only that, but there appeared to be a cultural resistance to innovation and adaptation which extended beyond them. Perhaps significantly, American historians of Britain advanced this argument with most vigour. Decline seemed inexorable, and historians began to argue that it was not merely a phenomenon of the mid-twentieth century. At least in a relative sense, it might already have been going on for a century. There were even traces of the belief that if Britain had ever been the 'workshop of the world' it had only been for a very short period. Economic historians were not given to much optimism. Their analyses in part reflected the political/economic conflicts of the period. Britain appeared strike-bound and even, in the view of some, 'ungovernable'. So much for a historic reputation for stability and political pragmatism.

It was in these decades, too, that 'reform of parliament' moved onto the political agenda and the hallowed traditions of the Civil Service were subjected to scrutiny and debate. The Fulton Report which appeared in 1968 after two years of enquiry into the Civil Service cast doubt, amongst other things, on the notion of the 'generalist' and suggested that more specialist skills were required. There was, too, a rumbling discontent with the way in which Parliament operated. The 'Mother of Parliaments' no longer received the automatic approval which had been normal twenty years earlier. Nonetheless, despite debate and public discussion, radical change did not occur.

Some Labour and many Liberal commentators wished to go even further. It was alleged that Britain was suffering from institutional fatigue, a fatigue which even extended to its most hallowed inheritances.[10] The two-party system which had been so much lauded and which had been offered as an example to the world appeared to cramp the expression of diverse opinions unduly. The crude character of the British electoral system was contrasted unfavourably with the various forms of proportional representation which operated in most European countries. During the 1960s, when the fortunes of the Liberal Party revived to some extent, it could not succeed in translating its share of the vote into a substantial bloc of MPs. How could such an electoral system be 'fair'? Later, it was noted that the prolonged period of Conservative government after 1979 did not rest on a firm majority in Britain as a whole, though the Conservatives were the largest minority amongst the voters. What kind of 'representation' was this? Likewise, it was felt to be absurd that Britain had a second chamber which still rested fundamentally on the hereditary principle, despite the advent of 'life' peers. It was time to remove such an anomalous institution, though there was little agreement about what should replace it. It was acknowledged that the watchword of 'English liberty' as it had echoed down the centuries was not a sham, that tyranny and dictatorship had not blotted modern British history as it had the history of other European states, but nevertheless those states were now in advance of Britain in giving firm constitutional anchorage to human rights.[11]

The advent of the Thatcher governments after 1979 produced a paradoxical situation. In some measure Mrs Thatcher accepted the diagnoses of those who argued that Britain was stuck in the past without a clear vision of the future. In a general sense, a Conservative Party does aim to conserve what are held to be the essential structures and institutions underpinning na-

---

[10] And some of those inheritances were thought to be hollow or even sinister. There was much discussion from this period, subsequently reflected in historiography, on 'control' and 'secrecy' perceived to be as much characteristic of 'Britishness' as 'liberty'. See, for example, C. Townshend, *Making the Peace: Public Order and Public Security in Modern Britain* (Oxford, 1993); D. Feldman, *Civil Liberties and Human Rights in England and Wales* (Oxford, 1992); L. Lustgarten and I. Leigh, *In from the Cold: National Security and Parliamentary Democracy* (Oxford, 1994); B. Porter, *Plots and Paranoia: A History of Political Espionage in Britain, 1790–1988* (London, 1992); A. Simpson, *In the Highest Degree Odious: Detention without Trial in Wartime Britain* (Oxford, 1993).

[11] J. and A. Lively, *Democracy in Britain: A Reader* (Oxford, 1994); A. Wright, *Citizens and Subjects: An Essay on British Politics* (London, 1993).

tional life. Mrs Thatcher's Conservatism was not very conservative. Indeed, she seemed to have a definite aversion to the 'great institutions', whether the BBC, the Inns of Court, the Foreign and Commonwealth Office or the ancient universities. She was not in office to manage decline and her agenda necessarily entailed challenges to existing shibboleths. 'Cart-horses' were not exclusively located in trade union stables. Yet at the same time, she made potent use of the language of patriotism, most notably during the Falkland Islands crisis. She relished at least certain aspects of the national past, even as she tried to tilt the country in a new direction. She appealed sometimes to 'Victorian values' and appeared to believe that it was possible to return to the past. She was, of course, the first woman Prime Minister in British history, yet she had scant interest in what might be called a feminist agenda. A Methodist by origin, she displayed Christian conviction but found herself at loggerheads with the leaders of the main churches in Britain.

Church and Crown

There was objection to the continuance of 'Establishment' in religion in both England and, in a different form, in Scotland. The Established Churches, it was argued, had ceased to be the 'churches of the people' and it was wrong that this fiction should continue to receive constitutional sanction. 'Britain' had detached itself from its Christian past and neither Protestantism nor even Christianity itself could now serve as a source of common identity. It was indeed recognized within the churches that their position within society was changing rapidly. It is always difficult to give precision to 'church membership', but with the exception, for a time, of the Roman Catholic Church, other Christian churches suffered losses. There were more Roman Catholics than active Anglicans, though the Church of England could still be said to be the Church from which the English stayed away but still recognized as 'theirs' for the purpose of rites of passage. The strength of the Roman Catholic Church now made it impossible to think in terms of a simple identification of Britain as 'Protestant'. The fact that it had largely come into the mainstream of British life, however, did mean that it too began to suffer some erosion of support. Its previous status as a clear sub-culture was becoming blurred. By the late 1980s, those who acknowledged a specific church allegiance amounted to perhaps 15 per cent of the population – England being more 'secular' than either Scotland or Wales, though decline in attendance was also being recorded in the latter countries. It did look, therefore, that the churches were being pushed to the margin, at least as compared with the prominence given to theological and ecclesiastical debates in previous centuries which have required attention in this book. It was a pattern much closer to what was happening in Western Europe as a whole than in the

United States. In this respect, at least, the 'European' character of Britain was evident. Whether this amounted to 'secularization' remains contentious because relatively high levels of belief existed alongside low levels of practice. And, if the churches were pushed to the margin, they were still able to mount a sustained critique of government policy during the period when Mrs Thatcher was Prime Minister.[12]

In England, though less so in Scotland and Wales, the ecumenical movement made considerable progress. Differences between Anglicans, Roman Catholics and the Free Churches remained but there was far greater mutual understanding and respect than had been apparent in the past. The Free Churches were in a generally weaker condition and had long abandoned the notion that they might overtake the Established Church. It appeared to many church leaders that only by working together could they meet the challenges posed by indifference or hostility in late-twentieth-century Britain. Even so, there was no unanimity about the extent to which Christians should extricate themselves from their own past understandings of either their faith or of aspects of church order. The failure of the churches to give a 'clear lead', particularly on family issues and questions of individual personal morality, aroused the ire of sections of the Conservative Party in particular. It could certainly no longer be said, as it could have been plausibly maintained even half a century earlier, that the Church of England had a close alignment with the Tory Party. Bishops replied that they were trying to take stock of social change in a way that preserved Christian insights but did not perpetuate the past uncritically. The issue of women priests in the Church of England was one such example. Opponents of female ordination argued that there was no past precedent for such a step, a fact which did not in itself alarm supporters.

The pattern of immigration, alluded to earlier in this chapter, also brought about a religious pluralism on a scale without precedent in previous British history. Precision remains difficult, but besides the much more long-standing Jewish community there now existed Hindu, Sikh, Buddhist and above all Islamic communities. It was the size of the last-mentioned, over 1 million, which made it a very significant aspect of British life. The existence of these different communities raised profound issues for the nature of 'Britain'. The surface of British life still remained formally Christian but could the beliefs and assumptions of different religions be 'incorporated' into Britishness? To this there was no clear answer. The past had seen a struggle for 'religious liberty' but, in an old conundrum, how far could liberty be extended to

---

[12] A.D. Gilbert, *The Making of Post-Christian Britain* (London, 1980); G. Davie, *Religion in Britain since 1945: Believing without Belonging* (Oxford, 1994); K.N. Medhurst and G. Moyser, eds, *Church and Politics in a Secular Age* (Oxford, 1988); M. Cowling, *Religion and Public Doctrine in Modern England* (Cambridge, 1980); G. Davie, ' "An Ordinary God": The Paradox of Religion in Contemporary Britain', *British Journal of Sociology* 41 (Sept. 1990).

groups or bodies which did not themselves accept 'toleration' as a desirable goal in itself? Which was more appalling, the offence against religious faith as evidenced by Rushdie's novel *The Satanic Verses* or the threats against Rushdie himself? Was a condition being reached in which all faiths were in some sense united, with a future king as 'defender of the faiths', in opposition to the rampant hedonism and secularity of the late twentieth century? Or, put another way, was it not the case that the majority in Britain had shaken off the shackles of a religious past? The task, therefore, was to forge a new social morality devoid of religious connotations, though it was not clear how this could be achieved. It would be a society, perhaps already was a society, which could not relate to the Bible or the Koran as living texts from the past.

In the context of the developments that have already been mentioned it would have been surprising if the monarchy had emerged unscathed. The coronation of Elizabeth II in 1953 was accompanied by an upsurge of royalist sentiment – a new Elizabethan age was imminent. It was a mood which did not endure for very long. In the thought of the 1960s what Britain needed was not a reminder of continuity but a symbol of change. There followed a period of spasmodic reflection on the role of the Crown. The Conservative Party invented for itself a mechanism for selecting its leader and thus removed one residual role for the monarch. By 1977, when the Jubilee celebrations took place, it appeared that there was an affectionate if distant relationship between queen and people. Few would have then guessed that within a decade the monarchy would be looked at in a very different spirit. The role of the Crown as an inspiring example of 'family values', carefully cultivated since the late 1930s, collapsed. The marriages of three of the queen's children failed. Questions were increasingly asked about the royal finances. Although it would be wrong to place too much reliance on fickle opinion polls in the early 1990s, they did suggest that a dramatic change had taken place, with perhaps only a quarter of the population subscribing to the view that monarchy was 'something to be proud of'. The queen herself acknowledged that 1992 had been her 'annus horribilis'. It appeared that around 10 per cent of the population aggressively wanted the monarchy to end. Quite apart from the conduct of individuals, the monarchy was arguably a victim of the uncertainties now surrounding 'Britishness'. It was no longer self-evident that the kind of past which the monarchy inescapably transmitted was any longer attractive or viable. Even so, despite all the upheavals surrounding individual members of the royal family, there was little doubt that the monarchy would continue, though an heir to the throne who was divorced constituted a new development.[13]

---

[13] T. Nairn, *The Enchanted Glass: Britain and its Monarchy* (London, 1988); K. Harris, *The Queen* (London, 1994); M. Charlot, ed., *The Monarchy in Britain in the 20th Century* (Paris, 1993).

Regions and nations

Constitutional discussion at the end of the twentieth century sometimes had an even more extended dimension. Some academics and politicians wanted to go back into a more distant British past as they sketched their plans for the future. In their opinion, 'Britain' had come to the end of its useful life. To a degree only remotely conceivable in 1945, regional/national issues had moved to the fore. By the 1960s, both in Scotland and Wales, national parties, hitherto miniscule, had obtained considerable prominence and some parliamentary seats at Westminster. The 'break-up' of Britain moved onto the political agenda. Commentators began to suggest that 'Britain' was a construct which related to a world now gone and irrecoverable. It had at least to be recognized that 'Britain' was a multinational state and its administrative and governmental structures should be fashioned accordingly. In the 1960s Wales 'caught up' Scotland with the establishment of the office of Secretary of State for Wales with a seat in the Cabinet. Cardiff had at length been recognized a few years earlier as the capital of Wales and was host to an expanding Welsh Office. By the later 1970s, the air was thick with talk of devolution, though in the end, when put to a referendum in 1979, the schemes proposed for Scotland and Wales failed, in the case of Wales comprehensively.

After a further decade, there was more talk of devolution. The European framework had come to seem particularly attractive in Scotland and Wales and both the Scottish National Party and Plaid Cymru looked for 'Independence in Europe', bypassing the incubus which 'Britain' and its remote London-based Parliament was perceived in some quarters to have become. It was better, some supposed, to deal directly with Brussels. It was held to be easier for Scotland and Wales to be inhabited by 'Scottish Europeans' and 'Welsh Europeans' respectively than it was for England to be inhabited by 'English Europeans'. In contrast to England where three parties struggled for support, the politics of Scotland and Wales became firmly 'four-party' during these decades. It was difficult, however, to pin down precisely what constitutional change was desired. Support for the Scottish National Party fluctuated very considerably in the quarter of a century after 1970 and it found it hard going to consolidate any position in Scotland's major urban centres. In Wales, too, the support for Plaid Cymru was heavily concentrated in western Welsh-speaking constituencies. In both countries, the Labour Party became ever more dominant. In 1955, for example, the Conservatives held more seats in Scotland than Labour, whereas in 1992 Labour held more than four times the Conservative number. In Wales, likewise, Labour held more than four times the number held by the Conservatives. There had been occasions in the past when a non-Conservative government had been elected in Britain which had failed to win a majority of seats in England. However, the Conservative domination of British politics after 1979 increased a sense of frustration outside England. Scotland and Wales seemed doomed to have to live under policies for which they had not voted. The 'break-up of Britain' seemed the only way to escape from this position since Labour seemed unlikely to break the ascendancy of Mrs Thatcher.[14]

The continuing Labour ascendancy outside England, however, posed problems for the party. The devolution proposals which Labour had unavailingly championed in the late 1970s had been opposed by some prominent Labour figures. Some commentators could see no logic in a situation whereby Scottish MPs could continue to vote at Westminster on domestic matters relating to England whereas English MPs would not be able to vote on domestic matters in Scotland which had been devolved to a Scottish Assembly – shades of the 'Irish question' 100 years earlier. There was also some resentment in the north of England in particular that its problems of industrial regeneration were being neglected. As northerners perceived it, why should Scotland receive disproportionate attention and assistance? It seemed an extraordinary situation to some that it was only in Scotland and Wales that a referendum was held on schemes which would inevitably impact on the governance of Britain as a whole. Was there no room for an English referendum?

In the event, since nothing happened, English regional complaints did not come to any particular focus, but they continued to exist. Local government in Britain was reformed in the mid-1970s, allegedly to promote new units which would more efficiently deliver services. In the process, county boundaries and identities which had existed for many centuries were swept aside. To seek to preserve them was regarded as little more than antiquarianism. Twenty years later, however, it was concluded that further revision was needed. Many of the new structures were abandoned in a return to a much older past. It became evident that local government, particularly in England, was in crisis. Central government, confronted by what it regarded as profligate local spending, 'rate-capped' local authorities. Their freedom to initiate and innovate was further restricted in a context where they were in any case dependent upon 'rate support' from central government. It seemed increasingly difficult to know what local government was for and it often ceased to interest electors locally.

Even so, it was clear that the regions of England – difficult though they were to define – did have particular identifiable needs and aspirations. However, they lacked the regional governmental organs which existed in most other countries in the European Union. Yet, as has been noted in earlier chapters, England's historic cohesion ran counter to creation of effective regional bodies. What gave potency to the Scottish and Welsh claims, despite

---

[14] K. Robbins, 'State and Nation in the United Kingdom since 1945' in K. Robbins, *History, Religion and Identity in Modern Britain* (London, 1993); S. Haseler, *The End of the House of Windsor* (London, 1993).

continuing internal differences, was an appeal to a national past. No English region could make an effective appeal on this ground. It was against this rock that the redefinition of Britain in the late twentieth century stumbled. Once again, if Britain were to be 'federalized' into England, Scotland and Wales, England was the awkward element. The Labour Party, in the mid-1990s, in the context of renewed schemes for devolution in Scotland and Wales, advanced very unspecific notions of regional government in England.

There was, therefore, a sense that something needed to be done to retain unity but also to promote diversity, but no unanimity as to what that reconstruction should be. On the one hand, some critics argued that the 'traditions' of Britain should not so much be secured as shattered. Centralization of the government of Britain was not something to be proud of but something to be changed as quickly as possible, so that the regions and local authorities could take their proper place in the 'regional Europe' that beckoned. It was therefore necessary not to look merely at a couple of centuries of the British past but to see it in the kind of *longue durée* encompassed in this book. Structures would have to be evolved in the future which would truly give scope for all the peoples of Britain, both 'ancient' and 'modern'. A 'new Britain' would match a 'new Europe'. The result would be a very different structure not only for Britain but for Europe as a whole from the continent of 'nation-states' which had emerged from the nineteenth century.[15]

In other quarters, however, such visions and projects seemed dangerously and naïvely divisive. Centralization was not the result of some malign strategy but the inevitable outcome of the demand that there should be some semblance of common standards and common achievements throughout the United Kingdom. It was unduly starry-eyed to suggest that local authorities were full of energetic and visionary councillors. The level of local competence, it was suggested, left no alternative but to establish what became known as 'Quangos' composed, at least allegedly, of men and women with a proven capacity who could take forward policies energetically and consistently.

There was also some anxiety because, since the early 1970s, the United Kingdom had witnessed bloodshed and violence in Northern Ireland. The separate Northern Ireland Parliament was abolished by the British government and regional 'Home Rule' came to an end. The 'province' seemed still to be divided into two 'communities' locked in a conflict without end. Central to that conflict was the perception of identity – Protestant/Catholic, British/Irish – which has been discussed earlier. How could cultural and religious differences be reconciled, or at least be accommodated, within a common political structure which had sufficient acceptance to make it viable? Those

---

[15] W. Wallace, *The Transformation of Western Europe* (London, 1990); C. Harvie, *The Rise of Regional Europe* (London, 1994); A. Hannequart, *Economic and Social Cohesion in Europe* (London, 1992).

with a pessimistic turn of mind saw both 'Britain' and Northern Ireland becoming 'Balkanized'. The British Isles would become locked into internal inter-regional and inter-national disputes which would certainly be difficult to cope with and which might end in violence. The example of the dissolution of Yugoslavia was frequently – perhaps extravagantly – alluded to. In a quarter of a century of violence 'solution' after 'solution' was attempted.

By the mid-1990s as efforts were once again directed to promoting a 'peace process', the issue of 'identity' could still not be avoided, whatever progress had been made towards better understanding. In the face of this protracted crisis, attitudes in mainland Britain fluctuated between total commitment to that majority in Ulster which wished to remain in the Union and the view that the question could only be solved by 'troops out'. Some took the view that what Northern Ireland needed was not the mythical 'Britain' which still held such sway in the province but Britain as it actually existed. A Northern Ireland which was fully and unequivocally integrated in the United Kingdom would, paradoxically, be less 'British' than the majority community supposed. Others wished simply to see Britain's 'Irish question' finally laid to rest. The 'British' of Northern Ireland should be made to feel uncomfortable and alienated from Britain and left with no doubt that they should make whatever accommodation they could with the Republic of Ireland. Yet others, noting the improved relations between Britain and the Irish Republic, optimistically believed that there was scope for some kind of 'Council of the British Isles' which would be a more sensible structure than the existing governmental framework. Some English opinion never professed to understand the mindset of Protestant Ulstermen. What went on in Northern Ireland was a Scottish-Irish affair devoid of that conciliation and compromise which they liked to suppose was essentially English.[16]

By the mid-1990s all the political parties, except the Conservatives, now supported the 'restructuring' of Britain and supposed that Northern Ireland constituted a 'special case' with no bearing on devolved government as such. The Conservative government, weak though it was in parliamentary seats in both Wales and Scotland, still argued strongly that Britain, as a well-established coherent and integrated country, though diverse in important respects, was being undersold. John Major, as Prime Minister, spoke powerfully on this theme during the 1992 general election and subsequently.[17] It

---

[16] S. Bruce, *The Edge of the Union: The Ulster Loyalist Political Vision* (Oxford, 1994); J. Fulton, *The Tragedy of Belief: Division, Politics and Religion in Ireland* (Oxford, 1991); M. Cunningham, *British Government Policy in Northern Ireland 1969–1989* (London, 1991); J. McGarry and B. O'Leary, *Explaining Northern Ireland* (Oxford, 1995); D. Keogh and M. Haltzel, eds, *Northern Ireland the Politics of Reconciliation* (Cambridge, 1993). It scarcely needs to be added that the explanations differ strongly.

[17] In an echo of Labour leader Gaitskell's claim in 1962 that British membership of the 'Common Market' would mean 'the end of Britain as an independent nation

13.3 Fall-out: Bombs planted by the IRA had destroyed buildings in various British cities during the course of its campaign through the 1980s and 1990s, with inevitable casualties. The bombing of central Manchester in June 1996 (above) had devastating consequences. In 1867 there had been Fenian acts of terrorism in Great Britain, amongst which had been the shooting of an unarmed police sergeant in Manchester. The long fuse of the 'Irish Question' continued to extend into the life of Britain.

was not merely, as some supposed, the wreck of old glories, but it was a positive benefit to all its peoples. It would be folly to undo the work of centuries and unravel the consolidation of Britain – even though, in a party sense, it would benefit the Conservatives, who could aspire to be a permanent governing party in England. There was indeed some evidence that a sense of 'Englishness' was waxing stronger. It was reported, for example, that during the 'Euro'96' football championship held in England, English supporters purchased flags of St George – and spurned the Union Jack – on an unprecedented scale. It was England, not Britain, that was being supported. The Church of England was also reported to be taking steps to give St George a status in its calendar which he had not previously been accorded. There seemed to be a cry from the terraces, if not yet from Downing Street, that if Scotland and Wales wished to go their own way they should be encouraged to do so. England no longer bothered about Britain.

state, the end of a thousand years of history', Prime Minister Major in October 1996 told his Conservative party conference that Labour's constitutional plans 'would vandalise nearly 1,000 years of British history'. Neither man's grasp of 'British history' seems very firm. P.M. Williams, *Hugh Gaitskell* (London, 1979) pp. 734–5; *Daily Telegraph*, 12 October 1996.

The outcome of the 1997 general election was not only a victory for 'New Labour' but seemed likely to bring about that 'New Britain' which had been mooted, but never accomplished, for several decades. The new government embarked upon its proposals, to be initially placed before the electorate in referendums in Scotland and Wales respectively, to establish a Parliament and an Assembly in those two countries. The very large Labour parliamentary majority seemed to ensure that these schemes would go ahead and thus create a quite new framework for the governance of Britain. These arrangements in Scotland and Wales were, however, conceived and advocated not as a means of 'dissolving' Great Britain but of bringing government closer to the people in 'domestic' matters. Neither the Scottish National Party nor Plaid Cymru made significant electoral breakthroughs beyond their existing bases when they advocated 'independence in Europe'. For their part, critics of impending change wondered whether such 'lopsided' devolution was unstainable. the descent down the slippery path towards the break-up of Britain had begun. They therefore either advocated movement to a full-bodied 'Federal Britain' or the maintenance of the status quo. It remained to be seen whether any kind of English regional government would emerge which would allow 'the English' their own voice. What was most striking, however, was the parliamentary elimination of the Conservative Party, the party most committed to 'Union' from both Scotland and Wales. The party which had governed Britain since 1979 was reduced (in parliamentary terms) to being solely an English political party for the first time in its history – and it was not even a majority in England. It was perhaps this outcome, as much as the creation of new institutions in Scotland and Wales, which had most significance for the way in which Britain might be conceived and function in the future.

The referendum on the Labour government's proposals to establish a Scottish Parliament was held in September 1997. The turn-out was 60.1 per cent of the Scottish electorate. Three-quarters of those voting (74.3 per cent) were in favour and 63.5 per cent supported equipping it with tax-varying powers. All 32 local authority areas in Scotland voted strongly in favour of a parliament. Only Orkney, and Dumfries and Galloway, voted against tax-varying powers. This outcome was praised by the Prime Minister as good for Scotland and good for the UK (he did not use the word Britain). Westminster would continue to be responsible for foreign affairs, defence and national security, and macro-economic and fiscal matters. In other respects, however, Scotland would govern itself internally. The government maintained that 'Scotland would remain firmly part of the United Kingdom' but the Scottish National Party declared that the old system had been fundamentally breached. It would push for independence (albeit circumscribed by the European Union), hopefully to be achieved before the year 2007 (three hundred years after the Act of Union). Britain would be dead.

The outcome of the referendum in Wales, however, was far less clear-cut. There was a turn-out of only 50 per cent of the Welsh electorate and the majority in favour of the proposed Welsh Assembly (which would have substantially less authority than the Scottish Parliament) was only 0.3 per cent. Only a quarter of the Welsh electorate therefore positively backed the proposals. Cardiff, the capital city, voted against the Assembly and, taking Wales as a whole, the local authority areas divided evenly between the 'Yes' and the 'No' camps. Parts of Wales were strongly in favour while other parts were strongly against.

In the light of these outcomes, it remained to be seen how the government would attempt to tackle 'accountability' in the ill-defined 'regions' of England. It also remained to be seen, in longer perspective, whether what was taking place was indeed the decentralization of a united country or its disintegration.

The matter of Britain, in short, after 2,000 years, was still under debate. One century ago, in 1897, the then Bishop of London, with his historian's mind, took to musing about his country which he called 'England', though he was reflecting on the British Empire. It seemed to him that England was 'the most artificial of states'. He feared that a single disaster might crush her, as Athens had been crushed. Coal might run out or there could be a single devastating defeat at sea. He thought that if such an artificial fabric could escape a shock of some kind for thirty years that would be enough. The colonies would have navies of their own and England would gradually be able to retire. She would be the mother country visited by her rich children anxious to spend their money. There would be no great industries in England but she would be 'the intellectual centre of a vast empire, radiating culture to its fullest limits'.[18] It was that view that he was endeavouring to impress upon the British statesmen of his acquaintance. He had to confess, however, that when asked to find a professor of history to go out to a colonial university he could not get anybody to go! Which historian had a better grasp of past, present and future?

The future of Britain still remains obscure and its structure may yet be subjected to fresh stresses and strains, but it is scarcely conceivable that its history, as it has evolved over some 2,000 years, will not continue to have a powerful influence over the minds of the people who now inhabit these islands. Beyond that, a mere historian cannot with confidence go.

---

[18] L. Creighton, *Life and Letters of Mandell Creighton* (London, 1913) p. 499; W. Krieger, 'Die Britische Krise in Historischer Perspektive'. *Historische Zeitschrift* 247 (1988).

Bibliography

A complete bibliography of British history over two millennia to accompany a book of this kind is clearly impossible. Instead, this essay highlights some of the books and articles which have been used, with an emphasis on recent publication. Students of twentieth-century Britain are directed to K. Robbins, *Bibliography of British History 1914–1989* (Oxford, 1996) which provides a comprehensive guide. C. Cook and J. Stevenson, *The Longman Handbook of Modern British History 1714–1987* (3rd edn, London, 1996) contains a wealth of useful information.

The Addison Wesley Longman series *Foundations of Modern Britain*, edited by the late Geoffrey Holmes, covers the centuries from 1370 to 1992 in six volumes and provides in each case text, chronology, bibliography and a compendium of information. The volumes are J. Thomson, *The Transformation of Medieval England 1370–1529* (London, 1983); A. Smith, *The Emergence of a Nation State: The Commonwealth of England 1529–1660* (2nd edn, London, 1996); G. Holmes, *The Making of a Great Power: Late Stuart and early Georgian Britain 1660–1772* (London, 1993); G. Holmes and D. Szechi, *The Age of Oligarchy: Pre-industrial Britain 1722–1783* (London, 1993); E. Evans, *The Forging of the Modern State: Early Industrial Britain 1783–1870* (2nd edn London, 1995), K. Robbins, *The Eclipse of a Great Power: Modern Britain 1870–1992* (2nd edn, London, 1994). These books should lead the reader to other items which are relevant to the theme of this book.

Another Addison Wesley Longman series, *A Regional History of England*, edited by B. Cunliffe and D. Hey, is also recommended. It identifies ten 'regions' of England and the volumes cover pre- and post-1000 respectively.

The structure of this bibliographical essay follows the chapter sequence of the book closely, though some of the material, while listed in one section only, inevitably has relevance to more than one chapter. Items specifically referred to in the reference notes are only occasionally incorporated in this guide to further reading.

General

This initial section introduces works of comparable span and books which tackle issues of structure and methodology in writing the history of 'Great Britain'.

J. Black, *A History of the British Isles* (London, 1996) appeared after this book was completed. H. Kearney, *The British Isles: A History of Four Nations* (Cambridge, 1989) ranges from pre-Roman times to the twentieth century. R. Tompson, *The Atlantic Archipelago: A Political History of the British Isles* (Lewiston/Queenston, 1986) has a comparable scope. The contributors to A. Grant and K.J. Stringer, *Uniting the Kingdom: The Making of British History* (London, 1995), among them the present author, discuss both general and specific issues. D. Cannadine's opening chapter points to changing historiographical emphases, building on his other stimulating article 'British History: Past, Present – and Future?' *Past and Present* 116 (1987). See also P. R. Coss, W. Lamont and N. Evans, 'Debate: British History: Past, Present – and Future?', *Past and Present* 119 (1988). There is also a contribution from J.G. A. Pocock, whose two earlier articles raised important questions and have had a lasting impact: 'British History: A Plea for a New Subject', *Journal of Modern History* xlvii (1975) and 'The Limits and Divisions of British History: In Search of the Unknown Subject', *American Historical Review*, lxxxvii (1982).

Ronald G. Asch, ed., *Three Nations – A Common History? England, Scotland, Ireland and British History c. 1600–1920* (Bochum, 1993) and N. Evans, ed., *National Identity in the British Isles* (Harlech, 1989) are collections of articles which also relate to this theme. C. Björn, A. Grant and K.J. Stringer edited two volumes *Social and Political Identities in Western Europe* (Copenhagen, 1994) and *Nations, Nationalism and Patriotism in the European Past* (Copenhagen, 1994) which contain substantial contributions on aspects of British history. H. Schulze, *States, Nations and Nationalism: From the Middle Ages to the Present* (Oxford, 1996) also provides a helpful comparative perspective. J.B. Duroselle, *Europe: A History of its Peoples* (London, 1990) places 'Britain' in 'Europe'. The present author was the British member of an international committee which advised Professor Duroselle. M. Mann, ed., *The Rise and Decline of the Nation State* (Oxford, 1990) raises general issues.

D. Lowenthal, *The Past is a Foreign Country* (Cambridge, 1985), P. Wright, *On Living in an Old Country* (London, 1985), D. Horne, *The Great Museum* (London, 1984), D. Hooson, ed., *Geography and National Identity* (Oxford, 1994), J. Habermas, *The Past as Future* (Oxford, 1994) W. Connor *Ethnonationalism: The Quest for Understanding* (Princeton, 1993) W. Bloom, *Personal Identity, National Identity and International Relations* (Cambridge, 1990) and G. Tindall, *Countries of the Mind: The Meaning of Place to Writers* (London, 1991) all offer, in their different ways, stimulating reflections on issues which constantly recur in this book.

S. Gilley and W.J. Sheils, eds, *A History of Religion in Britain: Practice and Belief from the Pre-Roman Times to the Present* (Oxford, 1994), D. Chandler, ed., *The Oxford Illustrated History of the British Army* (Oxford, 1994), T. Mason, ed., *Sport in Britain: A Social History* (Cambridge, 1989), and F. McLynn, *Invasion: From the Armada to Hitler, 1588–1945* (London, 1987) provide useful introductions to their respective topics across substantial periods.

Two contrasting volumes attempt national 'audits': Sir Geoffrey Elton's *The English* (Oxford, 1992) is the work of an outsider/insider, while R. Porter, ed., *Myths of the English* (Cambridge, 1993) ranges from Guy Fawkes' Night to the operas of Gilbert and Sullivan. J.B. Priestley, *English Journey* (London, 1934) and A.G. Macdonell, *England, their England* (London, 1933) are interesting but rather different contemporary 'portraits'. K. Tidrick, *Empire and the English Character* (London, 1992) looks at the English 'out of area'. G.A. Williams, *When was Wales? A History of the Welsh* (London, 1985) perhaps answers his question. M. Lynch, *Scotland: A New History* (London, 1991) is the best recent single-volume account. F. Musgrove tackles a 'region' in *The North of England: A History from Roman Times to the Present* (Oxford, 1990). K. Robbins, 'Varieties of Britishness' in M. Crozier, ed., *Cultural Traditions in Northern Ireland* (Belfast, 1989) was originally a lecture given in Northern Ireland. R. Dahrendorf, *On Britain* (London, 1982) presents the reflections of another outsider/insider.

Prologue: ingredients assembled and framework established

Earlier approaches to 'national character' can be traced in the writings of M. Creighton, *The English National Character* (London, 1896), E. Barker, *National Character* (London, 1927) and A. Bryant, *The National Character* (London, 1934). Their tone can be contrasted with R. Porter, ed., *Myths of the English* (Cambridge, 1993), E.J. Hobsbawm and T.O. Ranger, eds, *The Invention of Tradition* (Cambridge, 1981) and R. Samuel, ed., *Patriotism: The Making and Unmaking of British National Identity* (London, 1989). The volume by various hands, *British Life and Thought* (London, 1941) can be intriguingly compared with J. Randle, *Understanding Britain: A History of the British People and their Culture* (Oxford, 1981). R. Rose, *The United Kingdom as a Multi-National State* (Glasgow, 1970) and *Understanding the United Kingdom: The Territorial Dimension in Government* (London, 1970) are political analyses. Anthony P. Cohen, ed., *Symbolizing Boundaries: Identity and Diversity in British Cultures* (Manchester, 1986) and B. Anderson, *Imagined Communities: Reflections on the Origin and Spread of Nationalism* (London, 1983) offer sociological and philosophical insight.

P. Sahlins, *Boundaries: The Making of France and Spain in the Pyrenees* (Berkeley, 1989) has not as yet stimulated a comparable comprehensive study by a historian of boundaries within Britain, though see R.R. Davies, 'Frontier Arrangements in Fragmented Societies: Ireland and Wales' in R. Bartlett and A. MacKay, eds, *Medieval Frontier Societies* (Oxford, 1989) and D. Hay, 'England, Scotland and Europe: The Problem of the Frontier', *Transactions of the Royal Historical Society* Fifth Series 25 (1975). A. Goodman, ed., *War and Border Societies in the Middle Ages* (Gloucester, 1992), S.R.J. Woodell, ed., *The English Landscape: Past, Present and Future* (Oxford, 1985) and M. Reed, *The Landscape of Britain* (London, 1990) are examples of work designed to make historians and geographers 'see' landscape in new ways. The concept of 'core' and 'periphery' has likewise proved fruitful for both geographers and historians. For Cornwall, see the general study by P. Payton, *The Making of Modern Cornwall* (Redruth, 1992) J. Hatcher, *Rural Economy and Society in the Duchy of Cornwall 1300–1500* (Cambridge, 1970) and A.L. Rowse, *Tudor Cornwall* (London, 1941).

Saxons and Scandinavians can be approached through S. Bassett, ed., *The Origins of Anglo-Saxon Kingdoms* (Leicester, 1989). There are influential assessments in H.R. Loyn, *The Vikings in Britain* (London, 1977), *The Making of the English Nation: From the Anglo-Saxons to Edward I* (London, 1991), *Anglo-Saxon England and the Norman Conquest* (London, 1991) and *Society and Peoples: Studies in the History of England and Wales c. 600–1200* (London, 1992), P. Stafford, *Unification and Conquest* (London, 1989) and A.P. Smyth, *Scandinavian Kings in the British Isles 850–80* (Oxford, 1977). *Bede's Ecclesiastical History of the English People* has been freshly edited by B. Colgrave and R. Mynors (Oxford, 1992 edn). Smyth's *King Alfred the Great* (Oxford, 1995) is contentious. J. Campbell, *Essays in Anglo-Saxon History* (London, 1986) sets a high standard.

The Normans are best approached through D.R. Bates, *Normandy before 1066* (London, 1982), *William I* (London, 1989) and the volume he edited with A. Curry, *England and Normandy in the Middle Ages* (London, 1994). R.H.C. Davis, *The Normans and their Myth* (London, 1976) looks further afield. A specific episode is treated in W.E. Kapelle, *The Norman Conquest of the North: The Region and its Transformation 1000–1135* (London, 1980). A. Williams considers *The English and the Norman Conquest* (Woodbridge, 1995) as does B. Golding, *The Normans in England 1066–1100* (London, 1993).

Linguistic matters are considered in the following: R. McKitterick, ed., *The Uses of Literacy in Early Medieval Europe* (Cambridge, 1990), R.M. Hogg, ed., *The Cambridge History of the English Language*, i (Cambridge, 1992), S. Hussey, 'Nationalism and Language in England, c.1300–1500' in Björn, Grant and Stringer, *Nations, Nationalism and Patriotism in the European Past*. M.T. Clanchy, *From Memory to Written Record: England 1066–1307* (London, 1979) and N. Orme, 'Lay Literacy in England, 1100–1300' in

A. Haverkamp and H. Vollrath, *England and Germany in the High Middle Ages* (London/Oxford, 1996). P. Burke and R. Porter, eds, *Language, Self and Society: A Social History of Language* (Oxford, 1991) raise issues which span periods. R. McCrum, W. Cran and R. MacNeil, *The Story of English* (London, 1986) and D. Crystal, *The English Language* (Harmondsworth, 1988) likewise cover a long span.

For Scotland, see D. Brown, 'When did Scotland become Scotland?' *History Today* (Oct. 1996), A.A.M. Duncan, *Scotland: The Making of the Kingdom* (Edinburgh, 1975), A.P. Smyth, *Warlords and Holy Men: Scotland AD 80–1000 (London, 1984)*, G.W.S. Barrow, *The Anglo- Norman Era in Scottish History* (Oxford, 1980) and *The Kingdom of the Scots: Government, Church and Society from the Eleventh to the Fourteenth Century* (London, 1973). Anglo-Scottish relations are discussed in R.A. Mason, ed., *Scotland and England 1286–1815* (Edinburgh, 1987).

M. Prestwich, *Edward I* (London, 1988) is standard. His 'La "France Anglaise" au Moyen Age' in *Tome 1 des Actes du III Congrès National des Societés Savantes, Poitiers, 1986* (Paris, 1986) can be interestingly compared with R. Frame, ' "Les Engleys Nées en Irelande": The English Political Identity in Medieval Ireland', *Transactions of the Royal Historical Society* Sixth Series 3 (1993). A. Curry tackles *The Hundred Years War* (London, 1993).

For Wales, see R.R. Davies, *Conquest, Coexistence and Change: Wales, 1066–1415* (Oxford/Cardiff, 1987), *Dominion and Conquest: The Experience of Ireland, Scotland and Wales, 1100–1300* (Cambridge, 1990), *The Revolt of Owain Glyn Dŵr* (Oxford, 1995) and ed., *The British Isles 1100–1500: Comparisons, Contrasts and Connexions* (Edinburgh, 1988). G. Williams, *Recovery, Reorientation and Reformation: Wales c.1415–1642* (Oxford/Cardiff, 1987) and S. Chrimes, *Henry VII* (London, 1972) take the story forward.

Rome and its aftermath can be approached through M. Millett, *The Romanization of Britain* (Cambridge, 1990), A.S.E. Cleary, *The Ending of Roman Britain* (London, 1989) and C.J. Arnold, *Roman Britain to Saxon England* (London, 1984).

C. Thomas illumines *Celtic Britain* (London, 1986) but there is a warning about the term 'Celtic' in M. Chapman, *The Celts: The Construction of a Myth* (London, 1992). D. Dumville, *The Celts* (Oxford, 1991) presents one interpretation. R. Frame, *The Political Development of the British Isles 1100–1400* (Oxford, 1900) looks at things in the round, and R. Bartlett, *The Making of Europe: Conquest, Colonization and Cultural Change 950–1350* (London, 1993) provides a different comparative perspective.

Religious and ecclesiastical matters can be approached through R. Hutton, *The Pagan Religions of the Ancient British Isles* (Oxford, 1991), H. Mayr-Harting, *The Coming of Christianity to Anglo-Saxon England* (London, 1972), V. Ortenberg, *The English Church and the Continent in the*

Tenth and Eleventh Centuries (Oxford, 1992), J. Burton, *Monastic and Religious Orders in Britain, 1000–1300* (Cambridge, 1994), R. Swanson, *Church and Society in Late Medieval England* (Oxford, 1993), P. Collinson, N. Ramsay and M. Sparks, *A History of Canterbury Cathedral* (Oxford, 1995), E. Duffy, *The Stripping of the Altars. Traditional Religion in England c.1400–c.1580* (London, 1992), N. Macdougall, ed., *Church, Politics and Society: Scotland 1408–1919* (Edinburgh, 1983), and I.B. Cowan, *The Medieval Church in Scotland* (Edinburgh, 1995).

On 'governance', see W.L. Warren, *The Governance of Norman and Angevin England, 1066–1272* (London, 1987), J. Maddicott, *Simon de Montfort* (Oxford, 1994), M. Clanchy, *England and its Rulers* (Glasgow, 1981), J. Le Patourel, *The Norman Empire* (Oxford, 1976), and J. Green, *The Government of England under Henry I* (Cambridge, 1986).

H.M. Jewell explores *The North–South Divide: The Origins of Northern Consciousness in England* (Manchester, 1994). M.E. James, *Lineage and Civil Society: A Study of Society, Politics and Mentality in the Durham Region, 1500–1640* (Oxford, 1974) studies a particularly distinctive northern region.

The role of historians in shaping the past can be found in the following: A. Briggs, *Saxons, Normans, and Victorians* (London, 1966), H. MacDougall, *Racial Myth in English History: Trojans, Teutons and Anglo-Saxons* (London, 1983), D. Douglas, *The Norman Conquest and British Historians* (Glasgow, 1946), C. Kingsley, *The Roman and the Teuton* (London, 1864) and *Hereward the Wake* (London, 1865), O. Anderson, 'The Political Uses of History in mid-nineteenth century England' *Past and Present* 36 (1967), C. Parker, *History as Present Politics* (Winchester, 1980), J.W. Burrow, *A Liberal Descent: Victorian Historians and the English Past* (Cambridge, 1981), S. Bann, *The Clothing of Clio: A Study of the Representations of History in Nineteenth-Century Britain and France* (Cambridge, 1984).

Creation, crisis, consolidation

Valuable essays on this theme are to be found in S. Ellis and S. Barber, eds, *Conquest & Union: Fashioning a British State 1485–1725* (London, 1995), P. Jenkins, *A History of Modern Wales 1536–1990* (London, 1992), B.P. Levack, *The Formation of the British State: England, Scotland and the Union 1603–1707* (Oxford, 1987), K. Brown, *Kingdom or Province? Scotland and Regal Union 1603–1707* (Basingstoke, 1992), C. Russell, *The Fall of the British Monarchies 1637–1642* (Oxford, 1991), F. Dow, *Cromwellian Scotland, 1651–1660* (Edinburgh, 1979), P.W.J. Riley, *The Union of England and Scotland* (Manchester, 1978), W. Ferguson, *Scotland's Relations with England: A Survey to 1707* (Edinburgh, 1977).

Precedents and rights: the British polity

R.A. Griffiths and R.S. Thomas explain *The Making of the Tudor Dynasty* (Gloucester, 1985). The following studies of individual rulers are recommended: S. B. Chrimes, *Henry VIII* (London, 1972), J. Scarisbrick, *Henry VII* (London, 1968), D. M. Loades, *The Reign of Mary Tudor* (London, 1979), M. Lynch, ed., *Mary Stewart: Queen in Three Kingdoms* (Oxford, 1988), C. Haigh, *Elizabeth I* (London, 1988), M. Lee, *Great Britain's Solomon: James VI and I in his Three Kingdoms* (Chicago, 1990), K. Sharpe, *The Personal Rule of Charles I* (London, 1993), B. Coward, *Oliver Cromwell* (London, 1991), R. Hutton, *Charles II: King of England, Scotland and Ireland* (Oxford, 1989), J.R. Jones, *Charles II: Royal Politician* (London, 1987), J. Miller, *James II: A Study in Kingship* (Hove, 1978), S.B. Baxter, *William III* (London, 1966), E. Gregg, *Queen Anne* (London, 1980), R. Hatton, *George I: Elector and King* (London, 1978), J.B. Owen, 'George II Reconsidered' in J.S. Bromley and P.G.M. Dickson, eds., *Statesmen, Scholars and Merchants: Essays in Eighteenth-Century History presented to Dame Lucy Sutherland* (Oxford, 1973).

Government can be approached through G.R. Elton, *Studies in Tudor and Stuart Politics and Government* (Cambridge, 1983), D.R. Starkey, *The Reign of Henry VIII: Personalities and Politics* (London, 1985), J. Guy, *Tudor England* (Oxford, 1988), A.G.R. Smith, *The Government of Elizabethan England* (London, 1967), P.H. Williams, *The Tudor Regime* (Oxford, 1979), M. Graves, *The Tudor Parliaments: Crown, Lords and Commons 1485–1603* (London, 1985), C. Haigh, ed., *The Reign of Elizabeth I* (London, 1984), J. Wormald, *Court, Kirk and Community: Scotland 1470–1625* (London, 1981), R. Sherwood, *The Court of Oliver Cromwell* (London, 1977), G.E. Aylmer, *The State's Servants* (London, 1973), J.P. Kenyon, ed., *The Stuart Constitution* (Cambridge, 1966), C. Russell, *The Causes of the English Civil War* (Oxford, 1990), J.H. Hexter, ed., *Parliament and Liberty from the Reign of Elizabeth to the English Civil War* (Stanford, Calif., 1992), R. Hutton, *The British Republic 1649–60* (London, 1990), R. Beddard, ed., *The Revolutions of 1688* (Oxford, 1991), W. Speck, *Reluctant Revolutionaries: Englishmen and the Revolution of 1688* (Oxford, 1988), J.C.D. Clark, *English Society, 1688–1832* (Cambridge, 1985), B. Lenman, *The Jacobite Risings in Britain 1689–1746* (London, 1980), E. Cruickshanks, ed., *Ideology and Conspiracy: Aspects of Jacobitism 1689–1759* (Edinburgh, 1982), J. Cannon, *Electoral Reform, 1640–1832* (Cambridge, 1973), C. Jones, ed., *A Pillar of the Constitution: The House of Lords in British Politics 1640–1784* (London, 1989), B.W. Hill, *The Growth of Parliamentary Parties 1689–1742* (London, 1976), L. Colley, *In Defiance of Oligarchy: The Tory Party 1714–60* (Cambridge, 1982), J.H. Plumb, *The Growth of Political Stability in England, 1675–1725* (London, 1967). For some individual figures see J. P. Kenyon, *Robert Spencer, Earl of Sunderland 1641–1702*

(London, 1958), A. MacInnes, *Robert Harley, Puritan Politician* (London, 1970), H.T. Dickinson, *Walpole and the Whig Supremacy* (London, 1973), J.H. Plumb, *Sir Robert Walpole: I. The Making of a Statesman* (London, 1956) and *Sir Robert Walpole: II. The King's Minister* (London, 1960).

Truth, uniformity and toleration

J.A.F. Thomson, *The Later Lollards, 1414–1520* (Oxford, 1965), A. Hudson, *Lollards and their Books* (London, 1985) and 'Lollardy: the English Heresy?' in S. Mews, ed., *Studies in Church History Vol. 18: Religion and National Identity* (Oxford, 1982), E. Duffy and B. Bradshaw, eds, *Humanism, Reform and Reformation* (Cambridge, 1989), M. Aston, *England's Iconoclasts* (Oxford, 1989), A. G. Dickens, *The English Reformation* (London, 1990) and C. Haigh, *The English Reformation Revised* (London, 1987) and *English Reformation: Religion, Politics and Society under the Tudors* (Oxford, 1993) present contrasting interpretations. R. Whiting, *The Blind Devotion of the People: Popular Religion and the English Reformation* (Cambridge, 1991) offers a fresh angle and M. Skeeters, *Community and Clergy: Bristol and the Reformation c. 1530–c. 1570* (Oxford, 1993) a local study. D. MacCulloch, *Thomas Cranmer* (London, 1996) is an impressive biography.

G. Williams, *Welsh Reformation Essays* (Cardiff, 1967) and *Recovery, Reorientation and Reformation: Wales c. 1415–1642* (Oxford, 1987) covers general aspects and J.G. Jones, *The Translation of the Scriptures into Welsh* (Cardiff, 1988) a specific aspect. G.H. Jenkins, *Literature, Religion and Society in Wales 1660–1730* (Cardiff, 1978) and *The Foundations of Modern Wales: Wales 1642–1780* (Oxford, 1987) see religion in its total context.

I.B. Cowan, *The Scottish Reformation* (London, 1982), J. Kirk, *Patterns of Reform: Continuity and Change in the Reformation Kirk* (Edinburgh, 1989), G. Donaldson, *The Scottish Reformation* (Cambridge, 1960), M. Lynch, 'Calvinism in Scotland, 1559–1638' in M. Prestwich, ed., *International Calvinism, 1541–1715* (Oxford, 1985), J. Buckroyd, *Church and State in Scotland, 1660–1681* (Edinburgh, 1980).

The fortunes of different ecclesiastical groupings can be traced in the following: M. Watts, *The Dissenters: From the Reformation to the French Revolution* (Oxford, 1978), K. Fincham, ed., *The Early Stuart Church, 1603–1642* (London, 1993), J. Davies, *The Caroline Captivity of the Church* (Oxford, 1992), J. Spurr, *The Restoration Church of England, 1646–1689* (London, 1991), J. Champion, *The Pillars of Priestcraft Shaken: The Church of England and its Enemies 1660–1730* (Cambridge, 1992), J. Bossy, *The English Catholic Community 1570–1850* (London, 1975).

Voices critical of orthodoxy are examined in the following: J. Redwood, *Reason, Ridicule and Religion: The Age of Enlightenment in England,*

1660–1750 (London, 1976/1996), M. Hunter, ed., *Atheism from the Reformation to the Enlightenment* (Oxford, 1992), R. Hutton, *The Rise and Fall of Merry England: The Ritual Year 1400–1700* (Oxford, 1994) tackle rather different issues.

New world power

British relations with Europe, both formal and informal, are examined in the following: D. Hay, *Europe: The Emergence of an Idea* (Edinburgh, 1968), J. Black, *Convergence or Divergence? Britain and the Continent* (London, 1994), T. Munck, *Seventeenth- Century Europe* (London, 1990), J.R. Jones, *Britain and Europe in the Seventeenth Century* (London, 1966), P. Langford, *The Eighteenth Century 1688–1815* (foreign policy) (London, 1976), J. Brewer, *War, Money and the English State 1688–1783* (London, 1989), J. Black, *Natural and Necessary Enemies: Anglo–French Relations in the Eighteenth Century* (London, 1986), *The British Abroad: The Grand Tour in the Eighteenth Century* (Stroud, 1992) and with J. Gregory, eds, *Culture, Politics and Society in Britain, 1660–1800* (Manchester, 1991).

J.H. Parry, *Trade and Dominion: The European Overseas Empires in the Eighteenth Century* (London, 1971), G.V. Scammell, *The First Imperial Age: European Overseas Expansion c. 1400–1715* (London, 1989).

M. Lewis, *The History of the British Navy* (London, 1957), N.A.M. Rodger, *The Wooden World: An Anatomy of the Georgian Navy* (London, 1986).

P. Clark, ed., *The Transformation of English Provincial Towns, 1600–1800* (London, 1984), P. Borsay, *The English Urban Renaissance: Culture and Society in the Provincial Town, 1660–1770* (Oxford, 1989).

Preservation, reform and progress

The following books deal with the main developments in the political system and party politics c. 1745–1945. For the monarchy in general see F. Hardie, *The Political Influence of the British Monarchy 1868–1952* (London, 1970), J. Golby and W. Purdue, *The Monarchy and the British people 1760 to the Present* (London, 1987) and J. Cannon, 'The Survival of the British Monarchy', *Transactions of the Royal Historical Society* Fifth Series 36 (1986).

For some individual monarchs see J. Brooke, *King George III* (London, 1972), E. Longford, *Victoria RI* (London, 1964), P. Magnus, *King Edward VII* (London, 1964), H. Nicolson, *King George V* (London, 1952), K. Rose, *King George V* (London, 1983), P. Ziegler, *King Edward VIII* (London, 1985), S. Bradford, *King George VI* (London, 1989).

P.D.G. Thomas, *The House of Commons in the Eighteenth Century* (Oxford, 1971), C. Jones, ed., *A Pillar of the Constitution: The House of Lords in British Politics, 1640–1784* (1989), F. O'Gorman, *The Emergence of the British Two-party System, 1760–1832* (London, 1982) and *Voters, Patrons and Parties: The Unreformed Electorate of Hanoverian England* (Oxford, 1989), W. Bagehot, *The English Constitution* (London, 1867), J. Brewer, *Party Ideology and Popular Politics at the Accession of George III* (Cambridge, 1976), J. Cannon, *Parliamentary Reform, 1640–1832* (Cambridge, 1973), H.T. Dickinson, *British Radicalism and the French Revolution 1789–1815* (Oxford, 1985) and *The Politics of the People in Eighteenth-Century Britain* (London, 1995), A. Goodwin, *The Friends of Liberty: The English Democratic Movement in the Age of the French Revolution* (London, 1979), M. Philp, ed., *The French Revolution and British Popular Politics* (Cambridge, 1991), M. Freeman, *Edmund Burke and the Critique of Political Radicalism* (Oxford, 1980), I. Christie, *Stress and Stability in Late Eighteenth-Century Britain: Reflections on the British Avoidance of Revolution* (Oxford, 1984), A. Mitchell, *The Whigs in Opposition, 1815–1830* (Oxford, 1967), M. Brock, *The Great Reform Act* (London, 1973), N. Gash, *Reaction and Reconstruction in English Politics, 1832–1852* (Oxford, 1965) and *Politics in the Age of Peel: A Study in the Technique of Parliamentary Representation 1830–50* (London, 1953), D. Thompson, *The Chartists* (London, 1984), M. Finn, *After Chartism: Class and Nation in English Radical Politics, 1848–1874* (Cambridge, 1993) H.J. Hanham, *Elections and Party Management: Politics in the Time of Disraeli and Gladstone* (London, 1959), J. Vincent, *The Formation of the Liberal Party 1857–1868* (London, 1966), R. Blake, *Disraeli* (London, 1966), H.C.G. Matthew, *Gladstone 1809–1874* and *Gladstone 1875–1898* (Oxford, 1986 and 1995), K. Robbins, *John Bright* (London, 1979), N. McCord, *The Anti-Corn Law League 1838–1846* (London, 1958), B. Porter, *Britannia's Burden: The Political Evolution of Modern Britain 1851–1990* (London, 1994), F.B. Smith, *The Making of the Second Reform Bill* (Cambridge, 1966), M. Cowling, *Disraeli, Gladstone and Revolution: The Passing of the Second Reform Bill* (Cambridge, 1967), R. Shannon, (*History of the Conservative Party series*) *The Age of Disraeli, 1867–1881* (London, 1992) and *The Age of Salisbury 1881–1902: Unionism and Empire* (London, 1996), D. Hamer, *Liberal Politics in the Age of Gladstone and Rosebery* (Oxford, 1972), J.P. Parry, *Democracy and Religion: Gladstone and the Liberal Party, 1867–1875* (Cambridge, 1986), D.W. Bebbington, *The Nonconformist Conscience: Chapel and Politics 1870–1914* (London, 1982), B.H. Harrison, *Peaceable Kingdom: Stability and Change in Modern Britain* (Oxford, 1982), P.T. Marsh, *The Discipline of Popular Government* (Hassocks, 1978), M. Pugh, *The Tories and the People 1880–1935* (Oxford, 1985) and *State and Society: British Political and Social History 1870–1992* (London, 1994), B. Keith-Lucas, *English Local Government in the Nineteenth and Twentieth Centuries* (London, 1977), R. McKibbin, *The Evolution* of the Labour Party 1910–1922 (Oxford, 1974), P.F. Clarke, *Liberals and Social Democrats* (Cambridge, 1978), A. Seldon and S. Ball, eds., *Conservative Century: The Conservative Party since 1900* (Oxford, 1994), B.H. Harrison, *The Transformation of British Politics 1860–1995* (Oxford, 1996).

Pax Britannica

Imperial aspects are covered by B. Porter, *The Lion's Share: A Short History of British Imperialism 1850–1983* (London, 1984), D. Judd, *Empire* (London, 1996), P.J. Marshall, ed., *The Cambridge Illustrated History of the British Empire* (Cambridge, 1996), A.N. Porter, *Atlas of British Overseas Expansion* (London, 1991), L. James, *The Rise and Fall of the British Empire* (London, 1994), A.P. Thornton, *The Imperial Idea and its Enemies* (London, 1959), P.J. Cain and A.G. Hopkins, *British Imperialism: Innovation and Expansion 1688–1914* and *British Imperialism: Crisis and Deconstruction 1914–1990* (London, 1993), A. Calder, *Revolutionary Empire: The Rise of the English-speaking Empires from the Fifteenth Century to the 1780s* (London, 1981), R. Anstey, *The Atlantic Slave Trade and British Abolition, 1760–1810* (London, 1975), C.A. Bayly, *Imperial Meridian: The British Empire and the World 1780–1830* (London, 1989), I. Christie, *Crisis of Empire: Great Britain and the American Colonies, 1754–1783* (London, 1966), J.M. Ward, *Colonial Self-Government: The British Experience 1759–1856* (London, 1976), J. Eddy and D. Schreuder, eds, *The Rise of Colonial Nationalism* (Sydney, 1988), P. Lawson, *The East India Company* (London, 1993), A. Seal, *The Emergence of Indian Nationalism* (Cambridge, 1968), J. Brown, *Modern India: The Origins of an Asian Democracy* (Oxford, 1985), P.D. Curtin, *The Image of Africa: British Ideas and Action 1780–1850* (London, 1964).

General foreign policy can be approached through K. Bourne, *The Foreign Policy of Victorian England* (Oxford, 1970), M. Chamberlain, '*Pax Britannica*'?: *British foreign policy 1789–1914* (London, 1988), C.J. Bartlett, ed., *Britain Pre-Eminent: Studies in British World Influence in the Nineteenth Century* (London, 1969), J. Clarke, *British Diplomacy and Foreign Policy 1782–1865* (London, 1989), P. Kennedy, *The Rise of the Anglo-German Antagonism, 1860–1914* (London, 1980), F.H. Hinsley, ed., *British Foreign Policy under Sir Edward Grey* (Cambridge, 1977), J. Bourne, *Britain and the Great War 1914–1918* (London, 1989), M. Dockrill and D. Goold, *Peace without Promise: Britain and the Peace Conferences 1919–23* (London, 1981), D. Reynolds, *Britannia Overruled: British Policy & World Power in the 20th Century* (London, 1991), R. Holland, *The Pursuit of Greatness: Britain and the World Role 1900–1970* (London, 1991).

Believing in Britain

The following books deal with central aspects of religious belief and practice in the period: M. Watts, *The Dissenters: Vol. 2 The Expansion of Evangelical Nonconformity* (Oxford, 1995), J. Bradley, *Religion, Revolution and English Radicalism: Non-conformity in Eighteenth-Century Politics and Society* (Cambridge, 1990), C. Haydon, *Anti-Catholicism in Eighteenth-century England* (Manchester, 1993), D.M. Thompson, *Nonconformity in the Nineteenth Century* (London, 1972), W. Gibson, *Church, State and Society, 1760–1850* (London, 1994), O. Chadwick, *The Victorian Church* (London, 1966–70), G. Parsons, ed., *Religion in Victorian Britain* (4 vols, Manchester, 1988), D. Nicholls, *Church and State in Britain since 1820* (London, 1967), E.R. Norman, *Church and Society in England 1770–1970* (Oxford, 1976), *Anti-Catholicism in Victorian England* (London, 1968) and *The English Catholic Church in the Nineteenth Century* (Oxford, 1984), D.W. Bebbington, *Evangelicalism in Modern Britain: A History from the 1730s to the 1980s* (London, 1989), B. Hilton, *The Age of Atonement: The Influence of Evangelicalism on Social and Economic Thought 1785–1865* (Oxford, 1988), M. Wheeler, *Heaven, Hell and the Victorians* (Cambridge, 1994), E. Royle, *Victorian Infidels* (Manchester, 1974), G. Malmgreen, ed., *Religion in the Lives of English Women, 1760–1930* (London, 1986), C. Brown, *The Social History of Religion in Scotland since 1730* (London, 1987), S. Brown, *Thomas Chalmers and the Godly Commonwealth* (Oxford, 1982), G. Williams, *The Welsh and their Religion* (Cardiff, 1991), A. Hastings, *A History of English Christianity 1920–1985* (London, 1986), J. Wolffe, *God & Greater Britain: Religion and National Life in Britain and Ireland 1843–1945* (London, 1994), B. Stanley, *The Bible and the Flag: Protestant Missions and British Imperialism in the Nineteenth and Twentieth Centuries* (Leicester, 1990)

Aspects of national belief and identity are covered in L. Colley, *Britons: Forging the Nation 1707–1837* (London, 1992), M. Duffy, *The Englishman and the Foreigner* (Cambridge, 1986); G. Newman, *The Rise of English Nationalism: A Cultural History 1740–1830* (London, 1987), R. Samuel, ed., *Patriotism: The Making and Unmaking of British National Identity* (3 vols, London, 1989), K. Robbins, *Nineteenth- Century Britain: Integration and Diversity* (Oxford, 1988).

Epilogue

Readers are particularly referred to the bibliographies, books and articles referred to both in the reference notes and in the initial 'General' section of this guide to further reading.

Maps

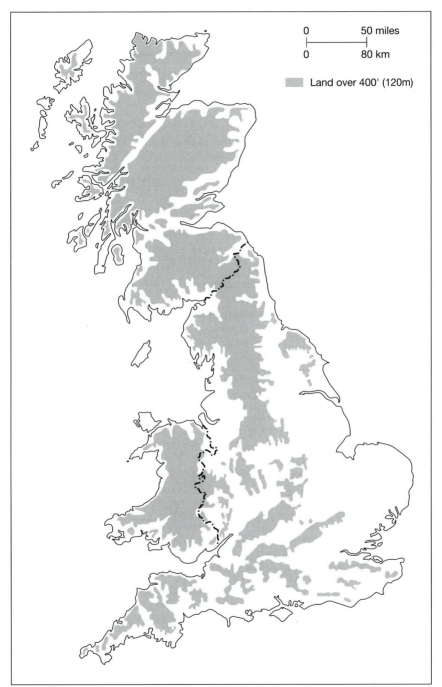

Map 1 England, Scotland and Wales

Maps

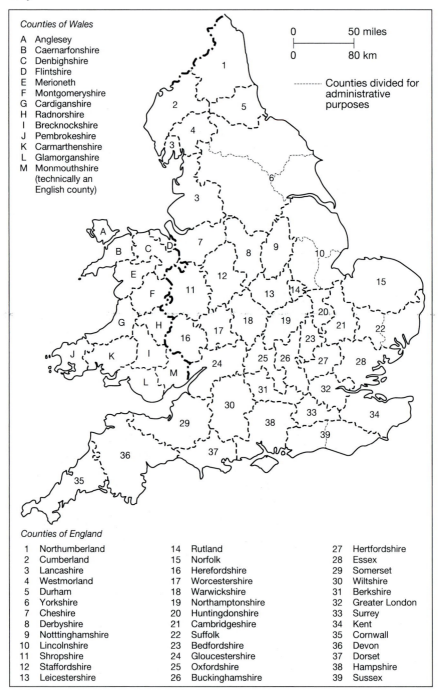

0   50 miles

0   80 km

-------- Counties divided for administrative purposes

Map 2   England and Wales – counties before 1975

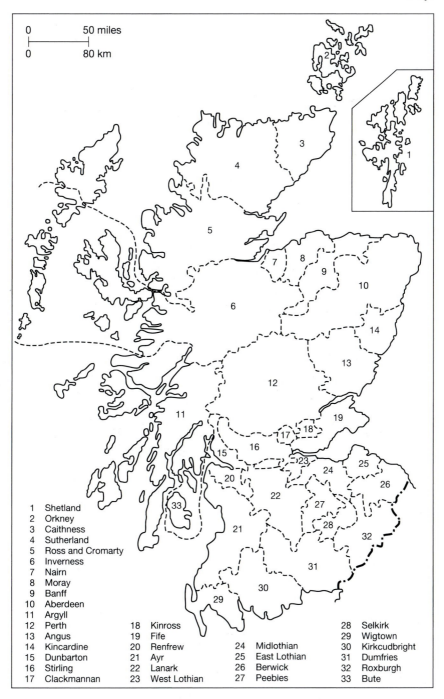

1   Shetland
2   Orkney
3   Caithness
4   Sutherland
5   Ross and Cromarty
6   Inverness
7   Nairn
8   Moray
9   Banff
10 Aberdeen
11 Argyll
12 Perth
13 Angus
14 Kincardine
15 Dunbarton
16 Stirling
17 Clackmannan
18 Kinross
19 Fife
20 Renfrew
21 Ayr
22 Lanark
23 West Lothian
24 Midlothian
25 East Lothian
26 Berwick
27 Peebles
28 Selkirk
29 Wigtown
30 Kirkcudbright
31 Dumfries
32 Roxburgh
33 Bute

Map 3 Scotland – counties before 1975

Map 4 England and Wales

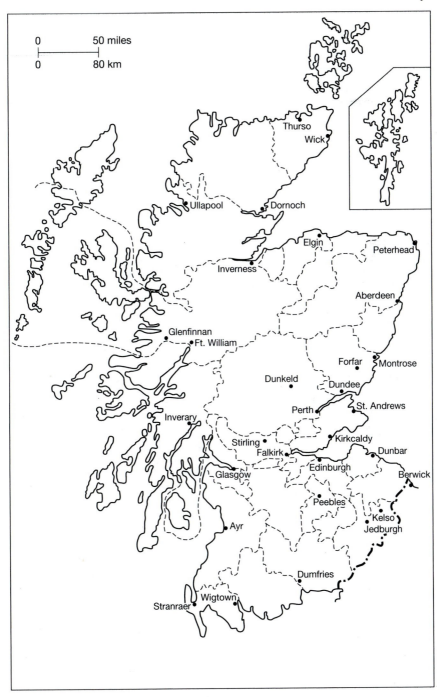

Map 5 Scotland

Index